# Native American Bibliography Series

*Advisory Board*

No. 1 *Bibliography of the Sioux*

Jack W. Marken, South Dakota State University
Herbert T. Hoover, University of South Dakota

# BIBLIOGRAPHY OF THE SIOUX

by

## Jack W. Marken

and

## Herbert T. Hoover

*Native American Bibliography Series,*
*No. 1*

THE SCARECROW PRESS, INC.
METUCHEN, N.J., & LONDON
1980

Library of Congress Cataloging in Publication Data

Marken, Jack Walter, 1922-
    Bibliography of the Sioux.

        (Native American bibliography series ; no. 1)
        Includes indexes.
        1.    Dakota Indians--Bibliography.    I.    Hoover, Her-
    bert T. , joint author.    II.    Title.    III.    Series.
    Z1210. D3M37    [E99. D1]    016. 97'000497            80-20106
    ISBN 0-8108-1356-4

# CONTENTS

## PUBLISHER'S NOTE

The idea for a series of bibliographies on Native Americans was inspired by Marken and Hoover's manuscript on the Sioux, here issued as the first volume of the series. Under the general editorship of Professor Marken, and with the help of a distinguished panel of experts, it is our goal to publish comprehensive bibliographies of service to scholarship, yet with all important items annotated to make them useful to students and others beginning research in the field.

Over the decade of the 1980's a score or more of these bibliographies will be published. Those planned definitely at this date are Papago, by Bernard Fontana, University of Arizona (1982); Cherokee, by James H. May, Sonoma State University (1983); Arapaho & Cheyenne, by Donald J. Berthrong, Purdue University (1984); Crow, by Peter Nabokov, Pacific Grove, California (1984); Menominee, by Patricia Ourada, Boise State University (1984); Zuni, by Theodore Frisbie, Southern Illinois University (1984); Choctaw, by Charles E. Roberts, California State University/Sacramento (1985); Osage, by Terry Wilson, University of California/Berkeley (1985); Potawatomi, by David Edmunds, Texas Christian University (1985); Lenni-Lenape, by James Ronda, Youngstown State University (1985); Apache, by Keith Basso, University of Arizona (1986); and Yaqui-Mayo, by N. Ross Crumrine, University of Victoria (1987).

## PREFACE

In this bibliography of the Sioux Indians we have attempted to list all the important books and articles published
through 1978.  We have not, however, attempted to list newspaper articles, articles in magazines published by reservation schools, or occasional publications by tribal councils or
government agencies, unless these have been published else-
where.  We have included the articles from The Great Plains
Observer and North Country Anvil, two newspaper-like publications that have focused on the Sioux in Minnesota and South
Dakota.  We have listed dissertations and theses that have
been published as articles or books, and we have listed regional bibliographies of theses that have appeared in journals.
We have not listed the nearly two hundred dissertations and
theses from Frederick and Alice Dockstader's The American
Indian in Graduate Studies, but we have included those dissertations that have appeared since the publication of their
bibliography in 1974.

About half of the entries are annotated.  We have not
commented on many of the articles and books in which the
title has indicated the nature of the contents.  The annotations are nearly equally divided between those describing and
those evaluating the contents.

We have organized the material under subject headings
with entries arranged alphabetically under each heading.  Because we have decided to list an entry only once, we have
placed some entries arbitrarily under one heading rather than
another.  For instance, articles and books by Charles A.
Eastman might be listed entirely under the heading "Indian
Authors," but we have also placed some of them under "Autobiographies," "Arts and Culture," and "Education," depending
upon the type or content of the entry.  The works by Stephen
R. Riggs appear under "Arts and Culture" and "Missionaries,"
as well as "Language."  The Name Index lists all these entries under the specific author.  The Subject Index also will
aid the reader by including subjects in addition to those
named in the Contents.

For some materials, such as those on dance, one must consider whether they belong under "Arts and Culture" or "Religion." We have assigned these to one or the other depending upon whether the material seems to emphasize by title or content either cultural or religious aspects. There is also a question of whether material ought to be listed under the heading "Contemporary Sioux" or "Reservation Affairs." We have assigned entries in the latter category if the content refers to a specific reservation and to the former if the content is general. But we cannot guarantee that every entry fits as conveniently into pattern as to make misplacement impossible. We refer readers to the Subject Index to find materials that are not classified as the user might expect.

We have a large section on George Custer. Our aim has been to list materials in this category that contain significant information concerning the Sioux, but we may have some entries that emphasize the military figure more than the Indians. We have erred on the side of liberality by including material in this section rather than omitting it; however, we have not attempted to provide a complete bibliography of Custer, nor have we attempted to supplement or extend the bibliographies in W. A. Graham's The Custer Myth (1953). We have supplied a useful list of materials on Custer, especially for someone who is interested in the Sioux battles against him.

Our list of materials in the area of fiction about the Sioux is incomplete. Our purpose in this section is to give a representative list of imaginative works of various kinds to illustrate most of the prejudices appearing in American literature about the Sioux. We have listed under "Types of Literature and Criticism" articles by scholars that point out these prejudices and make other judgments about the literature and history of the Sioux written by non-Indians.

We might discuss the individual characteristics of every heading in this bibliography, but we give explanatory comment on only two more. In the section "Bibliographies" we have listed major bibliographies useful for the study of the Sioux and the background of the Sioux, but we have not listed separately the entries from James Pilling's Bibliography of the Siouan Languages, the Dockstader bibliographies previously mentioned, nor Angeline Jacobson's Contemporary Native American Literature. Also, in our "History" section, we have listed all the early histories that have focused on the Plains Indians and the Sioux (since they have been used as secondary sources by many later writers), but we have not listed modern general histories which have material on the Sioux, unless there are extensive sections of these books devoted solely to the Sioux.

We have followed the bibliographic forms found in the MLA Handbook throughout the book. We have abbreviated journals and magazines and the names of special collections; see the key given following this preface. We have listed modern reprints of books on the Sioux to aid librarians as well as researchers. Though we have attempted to make this bibliography complete, we know that omissions are inevitable, and we ask that materials which we have overlooked be brought to our attention.

Jack W. Marken
South Dakota State University

Herbert T. Hoover
University of South Dakota

# ABBREVIATIONS FOR TITLES OF PERIODICALS, SERIES, AND COLLECTIONS

| | |
|---|---|
| AA | American Anthropologist |
| AAn | American Antiquity |
| AAOJ | American Antiquarian and Oriental Journal |
| AAW | Arizona and the West |
| ABR | American Benedictine Review |
| ACQR | American Catholic Quarterly Review |
| AD | Acta et Dicta |
| AH | American Heritage |
| AHI | American History Illustrated |
| AHR | American Historical Review |
| AI | American Indian |
| AIAM | American Indian Art Magazine |
| AICC | American Indian Crafts and Culture |
| AICRJ | American Indian Culture and Research Journal |
| AIH | American Indian Hobbyist |
| AIM | American Indian Magazine |
| AIo | Annals of Iowa |
| AIQ | American Indian Quarterly |
| AIT | American Indian Tradition |
| AJP | American Journal of Psychology |
| AJPA | American Journal of Physical Anthropology |
| AJPs | American Journal of Psychiatry |
| AL | American Literature |
| AlHR | Alberta Historical Review |
| ALi | American Libraries |
| AM | Atlantic Monthly |
| AMe | American Mercury |
| AMHS | Annals of the Minnesota Historical Society |
| AmI | American Indigena |
| AN | The American Naturalist |
| AnL | Anthropological Linguistics |
| AnQ | Anthropology Quarterly |
| ApA | Applied Anthropology |
| APAM | Anthropological Papers of the American Museum of Natural History |
| AQ | American Quarterly |
| ARBAE | Annual Reports of the Bureau of American Ethnology |

| | |
|---|---|
| ArQ | Arizona Quarterly |
| ARSI | Annual Reports of the Board of Regents of the Smithsonian Institution |
| AS | Archaeological Studies. Pierre, SD: South Dakota Archaeological Commission |
| ASR | American Sociological Review |
| AW | American West |
| AWy | Annals of Wyoming |

| | |
|---|---|
| B | Beaver, Magazine of the North |
| BAMNH | Bulletin of the American Museum of Natural History |
| BB | The Book Buyer |
| BBAE | Bureau of American Ethnology Bulletin |
| BCQ | Blue Cloud Quarterly |
| BM | Booklover's Magazine |
| BMANS | Bulletin of the Minnesota Academy of Natural Sciences |
| BMHS | Bulletin of the Missouri Historical Society |

| | |
|---|---|
| C | The Craftsman |
| CA | Current Anthropology |
| CC | Cross Currents |
| CCC | College Communication and Composition |
| CCS | Colorado College Studies |
| ChC | Christian Century |
| CHR | Canadian Historical Review |
| CHSMo | Contributions to the Historical Society of Montana |
| CHSND | Collections of the Historical Society of North Dakota |
| CHSSD | Collections of the Historical Society of South Dakota |
| CM | Canadian Magazine |
| CMag | Century Magazine |
| CMAI | Contributions from the Museum of the American Indian |
| CMHS | Collections of the Minnesota Historical Society |
| CMo | Continental Monthly |
| CNAE | Contributions of North American Ethnology |
| CO | Chronicles of Oklahoma |
| ColM | Colorado Magazine |
| CRAS | Canadian Review of American Studies |
| CRD | Civil Rights Digest |
| CuA | Current Anthropology |

CuL          Current Literature
CWHS         Collections of the Wisconsin Historical Society


DBN          Dakota Book News
DW           Dakota West


E            Ethnohistory
Ed           Education
EE           Elementary English
EJ           English Journal


FN           Fellow Newsletter


GH           Gopher Historian
GPJ          Great Plains Journal
GPO          Great Plains Observer


H            Harper's New Monthly, or Harper's Monthly
HBR          Harvard Business Review
HGM          Home Geographic Monthly
Historian    The Historian:  A Journal of History
HO           Human Organization
HR           History of Religions
HRS          Historical Records and Studies
HT           History Today
HW           Harper's Weekly


IAVE         Indian Arts and Vocational Education
ICA          International Congress of Americanists
IHR          Iowa Historical Record
IJAL         International Journal of American Linguistics
IJHP         Iowa Journal of History and Politics
IN           Indian Notes
InH          The Indian Historian
INM          Indian Notes and Monographs
IS           The Indian Sentinel
IW           Indians at Work


JAAR         Journal of the American Academy of Religion
JAH          Journal of American History

| | |
|---|---|
| JAIE | Journal of American Indian Education |
| JASP | Journal of Abnormal and Social Psychology |
| JCP | Journal of Cross-Cultural Psychology |
| JES | Journal of Ethnic Studies |
| JFI | Journal of the Folklore Institute |
| JHE | Journal of Higher Education |
| JP | Journal of Psychology |
| JPC | Journal of Popular Culture |
| JQ | Journalism Quarterly |
| JR | Journal of Reading |
| JRe | Journalism Review |
| JSAP | Journal de la Société des Américanistes |
| JSP | Journal of Social Psychology |
| JW | Journal of the West |

| | |
|---|---|
| KHQ | Kansas Historical Quarterly |
| KQ | Kansas Quarterly |

| | |
|---|---|
| LD | Literary Digest |
| LHJ | Ladies Home Journal |
| LJ | Library Journal |
| LM | The Little Missionary |
| LUR | Lakehead University Review |
| LWLR | Land and Water Law Review |

| | |
|---|---|
| MA | Minnesota Archaeologist |
| McM | McClure's Magazine |
| MH | Mental Hygiene |
| MHB | Minnesota History Bulletin |
| Mid | Mid-America |
| MiH | Minnesota History |
| MLS | Modern Language Studies |
| MM | Midland Monthly |
| MNAs | Memoirs of the National Academy of Sciences |
| Montana | Montana: The Magazine of Western History |
| MRW | Missionary Review of the World |
| MVHR | Mississippi Valley Historical Review |
| MWH | Magazine of Western History |

| | |
|---|---|
| NAM | North American Mentor |
| NaR | National Review (London) |
| NAR | North American Review |
| NaRe | National Review (United States) |

NCA          North Country Anvil
NDH          North Dakota History
NDHQ         North Dakota Historical Quarterly
NDLR         North Dakota Law Review
NDQ          North Dakota Quarterly
NEQ          New England Quarterly
NFP          Nebraska Folklore Pamphlets
NH           Nebraska History
NHi          Natural History
NHM          Nebraska History Magazine
NM           Northwest Magazine
NMa          National Magazine
NMSJ         Northwestern Medical and Surgical Journal
NR           New Republic


OC           Open Court
OH           Ontario History
OL           Outdoor Life
OM           Outing Magazine
OTT          Old Travois Trails
Out          Outlook


PA           Practical Anthropology
PAAAS        Proceedings for the American Association for
                 the Advancement of Science
PAPS         Publications of the American Philosophical So-
                 ciety
PCWHS        Pacific Center for Western Historical Studies
PE           Progressive Education
PIL          Papers in Linguistics
PlA          Plains Anthropologist
PM           Pembroke Magazine
PMAS         Proceedings of the Minnesota Academy of Science
PMP          Peabody Museum Papers
PMR          Peabody Museum Records
PMVHA        Proceedings of the Mississippi Valley Historical
                 Association
PNQ          Pacific Northwest Quarterly
PNSHS        Publications of the Nebraska State Historical
                 Society
PrM          Primitive Man
Prologue     Prologue:  The Journal of the National Archives
PRRB         Pine Ridge Research Bulletin
PS           Prairie Schooner
PSM          Popular Science Monthly

| | |
|---|---|
| PT | Psychology Today |
| PUMB | Pennsylvania University Museum Bulletin |
| PUSNM | Proceedings of the United States National Museum |
| PW | Publishers Weekly |

| | |
|---|---|
| QJSAI | The Quarterly Journal of the Society of American Indians |

| | |
|---|---|
| RCH | Ramsey County History |
| RHAF | Revue d'Histoire de l'Amérique Française |
| RR | Review of Reviews, American Monthly |

| | |
|---|---|
| S | Science |
| School | Information Respecting the History, Condition, and Prospects of the Indian Tribes of the United States. Ed. Henry R. Schoolcraft. 6 Parts. Philadelphia, 1851-1857; rpt. New York: Paladin Press, 1969. |
| SCK | Smithsonian Contribution to Knowledge |
| SDBJ | South Dakota Bar Journal |
| SDFHR | South Dakota Farm and Home Research |
| SDH | South Dakota History |
| SDLR | South Dakota Law Review |
| SDR | South Dakota Review |
| SEd | Social Education |
| SEP | Saturday Evening Post |
| SFQ | Southern Folklore Quarterly |
| SJA | Southwestern Journal of Anthropology |
| SL | School Libraries |
| SM | Scientific Monthly |
| SMa | Scribner's Magazine |
| SMC | Smithsonian Miscellaneous Collections |
| SR | Southwest Review |
| SRe | Saturday Review |
| SS | Social Studies |
| StN | Saint Nicholas |

| | |
|---|---|
| TAM | Theatre Arts Monthly |
| TAPS | Transactions of the American Philosophical Society |
| TASW | Transactions of the Anthropological Society of Washington |
| TB | The Tepee Book |

| THSSM | Transactions of the Historical and Scientific Society of Manitoba |
| TKHS | Transactions of the Kansas Historical Society |
| TS | The Texaco Star |

| UCP | University of California Publications in American Archeology and Ethnology |
| UCPAR | University of California Publications in Anthropological Records |
| UCPL | University of California Publications in Linguistics |
| USDMN | Museum News, University of South Dakota |

| WA | Wisconsin Archeologist |
| WAL | Western American Literature |
| WBB | Westerner's Brand Book |
| WHQ | Western Historical Quarterly |
| WM | Western Magazine |
| WMH | Wisconsin Magazine of History |
| WT | Weewish Tree |
| WWS | Western Writers Series |

| YR | Yale Review |
| YSE | Yale Studies in English |
| YUPA | Yale University Publications in Anthropology |

# FOREWORD

I assume I was asked to write this foreword to Jack Marken and Herbert Hoover's <u>Bibliography of the Sioux</u> because I am a member of that tribe and a writer. I didn't think the assignment would be difficult so I agreed to do it.

But I leafed through the typescript pages with growing unease and by the time I turned over the last page, I was distressfully stunned. The enormity, the sheer number of the listings gathered by the authors, overwhelmed me.

Of course I had known that my tribe had been a popular subject ever since the Europeans made that first contact. But I was unprepared for the mass of data this bibliography represents. Some of what is listed is useful, some of it worthless. But whether good or bad, serious or humorous, there have been millions of words written on every possible aspect, angle, custom, and episode of the Sioux Indians: scholarly studies, stereotypical farces, factual, mythical, untruths, music, fiction and poetry. Everything that anyone has ever and will ever want to know about our past, present, and even future has to be in the listings contained herein.

The thought occurred to me, a relative newcomer to writing about the Sioux, that all of the words had been used and there were none left for me. I was humbled and frightened. What could I write about this immense gathering of titles, authors, and words?

Then from some part of me, deep within and perhaps from beyond my historic consciousness, came whispering fragments of Lakota phrases.

<u>Oyate nimkte wacin yelo.</u> I took up my Dakota and Lakota dictionaries (included in this bibliography) to be sure of the translation: "I want the people to live." And, of course, that's what it's all about. That which my grandmothers preserved in the oral tradition was now permanently and forever alive in the written word.

Wicaśa okinihanipi whispered in my mind and I agreed.
That is what must be said of Herb Hoover and Jack Marken,
long time friends to many Sioux and our sympathetic advo-
cates in their respective universities. "Honorable and re-
spected men," the Lakota words commend them for their efforts in finding and identifying the thousands of listings in this
most complete bibliography.

Then I heard simple statements: Waste. Pilamiye.
"Good. Thank you."

Virginia Driving Hawk Sneve

# BIBLIOGRAPHY OF THE SIOUX

## BIBLIOGRAPHIES

1. American Association of School Librarians, Committee on the Treatment of Minorities in Library Books and Other Instructional Materials. "Multi-Ethnic Media: Selected Bibliographies. " SL, 19 (Winter 1970), 49-57.

2. Andrews, H. A. , et al. "Bibliography of Franz Boas. " AA, 45:3, Pt. 2 (July-September 1943), 67-109. Contains sources on the Sioux.

3. ASD Adult Library Materials Committee Subcommittee on Materials for American Indians for the Use of Libraries and other Institutions. "Selective Bibliography of Bibliographies on Indian Materials for Adults. " ALi, 4 (February 1973), 115-117. Annotates approximately seventy bibliographies with short remarks.

4. Beidleman, Richard G. "A Partial, Annotated Bibliography of Colorado Ethnology. " CCS, No. 2 (Fall 1958), pp. 3-55. Contains a section on the Sioux.

5. "Bibliography on the Dakota. " In The Aborigines of Minnesota. A Report Based on the Collections of Jacob V. Brower, and on the Field Surveys and Notes of Alfred J. Hill and Theodore H. Lewis. Ed. N. H. Winchell. St. Paul, MN: The Minnesota Historical Society, 1911, pp. 575-579.

6. Boas, Franz. "Recent Work on American Indian Languages. " S, 75 (May 1932), 489-491. A valuable article listing works on Indian languages published in the Bureau of American Ethnology from 1911-1922.

7. Briggs, Harold E. "An Appraisal of Historical Writings on the Great Plains Region Since 1920. " MVHR, 34: 1 (June 1947), 83-100.

8.  Brudvig, Glenn. "The Catalog of the Orin G. Libby
    Historical Manuscripts Collection of North Dakota Li-
    brary." NDH, 31:1 (January 1964), 79-90. Contains
    material on the Sioux, including microfilms of cor-
    respondence from Sioux agencies.

9.  Bryde, John F. Bibliography of Indian Education. Ver-
    million, SD: Institute of Indian Studies, 1969. Short
    list of articles and books on Indian education.

10. Byler, Mary G. American Indian Authors for Young
    Readers: A Selected Bibliography. New York: Asso-
    ciation on American Indian Affairs, 1973.

11. Center for the Study of Man. Smithsonian Institution.
    [Blew, Carol H., Bess C. Keller, Carol Ballentine,
    and Marianna Kouskouras.] "Current North Ameri-
    can Indian Periodicals." SEd, 36 (May 1972), 494-
    500. Good list of some 150 entries.

12. DeMallie, Raymond J., Jr. "Appendix III: A Partial
    Bibliography of Archival Manuscript Material Relating
    to the Dakota Indians." See entry no. 528, pp. 312-
    43.

13. Dockstader, Frederick J. The American Indian in
    Graduate Studies. A Bibliography of Theses and Dis-
    sertations. Part 1. 2nd ed. New York: Museum of
    the American Indian, Heye Foundation, 1973. 362 pp.

14. Dockstader, Frederick J., and Alice W. Dockstader.
    The American Indian in Graduate Studies. A Bibli-
    ography of Theses and Dissertations. Part 2. New
    York: Museum of the American Indian, Heye Founda-
    tion, 1974. 426 pp.

15. Edgerton, Franklin. "Notes on Early American Work
    in Linguistics." PAPS, 87:1 (July 1943), 25-43.
    Valuable.

16. Fontana, Bernard L. The Indians of North America:
    Bibliographical Sources. Arizona State Museum.
    Tucson: The University of Arizona, 1972. Anthro-
    pology--American Indian Studies, No. 217.

17. Freeman, John F., and Murphy D. Smith. A Guide to
    Manuscripts Relating to the American Indian in the

Library of the American Philosophical Society. Philadelphia: The American Philosophical Society, 1966.
407 pp., index, annotations.

18. Gibson, A. M. "Sources for Research on the American
    Indian." E, 7 (1960), 121-136. A valuable guide to
    publications on the Sioux and other Indians.

19. GLR/Bibliography, No. 5. "The Indians of the Midwest:
    A Partially Annotated Bibliography." GPR, 2:2 (Win-
    ter 1976), 54-74. Contains a section on the Sioux.

20. Goodman, R. Irwin. Bibliography of Nonprint Instruc-
    tional Materials on the American Indian. Provo, Utah:
    Brigham Young University Press, 1972.

21. Henry, Jeannette, et al. Index to Literature on the
    American Indian 1970. San Francisco: Indian His-
    torian Press, Inc., 1972. 1971 (published in 1972)
    and 1972 (published in 1974) editions are also avail-
    able.

22. Hirschfelder, Arlene B. American Indian Authors. A
    Representative Bibliography. New York: Association
    on American Indian Affairs, Inc., 1970. 45 pp.
    Good, short bibliography.

23. Hirschfelder, Arlene B. "Bibliography Sources and Ma-
    terials for Teaching About American Indians." SEd,
    36 (May 1972), 488-493. Lists visual materials (film-
    strips, photographs, etc.), documents, and bibliogra-
    phies.

24. Hodge, William H. A Bibliography of Contemporary
    North American Indians. Selected and partially an-
    notated with study guides. New York: Interland,
    1976.

25. Hoover, Herbert T. "Indian Books--A Guide." NCA,
    No. 4 (February-March 1973), pp. 51-52.

26. Hoover, Herbert T. Sioux Contact-History and Culture:
    A Critical Bibliography. Bloomington: Indiana Uni-
    versity Press, 1979. Published for the Newberry
    Library.

27. Jacobson, Angeline. Contemporary Native American

Literature.   Metuchen,  N. J. :   Scarecrow Press, Inc. ,
1977.   262 pp.   A selected and partially annotated
bibliography which concentrates on literature published
between 1960 and 1976.   The 2024 entries are arranged
by genre.

28.  Johnson, Harry A.   Ethnic American Minorities:   A
     Guide to Media and Materials.   New York:   Bowker,
     1976.   304 pp.   Section on Native Americans, pp.
     133-187, includes purchase and rental prices.

29.  Johnson, Steven L.   Guide to American Indian Docu-
     ments in the Congressional Serial Set:   1817-1899.
     New York:   Clearwater Publishing Co. , 1977.   503 pp.
     Over 10, 000 items.   With a subject index organized
     under tribal headings, a valuable guide to 19th- century
     federal documents relating to Indian affairs.

30.  Jones, Clifton H.   "Manuscript Sources in Religious His-
     tory at the Historical Resource Center. "   SDH,  7:3
     (Summer 1977), 325-333.   Identifies records of the
     work of missionaries among the Sioux preserved by
     the South Dakota Historical Resource Center in Pierre.

31.  Klein,  Barry T.   Reference Encyclopedia of the Ameri-
     can Indian.   2nd ed.   Vol. I.   Rye, NY:   Todd Publi-
     cations, 1973.   547 pp.   Lists agencies, museums,
     tribal councils, etc. and bibliography of secondary
     sources.

32.  Lawson, Michael J.   "Recent Research in Dakota His-
     tory:   A Bibliography, 1970-1974. "   SDH,  6:3 (Summer
     1976), 353-362.   Sources on the Sioux are mainly
     Master's theses and doctoral dissertations.

33.  Lydenberg, Harry M.   "The Society's Program in Amer-
     ican Linguistics and Archaeology:   I American Lin-
     guistics. "   PAPS,  92:2 (May 1948), 124-26.

34.  Mackay, Mercedes B.   South Dakota Indian Bibliography.
     Pierre, SD:   State Library Commission, 1969.   Anno-
     tated.   Arranged by broad subject areas.

35.  Malan, Vernon D.   An Annotated Bibliography of Culture
     Change for the Teton Dakota Indians.   Pamphlet No.
     120, Rural Sociology Department.   Brookings, SD:
     South Dakota State College, 1959.

36. Marken, Jack. The American Indian: Language and
    Literature. Goldentree Bibliographies in Language and
    Literature. Arlington Heights, IL: AMS Publishing
    Corp., 1978. 205 pp. Nearly 3700 entries, with a
    major section on Sioux and other Great Plains Indians.

37. The Minnesota Historical Society. Chippewa and Dakota
    Indians. A Subject Catalog of Books, Pamphlets, Peri-
    odical Articles, and Manuscripts in the Minnesota His-
    torical Society. St. Paul: Minnesota Historical So-
    ciety, 1969. 131 pp.

38. Moorehead, Warren K. American Indian in the United
    States, Period 1850-1914. Facsimile ed. Freeport,
    NY: Books for Libraries, Inc., 1970.

39. Murdock, George P. Ethnographic Bibliography of
    North America. 4th ed. Rev. Timothy J. O'Leary.
    5 vols. New Haven: Human Relations Area Files,
    1975. Standard bibliography.

40. Naumer, Janet N. "American Indians: A Bibliography
    of Sources." ALi, 1 (1970), 861-864. Select bibli-
    ography of books, articles and pamphlets, plus photo-
    graphs, slides, transparencies, and recordings.

41. Neuman, Robert W. "Additional Annotated References:
    An Archeological Bibliography of the Central and
    Northern Plains Prior to 1930." PlA, 13:40 (May
    1968), 100-102.

42. Neuman, Robert W. "An Archaeological Bibliography:
    The Central and Northern Great Plains Prior to
    1930." PlA, 7:15 (February 1962), 43-57.

43. Newberry Library. Narratives of Captivity Among the
    Indians of North America. A List of Books and Manu-
    scripts on the Subject in the Edward E. Ayer Collec-
    tion of the Newberry Library. With Supplement.
    1928; rpt. Highland Park, NJ: Gryphon Press, 1970;
    also New York: Burt Franklin, Pub., 1970.

44. Nickerson, Gifford S. Native Americans in Doctoral
    Dissertations, 1971-75: A Classified and Indexed Re-
    search Bibliography. Monticello, IL: Council of
    Planning Libraries, 1977.

45.  Nute, Grace L. Calendar of the American Fur Com-
     pany's Papers. 2 vols. Washington: Government
     Printing Office, 1945. Numerous references to trad-
     ers and outposts in Sioux country.

46.  Parker, Watson. "A Black Hills Bibliography." CHSSD,
     35 (1970), 169-301. Comprehensive. Contains ma-
     terial on the Sioux in annual, alphabetical listings.

47.  Pilling, James. Bibliography of the Siouan Languages.
     Washington: Government Printing Office, 1887. 87
     pp.

48.  "Pine Ridge Research Bulletins 1-10, Subject Index."
     PRRB, 11 (January 1970), 74-79.

49.  Prucha, Fr. Francis P. A Bibliographical Guide to the
     History of Indian-White Relations in the United States.
     Chicago: University of Chicago Press, 1977. 454 pp.
     Contains a section on the Sioux.

50.  Prucha, Fr. Francis P. "Note: Books on American
     Indian Policy, A Half-Decade of Important Work,
     1970-1975." JAH, 63:3 (December 1976), 658-669.

51.  Richburg, James R. , and Phyllis R. Hastings. "Media
     and the American Indian: Ethnographical, Histor-
     ical, and Contemporary Issues." SEd, 36 (May 1972),
     526-533, 562. Includes descriptions of films, evalua-
     tions, recommended grade levels, and distributor in-
     formation.

52.  Rose, Margaret. "Manuscript Collections of the State
     Historical Society of North Dakota." NDH, 30:1 (Janu-
     ary 1963), 17-61. Contains both original and copied
     sources that deal with the Sioux.

53.  Ryan, Carmelite S. "The Written Record and the Amer-
     ican Indian: The Archives of the United States."
     WHQ, 6:2 (April 1975), 163-173.

54.  Schusky, Ernest L. , and Mary Sue Schusky. "A Cen-
     ter of Primary Sources for Plains Indian History."
     PlA, 15:48 (May 1970), 104-108. Most primary
     sources on the Sioux are housed in the Federal Rec-
     ords Centers at Kansas City and Denver.

55. Shapiro, Beth J. Directory of Ethnic Publishers and
    Resource Organizations. Rev. ed. New York: Amer-
    ican Library Association, 1976. 89 pp. Contains a
    subject index; lists non-traditional publishers and or-
    ganizations, archival and research centers, distribu-
    tors, etc. Many new publishers not listed.

56. South Dakota State Library Commission. South Dakota
    Indian Bibliography. Pierre, SD: South Dakota State
    Library Commission, 1971-1972.

57. Stensland, Anna Lee. Literature By and About the
    American Indian. Urbana, IL: National Council of
    Teachers of English, 1973. Prepared primarily for
    teachers of high schools, this annotated bibliography
    describes novels and other books on American Indians.

58. "Theses in the Library of the State Historical Society
    of North Dakota." NDH, 31:2 (April 1964), 135-139.
    Largely Master's theses, many on the Sioux. From
    North Dakota and elsewhere.

59. Ullom, Judith C. Folklore of the North American In-
    dians. Washington: Government Printing Office,
    1969. 126 pp. Includes annotations and index.

60. Useem, Ruth Hill, and Ethel Nurge. "Bibliography."
    See entry no. 528, pp. 291-297.

61. Van Balen, John. The Sioux: A Selected Bibliography.
    Vermillion, SD: Institute of Indian Studies, 1978.
    168 pp. A list of primary and secondary sources on
    the Sioux housed by the I. D. Weeks Library at the
    University of South Dakota.

62. Vizenor, Gerald R. A Selected Bibliography of the
    Dakota and Ojibway Indians of Minnesota, with a
    General Selection of References about the Indians of
    North America. Minneapolis: Curriculum Resource
    Center, Grant Elementary School, 1967. 24 pp.

63. Voegelin, C. F. "A Decade of American Indian Lin-
    guistic Studies." PAPS, 93:2 (May 1949), 137-140.

64. Wehrkamp, Tim. "Manuscript Sources in Sioux Indian
    History at the Historical Resource Center." SDH,
    8:2 (Spring 1978), 143-156. Contains accession num-

bers and brief descriptions of collections held by the
South Dakota State Historical Resource Center in
Pierre.

65.  Williams, John F.  "Bibliography of Minnesota."
     CMHS, 3 (1880), 13-75.


JOURNALS, NEWSPAPERS, AND
SPECIAL REPORTS

66.  Akwesasne Notes.  Mohawk Nation, via Rooseveltown,
     New York, 1969-  .  Published five times a year.
     Articles on contemporary issues of all tribes.

67.  American Board of Commissioners for Foreign Mis-
     sions.  Annual Report.  Boston:  ABCFM, 1811-  .

68.  American Board of Commissioners for Foreign Mis-
     sions.  Annual Sermons.  Boston:  ABCFM, 1813-
     1909.

69.  American Board of Commissioners for Foreign Mis-
     sions.  Commemorative Volume.  In Connection with
     the Seventy-Fifth Anniversary ... of the American
     Board of Commissioners for Foreign Missions.  Bos-
     ton:  ABCFM, 1885.

70.  American Board of Commissioners for Foreign Mis-
     sions.  Maps and Illustrations of the Missions of the
     American Board of Commissioners for Foreign Mis-
     sions, 1841.  Boston:  ABCFM, 1841.

71.  American Board of Commissioners for Foreign Mis-
     sions.  The Missionary Herald, 1805-1944.  These
     proceedings of the ABCFM originally were published
     under the title Panopist, which absorbed the Massa-
     chusetts Missionary Magazine in 1808 and became
     Panopist and Missionary Magazine, 1809-17.  It was
     then Panopist and Missionary Herald, 1818-20, and
     finally The Missionary Herald, 1821-1944.

72.  American Indian Index, 1956-  .

73.  American Traveller's Journal, Devoted to Travel, De-
     scriptions and Illustrations of American and Foreign

Slavery. New York: The American Traveller's Publishing Co., 1881. 16 pp. Report on visit to the Sisseton Agency.

74. Anpaokin, or The Daybreak. 8 vols. Protestant Episcopal Church mission paper published monthly from Yankton Agency and Niobrara Missions, 1880-1895.

75. Bishop Seabury Mission. Missionary Paper. Protestant Episcopal mission paper published 1859-1868, Faribault, MN: Holly and Brown Book and Job Printers, 1859-1868.

76. Blue Cloud Quarterly. Blue Cloud Abbey, Marvin, SD, 1954- . Beautifully designed small booklets containing writings by Sioux and other tribal writers.

77. Board of Missions. Annual Report of Board of Missions of the Protestant Episcopal Church. New York: Sanford Harroun and Co., 1865-1869.

78. The Catholic Indian Herald. Newspaper published by Marty Mission on Yankton Reservation, 1932-1978.

79. Chanta Anumpa. Rapid City, SD. Newspaper of American Indian Leadership Council. Good on Indian news.

80. The Children's Magazine. 4 vols. New York: General Protestant Episcopal Sunday School Union, 1857.

81. The Daily Journal, New Ulm, Minnesota. Sioux Centennial Edition. New Ulm, MN: The Daily Journal, 1962. Minnesota Sioux War centennial.

82. Dakota Tawaxitku kin, or The Dakota Friend. Newspaper published in Minnesota by Gideon H. Pond, February 1851 to August 1852 (no issue in November-December, 1851).

83. Dominion of Canada. Department of Indian Affairs. Annual Reports. 1879-1943.

84. Dominion of Canada. Department of the Interior. Annual Reports. 1875-1879.

85. Dominion of Canada. Parliament. Sessions Papers. 1868- .

86. Ethnic American Notes. Pittsburgh, PA. Contains
    lists and reviews of books and recordings in all
    phases of ethnic studies.

87. The Fairfax Standard, Fairfax, Minnesota. "Souvenir
    Edition, Commemorating Fiftieth Anniversary of the
    Battle of Fort Ridgely." Issued August 15, 1912.
    32 pp.

88. Frontier Scout. Published at Fort Union and Fort Rice,
    Dakota Territory. July 14, 1864-October 12, 1865.

89. Iape Oaye, or The Word Carrier. Bilingual newspaper
    published from Greenwood on the Yankton Reservation
    and Santee Normal Institute, May, 1871-March, 1939.
    Principal editors John P. Williamson, Stephen Return
    Riggs, and Aldred L. Riggs.

90. The Little Bronzed Angel. Newspaper published by
    Marty Mission on Yankton Reservation, 1922-1978.

91. Minnesota Year Book for 1851-55. 5 vols. St. Paul:
    W. G. LeDuc, etc., 1851-55. Contains information
    on the treaties of Traverse des Sioux and Mendota,
    1851.

92. The Nor'wester, 1863-70. Fort Garry newspaper re-
    ported on Sioux exiles as they arrived in Canada fol-
    lowing the Minnesota Sioux War.

93. Scree. Duck Down Press. Missoula, MT. Devoted to
    publishing American Indian poetry.

94. Sina Sapa Wocekiye Taeyanpaha, and English language
    Supplement to the Eyanpoha. Bilingual monthly news-
    paper published at Fort Totten, North Dakota, 1892-
    1913.

95. The South Dakotan. Monthly magazine published by the
    South Dakota Historical Society, 1898-1904.

96. Sun Tracks: An American Indian Literary Magazine.
    University of Arizona, Tucson, 1971- . Sponsored
    by the American Indian Student Club. Contains litera-
    ture by Indians of the southwest primarily, but also of
    others, including the Sioux.

97.  Wassaja:  A National Newspaper of Indian America.
     The American Indian Historical Society.  San Fran-
     cisco, 1973- .  Contains current affairs, miscel-
     laneous articles, section on arts, education, edi-
     torials, etc.


                 APPRAISALS AND CESSIONS

98.  Arneson, Harry E.  Appraisal of a Tract of Land in
     Lyman County, South Dakota, 1890-1900.  New York:
     Clearwater Publishing Co., 1973.  140 pp.  Indian
     Claims Commission report No. 78.

99.  Case, Francis H.  The Sioux Indians are Entitled to
     Settlement of their Claims.  Washington:  Govern-
     ment Printing Office, 1939.  16 pp.  Speech before
     the House of Representatives, July 6, 1939.

100. Elmquist, Gordon E.  Appraisal of the Lands of the
     Lower Sioux Community in Minnesota, Located in
     Northeast North Dakota near Devil's Lake, Based on
     the Treaties [Agreements] of 1884, 1885, 1895, 1897,
     1904, 1906, 1908, 1910.  New York:  Clearwater
     Publishing Co., 1974.  142 pp.  Indian Claims Com-
     mission report No. 363.  Contains maps, bibliogra-
     phies.

101. Fenton, Harry R.  Appraisal of the Black Hills Area
     of South Dakota, 1877.  New York:  Clearwater Pub-
     lishing Co., 1973.  190 pp.  Indian Claims Commis-
     sion report No. 74-B.  Contains maps.

102. Griffiths, Thomas M.  Yankton Sioux Tribe:  Appraisal
     of Lands in Nebraska, Iowa, Minnesota, South Da-
     kota and North Dakota, As of 1858.  New York:
     Clearwater Publishing Co., 1976.

103. Hickerson, Harold.  Anthropological Report on the In-
     dian Occupancy of Area 243 and 289 in Iowa, Min-
     nesota, South Dakota and Wisconsin, Ceded by the
     Mdewakanton Band of Sioux under the Treaty of Sep-
     tember 29, 1837.  New York:  Clearwater Publish-
     ing Co., 1973.  301 pp.  Indian Claims Commission
     report No. 360.  Contains maps, bibliographies.

104.  Hickerson, Harold. Anthropological Report on the In-
      dian Occupancy of Royce Area 289, Ceded by the Sis-
      seton and Wahpeton Bands of the Sioux Indians under
      the Treaty of July 23, 1851, and by the Mdewakanton
      and Wahpakoota Bands under the Treaty of August 5,
      1951. New York: Clearwater Publishing Co., 1973.
      75 pp. Indian Claims Commission report No. 362.
      Appears as pp. 226-301 of entry no. 96 above.

105.  Hilliard, Sam B. "Indian Land Cessions West of the
      Mississippi." JW, 10:3 (1971), 493-510. Includes
      Sioux.

106.  Hurt, Wesley R. Anthropological Report on Indian
      Occupancy of Certain Territory Claimed by the Da-
      kota Sioux Indians and by Rival Tribal Claimants in
      North and South Dakota, Colorado, Nebraska, Wyom-
      ing and Montana, 1868. New York: Clearwater Pub-
      lishing Co., 1973. 254 pp. Indian Claims Commis-
      sion report No. 74.

107.  Kleinman, Frank R., and Donald D. Myers. Apprais-
      al of Lands of the Sioux Nation in North and South
      Dakota, Wyoming, Nebraska and Montana, Acquired
      by the U.S. under the Treaty of April 29, 1868.
      New York: Clearwater Publishing Co., 1973. 354
      pp. Indian Claims Commission report No. 74.

108.  Murray, William G. Sioux Cession in Iowa and Min-
      nesota. New York: Clearwater Publishing Co.,
      1973. Appraisal of Royce Area No. 153, 1831.

109.  Murray, William G. Sioux Indian Tribe: Appraisal of
      Lands in North Dakota, South Dakota, Nebraska,
      Wyoming and Montana in 1869. New York: Clear-
      water Publishing Co., 1973. Indian Claims Com-
      mission report No. 74.

110.  Muske, William H. Appraisal of the Lands of the
      Sisseton and Wahpeton Tribes of North Dakota: Ap-
      praisal of Lands Disposed of under the Act of April
      27, 1904 and Land Excluded from the Devil's Lake
      Reservation by Erroneous Survey. New York:
      Clearwater Publishing Co., 1974. 100 pp. Indian
      Claims Commission report No. 363 (P).

111.  Myers, Donald D., and Frank R. Kleinman. Appraisal

of the Black Hills Lands of the Sioux Nation in South
Dakota. New York: Clearwater Publishing Co.,
1973. 132 pp. Indian Claims Commission report
No. 74-B.

112. Newcombe, Dewey, and Howard Lawrence. Sisseton
and Wahpeton Bands: Royce Area 413, 1859; Royce
Area 243, 1838; Royce Area 413, 1859; Pike's Pur-
chase Areas A and B, 1808; Appraisal of Lands in
Minnesota, Wisconsin, South Dakota, and Iowa. New
York: Clearwater Publishing Co., 1973. 346 pp.
Indian Claims Commission report No. 360.

113. Oberbillig, Ernest. Sioux Lands in the Black Hills,
South Dakota: Mineral Value as of 1877. New
York: Clearwater Publishing Co., 1973. 177 pp.
Indian Claims Commission report No. 74-B.

114. Shenon, P. J., and R. P. Full. Appraisal of the
Mineral Resources in the Lands of the Sioux Nation
in North and South Dakota, Montana, Wyoming and
Nebraska, Acquired under the Treaty of April 26,
1868. 4 vols. New York: Clearwater Publishing
Co., 1973. 2092 pp. Indian Claims Commission
report No. 74.

115. Tanner, Helen H. Ethnohistorical Report on the Sisseton and Wahpeton Tribes in North Dakota and South
Dakota and the Treaty of 1867 and the Agreement of
1872. New York: Clearwater Publishing Co., 1974.
134 pp. Indian Claims Commission report No.
363(P).

116. United States. Bureau of Indian Affairs. Appraisal
of Indian Property on the Oahe Reservoir Site Within the Cheyenne River Indian Reservation, South
Dakota. Billings, MT: Missouri River Basin Investigations Project, 1952. 31 pp.

117. United States Congress. House. Committee on Indian
Affairs. Sisseton and Wahpeton Payment for Lands.
76 Cong., 1st Sess., Hearings on H.R. 793, lands
ceded in 1851. 28 pp.

118. United States President (Johnson). Lands for Sioux
Indians: Message from the President of the United
States, in Answer to a Resolution of the House of

21st Ultimo, Transmitting a Report from the Secretary of the Interior Relative to Lands for Sioux Indians. Washington: Government Printing Office,
1866. 10 pp. Deals with the removal of Sioux from
Crow Creek, Minnesota and Iowa to Santee Reservation in Nebraska.

119. United States President (Harrison). Message from the
President of the United States, Transmitting Reports
Relative to the Proposed Division of the Great Sioux
Reservation, and Recommending Certain Legislation.
Washington: Government Printing Office, 1890. 308
pp. 51st Cong., 1st Sess., Sen. Ex. Doc., No.
51.

120. Woolworth, Alan R. Ethnohistorical Report on the Indian Occupancy of Royce Area 410, Yankton Sioux
in South Dakota. New York: Clearwater Publishing
Co., 1973. 236 pp. Indian Claims Commission report No. 332-A.


ARCHEOLOGY

121. Bass, William M. "The Variation in Physical Types
of the Prehistoric Plains Indians." PlA, 9:24 (April
1964), 64-145. Brief mention of the Sioux.

122. Bass, William M., and Donald C. Lacy. "Three Hu-
man Skeletons from the PK Burial Sheridan County,
Wyoming." PlA, 8:21 (August 1963), 142-157.
Skulls buried 300-800 years ago appear to be Siouan.

123. Chapman, Carl H., and Eleanor F. Chapman. Indians
and Archaeology of Missouri. Columbia: University
of Missouri Press, 1964.

124. Comfort, A. J. "Indian Mounds Near Fort Wadsworth,
Dakota Territory." ARSI (1871), pp. 389-402.

125. Cooper, Paul L. "Recent Investigations in Fort Randall and Oahe Reservoirs, South Dakota." AAn, 14:
4, Pt. 1 (1949), 300-310.

126. Daniel, Z. T. "Mounds in South Dakota." AA, 4:4
(October 1891), 327-328. Sioux say they were erected
by Rees as military defenses.

127.   Gilder, Robert F.   "Archeology of the Ponca Creek
       District, eastern Nebraska. "   AA, N. S.   9 (1907),
       702-719.

128.   Gregg, John B. , M. D. , and Ann Holzhueter.   "An
       Archeological Detective Story. "   PlA, 8:21 (August
       1963), 164-166.   On injuries found in the skull of
       Last Child, buried near Big Stone Lake.

129.   Gregg, John B. , M. D. , James P. Steele, M. D. , and
       Sylvester Clifford, Ph. D.   "Ear Diseases in Skulls
       from the Sully Burial Site. "   PlA, 10:30 (November
       1965), 233-239.   Probably Sioux.

130.   Gregg, John B. , M. D. , James P. Steele, M. D. , and
       Ann Holzhueter.   "Roentgenographic Evaluation of
       Temporal Bones from South Dakota Indian Burials. "
       AJPA, 23:1 (March 1965),  51-61.

131.   Griffin, James B.   "An Interpretation of Siouan Archae-
       ology in the Piedmont of North Carolina and Vir-
       ginia. "   AAn, 10 (1945), 321-330.   Siouan tribes of
       North Carolina in the period 1650-1700 had a rela-
       tively homogeneous archeological culture.

132.   Hill, Alfred J.   "Mounds in Dakota, Minnesota and
       Wisconsin. "   CMHS, 6 (1894), 311-319.

133.   Howard, James H.   "Archeological Investigations at
       the Spawn Mound, 39LK201, Lake County, South
       Dakota. "   PlA, 13:40 (May 1968), 132-139.   Appears
       to be a Plains woodland burial mound used later by
       Sioux for "secondary internments. "

134.   Hughes, Jack T.   "Investigations in Western South
       Dakota and Northeastern Wyoming. "   AAn, 14:4, Pt.
       1 (April 1949), 266-277.

135.   Hurt, Wesley R.   "Report of the Investigation of the
       Scalp Creek Site, 39GR1, and the Ellis Creek Site,
       39GR2, Gregory County, South Dakota. "   AS, 4
       (1952).

136.   Hurt, Wesley R.   "Report of the Investigation of the
       Spotted Bear Site, 39HU26, and the Cottonwood Site,
       39HU43, Hughes County, South Dakota. "   AS, 6
       (1954).

137.  Hurt, Wesley R.   "Report of the Investigation of the
      Swanson Site, 39BR16, Buffalo County, South Dakota."
      AS, 3 (1951).

138.  Hurt, Wesley R.   "Report of the Investigation of the
      Thomas Riggs Site, 39HU1, Hughes County, South
      Dakota."  AS, 5 (1953).

139.  Miller, Carl F.   "The Excavation and Investigation of
      Fort Lookout Trading Post II (39LM57) in the Fort
      Randall Reservoir, South Dakota."  BBAE, 176
      (1960), 49-82.

140.  Mills, John E.   "Historic Sites Archeology in the
      Fort Randall Reservoir, South Dakota."  BBAE, 176
      (1960), 25-48.

141.  Montgomery, Henry.   "Remains of Prehistoric Man in
      the Dakotas."  AA, N.S. 8 (1906), 640-651.  On
      forty mounds in Dakota Territory.

142.  Neuman, Robert W.   "The Good Soldier Site (39LM238)
      Big Bend Reservoir, Lyman County, South Dakota."
      BBAE, 189 (1964), 291-318.

143.  Pettigrew, F. W.   "A Pre-historic Indian Village."
      BMANS, 3 (1901), 348-355.

144.  Pond, Gideon H.   "Iowa Indians and Mounds."  CMHS,
      1 (1872), 144-146.   More on the Sioux than on Iowas.

145.  Riggs, Stephen R.   "Mounds of Minnesota Valley."
      CMHS, 1 (1872), 149-152.   Natural elevations used
      by Sioux for burial.

146.  Smith, Carlyle S.   "The Temporal Relationships of
      Coalescent Village Sites in Fort Randall Reservoir,
      South Dakota."  ICA, 33 (1958), 111-123.

147.  Smith, Harlan I.   "The Data of the Archaeology of the
      Dakotas."  CHSND, 1 (1906), 74-88.   Contains draw-
      ings of boulder mosaics and list of mounds in various
      counties.

148.  Weakly, Ward F.   "A Site in the Fort Randall Reser-
      voir, Brule County, South Dakota."  PlA, 6:14 (No-
      vember 1961), 230-241.

149.    Wedel, Waldo R.   "Archeological Materials from the
        Vicinity of Mobridge, South Dakota." BBAE, 157
        (1955), 69-188.

150.    Wedel, Waldo R.   "Prehistory and the Missouri Val-
        ley Development Program:  Summary Report on the
        Missouri River Basin Archeological Survey in 1948."
        BBAE, 154 (1953), xv-60.

151.    Wedel, Waldo R.   "Prehistory and the Missouri Valley
        Development Program:  Summary Report on the Mis-
        souri River Basin Archeological Survey, 1949."
        BBAE, 154 (1953), 61-102.

152.    Wilford, Lloyd A.   Burial Mounds of the Red River
        Headwaters.   St. Paul:  Minnesota Historical Society,
        1970.

153.    Wilford, Lloyd A.   Late Prehistoric Burial Mounds of
        the Red River Valley.   St. Paul:  Minnesota Histor-
        ical Society, 1970.

154.    Wilford, Lloyd A.   "The Prehistoric Indians of Min-
        nesota." MiH, 25 (June 1944), 153-157.

155.    Wilford, Lloyd A.   "The Prehistoric Indians of Min-
        nesota:  The Mille Lacs Aspect." MiH, 25 (Decem-
        ber 1944), 329-341.

156.    Wood, Raymond W., et al.   "The Paul Brave Site
        (32SI4) Oahe Reservoir Area, North Dakota." BBAE,
        (1964), ix-66.

157.    Woolworth, Alan R., et al.   "The Demery Site (39C01)
        Oahe Reservoir Area, South Dakota." BBAE, 189
        (1964), 67-138.

## ARTS AND CULTURE

158.    Alexander, Hartley B., ed.   Sioux Indian Painting.   2
        vols.   Nice, France:  C. Szwedzicki, 1938.

159.    Amiotte, Arthur, and Myles Libhart, eds.   Photographs
        and Poems by Indian Children, from the Porcupine
        Day School, Pine Ridge Indian Reservation, South

Dakota. Rapid City, SD: Tipi Shop Inc., 1971. 77
pp. Includes an essay by Arthur Amiotte.

160. Anderson, Harry. "A Sioux Pictorial Account of General Terry's Council at Fort Walsh, October 17,
1877." NDH, 22:3 (July 1955), 92-116. A group
photo contains Spotted Tail, Roman Nose, Old Man
Afraid of His Horse, Lone Horn, Whistling Elk, and
Pipe. Also, two pictographs.

161. Anderson, John A., comp. Among the Sioux. New
York: Albertype, 1896. Sixteen pages with photographs; no text.

162. Anderson, John A., Eugene Buechel, and Don Doll.
Crying for a Vision: A Rosebud Sioux Trilogy 1886-
1976. Ed. Don Doll and Jim Alinder. Dobbs Ferry,
NY: Morgan & Morgan, 1976. Over 100 pages of
photographs with foreword by Ben Black Bear, Jr.

163. Anderson, Myrtle M. Sioux Memory Game. Chicago:
University of Chicago Press, 1929. Descriptions
of recreational games.

164. Babcock, Thornton. "Primitive Customs." CHSSD, 6
(1912), 279. Information from Charles R. Crawford,
half-brother to Gabriel Renville, about the Sisseton-
Wahpeton tribe.

165. Baber, Bernard. "Acculturation and the Messianic
Movements." ASR, 6 (October 1941), 663-669.

166. Bad Heart Bull, Amos. A Pictographic History of the
Oglala Sioux. Text Helen M. Blish; intro. Mari
Sandoz. Lincoln: University of Nebraska Press,
1967. Bad Heart Bull's drawings for the period
1890-1913.

167. Bates, Jane. "Things Got Turned Around." GPO,
March 1968, p. 9. Urges the perpetuation of Indian
culture.

168. Beach, Rex E. "The Great Sioux Festival." Apple-
ton's Magazine, September 1905, pp. 305-316.

169. Beckwith, Paul. "Notes on Customs of the Dakotahs."
ARSI, Pt. 1 (1886), pp. 245-257. Unreliable source.

170. Beede, Aaron McGaffey. "The Dakota Indian Victory
     Dance." NDHQ, 9:3 (April 1942), 167-178. Episco-
     pal missionary reports on a celebration near Fort
     Yates November 30, 1918, at the end of World War
     I.

171. Belitz, Larry. Step-by-Step Brain Tanning the Sioux
     Way. Hot Springs, SD: Larry Belitz, 1973. 16 pp.
     Techniques Belitz acquired on Pine Ridge Reserva-
     tion.

172. "Big Town of the Plains Indians." Hobbies, 63 (Janu-
     ary 1959), 114.

173. Boas, Franz. "Teton Sioux Music." JAFL, 38 (April-
     June 1925), 319-324.

174. "A Boulder Outline on the Upper Missouri." CHSND,
     3 (1910), 684-687. Located on the Missouri north
     of Mandan.

175. Bryde, John. "Indian Heritage: Adopt Old Values to
     New World." GPO, April 1968, pp. 4-6.

176. Bryde, John. "Indian Heritage: Bravery--A Way of
     Life." GPO, May 1968, pp. 10-11.

177. Bryde, John. "Indian Heritage: Brother to All of
     Nature." GPO, August 1968, pp. 4-5.

178. Bryde, John. "Indian Heritage: His Freedom to
     Choose Wisely, Surely." GPO, June 1968, pp. 10-
     13.

179. Bryde, John. "Indian Heritage: A Life Is Wakan."
     GPO, November 1968, pp. 10-14.

180. Bryde, John. "Indian Heritage: Look Deep into All."
     GPO, October 1968, pp. 12-13.

181. Bryde, John. "Indian Heritage: Sharing, to Survive,
     to Be Nature's Partner." GPO, July 1968, pp. 6-8.

182. Bryde, John. "Indian Heritage: Utter Acceptance of
     Others." GPO, September 1968, pp. 8-14.

183. Bushnell, David I. "The Various Uses of Buffalo Hair

by the North American Indians. " AA, N. S. 11:3
(July-September 1909), 401-425.

184.   Case, H. W.   "North Dakota's Sculptress and Artist,
       Ida Prokop Lee, Presents Sculptured Portraits of
       the Major North Dakota Indian Tribes to the State. "
       NDH, 24:2 (April 1957), 106-112.   Yanktonai Sioux
       Mary Louise Defender, of Standing Rock, was chosen
       as model.

185.   Cohen, Lucy Cramer.   "Big Missouri's Winter Count--
       A Sioux Calendar 1796-1926. "  IW, February 1939,
       pp. 16-20.   Interprets the symbols on this famous
       winter count of the Rosebud Sioux.

186.   Cohen, Lucy Cramer.   "Even in Those Days Pictures
       Were Important. "  IW, January 1942, pp. 19-21.

187.   Cohen, Lucy Cramer.   "Swift Bear's Winter Count. "
       IW, January 1942, pp. 18-21; and February 1942,
       pp. 30-31; and March 1942, pp. 29-30.

188.   Coler, Della.   "Crow Creek Bags. "  IW, 15 Decem-
       ber 1935, p. 12.   Searching for a saleable craft
       article, Crow Creek Sioux women make beaded wom-
       en's bags.

189.   Culin, Stewart.   "Games of the North American In-
       dians. "  ARBAE, 24 (1907), 846 pp.   Rpt. New
       York:  Dover, 1975.

190.   Curtis, Edward S.   The Sioux and the Apsaroke.
       From vols. 3 and 4 of The North American Indian.
       Ed. Stuart Zoll.  New York:  Harper, 1975.  100 pp.

191.   Daniels, Robert E.   "Cultural Identities Among the
       Oglala Sioux. "  See entry 528, pp. 189-245.

192.   Deloria, Ella, and Jay Brandon, trans.   "The Origin
       of the Courting-Flute, a Legend in the Santee Dia-
       lect. "  USDMN, 22:6 (1961), 1-7.

193.   Densmore, Frances.   "A Collection of Specimens from
       the Teton Sioux. "  INM, 11:3 (1948), 169-204, and
       24 plates.

194.   Densmore, Frances.   "Imitative Dances Among the

American Indians. " JAFL, 60 (January-March 1947),
73-78. Dances imitating animals and birds.

195. Densmore, Frances. "Music in Relation to the Religious Thought of the Teton Sioux. " In Holmes Anniversary Volume. Washington: Government Printing Office, 1916, pp. 68-78.

196. Densmore, Frances. Poems from Sioux and Chippewa
Songs. Washington: Government Printing Office,
1917. 23 pp. Poems from nine Sioux songs, most
of which are ceremonial.

197. Densmore, Frances. "Prelude to the Study of Indian
Music in Minnesota. " MA, 11 (April 1945), 27-31.

198. Densmore, Frances. "The Study of Indian Music. "
ARSI (1941), pp. 527-550.

199. Densmore, Frances. Teton Sioux Music. BBAE, 61
(1918); rpt. New York: Da Capo, 1972; St. Clair
Shores, Mich. : Scholarly Press, 1977. 516 pp.
An outstanding work.

200. Densmore, Frances. "Teton Sioux Music. " Nature,
28 August 1919, pp. 515-516.

201. Densmore, Frances. "The Use of Music in the Treatment of the Sick by American Indians. " ARSI (1952),
pp. 439-454. Photographs of two men who used
music in treatment.

202. Denver Public Library, Western History Department.
David F. Barry Catalog of Photographs. Denver:
Denver Public Library, 1960. 24 pp.

203. "Doctor Frances Densmore, Red Wing, Minnesota,
1867-1957. " MA, 20:2 (Spring 1957). Memorial
issue.

204. Dole, Gertrude Evelyn, and Robert L. Carneiro, eds.
Essays in the Science of Culture: In Honor of Leslie A. White, in Celebration of His Sixtieth Birthday
and His Thirtieth Year of Teaching at the University
of Michigan. New York: Crowell, 1960. 509 pp.
On Dakota Indians, see pp. 249-268.

205.   Dorsey, J. Owen. "Games of the Dakota Children. "
       AA, 4:4 (October 1891), 329-345.

206.   Dunn, Dorothy, ed.   1877:  Plains Indian Sketchbook
       of Zu-Tom and Howling Wolf.  Flagstaff, AZ:  North-
       land Press, 1969.

207.   Dyck, Paul.  Brule:  The Sioux People of Rosebud.
       Flagstaff, AZ:  Northland Press, 1970.  365 pp.
       Excellent collection of photographs with identifying
       texts.  Photos taken by John A. Anderson on Rose-
       bud Reservation between 1880 and 1920.

208.   Dyck, Paul. "The Plains Indian Shield. "  AIAM,  1:1
       (November 1975), 34-41.  The Sioux material beau-
       tifully illustrated.

209.   [Dykshorn, Jan, ed.]  "Sitting Bull Collection. "  SDH,
       5:3 (Summer 1975), 245-265.  Stereoptic views from
       the Stanley J. Morrow collection, copyrighted by
       Bailey, Dix and Mead.  The 24 views, of Ft. Ran-
       dall, were purchased by The Historical Society from
       Mrs. Leona Dix Wilber in 1932.

210.   Dykshorn, Jan. "William Fuller's Crow Creek and
       Lower Brule Paintings. "  SDH, 6:4 (Fall 1976), 411-
       420.  On Indian camp scenes, burials, and other
       traditional material.

211.   Easter, Georgia R.  "Badlands Soil Used to Decorate
       Indian Homes. "  IW, 21 June 1935, pp. 28-30.
       Badlands clay, long used by Indian women to decorate
       leather, was used to tint the walls of reservation
       homes.

212.   Easter, Georgia R. "Indian Ingenuity Leads to Unique
       Quilt Making. "  IW, 1 May 1935, pp. 38-39.  Mary
       Scout of Wounded Knee made eight-point star quilts
       from Bull Durham tobacco bags.

213.   Eastman, Charles A.  "The American Eagle:  An In-
       dian Symbol. "  AIM (Summer 1919), pp. 89-92.

214.   Eastman, Charles A.  "Indian Handicrafts. "  C, 8
       (August 1905), 658-662.

215.   Eastman, Charles A.  "The Language of Footprints. "
       StN, 44 (January 1917), 267-269.

216. Eastman, Charles A. "My People: The Indian's Con-
     tribution to the Art of America." The Red Man,
     December 1914, pp. 133-140.

217. Ewers, John C. Early White Influence upon Plains
     Indian Painting: George Catlin and Carl Bodmer
     among the Mandan. 1957; rpt. Seattle, WA:
     Shorey Publications, 1978.

218. Ewers, John C. "The George Catlin Collection of
     Painting in the U.S. National Museum." ARSI (1955),
     pp. 507-528.

219. Ewers, John C. "George Catlin, Painter of Indians
     and the West." ARSI (1955), pp, 483-528.

220. Ewers, John C. "Hair Pipes in Plains Indian Adorn-
     ment, A Study in Indian and White Ingenuity." BBAE,
     164 (1957), 29-86; rpt. Microfiche by NCR Micro-
     card, 1969.

221. Ewers, John C. Indian Art in Pipestone: George
     Catlin's Portfolio in the British Museum. Washing-
     ton, DC: Smithsonian Institution, 1978.

222. Ewers, John C. "Notes on the Weasel in Historic
     Plains Indian Culture." PIA, 22:Pt. 1 (November
     1977), 253-262.

223. Ewers, John C. Plains Indian Painting. Stanford:
     Stanford University Press, 1939.

224. Ewers, John C. "Plains Indian Painting." AW, 5:2
     (1968), 4-15, 74-76.

225. Ewers, John C. "Three Effigy Pipes by an Eastern
     Dakota Master Carver." AIAM, 3:4 (August 1978),
     51-55, 74.

226. Feder, Norman. Art of the Eastern Plains Indians:
     The Nathan Sturges Jarvis Collection. Brooklyn,
     NY: Brooklyn Institute of Arts and Sciences Museum,
     1964. 67 pp.

227. Feder, Norman. "Old Time Sioux Customs." AIH,
     4:3-4 (1957), 23-31.

228. Feder, Norman. "Plains Indian Metalworking with

Emphasis on Hairplates. " AIT, 8:2 (1962), 55-76.
On the flowering of metalwork, 1865-1880.

229.  Feder, Norman.  "Plains Indian Metalworking, Part
      II. "  AIT, 8:3 (1962), 93-112.

230.  Feder, Norman.  "Sioux Kettle Dance. "  AIH, 4:3-4
      (1957), 37-38.

231.  Fernberger, Samuel W. , and Frank G. Speck.  "Two
      Sioux Shields and Their Psychological Interpretation. "
      JASP, 33:2 (April 1938), 168-178.  Illustrated.

232.  Flecky, Michael, and Harold Moore, eds.  Photo Al-
      bum:  St. Francis Mission, School, and Community
      1886-1976.  St. Francis, SD:  Rosebud Educational
      Society, 1976.  61 pages of photos based on the
      Lakota Heritage Collection, which is largely unpub-
      lished.

233.  Forbes, [Major] William H.  "Traditions of Sioux In-
      dians. "  CMHS, 6 (1894), 413-416.

234.  Gilmore, Melvin R.  "Uses of Plants by the Indians
      of the Missouri River Region. "  ARBAE, 33 (1919),
      43-154; rpt. Lincoln:  University of Nebraska Press,
      1977.  About the practical and symbolic uses of
      plants.

235.  Grange, Roger T.  "The Garnier Oglala Winter Count. "
      PIA, 8 (May 1963), 74-79.  Text from a Winter
      Count covering the period 1795-1908.

236.  Grant, Campbell.  Rock Art of the American Indians.
      New York:  Crowell, 1967.

237.  Gundlach, Ralph H.  "A Quantitative Analysis of Indian
      Music. "  AJP, 44:1 (1932), 133-145.

238.  Hamilton, Henry W. , and Jean T. Hamilton, eds.  The
      Sioux of the Rosebud:  A History in Pictures.  Nor-
      man:  University of Oklahoma Press, 1971.  Excel-
      lent representation of life on Rosebud Reservation in
      the period 1880-1920 in some 200 plates of the pho-
      tographs of John A. Anderson.

239.  Hanson, James A.  Metal Weapons, Tools, and Orna-

ments of the Teton Dakota Indians. Lincoln: University of Nebraska Press, 1975. 118 pp. A comprehensive guide to the identification and use of
metal objects.

240. Herzog, George. "Plains Ghost Dance and Great
Basin Music." AA, 37:3 (July-September 1935), 403-
417.

241. Hlady, Walter M. "Some Dakota Songs." NDH, 19:2
(April 1952), 141-143. Words and music for three
songs.

242. Hoffman, Charles. "Frances Densmore and the Music
of the American Indian." JAFL, 49 (January-March
1946), 45-50.

243. Hoffman, J. Jacob. Comments on the Use and Dis-
tribution of Tipi Rings in Montana, North Dakota,
South Dakota, and Wyoming. Missoula: Montana
State University Press, 1953.

244. Holder, Preston. The Hoe and the Horse on the Plains:
A Study of Cultural Development Among North Amer-
ican Indians. Lincoln: University of Nebraska
Press, 1970.

245. Howard, James H. "The Compleat Stomp Dance."
USDMN, 26 (May-June 1965), 1-23.

246. Howard, James H. "The Cultural Position of the Dakota: A Reassessment." In Essays in the Science
of Culture, in Honor of Leslie A. White. Ed. Gertrude E. Dole and Robert L. Carneiro. New York:
Thomas Y. Crowell, 1960, pp. 249-268.

247. Howard, James H. "Dakota Fishing Practices."
USDMN, 12:5 (1951), 1-3.

248. Howard, James H. "The Dakota Indian Victory Dance
World War II." NDH, 18:1 (January 1951), 31-40.

249. Howard, James H. "Dakota Interpretations of Bird
Calls." USDMN, 27:11/12 (1961), 19.

250. Howard, James H. "Dakota Winter Counts as a Source
of Plains History." BBAE, 173 (1960), 335-420; rpt.
microfiche by NCR on microcard, 1969.

251.  Howard, James H.   "Drifting Goose's Village. "
      USDMN,  16:4 (1954),  2.

252.  Howard, James H.   "New Notes on the Dakota Earth
      Lodge. "  Plains Conference News Letter,  4 (1951),
      4-9.

253.  Howard, James H.   "The Northern Style Grass Dance
      Costume. "  AIH,  7 (1960),  18-27.

254.  Howard, James H.   "Notes on the Dakota Grass
      Dance. "  SJA,  7 (1951),  82-85.  This dance, which
      originated among the Omahas,  is among the ones
      most commonly practiced by the Sioux.

255.  Howard, James H.   "Plains Indian Feather Bonnets. "
      PlA,  No. 2 (December 1954),  23-26.

256.  Howard, James H.   "Two Dakota Dream Headdresses. "
      USDMN,  12:4 (1951),  1-4.

257.  Howard, James H.   "Two Dakota Winter Count Texts. "
      PlA,  No. 5 (December 1955),  13-30.   In Dakota
      with translation,  by Edward Roan Bear.

258.  Howard, James H.   "Two Teton Dakota Winter Count
      Texts. "  NDH,  27:2 ( Spring 1960),  66-79.   Explains
      the nature and purpose of these Sioux pictographs.

259.  Howard, James H.   "The White Bull Manuscript. "
      PlA,  6: Pt. 2 (May 1961),  115-116.   With pictographs
      and Sioux language text,  confirms Stanley Vestal's
      belief that Minneconjou Joseph White Bull killed
      Custer.

260.  Howard, James H.   "Yanktonai Dakota Eagle Trapping. "
      SJA,  10:1 (1954),  69-74.

261.  Howard, James H.   "Yanktonai Ethnohistory and the
      John K. Bear Winter Count. "  PlA,  21:pt. 2 (August
      1976).   78 pp.   A winter count,  probably done by
      Yanktonai Chief Drifting Goose for the period 1682-
      1833,  is the longest in existence.

262.  Howe, Oscar.   Artist/Paintings and Commentaries.
      Intro. John Milton.   Vermillion:   University of South
      Dakota, 1974.   40 pp.

263.  Hrdlicka, Ales.  "Indian Trap Pits Along the Missouri."
      AA, 18:4 (October-December 1916), 546-547.  About
      Sioux bird traps.

264.  Hulsizer, Allen L.  Region and Culture in the Cur-
      riculum of the Navajo and the Dakota.  Federalsburg,
      MD: J. W. Stowell Co., 1940.

265.  Humphrey, Norman D.  "A Characterization of Certain
      Plains Associations."  AA, 43:3 (July-September 1941),
      428-436.

266.  Hunt, W. B.  "Sioux Ghost Shirt: With Drawings and
      Instructions."  IAVE, 30 (September 1941), 308-309.

267.  Hurt, Wesley R., and James H. Howard.  "Two New-
      ly-Recorded Dakota House Types."  SJA, 6 (1950),
      423-426.  Reveals, with information from John Saul,
      that around Crow Creek Yanktons, Yanktonais, Wah-
      pekutes, Wahpetons and Mdewakantons once lived
      in earth lodges and log structures.

268.  Hurt, Wesley R., and William E. Lass.  Frontier
      Photographer: Stanley J. Morrow's Dakota Years.
      Vermillion: University of South Dakota, 1956.  135
      pp.

269.  Johnson, Elden.  "Notes on the Mdewakanton Bark
      House."  MA, 24 (April 1962), 48-52.

270.  Joyes, Dennis C.  "The Thunderbird Motif at Writing
      Rock State Historic Site."  NDH, 45:2 (Spring 1978),
      22-25.  In the northwest corner of North Dakota.

271.  Kant, Joanita.  Old Style Plains Indian Dolls from Col-
      lections in South Dakota.  Vermillion: University of
      South Dakota, 1975.  50 pp.

272.  Karol, Joseph S., ed.  Red Horse Owner's Winter
      Count: The Oglala Sioux 1786-1968.  Martin, SD:
      Boster Publishing Co., 1969.  67 pp.  Photographs
      of the winter count of Moses Red Horse Owner, who
      died in 1908 at age 72.

273.  Kehoe, Thomas F., and Alice B. Kehoe.  "Boulder
      Effigy Monuments in the Northern Plains."  JAFL,
      72 (April-June 1959), 115-127.

274.   Koch, Ronald P.   Dress Clothing of the Plains Indians.
       Norman:   University of Oklahoma Press, 1977.   219
       pp.

275.   Krieger, Herbert W.   "Aspects of Aboriginal Decora-
       tive Art in America Based on Specimens in the
       United States National Museum. "   ARSI (1930), pp.
       519-556.

276.   Kroeber, Alfred L.   "The Ceremonial Organization of
       the Plains Indians of North America. "   ICA, 15: Vol.
       2 (1906),   53-63.

277.   Laubin, Reginald, and Gladys Laubin.   American In-
       dian Archery.   Norman:   University of Oklahoma
       Press, 1978.

278.   Laubin, Reginald, and Gladys Laubin.   Indian Dances
       of North America:   Their Importance to Indian Life.
       Norman:   University of Oklahoma Press, 1977.   538
       pp.   Although the historical text is weak, the de-
       scriptions of dances and their religious cultural sig-
       nificance are excellent.   The work of two experienced
       dancers who have done much of their work among the
       western Sioux.

279.   Laubin, Reginald, and Gladys Laubin.   The Indian Tipi:
       Its History, Construction, and Use.   Norman:   Uni-
       versity of Oklahoma Press, 1957; rpt. 1969; 2nd ed.
       Norman:   University of Oklahoma Press, 1977.   208
       pp.   Best publication on the topic.

280.   Laubin, Reginald, and Gladys Laubin.   "Old Chief's
       Dance. "   Nine-minute color film of a dance recount-
       ing a chief's deeds, as taught the Laubins by One
       Bull, nephew of Sitting Bull.   Available in Film
       Series:   Plains Indian Culture by purchase only.

281.   Laubin, Reginald, and Gladys Laubin.   "Talking
       Hands. "   Twenty-minute color film on inter-tribal
       sign language.   Available in Film Series:   Plains In-
       dian Culture by purchase only.

282.   Laubin, Reginald, and Gladys Laubin.   "War Dance. "
       Twelve-minute color film on the Grass Dance, which
       the Sioux acquired from the Omahas.   Available in
       Film Series:   Plains Indian Culture by purchase only.

283.  Lewis, Theodore H.  "Bowlder Outline Figures in the
      Dakotas, Surveyed in the Summer of 1870. " AA, 4:
      1 (January 1891), 19-24.

284.  Lewis, Theodore H.  "Stone Monuments in Southern
      Dakota. " AA, 2:2 (April 1889), 159-164.

285.  Linck, Olaf.  En Sommar bland Siouxindianer.  Stock-
      holm: Almquist and Wiksells Forlag, 1926.  178 pp.
      Contains Sioux music.

286.  Linton, Ralph, ed.  Acculturation in Seven American
      Tribes.  New York:  Appleton-Century-Crofts, 1940;
      rpt. Gloucester, MA:  Peter Smith, 1970.

287.  Linton, Ralph.  "The Origin of the Plains Earth
      Lodge. " AA, 26:2 (April-June 1924), 247-257.

288.  Little Duck.  "How the First White Man Came to
      America. " Trans. Roger St. Pierre.  CHSND, 3
      (1910), 725-727.

289.  Lowie, Robert H.  "Dance Associations of the Eastern
      Dakota. " APAMN, 11:Pt. 2 (1913), 101-142.  De-
      scribes some twenty dances.

290.  Lyford, Carrie A.  Quill and Beadwork of the Western
      Sioux.  Lawrence, KS:  Printing Department, Haskell
      Institute, 1940.  116 pp.

291.  Lyford, Carrie A.  Sioux Beadwork.  Lawrence, KS:
      Haskell Institute, 1933.  27 pp.

292.  Lyford, Carrie A.  " Sioux Designs and Their Ori-
      gins. " IW, 15 February 1933, p. 33.

293.  McDermott, John Francis.  Seth Eastman:  Pictorial
      Historian of the Indian.  Norman:  University of
      Oklahoma Press, 1961.

294.  Malan, Vernon D.  Acculturation of the Dakota Indians.
      Rev. James L. Satterlee.  2nd ed.  Brookings, SD:
      Agriculture Experiment Station, South Dakota State
      University, 1968.  46 pp.

295.  Malan, Vernon D.  "Theories of Culture Change Rele-
      vant to the Study of the Dakota Indians. " PlA, 6
      (1961), 13-20.

296.   Malan, Vernon D.   "To Change a Culture."  SDFHR,
       3 (Fall 1962), 12-14.

297.   Malan, Vernon D.   To Change a Culture.   Brookings,
       SD:   Agriculture Experiment Station, South Dakota
       State University, n. d.   On the difficulties the Pine
       Ridge Sioux have in adjusting to the white world.

298.   Malan, Vernon D.   "The Value System of the Dakota
       Indians. "  JAIE,  3 (1963),  21-25.

299.   Malan, Vernon D. , and Martin Kallich.   "A Changing
       Dakota Indian Culture. "  SDFHR,  8 (May 1957),  11-
       15.

300.   Malan, Vernon D. , and R. Clyde McCone.   "The
       Time Concept, Perspective, and Premise in the
       Socio-Cultural Order of the Dakota Indians. "  PlA,
       5:9 (May 1960),  12-15.

301.   Meeker, Louis L.   Oglala Games.   PUMB,  3 (1901),
       23-46.

302.   Milligan, Edward A.   Petroglyphs, Pictographs, and
       Prehistoric Art in the Upper Missouri River and the
       Red River of the North Valley Areas.   Bottineau,
       ND:   Published Privately, 1968.   20 pp. , with photo-
       graphs.

303.   Milwaukee Public Museum.   Miller Collection of Sioux
       Indian Drawings.   Milwaukee, WI:  Moebius Printing
       Co. , 1961.   8 pp.

304.   Morgan, Alfred.   "A Description of a Dakota Calendar,
       With a Few Ethnographical and Other Notes on the Da-
       kotas, or Sioux Indians, and Their Territory. "  Pro-
       ceedings of the Literary and Philosophical Society of
       Liverpool.   33 (1879), 233-253.

305.   Morgan, Lewis H.   The Houses and House Life of the
       American Aborigine.   Chicago:   University of Chi-
       cago Press, 1966.

306.   Murray, Robert A.   Pipes on the Plains.   Pipestone,
       MN:  Pipestone Indian Shrive Association, 1968.   41
       pp.   With photographs, relates the origin of the
       Pipe legend and describes the manufacture of pipes.

307. Newell, Cicero. Life Among the Sioux Indians. New York: New York Popular Publishing Co., 1889. 13 pp.

308. Newell, Sylvia. "Dancing at Standing Rock." IW, 1 August 1935, p. 32. During the early 1930s.

309. Nydahl, Theodore L. "The Pipestone Quarry and the Indians." MiH, 31:4 (December 1950), 193-208.

310. Oliver, Symmes C. "Ecology and Cultural Continuity as Contributing Factors in the Social Organization of the Plains Indians." UCP, 41:1 (1962). 70 pp.

311. Orchard, William C. "The Technique of Porcupine-Quill Decoration Among the North American Indians." CMAI, 4:1 (1916), 1-54.

312. Over, W. H. Indian Picture Writing in South Dakota. Vermillion: University of South Dakota, 1941.

313. Page, Jean J. "Frank Blackwell Mayer: Painter of the Minnesota Indian." MiH, 46:2 (Summer 1978), 66-74. Contains many Sioux, including Chiefs Little Crow and Male Raven.

314. Paige, Harry W. Songs of the Teton Sioux. Los Angeles, CA: Westernlore Press, 1969. 201 pp.

315. "Paintings Done by Students at Santa Fe Indian School Receive Wide Recognition." IW, October 1937, p. 22. On "Warriors," a painting by Oscar Howe.

316. Partridge, William L. "Analysis of Crow Enculturation (As Compared to Sioux Enculturation) 1868 to 1880." Florida Anthropologist, 18 (1965), 225-34.

317. Petersen, Eugene. "Tipi How." Norman: University of Oklahoma Press, 1977. A ten-minute color film, available through purchase only, featuring Reginald and Gladys Laubin, on the virtues of Tipi living.

318. Petersen, Karen D. Plains Indian Art from Fort Marion. Norman: University of Oklahoma Press, 1971. 340 pp.

319. "Photographic Portraits of North American Indians in

the Gallery of the Smithsonian Institution. " SMC, 14 (1878). 42 pp.

320.   Poatgieter, Alice H.   "The Sioux Tepee. "  GH,  22 (Winter 1967-68),  17-23.

321.   Pohrt, Richard A.   "The Indian and the American Flag. "  AIAM,  1:2 (February 1976),  42-48.   Primarily on the Sioux.

322.   Pohrt, Richard A.   "Plains Indian Moccasins with Decorated Soles. "  AIAM,  2:3 (Summer 1977),  32-39, 84.

323.   Powers, William K.   "Contemporary Oglala Music and Dance:   Pan-Indianism Versus Pan-Tetonism. "  See entry no. 528, pp. 268-290.

324.   Powers, William K.   "The Rabbit Dance. "  AIT,  8:3 (1962), pp.  113-118.

325.   Powers, William K.   "The Sioux Omaha Dance. "  AIT, 8:1 (1961),  24-33.

326.   Powers, William K.   "Sneak-up Dance, Drum Dance, and Flag Dance. "  AIT,  8:4 (1962),  166-171.

327.   Powers, William K.   "A Winter Count of the Oglala. " No. 52 (1963),  27-37.

328.   Praus, Alexis.   The Sioux, 1798-1922:   A Dakota Winter Count.   Bloomfield Hills, Mich. :   Cranbrook Institute of Science, 1962.   31 pp.   On the Tetons.

329.   Prescott, Philander.   "Manners, Customs, and Opinions of the Dacotahs. "  In School, Pt. IV, pp. 59-72.

330.   Primbs, Charles.   The Sunflower Dance of the Sioux Indians of the Upper Missouri.   Norfolk, VA:   Landmark Office, 1876.   15 pp.

331.   Provinse, John J.   "The Underlying Sanctions of Plains Indian Culture. "  In Social Anthropology of North American Tribes.   Ed. Fred Eggan.   Chicago:   University of Chicago Press, 1937, pp. 341-374.

332.  Rau, Charles.  "Ancient Aboriginal Trade in North
      America."  ARSI (1872), pp. 348-394.  About the
      Sioux and the use of Pipestone.

333.  Remington, Frederic.  Artist Wanderings Among the
      Cheyennes.  1889; rpt. Seattle, WA:  Shorey Pub-
      lications, 1970.

334.  Remington, Frederic.  Pony Tracks.  Rpt. Columbus,
      OH:  Long's College Book Co., 1951; Norman:  Uni-
      versity of Oklahoma Press, 1969.

335.  Remington, Frederic.  Remington's Frontier Sketches.
      1898; rpt. New York:  Burt Franklin Pub., 1970.

336.  Remington, Frederic.  The Way of an Indian.  1906;
      rpt. Upper Saddle River, NJ:  Literature House/
      The Gregg Press, 1971.

337.  Reynolds, Sam.  "A Dakota Tipi."  NDH, 40:4 (Fall
      1973), 20-29.  With many photographs.

338.  Ritzenthaler, Robert E., ed.  Sioux Indian Drawings:
      The Miller Collection.  Milwaukee, WI:  Milwaukee
      Public Museum, 1961.  8 pp.  36 Plates.  Pen and
      ink drawings by the Sioux Red Hawk, on warfare,
      counting coup, and capturing horses.

339.  Rodee, Howard D.  "The Stylistic Development of
      Plains Indian Painting and Its Relationship to Ledger
      Drawings."  PlA, 10 (November 1965), 218-232.

340.  Roehm, Marjorie C., ed.  The Letters of George Cat-
      lin and His Family:  A Chronicle of the American
      West.  Berkeley:  University of California Press,
      1966.

341.  Rooks, Mable A.  Collections of Dakota Sioux Designs.
      Nemo, SD:  The Black Hills Recreation Laboratory,
      1958.  51 pp.

342.  Ross, Marvin C., ed.  George Catlin:  Episodes From
      Life Among the Indians and Last Rambles.  Norman:
      University of Oklahoma Press, 1959.  354 pp.

343.  Selmser, James L.  The Dakota Indian:  His Culture
      and His Religion.  Cambridge, MA:  Harvard College
      Library, 1955.  Microfilm publication.

344.  Sharp, J. H. "The Voice of the Great Spirit." TB,
      1:9 (September 1915), 275-276. On painting a Sioux
      burial and mourner.

345.  Sheldon, Addison E. "Ancient Indian Fireplaces in
      South Dakota Bad-Lands." AA, 7:1 (January-March
      1905), 44-48.

346.  Sheldon, Addison E. "Ancient Indian Fireplaces in
      South Dakota Bad-Lands." CHSSD, 6 (1912), 215-
      223.

347.  "Shinny and 'Snakes' on Rosebud." IW, 1 August 1935,
      pp. 30-31.

348.  "Sioux Designs." IW, 15 February 1935, pp. 34-38.
      Sketches of Sioux artistic designs.

349.  Skinner, Alanson. "A Sketch of Eastern Dakota Eth-
      nology." AA, 21:2 (April-June 1919), 164-174. On
      utensils, picture writing, tanning, games, naming,
      marriage, etc.

350.  Speck, Frank G. "Notes on the Functional Basis of
      Decoration and the Feather Technique of the Oglala
      Sioux." IN, 5 (1928), 1-42.

351.  Speck, Frank G., and Royal B. Hassrick. "A Plains
      Indian Shield and Its Interpretation." PrM, 21
      (1948), 74-79.

352.  Squires, John L., and Robert E. McLean. American
      Indian Dances: Steps, Rhythms, Costumes, and In-
      terpretation. New York: The Ronald Press, 1963.
      132 pp.

353.  Stipe, Claude E. Eastern Dakota Acculturation: The
      Role of Agents in Culture. Minneapolis: University
      of Minnesota Press, 1968. 296 pp.

354.  Strong, William D. "The Plains Culture Area in the
      Light of Archaeology." AA, 35:2 (April-June 1933),
      271-287.

355.  Sutton, Royal, ed. The Face of Courage: The Indian
      Photographic of Frank A. Rinehart. Fort Collins,
      CO: Old Army Press, 1972.

356. Taylor, Colin. "Early Plains Indian Quill Techniques in European Museum Collections." PlA, 7 (February 1962), 58-69.

357. Thayer, Burton W. "The Sioux Quill Iron." MA, 23 (1961), 33-37.

358. Theisz, Ronnie. "The Contemporary 'Traditional Style' of the Lakota." AICC, 8:6 (June 1974), 2-7. Photographs and drawings of costumes.

359. Todd, James E. "Boulder Mosaics in Dakota." CHSSD, 6 (1912), 205-214. Contains plates of several.

360. Tucker, Michael S. Old Time Sioux Dances. Panorama City, CA: n.p., 1969. 17 pp.

361. United States. Indian Arts and Crafts Board. Contemporary Sioux Painting: An Exhibition Organized by the Indian Arts and Crafts Board of the United States Department of the Interior. Rapid City, SD: Tipi Shop, 1970. 80 pp.

362. Vincent, John R. "Midwest Indians and Frontier Photography." AI, 38:1 (Summer 1965), 26-35. Contains photographs of famous Sioux.

363. Walker, James R. "Dakota Offering Sticks." IN, 3 (1926), 199-200.

364. Walker, James R. "Sioux Games. I." JAFL, 18 (October-December 1905), 277-290; "Sioux Games. II." JAFL, 19 (January-March 1906), 29-36.

365. Walker, James R. "Sioux Games." CHSSD, 9 (1918), 486-513.

366. Wheeler, Richard P. "'Quill Flattners' or Pottery Modeling Tools." PlA, No. 6 (April 1956), 17-20. What has been regarded as flattners may have been modeling tools.

367. White, Mary. How to Do Bead Work. 1904; abridged rpt. New York: Dover Publications, 1972. 142 pp.

368. White, Robert A. "Value Themes of the Native American Tribalistic Movement Among the South Dakota

Sioux. " CA, 15 (September 1974), 284-303. Various comments, with rejoinder by White and Karl Schlesier.

369. Will, George F. "Some Observations Made in Northwestern South Dakota. " AA, 11:2 (April-June 1909), 257-265. On land, petroglyphs, cave hills, Big Cave, etc.

370. Will, George F. , and George E. Hyde. Corn Among the Indians of the Upper Missouri. 1917; rpt. Lincoln: University of Nebraska Press, 1960 and Gloucester, MA: Peter Smith, 1971. 323 pp.

371. Williamson, T. H. "Dakota Scalp Dances. " CMHS, 6 (1894), 409-412.

372. Winchell, Newton H. "Habitations of the Sioux in Minnesota. " WA, 7:4 (1908), 155-164.

373. Wing, David. "Scenes from the Dakota Missions: Rosebud and Pine Ridge Photographs, 1922-1942 by David Buechel, S. J. [sic]. " The Critic, 34:4 (Summer 1976), 48-53. Photographs from the Eugene Buechel collection, St. Francis Indian Mission on the Rosebud Reservation.

374. Wissler, Clark. "Costumes of the Plains Indians. " APAM, 17:Pt. 2 (1915), 38-91.

375. Wissler, Clark. "Decorative Art of the Sioux Indians. " BAMNH, 18:Pt. 3 (December 1904), 231-278.

376. Wissler, Clark. "Diffusion of Cultures in the Plains of North America. " ICA, 15:Vol. 2 (1906), 39-52.

377. Wissler, Clark. "Distribution of Moccasin Decorations Among the Plains Tribes. " APAM, 29 (1927), 1-23.

378. Wissler, Clark. Indian Costumes in the United States. A Guide to the Study of the Collections in the Museum. New York: The American Museum of Natural History, 1931. 31 pp.

379. Wissler, Clark. "The Influence of the Horse in the Development of Plains Culture. " AA, 16:1 (January-March 1914), 1-25.

380. Wissler, Clark. Relations of Nature to Man in Aboriginal America. 1926; rpt. New York: AMS Press, 1970.

381. Wissler, Clark. "Societies and Ceremonial Associations in the Oglala Division of the Teton Dakota." APAM, 11: Pt. 2 (1912). 99 p.

382. Wissler, Clark. "Some Protective Designs of the Dakota." APAM, 1: Pt. 2 (1907), 19-53. Includes many drawings.

383. Wissler, Clark. "Structural Basis to the Decoration of Costumes Among the Plains Indians." APAM, 17: Pt. 3 (1916), 91-114.

384. Woodruff, K. Brent. "Material Culture of the Teton Dakota." CHSSD, 17 (1934), 604-646.

385. Woodyard, Darrel. Dakota Indian Lore. San Antonio, TX: Naylor Co., 1968. 164 pp. Juvenile literature.

## AUTOBIOGRAPHIES

386. Black Elk, [Nicholas]. Black Elk Speaks: Being the Life Story of a Holy Man of the Oglala Sioux, As Told to John G. Neihardt. 1932; rpt. Lincoln: University of Nebraska Press, 1961. 280 pp. His life from mid 1860's to Wounded Knee I. Not a verbatim account, but an approximation of the religious experiences of a western Sioux. Translated into many languages. Important source of knowledge of life among the Oglalas.

387. Carlson, Robert. "Interview with Grace Lambert." NDH, 44:4 (Fall 1977), 8-10. About growing up on Fort Totten Indian Reservation.

388. Deloria, Vine, Sr. "The Standing Rock Reservation: A Personal Reminiscence." In The Literature of South Dakota. Ed. John R. Milton. Vermillion, SD: Dakota Press, 1976, pp. 303-320.

389. Eastman, Charles A. "First Impressions of Civiliza-

tion. " H̲, 108 (March 1904), 587-592. A Flandreau
Santee, physician, tribal spokesman, and famous
writer.

390. Eastman, Charles A. From the Deep Woods to Civilization: Chapters in the Autobiography of an Indian.
Boston: Little, Brown, 1916; rpt. Lincoln: University of Nebraska Press, 1977. 205 pp. A sequel to
Indian Boyhood, no. 392.

391. Eastman, Charles A. "Hakadah's First Offering. "
CuL̲, 34 (January 1903), 29-32.

392. Eastman, Charles A. Indian Boyhood. 1902; rpt.
Rapid City, SD: Fenwyn Press Books, 1970; New
York: Dover Publications, 1971; Glorietta, NM: Rio
Grande Press, 1976; New York: Peter Smith, 1977.
Deals with the period of the Minnesota Sioux War and
retreat to Canada.

393. Eastman, Charles A. Indian Child Life. Boston: Little, Brown, and Co. , 1926. 160 pp.

394. Eastman, Charles A. "Life in the Woods: Boyhood
Memories of Autumnal Tribal Activities (C. 1870-
72). " See entry no. 1936, pp. 54-59.

395. Eastman, Charles A. Old Indian Days. New York:
McClure Co. , 1907; rpt. Rapid City, SD: Fenwyn
Press Books, 1970. 279 pp.

396. Eastman, Charles A. "The School Days of an Indian. "
Out̲, 85 (April 1907), 851-855; 894-899.

397. Eastman, Charles A. The Soul of the Indian: An Interpretation. Boston: Houghton Mifflin, 1911; rpt.
New York: Johnson Reprint Corp. , 1971.

398. Fire, John (Lame Deer), and Richard Erdoes. Lame
Deer Seeker of Visions. New York: Simon and
Schuster, 1972. 288 pp. Life of an Oglala medi-
cine man of the present. Now deceased.

399. Flying Hawk. Chief Flying Hawk's Tales: The True
Story of Custer's Last Fight as Told by Chief Flying
Hawk to M. E. McCreight (Tchamta Tanka). New
York: Alliance Press, 1936. 56 pp.

400.  Hilger, M. Inez, ed. "The Narrative of Oscar One
      Bull." Mid, 28:3 (July 1946), 147-172. Autobi-
      ography of an Hunkpapa, adopted son of Sitting Bull,
      born in the 1850's.

401.  "Indian Stories as Related by Andrew Knife at Pine
      Ridge Reservation...." IW, 15 April 1936, pp. 43-
      44. Relates his boyhood reaction to reservation
      schools in the 1880's, response to Wounded Knee,
      etc.

402.  Jordan, William Red Cloud. "Eighty Years on the
      Rosebud." Ed. Henry W. Hamilton. CHSSD, 35
      (1970), 322-383. Born in 1884 the son of Colonel
      Charles P. Jordan and an Oglala woman from Red
      Cloud's clan.

403.  Keleher, Leroy (Oytasita). The Soul of the American
      Indian. San Diego, CA: Frye and Smith, 1927. 94
      pp. Autobiography of an Indian born along the west-
      ern edge of Standing Rock Reservation.

404.  Libby, O. G., ed. The Arikara Narrative of the Cam-
      paign Against the Hostile Dakotas, June, 1876.
      CHSND, 6 (1920), 5-209; rpt. Glorietta, NM: Rio
      Grande Press, 1976; New York: AMS Press, 1977.
      Contains autobiographical accounts by many Indian
      participants.

405.  Marquis, Thomas B., ed. "The Autobiography of a
      Sioux: An Indian with a Sense of Humor." CMag,
      113:2 (December 1926), 182-188.

406.  Marquis, Thomas B. Cheyenne and Sioux: The
      Reminiscences of Four Indians and a White Soldier.
      Ed. Ronald H. Limbaugh. Stockton, CA: Univer-
      sity of the Pacific, 1973. 79 pp. Includes a brief
      autobiography of a western Sioux farmer.

407.  Praus, Alexis A., ed. "A New Pictographic Auto-
      biography of Sitting Bull." SMC, 123:6 (1955). 4
      pp. See entry no. 1862.

408.  Riegert, Wilbur A. I Am a Sioux. Illustrated by
      Vincent Hunts Horse. Rapid City, SD: Fenwyn
      Press, 1967. 24 pp.

409.   Riggs, Stephen R. , trans.   "Narrative of Paul Maza-
       kootemane. "   CMHS, 3 (1870-1880), 82-90.

410.   Standing Bear, Luther.   The Land of the Spotted Eagle.
       Boston:  Houghton Mifflin, 1933; rpt. Lincoln:  Uni-
       versity of Nebraska Press, 1978.   259 pp.   Written
       to non-Indians by a western Sioux, an excellent ac-
       count of Indian life that contrasts Indian and non-
       Indian civilization.

411.   Standing Bear, Luther.   My Indian Boyhood.   Boston:
       Houghton Mifflin, 1928.   288 pp.

412.   Standing Bear, Luther.   My People, the Sioux.   Ed.
       E. A. Brininstool.   Boston:  Houghton Mifflin,
       1931.   189 pp.

413.   White Bull, Joseph.   The Warrior Who Killed Custer:
       The Personal Narrative of Chief Joseph White Bull.
       Ed. James H. Howard.   Lincoln:  University of
       Nebraska Press, 1968.   84 pp.

414.   Wooden Leg:  A Warrior Who Fought Custer.   Trans.
       Thomas B. Marquis.   Minneapolis:  The Midwest
       Co. , 1931; rpt. Lincoln:  University of Nebraska
       Press, 1962.   384 pp.

415.   Zitkala-Ša.   "Impressions of an Indian Childhood. "
       AM, 85 (January 1900), 37-47; rpt. in A Nation of
       Nations.   Ed. Theodore L. Gross.   New York:
       Macmillan, 1971, pp. 160-162.   Her Anglo name was
       Ethel Bonin.

416.   Zitkala-Ša.   "The School Days of an Indian Girl. "
       85 (January 1900), 185-194.


                        CANADIAN SIOUX


417.   Abbott, Frederick H.   Administration of Indian Affairs
       in Canada.   Washington, DC:  Board of Indian Com-
       missioners, 1915.

418.   Black, Norman F.   History of Saskatchewan, and the
       Old Northwest.   2nd ed.   Regina:  North West His-
       torical Co. , 1913.   605 pp.

419.  Gunn, Donald, and Charles R. Tuttle.  History of
      Manitoba:  From the Earliest Settlements to 1835;
      from 1835 to the Admission of the Province into the
      Dominion.  Ottawa:  Maclean, Roger and Co., 1880.
      482 pp.  Another volume was projected but not com-
      pleted.

420.  Kehoe, Alice B.  "Dakota Indian Ethnicity in Saskatche-
      wan. "  JES, 3:2 (Summer 1975), 37-42.

421.  Kehoe, Alice B.  "The Dakotas in Saskatchewan. "
      See entry no. 528, pp. 148-172.

422.  Kehoe, Alice B.  The Roads of Life:  Dakota and Cree
      Adaptations to Twentieth-Century Sasktachewan.
      Toronto:  Holt, Rinehart and Winston, 1977.

423.  Laviolette, Gontran.  The Sioux Indians in Canada.
      Regina, Sask.:  The Marian Press, 1944.  138 pp.
      Brief but fairly reliable survey history.

424.  Meyer, Roy W.  "The Canadian Sioux:  Refugees from
      Minnesota. "  MiH, 41 (Spring 1968), 13-28.  For the
      period 1863-1900.

425.  Sanderson, James F.  "Indian Tales of the Canadian
      Prairies. "  AlHR, 13:3 (Summer 1965), 7-21.  Some
      information on the Sioux in these tales told to San-
      derson.

426.  Wallis, Wilson D.  "The Canadian Dakota. "  In APAM,
      41 (1947-1949), New York:  American Museum of
      Natural History, 1952, pp. 1-225; rpt. New York:
      AMS Press, 1977.  Contains information about
      twentieth-century life, collected from Sioux at New
      Village and Long Plain Reserve near Portage la
      Prairie.

427.  Woolworth, Alan R.  "A Disgraceful Proceeding:  In-
      trigue in the Red River Country in 1864. "  B (Spring
      1969), pp. 54-59.  About the abduction from Canada
      of Little Six and Medicine Bottle.

CAPTIVITY LITERATURE:
HISTORY AND STORIES

428.   Allanson, George G.   Stirring Adventures of the
       Joseph R. Brown Family.   Wheaton, MN:   Wheaton
       Gazette, [1863]; rpt. in Garland Library of Narratives
       of North American Indian Captivities, Vol. 103.
       New York:   Garland, 1976.

429.   Barber, Mary.   The True Narrative of the Five Years'
       Suffering and Perilous Adventures, by Miss Barbara,
       Wife of "Squatting Bear," a Celebrated Sioux Chief.
       Philadelphia:   Barclay, [1872]; rpt. in Indian Captiv-
       ities, Vol. 86.   New York:   Garland, 1976.

430.   Barbier, Charles P.   "Recollections of Ft. La Fram-
       boise in 1862 and the Rescue of Lake Chetak Cap-
       tives."   CHSSD, 11 (1922), 232-242.

431.   Bishop, Harriet E.   See McConkey, Harriet E. B.,
       below.

432.   Brown, Samuel J.   In Captivity.   The Experience,
       Privations and Dangers of Sam'l J. Brown and Oth-
       ers, While Prisoners of the Hostile Sioux, During
       the Massacre and War of 1862.   Mankato, MN:
       n. p., [1896]; rpt. Washington, Government Printing
       Office, 1900; in Indian Captivities, Vol. 76.   New
       York:   Garland, 1977.

433.   Bryant, Charles S., and Abel B. Murch.   A History
       of the Great Massacre by the Sioux Indians, in Min-
       nesota, Including the Personal Narratives of Many
       Who Escaped.   Cincinnati:   Rickey and Carroll,
       1864.   504 pp.   The narratives of the captivities of
       Mrs. Helen Carrothers and Mary Schwandt.

434.   Captivities of Mrs. J. E. DeCamp Sweet, Nancy Mc-
       Clure, and Mary Schwandt.   In Indian Captivities,
       Vol. 99.   New York:   Garland, 1976.

435.   Carrigan, Wilhelmina (Winnie) Buce.   Captured by In-
       dians:   Reminiscences of Pioneer Life in Minnesota.
       Forest City, SD:   Forest City Press, 1907.   40 pp. ;
       rpt. Buffalo Lake, MN:   The News Print, 1912; in
       Indian Captivities, Vol. 109.   New York:   Garland,
       1977.

436.  Coleson, Ann.  Narrative of Her Captivity Among the
      Sioux Indians!  An Interesting and Remarkable Ac-
      count of the Terrible Sufferings and Providential
      Escape of Miss Ann Coleson, A Victim of the Lake
      Indian Outrages in Minnesota.  Philadelphia:  Bar-
      clay and Co., 1864.  70 pp.; rpt. in Indian Captiv-
      ities, Vol. 79.  New York:  Garland, 1977.

437.  Drimmer, Frederick, ed.  Scalps and Tomahawks:
      Narratives of Indian Captivity.  New York:  Coward-
      McCann, 1961.  378 pp.

438.  Eastlick, Mrs. Lavina (Dat).  Thrilling Incidents of the
      Indian War of 1862:  Being a Personal Narrative of
      the Outrages and Horrors Witnessed by Mrs. L.
      Eastlick, in Minnesota.  Lancaster, WI:  Herald
      Book and Job Office, 1864; rpt. Minneapolis:  Atlas
      Steam Press Printing Co., 1864, Mankato:  Free
      Press Printing Co., 1890, 1946.

439.  Ellis, Edward Sylvester.  Nathan Todd; Or, the Fate
      of the Sioux Captive.  New York:  Beadle and Co.,
      1860.  124 pp.; rpt. in Indian Captivities, Vol. 90.
      New York:  Garland, 1977.

440.  [Harlan, Edgar R.]  "Last Figure of the Spirit Lake
      Tragedy."  AI, 13:3 (January 1922), 219-222.  On
      Abigail Gardner Sharp's death.

441.  Heard, Joseph H.  White into Red:  A Study of the
      Assimilation of White Persons Captured by Indians.
      Metuchen, NJ:  Scarecrow Press, 1973.

442.  Hibschman, Harry Jacob.  The Shetek Pioneers and
      the Indians.  St. Paul, MN:  Pioneer Press, 1901;
      rpt. Indian Captivities, Vol. 104.  New York:  Gar-
      land, 1976.

443.  Hosmer, Margaret E.  The Child Captives.  In Indian
      Captivities, Vol. 83.  New York:  Garland, 1976.
      230 pp.

444.  Huggan, Nancy (McClure).  "The Story of Nancy Mc-
      Clure.  Captivity among the Sioux."  CMHS, 6 (1894),
      438-460.

445.  Johnson, Dorothy M.  Flame on the Frontier:  Short

Stories of Pioneering Women. New York: Dodd,
Mead and Co., 1967. 141 pp. Seven stories including one on captivity by the Sioux.

446.   Juni, Benedict. Held in Captivity: Experiences Related by Benedict Juni, of New Ulm, Minn., as an
Indian Captive During the Indian Outbreak of 1862.
New Ulm, MN: Liesch-Walter Print. Co., 1926;
rpt. New Ulm, MN: Kemske Paper Co., 1962.
23 pp.

447.   Kelly, Fanny. My Captivity Among the Sioux Indians.
Cincinnati: Wilstach, Baldwin and Co., 1871; rpt.
Toronto: Maclear, 1871; Chicago: Donnelley, Gas-
sette and Lloyd, 1880; New York: Corinth Books,
1962; Gloucester, MA: Peter Smith, 1971. A
prisoner during the Minnesota Sioux War, July 12 to
December 12, 1864. 285 pp.

448.   Kelly, Fanny. Narrative of My Captivity Among the
Sioux Indians: With a Brief Account of General
Sully's Expedition in 1864, Bearing Upon Events
Occurring in My Captivity. Hartford, CT: Mutual
Publishing Co., 1871; rpt. in Indian Captivities, Vol.
85. New York: Garland, 1976. 285 pp.

449.   Kelly, Fanny. To the Senators and Members of the
House of Representatives of Congress. Broadside,
copy preserved in the Graff collection at the Newberry Library in Chicago. A petition for compensa-
tion for suffering during captivity.

450.   Larimer, Sarah Luse. The Capture and Escape; or
Life Among the Sioux. Philadelphia: Claston, Rem-
sen and Haffelfinger, 1870; rpt. in Indian Captivities,
Vol. 84. New York: Garland, 1976. 252 pp.

451.   Lee, Lorenzo P. History of the Spirit Lake Massacre
and of Miss Abigail Gardiner's Three Month's Captivity Among the Indians. 1857; rpt. Seattle, WA: Ye
Galleon, 1968; in Indian Captivities, Vol. 72. New
York: Garland, 1976.

452.   McClure, Nancy. "Captivity Among the Sioux." CMHS,
6 (1894), 439-460; rpt. in Indian Captivities, Vol.
99. New York: Garland, 1977. Her mother was a
Dakota; her married name was Huggan.

453. McConkey, Harriet E. Bishop. Dakota War Whoop:
Or, Indian Massacres and War in Minnesota, of 1862-
3. Rev. ed. 1863; rpt. Minneapolis: Ross and
Haines, 1970. 429 pp.; in Indian Captivities, Vol.
78. New York: Garland, 1978. This famous contemporary account, by St. Paul's first school teacher, has been printed in these and other editions for
its vivid descriptions of events in the Minnesota
Sioux War.

454. Marsh, James B. Four Years in the Rockies; Or, the
Adventures of Isaac P. Rose. New Castle, PA:
W. B. Thomas, 1884; rpt. Columbus, OH: Long's
College Book Co., 1950; in Indian Captivities, Vol.
94. New York: Garland, 1978. 262 pp.

455. Pearce, Roy Harvey. "The Significance of the Captivity Narrative." AL, 19 (March 1947), 1-20. Significant article.

456. Petersen, William J. "Captives of the Sioux."
Palimpsest, 38:6 (June 1957), 236-252. About four
women captives from Abbie Gardner's account; rpt.
Palimpsest, 43:10 (October 1962), 433-449.

457. Petersen, William J. "Westward with the Gardners."
Palimpsest, 38:6 (June 1957), 209-20. Primarily
about Abbie Gardner and the Spirit Lake Uprising.

458. Renville, Mary (Butler). A Thrilling Narrative of Indian Captivity. Minneapolis: Atlas Company's Book
and Job Printing Office, 1863. 52 pp.

459. Robinson, Doane. "The Rescue of Frances Kelly."
CHSSD, 4 (1908), 108-17.

460. Robinson, Doane. "A Side Light on the Sioux." McM,
21:4 (August 1903), 426-431.

461. Russell, Jason A. "The Narratives of the Indian Captives." Ed, 51 (October 1930), 84-88. Captivity
stories give us an understanding of American Indian
character and ingenuity. He was not cruel nor
treacherous.

462. Schwandt, Mary. "Her Captivity During the Sioux
'Outbreak'--1862." CMHS, 6 (1894), 461-474; rpt.

in Indian Captivities, Vol. 99. New York: Garland, 1977.

463. Schwandt, Mary. The Captivity of Mary Schwandt. Fairfield, WA: Ye Galleon Press, 1975. 30 pp.

464. Sharp, Abbie Gardner. History of the Spirit Lake Massacre and Captivity of Miss Abbie Gardner. 4th ed. rev. Des Moines, IA: Iowa Printing Co., 1895. 352 pp. Reprinted often.

465. Sweet, Mrs. J. E. DeCamp. "Narrative of Her Captivity in the Sioux Outbreak of 1862." CMHS, 6 (1894), 354-380; rpt. in Indian Captivities, Vol. 99. New York: Garland, 1977.

466. Tarble, Mrs. Helen. The Story of My Capture and Escape During the Minnesota Indian Massacre in 1862. St. Paul: Abbott, 1904; rpt. in Indian Captivities, Vol. 105. New York: Garland, 1976. 65 pp.

467. Wakefield, Mrs. Sarah F. Six Weeks in the Sioux Tepees. Shakopee, MN: Argus Printing Office, 1864; rpt. in Indian Captivities, Vol. 79. New York: Garland, 1977.

468. White, Lonnie J. "White Women Captives of the Southern Plains Indians, 1866-1875." JW, 8:3 (1969), 327-354. Information about the Sioux, in spite of the title.

469. White, Urania S. "My Captivity Among the Sioux, August 18 to September 26, 1862." CMHS, 9 (1901), 395-426; rpt. in Indian Captivities, Vol. 104. New York: Garland, 1976. She and her husband homesteaded six miles from Little Crow's village.


CONTEMPORARY SIOUX

470. Artichoker, John. Indians of South Dakota. Rev. ed. South Dakota Department of Public Instruction Bulletin 67A. Pierre, SD: South Dakota Department of Public Instruction, 1956.

471. Barnett, Mrs. Webster. "Not the Thomas White Hawk We Knew. " GPO, March 1968, p. 5.

472. Becker, Eugene D. "Scenes of the Sioux War a Century Afterward. " MiH, 38 (September 1962), 154-156. Mostly pictures.

473. Braudy, S. "We Will Remember Survival School: A Visit with Women and Children of the American Indian Movement. " MS, 5 (July 1976), 77-80.

474. Brophy, William A. , Sophie D. Aberle, et al. , comps. The Indian: America's Unfinished Business. Norman: University of Oklahoma Press, 1966. 236 pp. Useful report of the Commission on the Rights, Liberties and Responsibilities of the American Indian that contains information about Sioux.

475. Bryde, John. "After Words. " GPO, August 1970, pp. 12-15; September 1970, pp. 12-15. From Modern Indian Psychology.

476. Cahn, Edgar S. , ed. Our Brother's Keeper: The Indian in White America. New York: World Publishing Co. , 1969. 193 pp. An indictment of the Indian Bureau and of non-Indian society.

477. Caldwell, Warren W. An Introduction to the Modern Oglala Sioux. Washington, DC: Department of Health, Education and Welfare, 1958.

478. Capps, Benjamin. The Trail to Ogallala. New York: Hawthorn Books, Inc. , 1964.

479. Cash, Joseph H. , and Herbert T. Hoover, eds. To Be an Indian: An Oral History. New York: Holt, Rinehart and Winston, 1971. 239 pp. Sioux respondents comment on the past hundred years.

480. Chronicles of American Indian Protest. Comp. and ed. by The Council on Interracial Books for Children. Greenwich, CT: Fawcett Publications, 1970. 374 pp.

481. Clark, LaVerne Harrell. Revisiting the Plains Indian Country of Mari Sandoz. Marvin, SD: Blue Cloud Abbey, 1977. 57 pp. Information from Sioux people who knew Mari Sandoz.

482.  Collier, John, Jr.  "Report of a Photographic Research
      Project. "  In Visual Anthropology:  Photography as
      a Research Method.  New York:  Holt, Rinehart and
      Winston, 1967, pp. 81-104.  Sioux are included in
      this photographic study of twenty-two Indian house-
      holds.

483.  Collins, Dabney O.  "A 'Happening' at Oglala. "  AW,
      6:2 (March 1969), 15-19.  On the involvement of Fr.
      Paul Steinmetz with Sioux culture on Pine Ridge
      Reservation.

484.  Crenshaw, Ronald W.  "Jury Composition--The Pur-
      poseful Inclusion of American Indians. "  SDLR, 16:1
      (Winter 1971), 214-221.  On Long Warrior v.  Pea-
      cock, Civil No.  69-122, to have Indians included in
      significant numbers on juries.

485.  Cress, Joseph N. , and James P. O'Donnel.  "Self-
      Esteem Inventory and the Oglala Sioux:  A Validation
      Study. "  JSP, 97 (October 1975), 135-136.

486.  DeMallie, Raymond J.  "Review Essay:  Sioux Eth-
      nohistory, A Methodological Critique. "  JES, 4:3
      (Fall 1976), 77-83.  Reviews Ernest Schusky's The
      Forgotten Sioux--says it is a significant work that
      brings Sioux history down to the present, but fails
      to do justice to the personal and cultural integrity
      to the Indians.

487.  [Dollar, Clyde.]  "Traps Still Plotted Against the In-
      dian. "  GPO, November 1969, p. 4.  Warns the
      Sioux about bad effects of government activities on
      the reservations.

488.  Dusenberry, V.  "Montanans Look at Their Indians. "
      Nation, 19 November 1956, pp. 75-76.

489.  Edmunds, R. David.  "Indian Humor:  Can the Red
      Man Laugh?"  See entry no. 1250, pp. 141-153.

490.  Erikson, Erik H.  "Erikson Among the Indians:  Sioux
      and Yurok Indians. "  Horizon, 14:4 (Autumn 1972),
      80-85.

491.  Fanshel, David.  Far from the Reservation:  The
      Transracial Adoption of American Indian Children.
      Metuchen, NJ:  Scarecrow Press, 1972.

492. Farber, William O. "Representative Government: Application to the Sioux." See entry no. 528, pp. 123-139.

493. Farber, William O. Study Paper on Election Problems. With the Assistance of Richard E. Brown. Vermillion: University of South Dakota, 1965. 44 pp. A government Research Bureau Report.

494. Farber, William O., P. A. Odeen, and R. A. Tschetter. Indians, Law Enforcement and Local Government: A Study of the Impact of the Off-Reservation Indian Problem on South Dakota Local Government with Special Reference to Law Enforcement. Report No. 37.

495. Feraca, Stephen E. "The Political Status of the Early Bands and Modern Communities of the Oglala Dakota." USDMN, 27:1/2 (1966), 1-26. Vermillion, SD: Government Research Bureau, in Cooperation with the Institute of Indian Studies, 1957.

496. Feraca, Stephen E., and James H. Howard. "The Identity and Demography of the Dakota or Sioux Tribes." PlA, 8 (1963), 80-84.

497. Fried, Morton H. The Notion of Tribe. Menlo Park, CA: Cummings Publishing Co., 1976. 136 pp. Includes information about tribes of the Great Plains.

498. Gladwin, Thomas. "Personality Structure in the Plains." AnQ, 30 (1957), 111-124.

499. Governor's Human Rights Commission. Minnesota's Indian Citizens (Yesterday and Today). St. Paul: n. p., 1965. 136 pp.

500. Hassrick, Royal B. "Teton Dakota Kinship System." AA, 46:3, Pt. 1 (1944), 338-348. An analysis of the familial relationships and their effects on rights and status of Indians.

501. Hettich, Leo. The Problem of Indian Vocations. Marvin, SD: Blue Cloud Abbey, 1966. 40 pp.

502. Hough, Henry W. Development of Indian Resources. Denver, CO: World Press, Inc., 1967. 285 pp.

A handbook produced by the National Congress of
American Indians while Vine Deloria, Jr. was Di-
rector.

503.   Hough, Walter.   "Racial Groups and Figures in the
       Natural History Building of the United States National
       Museum. "  ARSI, (1920), pp. 611-656.   Several
       pages of text and photographs on the Sioux.

504.   Howard, James H.   "Future Needs of Ethnological Re-
       search in the Great Plains. "  GPJ, 1 (Spring 1962),
       27-31.

505.   Hrdlička, Aleš.   "Catalogue of Human Crania in the
       United States National Museum Collections:   The
       Algonkin and Related Iroquois; Siouan, Caddoan,
       Salish and Sahaptin, Shoshonean and California In-
       dians. "  PUSNM, 69 (1927), 1-127.

506.   Hurt, Wesley R.   Anthropological Report on Indian
       Occupancy by the Dakota Sioux Indians and by Rival
       Tribal Claimants.   New York:   Clearwater Press,
       1973.

507.   Hurt, Wesley R.   "The Urbanization of the Yankton
       Indians. "  HO, 20 (Winter 1961-62), 226-231.

508.   Jessett, Frederick E.   "Sioux Farming Today. "  InH,
       3:1 (Winter 1970), 34-36.

509.   Johnson, Oscar Elden.   Kinship in a Contemporary
       Yanktonai-Dakota Indian Community.   Minneapolis:
       University of Minnesota, 1950.   Microfilm publica-
       tion by the Audio-Visual Educational Service.

510.   Kemnitzer, L. S.   "Familial and Extra-Familial So-
       cialization in Urban Dakota Adolescents. "  See en-
       try no. 528, pp. 246-267.

511.   Kent, Calvin, and Jerry Johnson.   Indian Poverty in
       South Dakota.   Business Research Bureau Bulletin
       #99.   Vermillion, SD:   Dakota Press, 1969.

512.   League of Women Voters of Minneapolis.   Indians of
       Minneapolis.   Minneapolis:   League of Women Voters,
       1968.   112 pp.

513.  League of Women Voters of Minnesota.  Indians in
      Minnesota.  St. Paul:  League of Women Voters,
      1971.  165 pp.

514.  Leonard, Bill.  "I Plead with You to Save His Life."
      GPO, February 1969, pp. 8-13.  On Thomas White
      Hawk.

515.  [Leonard, Jean D.]  "After Words."  GPO, August
      1969, p. 15.  On differences between the Lakota
      and non-Indians.

516.  Leonard, Jean D.  "Is a Voice Given to Be Used?"
      GPO, July 1969, pp. 8-9.  About the Sioux Sani-
      tarium in Rapid City and attempts to hire Indian
      employees.

517.  Leonard, Jean D.  "New Indian Act Isn't Fooling Any-
      one."  GPO, February 1967, p. 16.

518.  Lesser, A.  "Some Aspects of Siouan Kinship."  ICA,
      23 (1930), 563-571.  Describes three distinct types
      of social organization.

519.  Lesser, A.  Siouan Kinship.  Ann Arbor, MI:  Uni-
      versity Microfilms, 1958.

520.  "Little Brave and White Justice."  GPO, May 1969,
      p. 5.  Little Brave was shot and killed by prominent
      rancher Baxter Berry, near Belvidere, South Dakota.

521.  "Lonely Trail:  Sioux Indian Grows."  Newsweek, 17
      July 1961, p. 22.

522.  McCone, R. Clyde.  "Cultural Factors in Crime
      Among the Dakota Indians."  PlA, 11:32 (1966), 144-
      151.  There are twice as many crimes against per-
      sons as against property.

523.  Mails, Thomas E.  The Mystic Warriors of the Plains.
      New York:  Doubleday and Co., 1972.  618 pp.

524.  Malan, Vernon.  The Dakota Indian Family.  South
      Dakota Experiment Station.  Bulletin 470.  Brookings,
      SD:  South Dakota State College, 1958.

525.  Maynard, Eileen.  "Growing Negative Image of the

Anthropologist Among American Indians. " HO, 33
(Winter 1974), 402-404. Remarks about Sioux. Non-
Indians were excluded from 1973 Sun Dance.

526.  Meyer, William.  Native Americans:  The New Indian
Resistance.  New York:  International Publishers Co. ,
1971.

527.  Nurge, Ethel.  "Dakota Diet:  Traditional and Contemporary. "  See entry no. 528, pp. 35-91.

528.  Nurge, Ethel, ed.  The Modern Sioux:  Social Systems
and Reservation Culture.  Lincoln:  University of
Nebraska Press, 1970.  352 pp.  Informative and
very useful articles by modern scholars.

529.  Ogden, Peter S.  Traits of American Indian Life and
Character.  2nd ed.  1933; rpt. New York: AMS,
1970.

530.  Oliver, Symmes C.  Ecology and Cultural Continuity
as Contributing Factors in the Social Organization
of the Plains Indians.  UCP,  48:1 (1962).  90 pp.

531.  Ortiz, Roxanne Dunbar, ed.  The Great Sioux Nation:
Sitting in Judgment on America.  Berkeley, CA:
Moon Books, 1977, and Westminster, MD:  Random
House, 1977.  224 pp.  An important book on the
special hearing at Lincoln, Nebraska, in December
1974 to decide whether the Sioux Indians have sovereignty.  An aftermath of Wounded Knee II.  Includes the following articles:  Simon Ortiz, "Indian
Oral History:  A Sacred Responsibility, " pp.  14-15;
Vine Deloria, Jr. ,  "Sovereignty, " pp.  16-18, and
"The United States Has No Jurisdiction in Sioux Territory, " pp.  141-46; Alvin M. Josephy, Jr. ,  "Con-
cise History of the United States-Sioux Relations, "
pp.  19-28, and "Distortions of Indian History, " pp.
55-57; Wilbur R. Jacobs,  " Demography, " pp.  60-
61,  "Indian-White Relations, " pp.  79-88,  "The Sioux
Nation and the Treaty, " pp.  116-18, and "The Great
White Father, " p.  150; Father Peter Powell, "The
Sacred Way, " pp.  62-66, and "The Sacred Treaty, "
pp.  105-109; Roxanne Dunbar Ortiz, "Indian Political
Economy, " pp.  67-68, "Colonialist Programs, " pp.
71-73, "Oral History and Written History, pp. 100-
104, "Dispossession, " pp.  162-63, and "Nationhood

or Genocide, " p. 168; Raymond J. DeMallie, Jr.,
"Treaties Are Made Between Nations, " pp. 110-15.
Also included are statements and testimony from over
thirty Native Americans, most of whom are Sioux,
and statements by attorneys and the judge, who ren-
dered the decision in favor of the federal government. Concludes with the "Declaration of Continuing
Independence by the First International Indian Treaty
Council at Standing Rock Indian Country June 1974. "
Excludes all testimony opposing the Indian claim of
sovereignty.

532. Oswalt, Wendell H. This Land Was Theirs. New
York: John Wiley and Sons, 1966. On ten representative tribes across the country.

533. Reid, Kenneth C. "Psoralea Esculenta as a Prairie
Resource: An Ethnographic Appraisal. " PlA, 22:
78, Pt. 1 (November 1977), 321-327. About the
prairie turnip.

534. Ridgeway, James F. "The Lost Indians. " NR, 153:
23-24 (December 1965), 17-20, 19-22.

535. Rosenblith, Judy F. "A Replication of Some Roots of
Prejudice. " JASP, 44:4 (October 1949), 470-489.
Addresses prejudice against Indians and Blacks in
nine South Dakota colleges.

536. Rowan, Carl T. The Plight of the Upper Midwest Indian: 'The First Are Last' ... Reprinted from the
Minneapolis Tribune, February 17 through March 3,
1957. Minneapolis: Star and Tribune, 1957. 16 pp.

537. Schusky, Ernest L. "American Indians and the 1968
Civil Rights Act. " AmI, 29 (April 1969), 369-376.
In spite of the Act, "much change is still necessary
before Indians will have the same rights as other
citizens. "

538. Shorris, Earl The Death of the Great Spirit: An
Elegy for the American Indian. New York: Simon
and Schuster, 1971. 253 pp. Essays on current
Indians and their problems.

539. "Sioux Don't Give Up. " Newsweek, 19 November 1956,
pp. 75-76.

540.  Stephens, Harry. The Government of the Indians of
      South Dakota. Governmental Research Bureau Re-
      port #8. Vermillion: University of South Dakota,
      1942.

541.  Sullivan, Louis R. "Anthropometry of the Siouan
      Tribes. " APAM, 23, Pt. 3 (1920), 81-174.

542.  "Their Plight Is Our Worst Disgrace. " Look, 19
      April 1955, pp. 32-37.

543.  United States. Indians of the Dakotas. Washington,
      DC: Government Printing Office, 1966.

544.  U. S. Congress. House. Committee on Interior and
      Insular Affairs. Sioux Indian Tribes, North and
      South Dakota. Washington, DC: Government Print-
      ing Office, 1956. 147 pp. Hearings before the
      Subcommittee on Indian Affairs pursuant to House
      Resolution 30, to authorize the Committee on In-
      terior and Insular Affairs to make investigations into
      any matter with its jurisdiction, and for other pur-
      poses, September 9, 10, and 12, 1955.

545   U. S. Congress. House. Committee on Public Lands.
      Rehabilitation of the Devils Lake Sioux Tribe and the
      Turtle Mountain Band of Chippewa Indians, North
      Dakota. Washington, DC: Government Printing
      Office, 1950. 49 pp.

546.  U. S. Congress. Senate. Committee on Interior and
      Insular Affairs. Subcommittee on Indian Affairs.
      To Amend the Indian Claims Commission Act of Au-
      gust 13, 1946. Washington, DC: Government Print-
      ing Office, 1976. 64 pp. Hearing before the Sub-
      committee on Indian Affairs on Senate 2780, May 4,
      1976, pertaining to Sioux claims.

547.  U. S. Congress. Senate. Committee on Interior and
      Insular Affairs. Subcommittee on Indian Affairs.
      Submarginal Lands and Trust Lands for Certain In-
      dian Tribes: Hearing Before the Subcommittee on
      Indian Affairs. Washington, DC: Government Print-
      ing Office, 1975. Hearings on S. 241, S. 423, S.
      536 and S. 1327; Sioux are included.

548.  U. S. Indian Claims Commission. Commission Findings

on the Sioux Indians. New York: Garland Publishers, 1974. 360 pp.

549. Waddell, Jack O., and O. M. Watson. The American
Indian in Urban Society. Boston: Little, Brown and
Co., 1971.

550. Walker, Derwald E., Jr., ed. The Emergent Native
Americans: A Reader in Culture Contact. Boston:
Little, Brown and Co., 1971.

551. Watson, J. G., and C. D. Rose. "Company Seeks
Profits with a Sioux Indian Tribe." HBR, 54 (July
1976), 7-8.

552. Wax, Rosalie H. Doing Fieldwork, Warnings and Ad-
vice. Chicago: University of Chicago Press, 1971.
Adventures with the Sioux of South Dakota.

553. Wedel, Mildred Mott. "LeSueur and the Dakota Sioux."
In Aspects of Upper Great Lakes Anthropology in
Honor of Lloyd A. Wilford. Ed. Elden Johnson. St.
Paul: Minnesota Historical Society, 1974, pp. 157-
171.

554. White, Robert A. "The Lower Class 'Culture of Excitement,' Among the Contemporary Sioux." See entry no. 518, pp. 175-197.

555. White, Robert A., Karl H. Schlesier, et al. "Value
Themes of the Native American Tribalistic Movement
Among the South Dakota Sioux." CuA, 15 (September
1974), 284-303.

556. Wilcox, Lloyd. Group Structure and Personality Types
Among the Sioux Indians of North Dakota. Madison:
University of Wisconsin, 1942. Microfilm publica-
tion.

557. Work Projects Administration, South Dakota. "Anthropological Schedule on Fullblood and Mixblood
Cicanger-Dakota Sioux Culture." Unpublished materials prepared by the WPA and the University of
South Dakota Sociology Department, preserved by the
University of South Dakota Library Archives; contains personal histories and observations.

EDUCATION

558.  Anderson, Beverly L.  Pine Ridge Reservation Assess-
      ment of Educational Needs.  Albuquerque:  BIA, De-
      partment of the Interior, 1974.

559.  Artichoker, John, Jr., and Neil M. Palmer.  The
      Sioux Indian Goes to College.  An Analysis of Se-
      lected Problems of South Dakota Indian College Stu-
      dents.  Vermillion, SD:  Institute of Indian Studies,
      1959.  47 pp.

560.  Bebeau, Donald E.  "Administration of a TOEFL Test
      to Sioux Indian High School Students."  JAIE, 9
      (October 1969), 7-16.

561.  Brasch, Beatty.  "The Y-Indian Guide and Y-Indian
      Princess Program."  InH, 10:3 (Summer 1977), 49-
      61.

562.  Brennan, Mary R.  "The First School at Fort Totten."
      CHSND, 3 (1910), 237-241.  Established in 1872 for
      the Sioux.

563.  Bryde, John, ed.  An Indian Philosophy of Education.
      Vermillion, SD:  Dakota Press, 1974.

564.  Bryde, John.  Indian Students and Guidance.  Boston:
      Houghton Mifflin, 1971.

565.  Bryde, John.  "Indian Students:  Teenagers Caught in
      in the Clash."  GPO, August 1967, pp. 4-6.

566.  Bryde, John.  Modern Indian Psychology.  Vermillion:
      University of South Dakota Press, 1970.

567.  Bryde, John.  The Sioux Indian Student:  A Study of
      Scholastic Failure and Personality Conflict.  n. p.,
      1966.  Offset print.  196 pp.

568.  [Burke, Harold M., Byron J. Brophy, and R. W.
      Kraushaar.]  "Educating the Sioux Indian of South
      Dakota."  CHSSD, 18 (1936), 505-530.

569.  "CCC-ID Educational Program at Flandreau, South
      Dakota."  IW, May 1938, p. 36.  Special vocational
      training classes met twice weekly to learn meat-
      cutting, masonry, etc.

570. Commissioner of Indian Affairs. Annual Report of the
     Commissioner of Indian Affairs. For information
     about the transfer of Indian education to state sys-
     tems, see 1953, p. 38; 1954, p. 238; 1955, p. 242;
     1956, p. 209.

571. Cook, Elizabeth. "Indian Education in Urban Areas."
     SDR, 8:3 (Autumn 1970), 118-122. Replies to a
     questionnaire from teachers and counselors.

572. Cook, Elizabeth. "A Severe Indictment of Our School
     System." GPO, June 1970, pp. 8-11. Recorded
     at a conference in Rapid City, SD where she taught
     at Central High.

573. Dale, George A. Education for Better Living: A
     Study of the Effectiveness of the Pine Ridge Educa-
     tional Program. Lawrence, KS: U.S. Department
     of the Interior, Bureau of Indian Affairs, 1955.
     245 pp.

574. Deissler, K. "A Study of South Dakota Indian Achieve-
     ment Problems." JAIE, 1 (May 1962), 19-21.

575. Duncan, Kunigunde. Blue Star. Caldwell, ID: The
     Caxton Printers, Ltd., 1938. 211 pp. Teaching ex-
     periences of Corabella Fellows among Sioux and Chey-
     enne at Riggs' Santee Normal Training School and
     Oahe School on Cheyenne River Indian Reservation.

576. Eastman, Charles A. "Education Without Books."
     The Craftsman, 21 (January 1912), 371-373.

577. Eastman, Charles A. "The School Days of an Indian."
     Out, 13 April 1907, pp. 851-855.

578. Eastman, Charles A. "What Can the Out-Doors Do for
     Our Children." Ed, 41 (1920-1921), 599-605.

579. Eastman, Elaine Goodale. "Indian Girls in Indian
     Schools." Home-maker, 6:3 (June 1891), 199-205.

580. Eastman, Elaine Goodale. "Reminiscences of a Super-
     visor." IW, 15 September 1936, pp. 47-48. How
     she worked in schools in Western South Dakota dur-
     ing the early 1890's.

581. Eastman, Elaine Goodale. The Senator and the School-

House.   Philadelphia:   Indian Rights Association,
1886.   4 pp.

582.   Erikson, Erik H.   "Observations on Sioux Education. "
       JP, 7 (January 1939), 101-156.   On Pine Ridge and
       other Sioux reservations.

583.   Fletcher, Alice C.   Indian Education and Civilization.
       Washington, DC:   Commissioner of Education, 1888.

584.   Fuchs, Estelle, and Robert J. Havighurst   To Live
       on This Earth.   Garden City, NY:   Doubleday and
       Co. , 1973.   A major, technical report on the history
       of American Indian education that contains consider-
       able information about the experiences of the Sioux
       in the twentieth century.

585.   Gill, Joseph C.   A Handbook for Teachers of Sioux In-
       dian Students.   Vermillion:   University of South Da-
       kota, 1971.   176 pp.

586.   Gilmore, Melvin R.   "The Old-Time Method of Rear-
       ing a Dakota Boy. "   IN, 6 (1929), 367-72.

587.   Guenther, Richard L.   "The Santee Normal Training
       School. "   NH, 51:3 (Fall 1970), 359-378.

588.   Hansen, H.   "Scholastic Achievement of Indian Pupils. "
       Journal of Genetic Psychology, 50 (1937), 361-369.

589.   Hare, William H.   "Report of the Boarding Schools in
       Dakota. "   The Church and the Indian, Nos. 1-4
       (1874-1875).

590.   Harkins, Arthur M. , I. Karon Sherarts, and Richard
       G. Woods.   Public Education for the Prairie Island
       Sioux:   An Interim Report   Minneapolis:   Univer-
       sity of Minnesota, 1969.   72 pp.

591.   Havighurst, Robert J. , Minna Korol Gunther, and Inez
       Ellis Pratt.   "Environment and the Draw-A-Man
       Test:   The Performance of Indian Children. "   JASP,
       41 (1946), 50-63.   Involved some Sioux children.

592.   Havighurst, Robert J. , and Rhea R. Hilkevitch.   "The
       Intelligence of Indian Children as Measured by a Per-
       formance Scale. "   JASP, 39 (1944), 419-433.   In-
       volved some Sioux.

593.  Havighurst, Robert J., and Bernice L. Neugarten.
      American Indian and White Children:  A Sociopsycho-
      logical Investigation.  Chicago:  University of Chicago
      Press, 1955; rpt. 1969.  335 pp.

594.  "Home Economics Teaching in Service Day Schools,
      South Dakota." IW, 21 June 1935, pp. 31-34.
      Classes for women at Little Wound Day School at
      Kyle on the Pine Ridge Reservation.

595.  Hoover, Herbert T., ed.  Education and the Sioux.
      Vermillion:  University of South Dakota, 1975.  123
      pp.  Includes three articles on the history of educa-
      tion among the Sioux.

596.  "In Federal Boarding Schools 'Children Systematically
      Dehumanized.'" GPO, March 1969, pp. 10-11.

597.  Indian Education:  A National Tragedy--A National
      Challenge.  1969 Report of the Committee on Labor
      and Public Welfare.  United States Senate Special
      Subcommittee on Indian Education.  Report No. 91-
      501.  Washington, DC:  Government Printing Office,
      1969.  220 pp.

598.  Indian Schoolboys at Work on Community Day Schools--
      and Other Buildings, Pine Ridge." IW, 1 January
      1935, pp. 41-42.  Day school at Slim Butte on the
      Pine Ridge Reservation.

599.  Jensen, Kenneth.  "Few Indians in SD Colleges:  We're
      Not Tuned to Their Needs." GPO, February 1967,
      p. 12.

600.  Kutzlieb, Charles R.  "Educating the Sioux." NDH,
      32:4 (October 1965), 197-216.  About methods, rea-
      sons and politics associated with educating Sioux
      children.

601.  LaBrack, Bruce, and Elizabeth S. Grobsmith.  Sioux
      Education in Northwestern Nebraska.  Final Report
      on the 1971 Cross-Cultural Training Program.
      Lincoln:  University of Nebraska Press, 1974.

602.  Ludlow, Helen W.  "Indian Education at Hampton and
      Carlisle." H, 62 (1881), 659-675.  Praises positive
      results.

603.  McBride, Dorothy McFatridge.  "Hoosier Schoolmaster
      Among the Sioux."  Montana, 20:4 (October 1970),
      79-97.  At He Dog, South Dakota.

604.  McGaa, Ed.  "Modern Indian Psychology:  The Book
      Made a Change in Them."  GPO, June 1970, pp. 6-
      7.  Says John Bryde's book instilled pride in Indian
      students.

605.  McLachlan, James.  American Boarding Schools:  A
      Historical Study.  New York:  Scribner's, 1970.
      381 pp.

606.  Malan, Vernon D.  "Indian College Students Plan for
      the Future."  SDFHR, 10 (1959), 10-15.

607.  [Marken, Jack W.]  "To Acquaint Indian Youth with
      College."  GPO, March 1968, pp. 8-9.

608.  Mayo, Josephine C.  "Genoa Indian School."  IHR, 3:
      4 (October 1887), 553-555.  Attended by many Sioux.

609.  Mekeel, H. Scudder.  "An Anthropologist's Observa-
      tions on Indian Education."  PE, 13 (1936), 151-159.

610.  Miller, Wilbur W.  "A Report on the Ring Thunder
      Day School--Rosebud Agency--South Dakota."  IW,
      1 April 1936, pp. 25-26.  Activities at a New Deal
      Community School.

611.  Milne, Bruce G. and Herbert T. Hoover.  A Teaching
      Guide for the Cultural History and Geography of the
      Western Frontier and Upper Missouri Region.  Ver-
      million, SD:  Hill's Creative Printing, 1975.  240
      pp.  Contains a section on Sioux history and Sioux
      leaders.

612.  Morgan, Thisba Hutson.  "Reminiscences of My Days
      in the Land of the Ogalalla Sioux."  CHSSD, 29
      (1958), 21-62.  Served as a teacher at the boarding
      school in Pine Ridge in the period 1890-1895.  In-
      cludes pictures of Indian leaders and Wounded Knee.

613.  Olsen, Louise P.  "The Problem of Language in the
      Indian Schools of Dakota Territory, 1885-88."  NDH,
      20:1 (January 1953), 47-57.  On compulsory English
      instruction.

614. Orata, Pedro. Fundamental Education in an American
     Indian Community. Haskell, KS: Haskell Press,
     1953. An outgrowth of a year's activity as Principal of
     the Little Wound Day School on Pine Ridge Reservation.

615. Pike, William. "Modern Indian Psychology--The Best
     Text Available Today." GPO, July 1970, pp. 8-9.
     A Sioux praises John Bryde's book.

616. Platt, Elvira Gaston. "Reminiscences of a Teacher
     Among the Nebraska Indians, 1843-1855." PNSHS,
     3 (1892), 125-143. Includes incidents with the Sioux.

617. "Practical Construction Taught at Oglala High School,
     Pine Ridge Reservation." IW, 15 January 1936, 41-4.

618. Riggs, Stephen R. "Education Among the Dakotahs."
     In School, Pt. V, pp. 695-97.

619. Schuck, Cecilia, Burness G. Wenberg, and Margaret
     T. Boedeker. Evaluation of the Boarding School
     Diets of Indian Children of the Dakotas and Observa-
     tions on the Growth and Development of Adolescent
     Indian Girls. Brookings: College of Home Econom-
     ics, South Dakota State University, 1964. 25 pp.

620. "Sioux Day Schools First Ready." IW, 15 September
     1934, p. 15. On schools opened at Allen (Pine
     Ridge) and He Dog (Rosebud) Reservations.

621. "Some Notes on School Dropouts." PRRB, January
     1970, 1-6.

622. "Student Ranchers: The Oglala High School Cattle Project,
     Pine Ridge, South Dakota." IW, October 1938, pp. 21-
     25. Describes a major program that exemplified New
     Deal educational plans to train young people in skills
     that would lead to economic and social self-sufficiency.

623. Szasz, Margaret C. "Federal Boarding Schools and the
     Indian Child: 1920-1960." SDH, 7:4 (Fall 1977), 371-84.

624. United States. Bureau of Education. Indian Education
     and Civilization. Rpt. New York: Kraus Reprint, 1978.

625. United States. Bureau of Indian Affairs. Education
     Facilities: Cheyenne River Reservation, South Da-
     kota. Report No. 127. Billings, MT: Missouri
     River Basin Investigations Project, 1952. 32 pp.

626.    Viken, Jeffrey L.  "Quick Bear v.  Leupp:  Amalga-
        mation of Church and State on the Rosebud. "  CHSSD,
        38 (1977),  1-72.

627.    Wax, Murray Lionel, Rosalie H.  Wax and Robert V.
        Dumont, Jr.   Formal Education in an American In-
        dian Community.   With the Assistance of Roselyn
        Holyrock and Gerald Onefeather.   Atlanta, GA:
        Emory University, 1964.   126 pp.

628.    Wilson, Jim.  "Dormitory, Teacher Aides Are Big
        Help in South Dakota. "  JAIE, 9:2 (January 1970),
        3-9.


                    FICTION AND OTHER WORKS ON
                           THE SIOUX

629.    Anderson, Myrtle M.  Sioux Memory Gems.   Illus-
        trated by J. A. Anderson.   Chicago:  n. p. ,  1929.
        Poetry.

630.    Beede, Aaron McGaffey.   Heart-in-the-Lodge, "All a
        Mistake. "  Bismarck, ND:  Bismarck Tribune Co. ,
        1915.   61 pp.

631.    Billberg, Eddy E.   The War Cry of the Sioux:  A His-
        torical Romance from the Sioux Outbreak of 1862.
        Boston:   The Christopher Publishing House, 1930.
        162 pp.   On the Minnesota Sioux War.

632.    Bleeker, Sonia.   The Sioux Indians:  Hunters and War-
        riors of the Plains.   New York:  William Morrow
        and Co. ,  1962.   160 pp.

633.    Blue Eye.   A Story of the People of the Plains.   By
        Ogal Alla.   Portland, OR:   The Irwin-Hodson Co. ,
        1905.   245 pp.   A novel, partly in dialect.

634.    Brainard, J. C.   The Death-Face:  Or,  The Enchan-
        tress of the Wilderness;  An Episode of the Recent
        Indian Troubles in the West.   New York:   George
        Munro and Co. ,  1865.   92 pp.   Munro's Ten Cent
        Novel,  No.  8.

635.    Brooks, Asa Passavant.   The Reservation:  A Romance

of the Pioneer Days of Minnesota and the Indian Massacre of 1862.   Comfrey, MN:   Asa P. Brooks,
1907.   235 pp.

636.   Calkins,  Franklin  W.   Two  Wilderness  Voyagers:   A
True  Tale  of  Indian  Life.   Chicago:   F. H. Revell
Co., 1902.   359 pp.

637.   Carpentier, Emilie.   Captive! par Mille.   Paris:
Librairie de Theodore Lefevre et cie,  n. d.   212 pp.

638.   Chadwick, Joseph.   The Sioux Indian Wars.   Derby,
CT:   Monarch Books, 1962.   143 pp.

639.   Distad,  Andree.   Dakota Sons.   New York: Harper and
Row, 1972.   159 pp.

640.   Drago,  Harry S.   Montana Road.   New York:   W. Morrow and Co., 1935.   306 pp.   Story based on the
gold rush into the Black Hills, and George Custer's
campaigns.

641.   Ellis,  Edward  S.   Among  the  Redskins  or  Tracking
Friend  and  Foe  Through  the  Wilds.   New  York:
Street and Smith, 1894.   212 pp.

642.   Ellis,  Edward  S.   Indian  Jim:   A  Tale  of  the  Minnesota  Massacre.   London:   Beadle and Co., 1864.
100 pp.

643.   Gilman,  Samuel C.   The  Story  of  a  Western  Claim:
A  Tale  of  How  Two  Boys  Solved  the  Indian  Question.
Philadelphia:   J. B. Lippincott, 1893.   201 pp.

644.   Goshe,  Frederick,  and  Frank  Goshe.   The  Dauntless
and  the  Dreamers.   New York:   T. Yoseloff, 1963.
382 pp.   Historical novel.

645.   Hart,  John S.   The  Iris:   An  Illuminated  Souvenir  for
1852.   Philadelphia:   Lippincott, Grambo and Co.,
1852.   298 pp.   Tales, poems and illustrations by
Captain and Mary Eastman, subsequently reprinted.

646.   Henry,  Will.   The  Bear  Paw  Horses.   New York:
Lippincott, 1973.   As  Crazy  Horse  lay dying, his
last request was the re-capture of 400 ponies that
had been stolen by non-Indians.

647. Hunsinger, Ruth. "A Dakota Story." InH, 6:4 (Fall
     1973), 5-7.

648. Johnson, Dorothy M. Man Called Horse and Other
     Stories. New York: Ballantine Books, Inc. , 1970.
     173 pp.

649. Jones, Douglas C. Arrest Sitting Bull. New York:
     Charles Scribner's Sons, 1977. 249 pp. Dramatizes
     events on Standing Rock Reservation just before the
     assassination of Sitting Bull.

650. King, Charles. A Daughter of the Sioux: A Tale of
     the Indian Frontier. Illstr. Frederic Remington and
     Edwin W. Deming. New York: Grosset and Dunlap,
     1902. 306 pp.

651. King, Charles. "Laramie, " Or, The Queen of Bedlam.
     Philadelphia: J. B. Lippincott Co. , 1889. 277 pp.

652. King, Charles. A Soldier's Secret: A Story of the
     Sioux War of 1890; And An Army Portila. Philadel-
     phia: J. B. Lippincott, 1893. 293 p. Two novels.

653. Lange, Dietrich. The Lure of the Black Hills. Bos-
     ton: Lothrop, Lee and Shepard Co. , 1916. 267 pp.

654. Lange, Dietrich. On the Trail of the Sioux; Or, The
     Adventures of Two Boy Scouts on the Minnesota
     Frontier. Boston: Lothrop, Lee and Shepard Co. ,
     1912. 298 pp.

655. Lange, Dietrich. The Sioux Runner. Boston: Lothrop,
     Lee and Shepard Co. , 1924. 269 pp.

656. Lanners, Tip. Im Fernen Western; Oder, Manalupe,
     der Siouxhauptling; eine Erzählung ans Nordamerikas
     Virgangenheit. Milwaukee, WI: W. Wernich, n. d.
     192 pp.

657. Lenski, Lois. Little Sioux Girl. Philadelphia: Lip-
     pincott, 1958. Story of struggle against hunger,
     blizzards, floods and poverty.

658. Lott, Milton. Dance Back the Buffalo. New York:
     Pocket Books, 1975. Among the warmest and most
     understanding novels about Indians.

659.  McGovern, Ann.  If You Lived with the Sioux Indians.
      New York:  Four Winds Press, 1972.  Juvenile lit-
      erature.

660.  McKelvie, Martha.  Hills of Yesterday.  New York:
      Dorrance and Co., 1960.  117 pp.  Vignettes on the
      Black Hills.

661.  McKnight, Bob Stuart.  Rafe:  Modern Sioux Rebel.
      Brooklyn, NY:  Gaus Sons, 1970.  277 pp.

662.  Maine, Floyd S.  Long Eagle:  The White Sioux.
      Albuquerque:  University of New Mexico Press, 1956.
      208 pp.  About Great Plains camp life, the Ghost
      Dance, George Custer's death, etc.

663.  Manfred, Frederick.  Conquering Horse.  1959; rpt.
      New York:  The New American Library, 1965.  276
      pp.  Novel on the odyssey of a young Indian to get
      his name.

664.  Manfred, Frederick.  The Manly-Hearted Woman.
      New York:  New American Library, 1975.

665.  Manfred, Frederick.  Scarlet Plume.  New York:
      Pocket Books, 1968.  328 pp.  Novel about Judith
      Raveling's surviving the massacre of her family to
      become a chief's wife, and to become enraptured of
      Scarlet Plume.

666.  Manfred, Frederick.  Winter Count.  Limited ed.
      Minneapolis:  J. D. Thueson, 1966.

667.  Marriott, Alice.  Indians on Horseback.  New York:
      T. Y. Crowell Co., 1968.  Juvenile literature.

668.  Martino, Bill.  The Dreamer:  A Tale of the Sioux.
      Boston:  Branden Press, 1975.  76 pp.

669.  Mason, Augustus Lynch.  The Romance and Tragedy
      of Pioneer Life.  A Popular Account of the Heros
      and Adventurers Who, by Their Valor and War-
      craft, Beat Back the Savages from the Borders of
      Civilization and Gave the American Forests to the
      Plow and Sickle.  Cincinnati:  Jonas Brothers and
      Co., 1883.

670.  Miller, Mark.  The White Captive of the Sioux.  New
      York:  Holt, Rinehart and Winston, 1953.  Juvenile
      literature.

671.  Moorhead, Warren King.  Tonda:  A Stody of the Sioux.
      Cincinnati:  R. Clarke Co. , 1904.  309 pp.

672.  Moorehead, Warren King.  Wanneta:  The Sioux.  New
      York:  Dodd, Mead and Co. , 1890.  285 pp.

673.  Neihardt, John.  A Cycle of the West.  Vol. 2.
      Lincoln:  University of Nebraska Press, 1971.
      Poetry.

674.  Neihardt, John.  Eagle Voice:  An Authentic Tale of
      the Sioux Indians.  London:  Andrew Melrose, 1953.

675.  Neihardt, John.  The Song of the Indian Wars.  New
      York:  Macmillan Co. , 1925.  231 pp.

676.  Neihardt, John.  The Song of the Messiah.  New York:
      Macmillan Co. , 1935.  110 pp.

677.  Neihardt, John.  The Twilight of the Sioux.  1925;
      rpt.  Lincoln:  University of Nebraska Press, 1971.
      Poetry.

678.  Neihardt, John.  When the Tree Flowered.  Fictional
      autobiography of Eagle Voice, a Sioux Indian.  1951;
      rpt.  Lincoln:  University of Nebraska Press, 1970.
      248 pp.

679.  Northrop, Joseph A.  Wawina:  A Beautiful Story of
      an Indian Princess.  Carlton, MN:  W. H. Hassing,
      1937.  83 pp.

680.  Pearson, M. J.  Ride the Red-Eyed Wing.  Minneapo-
      lis:  Dillon Press, 1978.  An unconvincing novel,
      set in Faribault, about the Minnesota Sioux War.

681.  Poatgieter, Alice H.  The Dakota or Sioux.  St. Paul:
      Historical Society, 1970.  18 pp.  Juvenile litera-
      ture.

682.  Poatgieter, Alice H.  Gifts from the Indians.  St.
      Paul:  Minnesota Historical Society, 1969.  11 pp.

683. Russell, Don. Sioux Buffalo Hunters. Chicago: Ency-
     clopaedia Press, 1962. Juvenile literature.

684. Sandoz, Mari. Buffalo Hunters. rpt; New York: Hast-
     ings House Publishers, Inc., 1971.

685. Sandoz, Mari. These Were the Sioux. New York:
     Dell Publishing Co., 1967.

686. Sanford, Paul. Sioux Arrows and Bullets. San An-
     tonio, TX: Naylor Co., 1969. 171 pp. Campaign
     against Little Crow based on documents and personal
     letters.

687. Seymour, Flora Warren. The Story of the Sioux In-
     dians. Girard, KS: Haldeman-Julius Co., 1924.
     64 pp.

688. Sinclair, Bertha (Muzzy). The Heritage of the Sioux.
     New York: Grosset and Dunlap, 1916. 312 pp.

689. Smith, A. "Ride, Dakota! A Sioux Legend." Col-
     lier's, 31 October 1925, pp. 26-27.

690. Stephens, Alan. White River Poems: Conversations,
     Pronouncements, Testimony, Recollections and Medi-
     tations on the Subject of the White River Massacre,
     Sept. 29, 1879. Chicago: Swallow Press, 1975.

691. Stoddard, William O. Little Smoke: A Tale of the
     Sioux. New York: D. Appleton and Co., 1891,
     1896. 295 pp.

692. Ude, Wayne. Buffalo and Other Stories. Amherst,
     MA: Lynx House, 1975. 68 pp.

693. Veglahn, Nancy. The Buffalo King; Or the Story of
     Scotty Philip. New York: Scribner's, 1971. 180
     pp.

694. Voss, Carroll. White Cap for Rechinda. New York:
     Ives Washburn, 1966. Contemporary novel about a
     Sioux girl attempting to get through nursing school
     while adjusting to cultural conflicts.

695. Waters, Gay. Alma: Or, Otonkah's Daughter; A Story

of the 20, 000 Sioux.   Chicago:   T. S. Denison,
1888.   170 pp.

696.   Watkins, J. P. C.   Wenonah:   The Story of an Indian
       Maid.   Winona, MN:   n. p. , 1919.   16 pp.

697.   Weyer, Montana H.   Trailing the Teepees.   New York:
       Vantage Press, 1968.


               FORTS AND MILITARY POSTS IN
                     SIOUX COUNTRY

698.   Anderson, Harry H.   "A Fortified Earthlodge Village
       Near Fort Thompson, South Dakota, as It Appeared
       in 1866. "   PlA, 13:39 (1968), 26-28.   Where Santees
       and Winnebagos were relocated in 1863.

699.   Anderson, Harry H.   "A History of the Cheyenne
       River Indian Agency and Its Military Post, Fort
       Bennett, 1868-1891. "   CHSSD, 28 (1956), 390-551.
       From his M. A. history thesis of 1954.

700.   Athearn, Robert G.   Forts of the Upper Missouri.
       Lincoln:   University of Nebraska Press, 1967.   293
       pp.   Better than any other source, this describes
       the movement of the United States Army into Sioux
       country during the 19th century.

701.   Babcock, Willoughby M. , ed.   "Up the Minnesota Val-
       ley to Fort Ridgely in 1853. "   MiH, 11:2 (June 1930),
       161-184.

702.   Burdick, Usher L.   Tales from Buffalo Land:   The
       Story of Fort Buford.   Baltimore, MD:   Wirth Broth-
       ers, 1940.   215 pp.   A key fort on the upper Mis-
       souri, where Sitting Bull surrendered.

703.   Clark, Dan E.   "Early Forts on the Upper Missis-
       sippi. "   PMVHA, 4 (1910-11), 91-101.

704.   "Dakota Military Posts. "   CHSSD, 8 (1916), 77-99.

705.   DeNoyer, Charles.   "The History of Fort Totten. "
       CHSND, 3 (1910), 178-236.   Established by General
       Alfred A. Terry in 1867.

706.   Dunn, Adrian R. "A History of Old Fort Berthhold."
       NDH, 30:4 (October 1963), 156-240. Especially
       valuable for the 1860's.

707.   Edwards, Paul M. "Fort Wadsworth and the Friendly
       Santee Sioux, 1864-1892." CHSSD, 31 (1962), 74-
       136.

708.   Folwell, William Watts. "The Sale of Fort Snelling,
       1857." CMHS, 15 (1915), 392-410. Describes the
       purchase of the land from the Sioux, and its later
       disposition.

709.   Forsyth, Thomas. "Fort Snelling. Col. Leaven-
       worth's Expedition to Establish It, in 1819." CMHS,
       3 (1870-1880), 139-167.

710.   "Fort Abercrombie, 1857-1877." CHSND, 2:2 (1908),
       1-34.

711.   Fort Sisseton Memorial Association, Britton, S. D.
       Fort Sisseton, First Called Fort Wadsworth, in the
       Heart of the Dakota Lake Region.   Britton, SD:
       Fort Sisseton Memorial Association, 1935.   20 pp.

712.   Foughty, Helen.  Fort Totten: History, Legends,
       Points of Interest. n. p. , n. d.  16 pp.  A project
       of the Devil's Lake Branch of the American Asso-
       ciation of University Women.

713.   Goplen, Arnold O.  "Fort Abraham Lincoln: A Typ-
       ical Frontier Military Post." NDH, 13:4 (1946),
       176-221.  Contains information about George Custer
       and his dealings with Sioux.

714.   Hedren, Paul L.  "On Duty at Fort Ridgely, Min-
       nesota:  1853-1867." SDH, 7:2 (Spring 1977), 168-
       192.  Established in 1853.

715.   Henry, Will.  The Day Fort Larking Fell:  The Leg-
       end of the Last Great Indian Fight.  Philadelphia:
       Chilton Book Co. , 1969.  Juvenile literature.

716.   Hoekman, Steven. "The History of Fort Sully."
       CHSSD, 26 (1952), 222-277.  The fort operated in
       the period 1863-1894 to control the Sioux.

717.  Holmes, Louis A.  Fort McPherson, Nebraska Terri-
      tory.  Lincoln, NE:  Johnsen Publishing Co., 1963.

718.  Johnson, Richard W.  "Fort Snelling from Its Founda-
      tion to the Present Time."  CMHS, 8 (1898), 427-
      448.  Contains an account by General Johnson of the
      murder of Philander Prescott.

719.  Johnson, Willis F.  The Red Record of the Sioux:
      Life of Sitting Bull and History of the Indian War of
      1890-91.  Philadelphia:  Edgewood Publishing Co.,
      1891; rpt. New York:  AMS Press, 1977.

720.  Jones, Evan.  Citadel in the Wilderness:  The Story of
      Fort Snelling and the Old Northwest Frontier.  New
      York:  Coward-McCann, 1966.

721.  Kellogg, Louise P.  "Fort Beauharnois."  MiH, 8:3
      (September 1927), 232-246.  Established among the
      Sioux of the Minnesota River Valley in 1727.

722.  Kimball, James P.  "Fort Buford."  NDHQ, 4:2 (Jan-
      uary 1930), 73-77.  Contains information on Bear's
      Rib, Sitting Bull, Running Bear and other leaders.

723.  Kitchen, Dick.  "Fort Sisseton.  Social Center of Da-
      kota Territory."  DW, 2:1 (Spring 1976), 8-10.

724.  Macgregor, Gordon.  "Attitudes of the Fort Berthhold
      Indians Regarding Removal from the Garrison Reser-
      voir Site and Future Administration of Their Reser-
      vation."  NDH, 16:1 (January 1949), 31-60.

725.  Mattison, Ray H.  "Fort Rice--North Dakota's First
      Missouri River Military Post."  NDH, 20:2 (April
      1963), 87-108.

726.  Mattison, Ray H.  "Old Fort Stevenson--A Typical
      Missouri River Military Post."  NDH, 18:2 and 3
      (April-July 1951), 53-91.  To protect other North
      Dakota tribes from the Sioux.

727.  Mullin, Cora P.  "The Founding of Fort Hartsuff."
      NH, 12:2 (April-June 1924), 128-140.  Built in 1874-
      75 about 200 miles west of Omaha to protect settlers
      from the Sioux.

728.  Murray, Robert A.  Military Posts in the Power River
       Country of Wyoming, 1865-1894.  Lincoln:  Univer-
       sity of Nebraska, 1968.

729.  Nadeau, Remi.  Fort Laramie and the Sioux Indians.
       Englewood Cliffs, NJ:  Prentice-Hall, 1957.  335 pp.

730.  Neill, Edward D.  "Early French Forts and Footprints
       of the Valley of the Upper Mississippi."  CMHS, 2:
       Pt. 2 (1879), 89-101.

731.  Neill, Edward D.  The Last French Post in the Valley
       of the Upper Mississippi, near Frontenac, Minn. :
       With Notices of it Commandants.  St. Paul:  The
       Pioneer Press Co., 1887.  23 pp.; also as "The
       Last French Post in the Upper Mississippi Valley,
       Lake Pepin, Minnesota."  MWH (November 1887),
       pp. 17-29.  On Fort Beauharnois in Goodhue County.

732.  Pfaller, Fr. Louis.  "The Fort Keogh to Bismarch
       Stage Route."  NDH, 21:3 (July 1954), 91-125.

733.  "Records of Fort Tecumseh."  CHSSD, 9 (1918), 93-
       167.  Founded on the upper Missouri at Bad River
       in 1822.  From the journal of Jacob Halsey; notes
       by Doane Robinson.

734.  Slaughter, Linda W.  "Fort Abercrombie."  CHSND,
       1 (1906), 412-423.  Established 1857, abandoned
       1859, re-established 1862 to deal with Sissetons and
       Yanktons.  Information on Sitting Bull.

735.  Smith, G. Hubert.  "Fort Pierre (39 St 217) A His-
       toric Trading Post in the Oahe Dam Area, South
       Dakota."  BBAE, 176 (1960), 83-158.

736.  Smith, G. Hubert.  "A Frontier Fort in Peacetime."
       MiH, 45:3 (Fall 1976), 116-128.

737.  Taylor, Joseph H.  "Fort Berthold Agency in 1869."
       NDHQ, 4:4 (July 1930), 220-226.

738.  Taylor, Joseph H.  "Fort Totten Trail."  NDHQ, 4:4
       (July 1930), 239-246.

739.  Thomson, William D.  "History of Fort Pembina:
       1870-1895."  NDH, 36:1 (Winter 1969), 4-39.  Es-

tablished along the Red River near the Canadian
border out of concern for hostiles from the Minnesota Sioux War.

740.   Walker, James F.  "Old Fort Berthold as I Knew It."
       NDH, 20:1 (January 1953), 25-46.

741.   [Warren, G. K.]  "Explorations in Nebraska and Da-
       kota ... Military Posts--Routes for Military Opera-
       tions, Etc."  CHSSD, 11 (1922), 206-219.  Describes
       Sioux bands and gives population figures in 1860.

742.   Wertenberger, Mildred.  "Fort Totten, Dakota Terri-
       tory, 1867."  NDH, 34:2 (Spring 1967), 125-146.
       One hundred years of history.

743.   Wright, Dana.  "The Fort Totten-Fort Stevenson
       Trail."  NDH, 20:2 (April 1953), 67-86.

744.   Wright, Dana.  "Military Trails in North Dakota.
       Fort Abercrombie to Fort Ransom.  With Notes on
       the History of Fort Ransom."  NDH, 17:4 (October
       1950), 241-252.

745.   Wright, Dana.  "Military Trails in North Dakota, Fort
       Abercrombie to Fort Wadsworth, 1864."  NDH, 18:
       2 and 3 (April-July 1951), 156-170.

746.   Wright, Dana.  "Military Trails in North Dakota.
       Fort Ransom to Fort Totten."  NDH, 16:4 (October
       1949), 203-210.  Used during punitive expeditions
       in 1863.


FUR TRADERS AND SCOUTS

747.   Ackermann, Gertrude W.  "George Northrup, Frontier
       Scout."  MiH, 19:4 (December 1938), 377-392.  In-
       formation on the Sioux from Northrup's letters of
       the 1850s and 1860s.

748.   Anderson, Harry H.  "The Fort Lookout Trading Post
       Sites--a Reexamination."  PlA, 6:14 (November 1961),
       221-229.  Established in 1822, Fort Lookout served
       as an outpost for Sioux trade for many years in the
       area north of Chamberlain, SD.

749.  Anderson,  Harry  H.  "Fur  Traders  as  Fathers:  The
      Origins  of  the  Mixed-Blooded  Community  Among  the
      Rosebud  Sioux. "  SDH,  3:3  (Summer  1973),  233-270.
      One  of  the  few  pieces  on  the  importance  of  mixed-
      bloods  in  Sioux  society.

750.  "The  Astorians  in  South  Dakota. "  CHSSD,  10  (1920),
      196-247.  Contains  information  about  Indians  en-
      countered  by  the  Astorians  on  their  expedition  of
      1810-11.

751.  Babcock,  Willoughby  M.  "Louis  Provencalle,  Fur
      Trader. "  MiH,  20  (September  1939),  259-268.

752.  Baker,  James  H.  "Lake  Superior:  Its  History--
      Romance  of  the  Fur  Trade--Its  Physical  Features--
      Treaties--the  Voyageurs,  Etc. "  CMHS,  3  (1889),
      333-355.  Contains  observations  about  the  origin  of
      the  Sioux-Chippewa  war,  and  other  information  about
      the  Sioux.

753.  Bell,  Charles  N.  "The  Earliest  Fur  Traders  on  the
      Upper  Red  River  and  Red  Lake,  Minn.  [1783-1810]. "
      THSSM.  N. S.  1  (November  1926).  16  pp.

754.  Campbell,  Marjorie  W.  The  North  West  Company.
      New  York:  St.  Martin's  Press,  1957.  295  pp.

755.  Caruso,  John  A.  The  Mississippi  Valley  Frontier:
      The  Age  of  French  Exploration  and  Settlement.  In-
      dianapolis:  Bobbs-Merrill,  1966.  432  pp.

755a.  Collins,  Ethel  A.  "Pioneer  Experiences  of  Horatio  H.
      Larned. "  CHSND,  7  (1925),  1-58.  Collins  took  part
      in  the  Fisk  Expedition  of  1864,  and  worked  in  the
      fur  trade.

756.  Dean,  Cora.  "Early  Fur  Trading  in  the  Red  River
      Valley.  From  the  Journals  of  Alexander  Henry,  Jr. "
      CHSND,  3  (1910),  350-368.  Information  about  the
      Sioux  during  the  period  1799-1814.

757.  Galbraith,  John  S.  "British-American  Competition  in
      the  Border  Fur  Trade  of  the  1820s. "  MiH,  36  (1929),
      241-249.

758.  Gates,  Charles  M. ,  ed.  Five  Fur  Traders  of  the

Northwest:  Being the Narrative of Peter Pone and
the Diaries of John Macdonell, Archibald N. McLeod,
Hugh Faries, and Thomas Connor.   Intro.  Grace L.
Nute.   Fwd. Theodore C. Blegen.   St. Paul:   Minnesota Historical Society, 1965.   296 pp.

759.   Gray, John S.   "Honore Picotte, Fur Trader."   SDH,
       6:2 (Spring 1976), 186-202.   Served in the fur trade
       from 1820 to 1865, and married the sister of Struck-
       by-the-Ree, last Head Chief of the Yankton tribe.
       After her death, he married the daughter of Two
       Lance, a Hunkpapa Chief.   Lived for years at Fort
       Pierre.

760.   Henry, Alexander.   New Light on the Early History of
       the Greater Northwest.   The Manuscript Journals of
       Alexander Henry, Fur Trader of the Northwest Com-
       pany, and of David Thompson, Official Geographer
       and Explorer of the Same Company, 1799-1814;   Ex-
       ploration and Adventure Among the Indians on the
       Red, Saskatchewan, Missouri, and Columbia Rivers.
       3 vols.   Ed. Elliott Coues.   New York:   Francis P.
       Harper, 1897; rpt. Minneapolis:   Ross and Haines,
       1965, 2 vols.

761.   Hughes, Thomas, and William C. Brown.   Old Traverse
       des Sioux.   St. Peter, MN:   Herald Publishing Co.,
       1929.   177 pp.   A history of early exploration, trad-
       ing posts, missions, and treaties among the eastern
       Sioux.

762.   Innis, Harold A.   Peter Pond:   Fur Trader and Ad-
       venturer.   Toronto:   Irwin and Gordon, 1930.   153
       pp.

763.   Jensen, Margeurite.   "Fur Trading Post."   DW, 2:4
       (Winter 1976), 6-9.   On Fort Pierre, with informa-
       tion about the Sioux.

764.   Johnson, Roy P.   "Fur Trader Chaboillez at Pembina."
       NHD, 32 (April 1965), 82-99.

765.   Kurz, Rudolph F.   The Journal of Rudolph Friederich
       Kurz:   An Account of His Experiences Among Fur
       Traders on the Upper Mississippi and the Upper
       Missouri Rivers During the Years 1846 to 1852.   Ed.
       J. N. Newitt.   Trans. Myrtis Jarrell.   1937; rpt.
       Lincoln:   University of Nebraska Press, 1970.

766. Larpenteur, August L. "Recollections of the City and People of St. Paul, 1843-1898." CMHS, 9 (1901), 363-394. Information about Sioux treaties, etc.

767. Larpenteur, Charles. Forty Years a Fur Trader on the Upper Missouri. Minneapolis: Ross and Haines, 1970.

768. Miller, David. "The Fur Men and Explorers Meet the Indians." See entry no. 1250, pp. 25-45.

769. Neill, Edward D. "Early French Forts and Footprints of the Valley of the Upper Mississippi." CMHS, 2 (1889), 89-101. Contains information about explorers' dealings with Sioux.

770. Nelson, George. "A Fur Trader's Reminiscences." MiH, 38 (1947), 1-14, 142-159, 225-240. Deals with trade in the St. Croix valley.

771. Nute, Grace L. "Posts in the Minnesota Fur-trading Area, 1660-1855." MiH, 11 (December 1930), 353-385; rpt. MA, 15 (July 1949), 61-77.

772. Oglesby, Richard Edward. Manuel Lisa and the Opening of the Missouri Fur Trade. Norman: University of Oklahoma Press, 1963. With his St. Louis Fur Company, Lisa dominated trade among the Sioux on the Missouri from 1807 to his death in 1820, and also served among them as special Indian agent.

773. Parker, Donald D. "Early Explorations and Fur Trading in South Dakota." CHSSD, 25 (1950), 1-211. Much information on the Sioux, including the experiences of Charles Le Ray, who was captive among them 1801-1805.

774. Parker, Watson. "The Report of Captain John Mix of a Scout to the Black Hills, March-April 1875." SDH, 7:4 (Fall 1977), 385-401.

775. Porter, T. R. "A Story of Crook's Scouts." TB, 2 (June 1916), 575-576, 610.

776. Reid, Russell, and Clell G. Gannon, eds. "Journal of the Atkinson-O'Fallon Expedition." NDHQ, 4:1 (October 1929), 4-56. Sioux volunteers accompanied this

punitive expedition up the Missouri to avenge an attack on William Ashley's traders by Arikaras.

777.    Remington, Frederic. "Lieutenant Casey's Last Scout. "
        HW, 31 January 1891, pp. 85-89.

778.    Saum, Lewis O.    The Fur Trader and the Indian.
        Seattle: University of Washington Press, 1965.
        324 pp.

779.    Sunder, John E.   Fur Trade on the Upper Missouri,
        1840-1865.   Norman:   University of Oklahoma Press,
        1965.

780.    Sunder, John E.    Joshua Pilcher:  Fur Trader and
        Indian Agent.   Norman:   University of Oklahoma
        Press, 1968.   203 pp.   Served as Indian agent
        among the Sioux, at Fort Lookout and elsewhere,
        during the 1830's.

781.    Tohill, Louis A.    "Robert Dickson, British Fur Trader
        on the Upper Mississippi. "   NDHQ, 3:1 (October 1928),
        5-49; 3:2 (January 1929), 83-128; 3:3 (April 1929),
        182-203.    About Dickson, who was married to a
        Yanktonai, traded among the eastern and middle
        Sioux, and led Sioux into the War of 1812 on the
        side of the British.

782.    Tohill, Louis A.   Robert Dickson, British Fur Trader
        on the Upper Mississippi:   A Story of Trade, War,
        and Diplomacy.   Ann Arbor, MI:   Edwards Brothers,
        1927.   124 pp.

783.    Trennert, Robert A.    "The Fur Trader as Indian Ad-
        ministrator:   Conflict of Interest or Wise Policy?"
        SDH, 5:1 (Winter 1974), 1-11.   Speaks of traders
        among Sioux of the Dakotas, and contends that traders
        held higher opinions of, and dealt more kindly with,
        Indians than did other non-Indian groups.

784.    "The War on Whiskey in the Fur Trade. "   CHSSD, 9
        (1918), 168-233.

785.    Wells, Philip F.    "Ninety-Six Years Among the Indians
        of the Northwest--Adventurers and Reminiscences of
        an Indian Scout and Interpreter in the Dakotas. "   As
        told to Thomas E. Odell.   NDH, 15:2 (April 1948),

85-133; 15:3 (July 1948), 169-215; 15:4 (October
1948), 265-312.   Contains biographies of numerous
Indians and mixed-bloods, including Jane Graham
Wells, Struck-by-the-Ree, Little Crow, Martin
Charger, Shakapa, Big Foot, Brave Bear; Fetter-
man fight, Custer War, and other episodes mentioned.

GEORGE A. CUSTER AND HIS
SIOUX WARS

786.  Adams, Jacob.  A Story of the Custer Massacre.  Vin-
      cennes, IN:  Printed Privately, 1930.  39 pp.  Adams
      fought with Custer in Benteen's troop.

787.  Anderson, Harry H.  "Cheyennes at the Little Big
      Horn--A Study of Statistics."  NDH, 27:2 (Spring
      1960), 81-93.

788.  Barry, David F.  "The Custer Battle."  TB, 2 (June
      1916), 611-613.

789.  Barry, David F.  David F. Barry's Indian Notes on
      'The Custer Battle.'"  Ed. Usher L. Burdick.  Balti-
      more:  Proof Press, 1937.  35 pp.

790.  Bates, Charles Francis.  Custer's Indian Battles.
      Bronxville, NY:  Printed Privately, 1936.  36 pp.

791.  Bates, Charles Francis.  Fifty Years After the Little
      Big Horn Battle.  New York:  Printed Privately,
      1926.  19 pp.  Recollections of Colonel Bates, re-
      printed from the New York Herald Tribune, June 20,
      1926.

792.  Beede, Aaron McGaffey.  Sitting Bull--Custer.  Bis-
      marck, ND:  Bismarck Tribune Co., 1913.  An
      Episcopal missionary presents the Battle of the Little
      Bighorn in a play, based upon oral research, which
      is very sympathetic to Sitting Bull and his followers.

793.  Bell, Gordon L., and Beth L. Bell.  "General Custer
      in North Dakota."  NDH, 31:2 (April 1964), 101-113.

794.  Bowen, William Holman Cary.  Custer's Last Fight.
      Caldwell, ID:  Caxton Printers, 1935; rpt.

Grand Rapids, MI: Custer Ephemera Society, 1973.
13 pp.

795.    Boyes, William. Custer's Black White Man. Washing-
        ton, DC: South Capital Press, 1972. 46 pp.

796.    Brackett, William S. "Custer's Last Battle. " CHSMo,
        4 (1903), 259-276.

797.    Bradley, James H. The March of the Montana Col-
        umn: A Prelude to the Custer Disaster. Ed. Edgar
        I. Stewart. Norman: University of Oklahoma Press,
        1961. 182 pp. Shows Custer's men were not muti-
        lated after the Battle of Little Bighorn.

798.    Brigham, Earl K. "Custer's Meeting with Secretary of
        War Belknap at Fort Abraham Lincoln. " NDH, 19:
        2 (April 1952), 129-131. Occurred during the sum-
        mer of 1875.

799.    Brininstool, E. A. "Charley Reynolds--Hunter and
        Scout. " NDHQ, 7:2 and 3 (1933), 73-81. On "Lone-
        some Charley, " Chief of Scouts for Custer.

800.    Brininstool, E. A. "The Custer Battle Continues. "
        Montana, 4:4 (Autumn 1954), 62-63. Contrary to re-
        ports that Major Reno was drunk after the Battle of
        the Little Bighorn, this says he was not.

801.    Brown, Dee. Showdown at Little Big Horn. New York:
        Berkley Publishing Corp. , 1970. 190 pp.

802.    Burdick, Usher L. The Last Battle of the Sioux Na-
        tion. Stevens Point, WI: Worzalia Publishing Co. ,
        1929. 164 pp. Includes names of those who died
        with Custer, and were wounded with Reno.

803.    Burrows, Jack. "From Bull Run to the Little Big
        Horn. " AW, 5:2 (1968), 51, 61, 64. A review of
        two books on the subject.

804.    Byrne, P. E. "The Custer Myth. " NDHQ, 6:3 (April
        1932), 187-200.

805.    Caras, Roger A. The Custer Wolf. Boston: Little,
        Brown and Co. , 1966. 175 pp.

806. Carroll, John M., ed. The Benteen-Goldin Letters on Custer and His Last Battle. New York: Liveright, 1974. 312 pp.

807. Coburn, Wallace D. "The Battle of the Little Bighorn." Montana, 6:3 (July 1956), 28-41. As told to the author by Major Will A. Logan.

808. Cockerill, John A. "The Custer Battle Field." TB, 2 (June 1916), 583-586. By a newsman sent out by the New York Herald.

809. Collections of Reminiscences by Sioux, Cheyenne, and Arapaho Indians Who Fought at Little Big Horn." AH, 22:4 (1971), 28-41.

810. Crawford, Lewis F. Ranching Days in Dakota and Custer's Black Hills Expedition of 1874. Baltimore: Wirth Bros., 1950. Contains material on the Sioux-- particularly their resentment toward the expedition.

811. "Curley's Statement." TB, 2 (June 1916), 602. A famous Crow scout speaks about the Custer Battle.

812. Custer, Elizabeth C. Boots and Saddles: Or Life in Dakota with General Custer. 1885; rpt. Norman: University of Oklahoma Press, 1968; New York: Harper-Row, 1970.

813. Custer, Elizabeth C. Following the Guidon. Rpt. Norman: University of Oklahoma Press, 1966.

814. Custer, Elizabeth C. Tenting on the Plains. Rpt. Norman: University of Oklahoma Press, 1970.

815. Custer, George A. My Life on the Plains; Or Personal Experiences with the Indians. New ed. Norman: University of Oklahoma Press, 1962; rpt. Ed. Milo M. Quaife. Lincoln: University of Nebraska Press, 1966; Gloucester, MA: Peter Smith, 1970.

816. Custer, George A. Wild Life on the Plains and Horrors of Indian Warfare. Being a Complete History of Indian Life, Warfare, and Adventure in America. 1891; rpt. Chicago: Library Resources, 1971. Reprint with additional chapters of My Life on the Plains.

817. Deming, E. "Custer's Last Stand: Indians' Version."
     The Mentor, 14 (July 1926), 56-57.

818. Diehl, Charles. "Crazy Horse's Story of Custer Bat-
     tle." CHSSD, 6 (1912), 224-228. Diehl, a news-
     man, interviewed Crazy Horse on May 24-25, 1877,
     before the Sioux leader's death at Camp Robinson in
     1877.

819. Dippie, Brian W. "Bards of the Little Bighorn."
     WAL, 1:3 (Fall 1966), 175-195. Examines "poetic
     celebrations of Custer, his last stand, and the leg-
     ends that surround both."

820. Dippie, Brian W. "Brush, Palette and the Custer
     Battle: A Second Look." Montana, 24:1 (January
     1974), 55-67. See entry no. 874.

821. Dippie, Brian W. "Jack Crabb and the Sole Survivors
     of Custer's Last Stand." WAL, 4:3 (Fall 1969), 182-
     202.

822. Dippie, Brian W. "The Southern Response to Custer's
     Last Stand." Montana, 21:2 (Spring 1971), 18-31.

823. Dippie, Brian W. "'What Will Congress Do About It?'
     The Congressional Reaction to the Little Big Horn
     Disaster." NDH, 37:3 (Summer 1970), 160-189.

824. Dustin, Fred. The Custer Tragedy. Ann Arbor, MI:
     Printed Privately, 1939.

825. Eastman, Charles A. "The Story of the Little Big
     Horn." The Chautauquan, 31 (July 1900), 353-358.

826. Ege, Robert J. "Braves of All Colors: The Story of
     Isaiah Dorman, Killed at Little Big Horn." Montana,
     16:1 (January 1966), 35-40.

827. Epple, Jess C. Custer's Battle of the Washita and
     the History of the Plains Indians. Jericho, NY: Ex-
     position Press, Inc., 1970.

828. Fife, Austin, and Alta Fife. "Ballads of the Little
     Big Horn." AW, 4:1 (1967), 46-49, 86-89. Both
     texts and music.

829. Frast, Lawrence A. The Court-Martial of General
George Armstrong Custer. Norman: University of
Oklahoma Press, 1968. 280 pp.

830. Fynn, A. J. "The Custer Battle." ColM, 3:4 (October 1926), 138-142.

831. Garst, Doris Shannon. Custer: Fighter of the Plains.
New York: Julian Messner, 1944. Juvenile literature.

832. Gerber, Max E. "The Custer Expedition of 1874: A
New Look." NDH, 40:1 (Winter 1973), 4-23. Includes photographs.

833. Gibbon, John. "The Custer Battle Too!" Montana,
7:2 (April 1957), 57. Letter from General Gibbon
to Major D. W. Benham on June 28, 1876, shortly
after the Battle of the Little Bighorn.

834. Godfrey, Edward S. "Custer's Last Battle." TB, 2
(June 1916), 570-573, 614-643; rpt. CHSMo, 9 (1923),
144-225; Palo Alto, CA: L. Osborne, 1968. 86 pp.

835. Goes Ahead. "Reminiscences of an Indian Scout for
Custer." TB, 2:11 (November 1916), 838-843. A
Crow scout with Custer.

836. Graham, W. A. The Custer Myth. New York: Bonan-
za, 1953. 413 pp. Contains an extensive bibliography.

837. Gray, John S. "Arikara Scouts with Custer." NDH,
35:2 (Spring 1968), 442-478. Includes photographs,
plus names of thirty-seven Arikara, four Dakota,
and four mixed-blood scouts who accompanied Custer.

838. Gray, John S. Centennial Campaign: The Sioux War
of 1876. Fort Collins, CO: Old Army Press, 1976.
392 pp.

839. Gray, John S. "Custer Throws a Boomerang." Montana, 11:2 (April 1961), 2-12. About disagreement
between the Indian Office and the U. S. Army during
the 1870's.

840. Gray, John S. "The Pack Train on George A. Custer's

Last Campaign. "   NH,   57:1  (Spring  1976),  53-
68.

841.   Gray,  John  S.   "Sutler  on  Custer's  Last  Campaign. "
NDH,  43:3  (Summer  1976),  14-21.   He  was  Capt.
John  W.  Smith.

842.   Gray,  John  S.   "Veterinary  Service  on  Custer's  Last
Campaign. "   KHQ,  43:3  (Autumn  1977),  249-263.

843.   Great  Western  Indian  Fights.   Lincoln:   University  of
Nebraska  Press,  1966.   336  pp.   Prepared  by  the
Potomac  Corral  of  Westerners,  Washington,  DC.

844.   Hall,  Henry.   "Reminiscences. "   TB,  2  (June  1916),
579-582.   About  the  Custer  Battle.

845.   Hammer,  Kenneth,  ed.   Custer  in  '76:   Walter  Camp's
Notes  on  the  Custer  Fight.   Provo,  Utah:   Brigham
Young  University  Press,  1976.   303  pp.   Camp,
editor  of  Railway  and  Engineering  Review,  wrote
from  personal  observations  and  interviews.

846.   Hammer,  Kenneth.   "Notes  from  the  Custer  Battlefield:   W.  M.  Camp's  Interviews  with  Survivors  of
Little  Bighorn. "   AW,  13:2  (March-April  1976),  36-
45.

847.   "A  Haunting  New  Vision  of  the  Little  Big  Horn. "   AH,
22:4  (June  1970),  101-103.

848.   Heidenreich,  C.  A.   "The  Sins  of  Custer  Are  Not
Anthropological  Sins. "   AA,  74:4  (August  1972),
1032-1034.

849.   Henry,  Will.   Custer's  Last  Stand:   The  Story  of  the
Little  Big  Horn.   Philadelphia:   Chilton  Book  Co. ,
1966.   Juvenile  literature.

850.   Hixon,  John  C.   "Custer's  'Mysterious'  Mr.  Kellogg. "
NDH,  17:3  (July  1950),  145-176.   Includes  the  diary
of  Mark  Kellog,  a  newsman  who  died  with  Custer  at
the  Battle  of  the  Little  Bighorn.

851.   Hofling,  Charles  D.   "George  Armstrong  Custer:   A
Psychoanalytic  Approach. "   Montana,  21:2  (Spring
1971),  32-43.   Written  by  a  physician.

852. Hoopes, Alban W. The Road to the Little Big Horn--
     and Beyond. New York: Vantage Press, 1975.
     336 pp. With excessive emotion, Hoopes describes
     conflict between the Sioux and non-Indians from the
     mid-1860's to the surrender of Sitting Bull in 1881.

853. Hubbard, Elbert. "The Custer Battle." TB, 1:6
     (June 1915), 106-122.

854. Huggins, Eli L. "Custer and Rain In The Face."
     AMe, 9 (November 1926), 338-343. Contains con-
     versations of others with Rain-In-The-Face.

855. Hunt, Frazier, and Robert Hunt. I Fought with Custer:
     The Story of Sergeant Windolph. New York: Charles
     Scribner's Sons, 1947.

856. Innis, Ben. Bloody Knife! Custer's Favorite Scout.
     Fort Collins, CO: Old Army Press, 1973. 202 pp.
     Although written with anti-Indian bias, provides in-
     sight into why Indian scouts joined the U. S. Army
     with a description of the vendetta of Bloody Knife
     against Sitting Bull and Gall.

857. Jacker, Edward. "Who Is to Blame for the Little Big
     Horn Disaster?" ACQR, 1 (1876), 712-741.

858. Jackson, Donald. Custer's Gold: The United States
     Cavalry Expedition of 1874. New Haven: Yale Uni-
     versity Press, 1966; rpt. Lincoln: University of
     Nebraska Press, 1972.

859. Johnson, Dorothy M. "Custer Rides Again." Montana,
     17:1 (January 1967), 53-63.

860. Johnson, Roy P. "Jacob Horner of the 7th Cavalry."
     NDH, 16:2 (April 1949), 74-100. A survivor of the
     Battle of the Little Bighorn, who joined the pursuit
     of the Sioux afterward.

861. Jones, Archer, and Jerry Vanderlinde. "The United
     States in the Little Big Horn Campaign." NDH, 42:
     2 (Spring 1975), 22-27. Leaders ignored standard
     military tactics at the Battle of the Little Bighorn.

862. Josephy, Alvin M. "The Custer Myth." Life, 2 July
     1971, pp. 48-60.

863.  Josselyn, Daniel W.  "Indian Cavalry." GPJ, 2:2
      (Spring 1963), 77-79.  On Custer's unsuccessful
      campaign of 1868.

864.  Kanipe, Daniel A.  "A New Story of Custer's Last
      Battle." CHSMo, 4 (1903), 277-283.  Told by a
      messenger boy who survived.

865.  Kaufman, Fred S.  Custer Passed Our Way.  Aber-
      deen, SD:  North Plains Press, 1971.  365 pp.
      Sympathetic to the Sioux, despite the use of such
      unfortunate terms as "savage."

866.  Keenan, Jerry.  "Exploring the Black Hills:  An Ac-
      count of the Custer Expedition." JW, 6:2 (1967),
      248-261.

867.  Knight, Oliver.  "Mark Kellog Telegraphed for Custer's
      Rescue." NDH, 27:2 (Spring 1960), 95-99.

868.  Koury, Michael J.  Diaries of the Little Big Horn.
      Bellevue, NE:  Old Army Press, 1968.  82 pp.

869.  Kuhlman, Charles.  Did Custer Disobey Orders at the
      Battle of the Little Big Horn?  Harrisburg, PA:
      Stackpole Co., 1959.  56 pp.

870.  Kuhlman, Charles.  Gen. George A. Custer:  A Lost
      Trail and the Gall Saga.  Billings, MT:  Printed
      Privately, 1940.

871.  Kuhlman, Charles.  Legend into History:  The Custer
      Mystery.  Harrisburg, PA:  Stackpole Co., 1952.

872.  Kurtz, Henry L  "Custer and the Indian Massacre,
      1868." HT, 18:11 (November 1968), 169-178.

873.  Lampman, Evelyn S.  Once Upon the Little Big Horn.
      New York:  Crowell, 1971.  157 pp.

874.  Lane, Harrison.  "Brush--Palette and the Little Big
      Horn." Montana, 23:3 (July 1973), 66-80.  About
      paintings of the Battle of the Little Bighorn by many
      artists.  See entry no. 820.

875.  Lane, Harrison.  "Custer's Massacre:  How the News
      First Reached the Outer World." Montana, 3:3 (Sum-
      mer 1953), 46-53.

876. Lange, Dietrich. The Threat of Sitting Bull: A Story
     of the Time of Custer. Boston: Lothrop, Lee and
     Shepard, Co., 1920. 370 pp.

877. Langley, Harold D. "The Custer Battle and the Cri-
     tique of an Adventurer." Montana, 22:2 (April
     1972), 20-33.

878. Laubin, Reginald, Edgar I. Stewart, and Bigelow Neal.
     "More Rumblings from the Little Big Horn." Mon-
     tana, 9:1 (January 1959), 57-61.

879. McAndrews, Eugene V. "An Army Engineer's Journal
     of Custer's Black Hills Expedition, July 2, 1874-
     August 23, 1874." JW, 13:1 (1974), 78-85.

880. Maclean, Norman, and Robert M. Utley. "Edward S.
     Luce: 'Commanding General (Retired) Department of
     the Little Bighorn.'" Montana, 6:3 (July 1956), 51-
     55.

881. Magnussen, Daniel O., ed. Peter Thompson's Nar-
     rative of the Little Bighorn Campaign, 1876. Glen-
     dale, CA: Arthur H. Clark, 1974. 338 pp.

882. Marquis, Thomas B. Custer on the Little Bighorn.
     Ed. Anna R. Heil. Lodi, CA: Dr. Marquis Custer,
     Publ., 1969.

883. Marquis, Thomas B. She Watched Custer's Last Bat-
     tle: Her Story, Interpreted, in 1927. Hardin, MT:
     Custer Battle Museum, 1935. 12 pp.

884. Marquis, Thomas B. Sketch Story of the Custer Bat-
     tle: A Clashing of Red and Blue. Hardin, MT:
     Custer Battle Museum, 1933. 8 pp.

885. Marquis, Thomas B. Two Days After the Custer Bat-
     tle. Hardin, MT: Custer Battle Museum, 1935. 8
     pp.

886. Mattes, Merrill J. "The Riddle of the Little Bighorn:
     A Review Essay." WMH, 61:2 (Winter 1977-1978),
     144-148.

887. Merington, Marguerite, ed. The Custer Story: The
     Life and Intimate Letters of General George A.
     Custer and His Wife Elizabeth. New York: Devin

Adair, 1950.   339 pp.   Covers his years in Sioux country.

888.  Merritt, Wesley.  "Three Indian Campaigns."   H, 80
      (1890), 720-737.   One of these is the Custer campaign
      against the Sioux in 1876.

889.  Millbrook, Minnie Dubbs.   "The Boy General and How
      He Grew."   Montana, 23:2 (April 1973), 34-43.

890.  Millbrook, Minnie Dubbs.   "Custer's First Scout in the
      West."   KHQ, 39:1 (Spring 1973), 75-95.

891.  Millbrook, Minnie Dubbs.   "A Monument to Custer."
      Montana, 24:2 (April 1974), 18-33.

892.  Miller, David H.   Custer's Fall:   The Indian Side of
      the Story.   New York:   Duell, Sloan and Pearce,
      1957.

893.  Miller, David H.   "Echoes of the Little Big Horn,"
      AH, 22:4 (June 1971), 28-39.   Personal accounts
      by Henry Oscar One Bull, Joseph White Cow Bull,
      Joseph White Bull, and Dewey Beard.

894.  "More Rumblings from the Little Big Horn."   Montana,
      9:4 (October 1959), 45-51; 10:2 (April 1960),  46-47.
      The buffs argue about the Battle of the Little Big-
      horn.

895.  Morris, Robert E.   "Custer Made a Good Decision:
      A Leavenworth Appreciation."   JW, 16:4 (October
      1977), 5-11.

896.  Moyne, Ernest J.   "Fred Snow's Account of the Custer
      Expedition of 1874."   NDH, 27:3 and 4 (Summer-
      Fall 1960), 143-151.   Known as " Antelope Fred"
      while he worked as a wagon master, packer, and
      scout, he was part of the expedition.

897.  Myers, Rex C.   "Montana Editors and the Custer Bat-
      tle."   Montana, 26:2 (April 1976), 18-31.

898.  National Park Service.   Bibliography of the Battle of
      the Little Big Horn River, Montana, June 25-26,
      1876.   Comp. Edward S. Luce and Evelyn S. Luce.
      Crow Agency, MT:   Custer Battlefield National Monu-
      ment, 1946.

899.  Newson, Thomas M.  Thrilling Scenes Among the In-
      dians, with a Graphic Description of Custer's Last
      Fight with Sitting Bull.  Chicago:  Belford, Clarke
      and Co. , 1884.  241 pp.

900.  Noyes, Lee.  "Major Marcus A.  Reno at the Little
      Big Horn. "  NDH, 28:1 (Winter 1961), 4-11.

901.  Nye, Elwood L.  "Cavalry Horse. "  Montana, 7:2
      (April 1957), 40-45.  Incidents in the life of Charles
      Varnum, who fought through the Battle of the Little
      Bighorn.

902.  Nye, Elwood L.  Marching With Custer:  A Day-by-
      day Evaluation of the Uses, Abuses and Conditions
      of the Animals on the Ill-Fated Expedition of 1876.
      Glendale, CA:  Arthur H.  Clarke, 1964.  300 copies
      printed.

903.  Overfield, Lloyd J.  The Little Big Horn, 1876:  The
      Official Communications, Documents, and Reports,
      with Rosters of the Officers and Troops of the Cam-
      paign.  Glendale, CA:  Arthur H.  Clarke, 1971.

904.  Parks, Jack.  Who Killed Custer.  New York:  Tower
      Publications, Inc. , 1971.  154 pp.  About White Bull,
      supposed killer of Custer.

905.  Parmlee, Mary M.  "A Child's Recollections of the
      Summer of '76. "  TB, 1:6 (June 1915), 123-130.
      As a child, she recalled her father, an officer,
      ride off to his death in the Custer Battle.

906.  Pearson, Carl L.  "Sadie and the Missing Custer Bat-
      tle Papers. "  Montana, 26:4 (October 1976), 12-17.
      On Sadie Whiteman, Northern Cheyenne.

907.  Pickard, Edwin.  "I Rode with Custer. "  Ed.  Edgar
      I.  Stewart.  Montana, 4:3 (Summer 1954), 17-29.
      A biased account; Pickard was old when he told the
      story.

908.  Quihuis, L. L.  "Curly of Custer Fame. "  Hobbies,
      67 (April 1962), 113.

909.  Rawling, G. S.  "Custer's Last Stand. "  HT, 12:1
      (January 1962), 57-66.  Illustrated.

910.    "Recent Newspaper Items Concerning Custer's Last
        Battle. "  CHSMo, 4 (1903), 284-287.

911.    Rector, William G.  "Fields of Fire:  The Reno-
        Benteen Defense Perimeter. "  Montana, 16:2 (Spring
        1966),  65-72.

912.    Remsburg, John E. , and George J. Remsburg.  Char-
        ley Reynolds.  Kansas City, MO:  H. M. Sender,
        1931.

913.    Reusswig, William.  A Picture Report of the Custer
        Fight.  New York:  Hastings House, 1967.

914.    Richards, Raymond.  "The Human Interest of the Cus-
        ter Battle. "  TB, 2 (June 1916),  593-597.

915.    Roe, Charles Francis.  Custer's Last Battle on the
        Little Big Horn, Montana Territory,  June 25,  1876.
        New York:  R. Bruce, 1927.  40 pp.

916.    Romaine, L. B. , ed.  "Custer's Last Stand:  10th
        Anniversary; C. H. Barstow Letter, 1886. "  Hob-
        bies, 50 (October 1945), 109-110.

917.    Rosenberg, Bruce A.  Custer and the Epic of Defeat.
        University Park:  Pennsylvania State University Press,
        1974.  313 pp.

918.    Rosenberg, Bruce A.  "Custer and the Making of a
        Legend. "  In Interdisciplinary Essays.  Vol. 3.  Ed.
        Stephen H. Good and Olaf P. Tollefsen.  Emmits-
        burg, MD:  Mt. St. Mary's College, 1973.  pp. 5-
        10.

919.    Rosenberg, Bruce A.  "Custer:  The Legend of the
        Martyred Hero in America. "  JFI, 9 (1972), 110-132.

920.    Russell, W. A.  "Custer, the Egotist. "  OTT, 2:3
        (September-October 1941), 4-25.

921.    Ryan, J. C. , ed.  Custer Fell First:  The Adven-
        tures of John C. Lockwood.  San Antonio, TX:  Nay-
        lor Co. , 1970.  Juvenile literature.

922.    Sandoz, Mari.  The Battle of the Little Bighorn.  New
        York:  Modern Literary Editions Publishing Co. ,

1966; Philadelphia: J. B. Lippincott, 1966. 238 pp.
Analysis of the reason for the expedition by the U. S.
Army, and for the assembly of Indians on the Little
Bighorn that year.

923.  Saum, Lewis O. "Colonel Custer's Copperhead: The
'Mysterious' Mark Kellog. " Montana, 28:4 (October
1978), 12-25. A journalist who rode to his death
with Custer; information about his life and career.

924.  Schulte, Marie L. "Catholic Press Reaction to the
Custer Disaster. " Mid, 37:4 (October 1955), 205-
214.

925.  Shideler, Frank J. "Custer Country: One Hundred
Years of Change. " AW, 10:4 (1973), 25-31. About
photographs taken by Richard Sowell and Donald R.
Progulske 100 years later.

926.  Shiflet, Kenneth. The Convenient Coward. Harris-
burg, PA: Stackpole, 1960. About Major Reno
in the Battle of the Little Bighorn.

927.  Shoenberger, Dale T. "Custer's Scouts. " Montana,
16:2 (Spring 1966), 40-49.

928.  Sievers, Michael A. "The Literature of the Little
Bighorn: A Centennial Historiography. " AAW, 18:
2 (Summer 1976), 149-176.

929.  Slotkin, Richard. "... 'Then the More Will Go!' An
1875 Black Hills Scheme by Custer, Holladay, and
Benford. " JW, 15:3 (July 1976), 60-77.

930.  "Smoking the Peace-Pipe at Custer's Last Stand. "
LD, 10 July 1926, pp. 36-40.

931.  Stammel, Heinz J. Solange Gras Wächst und Wasser
Fliesst: Die Sioux und das Massaker am Little Big
Horn. Stuttgart: Deutsche Verlags-Austalt, 1976.
297 pp.

932.  "Statement of Goes Ahead. " TB, 2 (June 1916), 603-
604. A Crow scout with Custer.

933.  "Statement of Hairy Moccasin. " TB, 2 (June 1916),
600-601. A Crow scout with Custer.

934. "Statement of Thomas H. Laforge." TB, 2 (1916), 599-600. A scout with Custer.

935. "Statement of White-Man-Runs-Him." TB, 2 (June 1916), 598-599. A Crow scout with Custer.

936. Steckmesser, Kent L. "Custer in Fiction: George A. Custer, Hero or Villain." AW, 1:4 (Fall 1964), 47-52, 63-64.

937. Stewart, Edgar L "The Custer Battle and Widow's Weeds." Montana, 22:1 (January 1972), 52-59.

938. Stewart, Edgar L Custer's Luck. 1955; rpt. Norman: University of Oklahoma Press, 1967.

939. Stewart, Edgar L "Little Big Horn 90 Years Later." Montana, 16:2 (Spring 1966), 2-13.

940. Stewart, Edgar L "Major Brisbin's Relief of Fort Pease: A Prelude to the Bloody Little Bighorn Massacre." Montana, 6:3 (July 1956), 23-27.

941. Stewart, Edgar L "A Psychoanalytic Approach to Custer: Some Reflections." Montana, 21:2 (Spring 1971), 74-77. Believes Custer reacted normally as a military man, and attacked.

942. Stewart, Edgar L "The Reno Court of Inquiry." Montana, 2:3 (July 1952), 31-43.

943. Stewart, Edgar L "Variations on a Minor Theme: Some Controversial Problems of the Custer Fight." Montana, 1:3 (July 1951), 23-36.

944. Stewart, Edgar L "Which Indian Killed Custer?" Montana, 8:3 (July 1958), 26-32. Says no one knows.

945. Stewart, Edgar L , and E. S. Luce. "The Reno Scout." Montana, 10:3 (July 1960), 23-28. Recounts the scouting movements of Reno before the Custer Battle.

946. Swift, Mrs. Henry. "The Custer Massacre: A Contemporary View." Ed. Mildred Scott Adler. SR, 44:4 (Autumn 1959), 318-326. The wife of Rev.

Henry Swift, who lived in Dakota Territory at the time of the Custer Battle, wrote her account forty years later and gave it to C. H. Brown, whose daughter offered it for publication.

947. Talbot, James Joseph. "Custer's Last Battle." Penn Monthly, September 1877, pp. 679-699. A non-Indian named Howard interviewed Sitting Bull, who said the Battle of the Little Bighorn lasted only half an hour.

948. Taylor, Joseph H. "Lonesome Charley." NDHQ, 4: 4 (July 1930), 227-238. Information on the Custer Battle.

949. Tillett, Leslie, ed. Wind on the Buffalo Grass: The Indians' Own Account of the Battle at the Little Big Horn River, and the Death of Their Life on the Plains. New York: T. Y. Crowell, 1976. 158 pp. Pictorial and oral history of the Battle of the Little Bighorn. Useful but unscholarly.

950. Turner, C. Frank. "Custer and the Canadian Connections." B (Summer 1976), pp. 4-11. On the Battle of the Little Big Horn and the flight of Sioux into Canada.

951. Utley, Robert M. "The Custer Battle in the Contemporary Press." NDH, 22:2 (April 1955), 75-88.

952. Utley, Robert M. Custer Battlefield National Monument: Montana. Washington, DC: Government Printing Office, 1969. 93 pp.

953. Utley, Robert M. Custer and the Great Controversy. Los Angeles: Westernlore Press, 1970. Discusses legends surrounding the Battle of the Little Bighorn.

954. Utley, Robert M. Frontier Regulars: The United States Army and the Indian, 1886-1891. New York: Macmillan, 1974. 462 pp. Best general survey of Indian warfare in the post-Civil War period.

955. Utley, Robert M. "The Gatlings Custer Left Behind." AW, 11:2 (1974), 24-25.

956. Utley, Robert M., ed. Life in Custer's Cavalry:

Diaries and Letters of Albert and Jennie Barnitz,
1867-1868. New Haven: Yale University Press,
1977. 302 pp. Barnitz was an officer in the 7th
Cavalry up to the time of the Battle of the Washita.

957.  Utley, Robert M. "Twenty Years After the Little Big-
horn--What Happened to a Fighting People." AH, 22:
4 (January 1971), 40-41.

958.  Van de Water, Frederic F. Glory-Hunter: A Life of
General Custer. Indianapolis: Bobbs-Merrill, 1934.
394 pp.

959.  Vestal, Stanley. "The Duel with Yellow Hand." SR,
26:1 (Autumn 1940), 65-77. About the killing of
Yellow Hand by Buffalo Bill on July 17, 1876; Yellow Hand fought at the Little Bighorn.

960.  Vindex, C. "Who Cares About Custer?" AMe, 83
(November 1956), 75-80.

961.  Walker, Judson E. The Campaigns of General Custer
in the Northwest and the Final Surrender of Sitting
Bull. 1881; facsimile rpt. as The Final Surrender
of Sitting Bull. New York: Argonaut Press, 1966.
Trader Walker wrote from personal observation and
left valuable information, but demonstrated charac-
teristic anti-Indian bias.

962.  Webb, Laura S. Custer's Immortality: A Poem, With
Biographical Sketches of the Chief Actors in the Late
Tragedy of the Wilderness. New York: Evening
Post Steam Press, 1876. 72 pp.

963.  Wemett, William M. "Custer's Expedition to the Black
Hills in 1874." NDHQ, 6:4 (July 1932), 292-301.

964.  Wheeler, Olin Dunbar. "The Custer Battle Field."
NM, 20:1 (1903), 3-12.

965.  Willert, James. Little Big Horn Diary: Chronicle of
the 1876 Indian War. La Mirada, CA: Willert,
1977. 470 pp.

966.  Wright, Kathryn. "Indian Trader's Cache." Montana,
7:1 (Winter 1957), 2-7. Whether a letter at the
Custer Battlefield National Monument in the stone

marker for the grave of Two Moon contains a secret
account of the Battle of Little Bighorn.

967.  Wright, Kathryn.  "An Epilogue and a Final Answer
      Deferred. "  Montana, 26:4 (October 1976), 18-21.
      On her previous article; has not seen the letter.


## HISTORY

968.  Abel, Annie H.  A History of Events Resulting in In-
      dian Consolidation West of the Mississippi River.
      1908; rpt. New York: AMS Press, 1970.  Guide to
      removal and resettlement of the Indian.

969.  Albright, Samuel J.  "The First Organized Govern-
      ment of Dakota. "  CMHS, 8 (1898), 129-147.  Con-
      tains material on the Sioux and their reactions to
      non-Indian settlers.

970.  Allen, Clifford, et al.  A History of the Flandreau
      Santee Sioux Tribe.  Flandreau, SD:  Flandreau
      Santee Sioux Tribe, 1971.  194 pp.  Surveys the
      history of Flandreau tribal members since the first
      settlers moved to the Big Sioux Valley from Santee,
      Nebraska; prepared with aid of Joy Knutson, Vince
      Pratt, Arlene Stuart, Paul Stuart, and Duwayne Wes-
      ton, tribal members.

971.  Ames, J. H.  "The Sioux or Nadouesis. "  Macalester
      College Contributions, 1 (1890), 229-40.

972.  Anderson, Harry H.  "Challenge to Brown's Sioux In-
      dian Wars Thesis. "  Montana, 12:1 (1962), 40-49.

973.  Anderson, Harry H.  "Empire of the Dakota. "  See
      entry no. 1122, pp. 1-23.

974.  Anderson, Harry H.  "An Investigation of the Early
      Bands of the Saone Group of Teton Sioux. "  Journal
      of the Washington Academy of Sciences, 46:3 (March
      1956), 87-94.

975.  Andreas, Alfred Theodore.  Historical Atlas of Dakota.
      Chicago: R. R. Donnelley and Sons, Lakeside Press,
      1884.  212 pp.

976.  Andrist, Ralph D.  The Long Death:  The Last Days
      of the Plains Indians.  New York:  Macmillan, 1964.
      371 pp.

977.  Babcock, Willoughby M.  "Sioux Villages in Minnesota
      Prior to 1837. "  MA, 11 (October 1945), 126-146.

978.  Batchelder, George A.  "A Sketch of the History and
      Resources of Dakota Territory. "  CHSSD, 14 (1928),
      181-251. Contains much material on the Sioux.

979.  Bates, Charles Francis.  "Red Man and the Black
      Hills. "  Out, 27 July 1927, pp. 408-411.

980.  Berthrong, Donald J.  "Changing Concepts:  The In-
      dians Learn About the 'Long Knives' and Settlers
      (1849-1890's). "  See entry no. 1250, pp. 47-61.

981.  "Birth of a Nation. "  Newsweek, 26 March 1973, p.
      22.

982.  Blackthunder, Elijah, et al.  History of the Sisseton-
      Wahpeton Sioux Tribe.  Sisseton, SD:  Sisseton-
      Wahpeton Sioux Tribe, 1972.  130 pp.  Contains his-
      tory of the tribe to the outset of the twentieth cen-
      tury; published with a supplement on Sioux culture.

983.  Blair, Emma H. , ed. and trans.  Indian Tribes of the
      Upper Mississippi Valley and Region of the Great
      Lakes as Described by Nicolas Perrot.  Cleveland,
      OH:  Arthur Clark, 1911; rpt. New York: Kraus Re-
      print Corp. , 1970.  Sketchy with more on Algonquins
      and Iroquois than Sioux.

984.  Bland, Thomas Augustus.  A History of the Sioux
      Agreement:  Some Facts Which Should Not Be For-
      gotten.  Washington, DC:  n. p. , 1889.  32 pp.

985.  Bleeker, Sonia.  The Sioux Indians.  The Hunters and
      Warriors of the Plains.  New York:  William Mor-
      row, 1962.  Juvenile.

986.  Board of Indian Commissioners.  The Reports of the
      Board of Indian Commissioners for the Years 1880-
      1900.  Washington, DC:  Government Printing Office,
      1880-1900.

987.  Bosch, Aloysius. "Indians Again in Council. " The
      Messenger of the Sacred Heart, 1895, pp. 393-403.

988.  Bowler, Mary Jane. The Sioux Indians and the United
      States Government, 1862-1878.  St. Louis:  Washing-
      ton University, 1944.

989.  Boyd, Robert Knowles. The Battle of Birch Coulee:
      A Wounded Man's Description of the Battle with the
      Indians.  Eau Claire, WI:  Herges Printing Co.,
      1925.  23 pp.  Address delivered before a meeting
      of the Sons of Veterans at Eau Claire, January 1925.

990.  Boyd, Robert Knowles. "How the Indians Fought:  A
      New Era in Skirmish Fighting, by a Survivor of the
      Battle of Birch Cooley. "  MiH, 11 (September 1930),
      299-304.  Says the Sioux were the best skirmish
      fighters in the world.  Battle on September 2-3,
      1862.

991.  Brackett, Albert Gallatin. "The Sioux or Dakota In-
      dians. "  ARSI (1876), pp. 466-472.  Gives popula-
      tions of several Sioux tribes, totalling nearly 50, 000.

992.  Bradley, J. H. "History of the Sioux. "  CHSMo, 9
      (1923), 29-140.

993.  Brailsford, Barry. The Sioux.  New York:  Interna-
      tional Pub. Service, 1976.  Also appears as The
      Sioux:  A Way to Live, A Way to Die.

994.  Briggs, Harold E. "The Black Hills Gold Rush. "
      NDHQ, 5:2 (January 1931), 71-99.

995.  "The British Regime in Wisconsin, 1760-1800. "
      CWHS, 18 (1908), 349-354.  Useful early descrip-
      tion of Sioux life-style and culture.

996.  Bromert, Roger. "The Sioux and the Indian CCC. "
      SDH, 8:4 (Fall 1978), 340-356.

997.  Brower, J. V. "Prehistoric Man at the Headwaters
      of the Mississippi River. "  CMHS, 8 (1898), 232-
      270.  Contains information about the Sioux.

998.  Brownlee, Fred L. , and Charles B. Johnson. The In-
      dians of North and South Dakota.  Nashville, TN:
      Fisk University Press, 1941.

999.    Bryde, John, ed.  The Sioux Indians:  A Socio-
        ethnological History.  New York:  S. Lewis,  1973.
        138 pp.  Reprinted from reports of the U. S.
        Bureau of Ethnology, 1893 and 1897.

1000.   Burdick, Usher L.  Tragedy in the Great Sioux Camp.
        Baltimore, MD:  The Proof Press, 1936.

1001.   Burleigh, Walter Atwood.  Management of Indian Af-
        fairs.  Washington, DC:  Congressional Globe Of-
        fice, 1866.  16 pp.  Speech of Territorial Dele-
        gate Burleigh in the U. S. House of Representatives,
        June 9, 1866, on Sioux-government relations.

1002.   Burlingame, Merrill G.  "The Buffalo in Trade and
        Commerce. "  NDHQ, 3:4 (July 1929), 262-291.
        Contains information about the Sioux and the de-
        struction of the buffalo.

1003.   Bushnell, David L.  Villages of the Algonquian, Siouan,
        and Caddoan Tribes West of the Mississippi.  1922;
        rpt. Nashville, TN:  The Blue and Gray Press,
        1972; rpt. St. Clair Shores, MI:  Scholarly Press,
        1976.

1004.   Butterworth, F. Edward.  White Shadows Among the
        Mighty Sioux.  Vol. L  Independence, MO:  Inde-
        pendence Press, 1977.

1005.   Cash, Joseph H.  The Rosebud Sioux People.  Phoe-
        nix, AZ:  Indian Tribal Series, 1971.  106 pp.  A
        general survey of the history of the Rosebud Sioux
        tribe, with emphasis on Indian-government rela-
        tions.

1006.   Cass, Lewis.  Incident of Indian Life.  Washington,
        DC:  n. p. , 1852.  3 pp.

1007.   Caughey, John W.  The American West:  Frontier
        and Region.  Rpt. ed. Norris Hundley and John A.
        Schultz.  Los Angeles:  Ward Ritchie Press, 1969.

1008.   Chamberlain, M. C.  A Brief Biographical and His-
        torical Sketch of the Early History of Lac qui Parle
        County.  Montevideo, MN:  C. E. Mills, 1896.
        56 pp.

1009.  Charlevoix, Pierre.  History and General Description
       of New France.  Trans.  John Shea.  New York:
       John Gilmary Shea,  1866.

1010.  Clark,  Charles A.  "Indians of Iowa. "  AIo,  6:2 (July
       1903),  81-106.  Considerable information about the
       Sioux.

1011.  Clow,  Richmond L.  "Brule Indian Agencies,  1868-
       1878. "  CHSSD,  36 (1972),  143-204.

1012.  Clow,  Richmond L.  "The Sioux Nation and Indian
       Territory:  The Attempted Removal of 1876. "  SDH,
       6:4 (Fall 1976),  456-473.

1013.  Clow,  Richmond L.  "The Whetstone Indian Agency,
       1868-1872. "  SDH,  7:3 (Summer 1977),  291-308.
       Agency established for the Brules as a result of
       the negotiations of the Treaty of Fort Laramie in
       1868.

1014.  Cochell,  Shirley Holmes.  The Land of the Coyote.
       Ames:  Iowa State University Press,  1972.  193 pp.

1015.  Conard,  Jane.  "Charles Collins:  The Sioux City
       Promotion of the Black Hills. "  SDH,  2:2 (Spring
       1972),  131-171.  Contains information on the Sioux,
       including details about negotiations for the purchase
       of the Black Hills.

1016.  Conn,  William (Baron Mandat-Grancy).  Cow-Boys
       and Colonels,  Narrative of a Journey Across the
       Prairie and Over the Black Hills of Dakota,  with
       Additional Notes Not Contained in the Original Edi-
       tion.  London:  Griffith,  Farran,  Dkeden & Welsh,
       1887.  364 pp.  A French nobleman writes about
       the Indians and non-Indians.

1017.  Cordeal,  John F.  "Historical Sketch of Southwestern
       Nebraska. "  PNSHS,  17 (1913),  16-37.  Contains
       information on Sioux participation in several bat-
       tles,  including the Pawnee-Sioux conflict of 1873.

1018.  Creel,  G.  "To the Last Man. "  Collier's,  22 January
       1927,  pp.  11-12.

1019.  Culbertson,  Thaddeus A.  "An Explanation of the

Tabular View of the Indian Tribes of the Upper
Missouri. " ARSI (1850), pp. 138-140.

1020.  Culbertson, Thaddeus A. "A Tabular View of the
       Sioux Nation on the Upper Missouri, A. D. 1850. "
       ARSI (1850), pp. 141-42.

1021.  Cutler, Jervis. A Topographical Description ... and
       a Concise Account of the Indian Tribes West of the
       Mississippi. Boston: Published by Charles Wil-
       liams, 1812.

1022.  Danziger, Edmund J. "Civil War Problems in the
       Central and Dakota Superintendencies: A Case
       Study. " NH, 51:4 (Winter 1970), 411-424.

1023.  Danziger, Edmund J. "The Indian Office During the
       Civil War: Impotence in Indian Affairs. " SDH, 5:
       1 (Winter 1974), 52-72. Material on the Sioux,
       particularly on the background of the Minnesota
       Sioux War of 1862.

1024.  Davidson, Gordon C. The North West Company.
       Berkeley: University of California, 1918. 349 pp.

1025.  DeLand, Charles E. "Aborigines of South Dakota.
       Part I. " CHSSD, 3 (1906), 269-586. Some in-
       formation on the Sioux, although the article deals
       mainly with Arikaras and Pawnees.

1026.  DeLand, Charles E. "Aborigines of South Dakota.
       Part II. The Mandan Indians. " CHSSD, 4 (1908),
       272-730. Some information on the Sioux, although
       the article deals mainly with Mandans.

1027.  Delanglez, Jean. "A Mirage: The Sea of the West. "
       RHAF, 1:3 (December 1947), 346-381. On con-
       tacts of early settlers and explorers with Sioux.

1028.  Denig, Edwin Thompson. Five Indian Tribes of the
       Upper Missouri: Sioux, Arikaras, Assiniboines,
       Crees, Crows. Ed. John C. Ewers. Norman:
       University of Oklahoma Press, 1961. 217 pp.

1029.  DeVoto, Bernard. The Course of Empire. Boston:
       Houghton Mifflin Co. , 1952, 1962.

1030.  Dicks, Samuel E. "A Territory with Many Flags."
       See entry no. 1122, pp. 72-77. About the various
       nations that owned Dakota Territory, it contains
       some information about the Sioux.

1031.  Dixon, Joseph Kossuth. The Vanishing Race, the
       Last Great Indian Council: A Record in Picture
       and Story. Garden City, NY: Doubleday, Page,
       and Co., 1913; rpt. Chicago: Library Resources,
       1971 and Glorietta, NM: Rio Grande Press, 1978.
       Council was held in the valley of the Little Big
       Horn, Montana, September 1909.

1032.  Dodge, Richard I. Our Wild Indians: Thirty-three
       Years' Personal Experience Among the Red Men of
       the Great West. 1882; rpt. Freeport, NY: Books
       for Libraries, Inc., 1971. Contains some observa-
       tions about Sioux government, religion, life-style.

1033.  Dodge, Richard I. The Plains of the Great West and
       Their Inhabitants. 1877; rpt. New York: Archer
       House, 1959.

1034.  Dorsey, James Owen. "Migrations of the Siouan
       Tribes." TASW, 3 (1885), 65 ff. Defines the term
       "Siouan," and describes east-to-west migration
       across North America.

1035.  Dorsey, James Owen. "The Places of Gentes in
       Siouan Camping Circles." AA, (October 1889),
       375-379.

1036.  Douglas, Frederic Huntington. The Sioux or Dakota
       Nation: Divisions, History and Numbers. Denver:
       Denver Art Museum, 1932.

1037.  Ellis, George E. Red Man and the White Man in
       North America from Its Discovery to the Present
       Time. 1882; rpt. East Orange, NJ: Thomas
       Kelly, 1970.

1038.  Ellis, Richard N., ed. The Western American In-
       dian: Case Studies in Tribal History. Lincoln:
       University of Nebraska Press, 1972. 203 pp. An
       anthology of essays on western tribes, it contains
       articles about the Santees, Red Cloud and Indian
       Agent Valentine T. McGillicuddy.

1039.   Engel, Lorenz.   Among the Plains Indians.   Minne-
        apolis: Lerner, 1970.   Describes Indian life-style
        before the arrival of non-Indians.

1040.   Englund, Erik Uncas.   Siouxerna-ett Krigarfolk pa
        prarlerna.   Stockholm:   Natur Och Kultur, 1967.
        182 pp.

1041.   Erdoes, Richard.   The Sun Dance People:   The Plains
        Indians, Their Past and Present.   New ed.   New
        York: Random House, 1978.

1042.   Erikkson, Erik M.   "Sioux City and the Black Hills
        Gold Rush 1874-1877. "   IJHP, 20:3 (July 1922),
        319-347.   Much information about the Sioux, as
        well as about eastern South Dakota.

1043.   Eschambault, Antoine d'.   "La Vie Aventureuse de
        Daniel Greysolon, Sieur Dulhut. "   RHAF, 5:3 (De-
        cember 1951), 320-339.   Considerable information
        about Sioux of Minnesota.

1044.   Ewers, John C.   "Edwin T. Denig's 'Of the Sioux. '"
        BMHS, 7 (1971), 185-215.

1045.   Ewers, John C.   "The Emergence of the Plains In-
        dians as the Symbol of the North American Indian. "
        ARSI (1964), pp. 531-544.

1046.   Ewers, John C.   Indian Life on the Upper Missouri.
        Civilization of the American Indian Series, No. 89.
        Norman:   University of Oklahoma Press, 1968.
        222 pp.

1047.   Ewers, John C.   "Indian Views of the White Man
        Prior to 1850:   An Interpretation. "   See entry no.
        1250, pp. 7-23.

1048.   Ewers, John C.   Teton Dakota, Ethnology and History.
        Rev. ed.   United States National Park Service.
        Berkeley, CA:   Western Museum Laboratories, 1938.

1049.   Farb, Peter.   "Rise and Fall of the Indian of the
        Wild West. "   NHi, 77:8 (October 1968), 32-41.
        Illustrated; deals largely with the Sioux.

1050.   Farnham, Thomas J.   Travels in the Great Western

Prairies, the Anahuac and Rocky Mountains, and in the Oregon Territory. Poughkeepsie, NY: Killey and Lossing Printers, 1841. 197 pp. Printed in several editions in the United States and abroad; translated into German.

1051. Farrell, Alfred C. "A Calendar of Principal Events of the French and Indians of Early Dacotah." CHSND, I (1906), 293-296. Covers the period 1540-1870.

1052. Finster, David. The Hardin Winter Count. Vermillion, SD: W. H. Over Museum, University of South Dakota, 1968. 57 pp.

1053. Fiske, Frank B. The Taming of the Sioux. Bismarck, ND: Bismarck Tribune, 1917. 186 pp. Contains material on the Sioux War of 1862, the Custer Battle, Religion of the Sioux, the Messiah religion, and Wounded Knee 1890.

1054. Flandrau, Charles E. "Reminiscences of Minnesota During the Territorial Period." CMHS, 9 (1901), 197-222. Information on the Sioux, including place names from Sioux language and Sioux religion.

1055. Flandrau, Charles E. "State-Building in the West." CMHS, 8 (1898), 463-494. Contains a section on the Sioux, as they were observed by a noted magistrate.

1056. Fleetwood, Mary. "Dakota's First Historian: Moses K. Armstrong, 1832-1906." NDH, 37:3 (Summer 1970), 200-213.

1057. Folwell, William Watts. A History of Minnesota. 4 vols. Rev. ed. St. Paul: Minnesota Historical Society, 1956-69.

1058. Foster, Charles. "Sioux Commission of 1889." MWH, 12 (1890), 228.

1059. Foster, James L. Outlines of the History of the Territory of Dakota, an Emigrant's Guide to the Free Lands of the Northwest. Yankton, Dakota Territory: M'Intyre and Foster, 1870. 127 pp.

1060.  Fritz, Henry.  The Movement for Indian Assimilation,
       1860-1890.  Philadelphia:  University of Pennsyl-
       vania Press,  1963.

1061.  Fugle, Eugene, and James H. Howard.  "The Nebras-
       ka Santee. "  AIT,  8: 5  (1962),  215-217.

1062.  Fulton, Alexander R.  The Red Men of Iowa:  Being
       a History of the Various Aboriginal Tribes Whose
       Homes Were in Iowa.  Sketches of the Chiefs, Tra-
       ditions.  Des Moines:  Mills and Co. ,  1882.  559
       pp.

1063.  Flynn, A. J.  The American Indian as a Product of
       Environment.  1907; rpt. New York:  Augustus M.
       Kelley,  1969.

1064.  Gale, George.  Upper Mississippi:  Or, Historical
       Sketches of the Moundbuilders, the Indian Tribes,
       and the Progress of Civilization in the Northwest,
       from A. D.  1600 to the Present Time.  Chicago:
       Clarke and Company; New York:  Oakley and
       Mason, 1867.  460 pp.

1065.  Gallatin, Albert.  Hale's Indians of Northwest Amer-
       ica, and Vocabularies of North America, with an
       Introduction.  New York:  n. p. ,  1848.  13 pp.
       Contains reports on exploration, ethnography and
       ethnology by Horatio E. Hale; appeared also in
       Transactions of the American Ethnological Society,
       Vol. 2.

1066.  Gallatin, Albert.  "A Synopsis of the Indian Tribes
       Within the United States East of the Rocky Moun-
       tains, and in the British and Russian Possessions
       in North America. "  Archaeologia Americana
       Transactions and Collections, 2 (1836), 1-422.  Pub-
       lishing for the American Antiquarian Society, Gal-
       latin was first to classify the tribes of the federation
       as "Sioux. "

1067.  Gardner, W. H.  "Ethnology of the Indians of the Red
       River of the North. "  ARSI (1870), pp.  369-373.
       Early observations on the Sioux.

1068.  Gerber, Max E.  "The Steamboat and Indians of the
       Upper Missouri. "  SDH,  4: 2  (Spring 1974),  139-160.

1069.   Gillette, J. M. "The Advent of the American Indian .
        into North Dakota. " NDHQ, 6:3 (April 1932), 210-
        220.

1070.   Gilmore, Melvin R.  "The Aboriginal Geography of
        the Nebraska Country. " PMVHA, 6 (1912-1913),
        317-331.  Contains Sioux and other Indian names
        for places in the northern Great Plains area, plus
        information about the Sioux tribes.

1071.   Goldfrank, Esther.  "Historic Change and Social
        Character. " AA, 45:1 (January 1943), 67-83.

1072.   Goodale, Elaine.  "Western Sentiment on the Indian
        Question. " CHSSD, 22 (1946), 426-433.  Published
        originally in Hartford Courant, October 16, 1885,
        it concludes that the average westerner was as
        much concerned about the interests of Indians as
        were easterners, when "the urgent pressure of
        business necessities" were "comparatively unfelt. "
        A sensitive observer who later became the wife of
        Dr. Charles Eastman, Flandreau Santee Sioux.

1073.   Goodfellow, Ferd J.  "South Dakota's Early Surveys. "
        CHSSD, 5 (1910), 351-376.  Contains many ref-
        erences on the Sioux.

1074.   Goodrich, Albert M.  "Early Dakota Trails and Set-
        tlements at Centerville, Minn. " CMHS, 15 (1915),
        315-322.  On Sioux Indian settlements.

1075.   Green, Charles Lowell. "The Administration of the
        Public Domain in South Dakota. " CHSSD, 10 (1940),
        7-280.  From his dissertation at the University of
        Iowa.

1076.   Greenhaus, B.  "The Origin of the Anglo-Indian Alli-
        ance of 1812 on the Upper Mississippi " LUR, 2
        (Fall 1969), 135-149.

1077.   Grinnell, George B.  "The Indian on the Reservation. "
        Atlantic, 83 (1899), 255-267.  Tells about the reser-
        vation spoils system, whereby money was diverted
        to white men.

1078.   Grinnell, George B.  "The Wild Indian. " Atlantic,
        83 (1899), 20-29.  Says the wild Indian no longer

exists because wild game is gone. Includes information about family life and some legends.

1079. Hafen, LeRoy R. , ed. Relations with the Indians of
the Plains, 1857-1861. Glendale, CA: A. H.
Clark Co. , 1959.

1080. Hagan, William T. The Indian in American History.
Publication No. 50 of the American Historical Asso-
ciation's Service Center for Teachers of History.
New York: Macmillan Co. , 1963. 26 pp.

1081. Hagen, Everett E. , and Louis Shaw. The Sioux on
the Reservations: The American Colonial Problem.
Boston: Massachusetts Institute of Technology,
1960.

1082. Haines, Francis. The Plains Indians. New York:
Thomas Crowell, 1976. 213 pp. Contains selected bibliography.

1083. Haines, Francis. "Red Men of the Plains, 1500-
1870. " AW, 10:4 (1973), 32-37.

1084. Hamilton, Charles, ed. Cry of the Thunderbird:
The American Indian's Own Story. New York:
Macmillan, 1951; Norman: University of Okla-
homa Press, 1972.

1085. Hamilton, William T. My Sixty Years on the Plains
Trapping, Trading and Indian Fighting. 1905; rpt.
Western Frontier Library, No. 15. Norman: Uni-
versity of Oklahoma Press, 1965.

1086. Hans, Fred M. The Great Sioux Nation: A Complete
History of Indian Life and Warfare in America.
The Indians as Nature Made Them. 1907; rpt.
Minneapolis: Ross and Haines, 1964. 586 pp.
Contains some information about the Sioux. An un-
reliable source, valuable largely because it reflects
anti-Indian bias of the late nineteenth century.

1087. Harris, Ramon L , ed. Oyate Iyechinka Woglakapi.
An Oral History Collection. 3 vols. Vermillion,
SD: American Indian Research Project, 1970-1971.
Catalogue for a collection of 1, 050 taped interviews
with northern Great Plains tribes, including all of

the Sioux, preserved by the South Dakota Oral History Center, University of South Dakota.

1088.   Harwood, W. S.  "Opening of the Sisseton Reservation," HW, 16 April 1892, p. 374.

1089.   Hassrick, Royal B. , et al. The Sioux: Life and Customs of a Warrior Society. Norman: University of Oklahoma, 1967. 337 pp.

1090.   Hayden, Carl Trumbull. Mdewakanton and Wahpakoota (Santee) Sioux Indians. Washington, DC: Government Printing Office, 1912. 6 pp.

1091.   Hayter, Earl W. "The Ponca Removal. " NDHQ, 6: 4 (July 1932), 262-275. Much information on the Sioux.

1092.   Henry, G. V. "Sioux Indian Episode. " HW, 26 December 1896, pp. 1273-1275.

1093.   Hickerson, Harold. The Chippewa and Their Neighbors: A Study in Ethnohistory. New York: Holt, Rinehart and Winston, 1970.

1094.   Hickerson, Harold. Mdewakanton Band of Sioux Indians. New York: Garland Publishing Co. , 1974. Prepared for presentation before the Indian Claims Commission, Docket No. 360.

1095.   Hill, Alex S. From Home to Home: Autumn Wanderings of the North-West in the Years 1881, 1882, 1883, 1884. 1885; rpt. New York: Arno Press, 1966.

1096.   History of the Sisseton-Wahpeton Indian Reservation. Sisseton, SD: Sisseton-Wahpeton Sioux Tribe, 1967. Prepared for tribal centennial celebration, July 1-4, 1967.

1097.   Hoffman, Charles F. Winter in the West by a New Yorker. 2 vols. 1835; rpt. New York: Burt Franklin Publisher, 1968; St. Clair Shores, MI: Scholarly Press, 1970.

1098.   Holley, Frances. Once Their Home: Our Legacy from the Dahkotas. Chicago: Donahue and Henney-

berry, 1892. An unreliable source, valuable largely because it reflects late nineteenth-century anti-
Indian bias.

1099.   Howard, James H.   The Dakota or Sioux Indians:   A
        Study in Human Ecology.   Vermillion:   University
        of South Dakota, 1966.   Includes the anthropology
        of three divisions of Sioux and traces change in
        their cultural patterns when they migrated from the
        woodlands to the prairies and Great Plains during
        the eighteenth century.

1100.   Howard, James H.   "The Dakota or Sioux Tribe."
        USDMN, 27:5/6 (1966), 1-10; 27:7/8 (1966), 1-9;
        27:9/10 (1966), 1-9.

1101.   Howard, James H.   "The Dakota or Sioux Tribe:   A
        Study in Human Ecology."   Powwow Trails, 7:1
        (1970), 5-16.

1102.   Howard, James H.   "Notes on the Ethnography of the
        Yankton Dakota."   PlA, 17, Pt. 1 (November 1972),
        281-307.

1103.   Howland, Edward.   "Our Indian Brothers."   H, 56
        (1878), 768-776.   Admits problems in the manage-
        ment of Indian affairs but says the Indian Office is
        working on remedies.

1104.   Hunter, John.   The Manners and Customs of Several
        Indian Tribes West of the Mississippi.   1823; rpt.
        Facsimile ed.   Minneapolis:   Ross and Haines,
        Inc. , 1970.

1105.   Hurlbut, William J.   "Beyond the Border:   A Thou-
        sand Mile Tramp in Dakota on a Government Sur-
        vey, 1874. "   Ed. Dayton W. Canaday.   SDH, 1:1
        (Winter 1970), 1-32.   From manuscript diaries
        covering the period 1867-1878.

1106.   Hurt, Wesley Robert.   Dakota Sioux Indians.   New
        York:   Garland Publishers, 1974.   264 pp.   Pre-
        pared for presentation before the Indian Claims
        Commission, Docket No. 74.

1107.   Hyde, George E.   Indians of the High Plains from the
        Prehistoric Period to the Coming of Europeans.

Norman: University of Oklahoma Press, 1959; rpt.
1970. 228 pp.

1108. Hyde, George E. "The Mystery of the Arikaras. "
NDH, 18:4 (October 1951), 187-218; 19:1 (January
1952), 25-58. Contains information on the Sioux,
particularly in the second part.

1109. Hyde, George E. Red Cloud's Folk. Norman: University of Oklahoma Press, 1967. 331 pp. Surveys the history of Oglalas to the end of the nineteenth century.

1110. Hyde, George E. A Sioux Chronicle. Norman: University of Oklahoma Press, 1956. 334 pp. Surveys the early recorded history of the Oglalas.

1111. Hyde, George E. Spotted Tail's Folk: A History of
the Brule Sioux. Norman: University of Oklahoma Press, 1961. 325 pp. Surveys the history
of the Brules to the end of the nineteenth century.

1112. Indian Rights Association. Another Century of Dishonor? Philadelphia: Indian Rights Association,
1904. 23 pp. Deals with the management of land
on Rosebud Reservation.

1113. Indian Rights Association. A Contrast. Philadelphia:
Indian Rights Association, 1891. About legislation
for the Sissetons and Wahpetons.

1114. Indians of Minnesota. St. Paul: Minnesota Historical Society, 1971. 18 pp.

1115. "The Indians of North Dakota. " CHSND, 1 (1906),
431-478; 2:1 (1908), 461-492. Deals with the Sioux
and their war in 1862 as well as with the Mandans
and Gros Ventres.

1116. Israel, Marion. Dakotas. Chicago: Malmont Publishers, Inc., 1959. Juvenile literature.

1117. Jackson, Helen Hunt. A Century of Dishonor: The
Early Crusade for Indian Reform. Ed. Andrew F.
Rolle. Gloucester, MA: Peter Smith, 1971; rpt.
St. Clair Shores, MI: Scholarly Press, 1972. Re-
print of a classic indictment against federal Indian
policy published in 1881.

1118.  Jacobson, Daniel.  Great Indian Tribes.  Maplewood,
       NJ:  Hammond, Inc. , 1970.  Juvenile literature.

1119.  Jenks, Albert E.  "Recent Discoveries in Minnesota
       Prehistory. "  MiH, 16:1 (March 1935),  1-21.
       Deals with early Sioux culture.

1120.  Jenks, Albert E.  "The Wild Rice Gatherers of the
       Upper Great Lakes:  A Study in American Primi-
       tive Economics. "  ARBAE, 19 (1900),  1013-1137.
       About a woodland food-gathering technique.

1121.  Jenness, Theodora R.  "The Indian Territory. "  AM,
       43 (1879),  444-452.  A travelog on Indian country.

1122.  Jennewein, J.  Leonard, and Jane Boorman, eds.
       Dakota Panorama.  Pierre:  Dakota Territory Cen-
       tennial Commission, 1961; rpt.  Sioux Falls, SD:
       Brevet Press, 1973.  468 pp.  Articles on the
       Sioux are listed individually within this bibliography.

1123.  Johnston, Sr. Mary Antonio.  Federal Relations with
       the Great Sioux Indians of South Dakota,  1887-1933.
       Washington, DC:  Catholic University of America
       Press, 1948.  137 pp.  A published doctoral dis-
       sertation that shows how the loss of land affected
       Sioux societies prior to World War II.

1124.  Jorgenson, Gladys W.  Before Homesteads in Tripp
       County and the Rosebud.  Freeman, SD:  Pine Hill
       Press, 1974.  138 pp.  Much on Indians as well
       as non-Indians; weak on descriptions of Indian cul-
       ture.

1125.  Keating, William H.  Narrative of an Expedition to
       the Source of St. Peter's River, Lake Winnepeek,
       Lake of the Woods ... Performed in the Year 1823
       by Order of the Hon. J. C. Calhoun, Secretary
       of War, under the Command of Stephen H. Long.
       Compiled from the notes of Major Long, Messrs.
       Say, Keating, and Calhoun.  2 vols.  Philadelphia:
       H. C. Carey and L Lea, 1824.  Contains Sioux
       vocabulary.

1126.  Keefe, Harry L.  "How Shall the Indian Be Treated
       Historically. "  PNSHS, 17 (1913), 263-277.  Sympa-
       thetic toward the Indian viewpoint.

1127.  Kelley, William F.  Pine Ridge 1890.  Ed. Alexander
       Kelley and Pierre Bovis.  San Francisco:  Pierre
       Bovis, 1971.  267 pp.

1128.  Kennedy, Michael S. , ed.  The Red Man's West.
       True Stories of the Frontier Indians from Montana,
       The Magazine of Western History.  New York:
       Hastings House, 1965.  342 pp.

1129.  Kenner, Charles L.  A History of New Mexican-
       Plains Indian Relations.  Norman:  University of
       Oklahoma Press, 1969.  250 pp.

1130.  Kingsbury, George.  A History of Dakota Territory.
       Chicago:  S. J.  Clarke Co. , 1915.

1131.  Kraenzel, Carl.  The Great Plains in Transition.
       Norman:  University of Oklahoma Press, 1955.

1132.  Lamar, Howard R.  Dakota Territory, 1861-1889.
       New Haven:  Yale University Press, 1956.  304 pp.

1133.  Landes, Ruth.  The Mystic Lake Sioux:  Sociology of
       the Mdewakantonwan Santee.  Madison:  University
       of Wisconsin Press, 1968.  224 pp.  Interesting
       study of the traditional culture of the eastern Sioux.

1134.  Landman, Adrian M.  "Our Duty to the Sioux."
       Northern Oratorical League (1908), pp. 24-29.
       Commentary on Sioux-government relations.

1135.  Lass, William E.  "The Moscow Expedition. "  MiH,
       39 (1965), 227-240.

1136.  Lass, William E.  "The Removal from Minnesota of
       the Sioux and Winnebago Indians. "  MiH, 38 (De-
       cember 1963), 353-364.

1137.  Lee, Bob, and Dick Williams.  Last Grass Frontier.
       Rapid City, SD:  Black Hills Publishers, 1964.
       453 pp.  History of the development of the cattle
       industry in South Dakota, describing the opening of
       Sioux reservation grasslands, the settlement of the
       Sioux on the reservations, the relationships between
       cattlemen and Indians, treaties of the Sioux, the
       battle at Wounded Knee, and a history of the South
       Dakota Stock Growers' Association from 1880 to
       1964.

1138.   Leupp, Francis E.   The Indian and His Problems.
        1910; rpt. New York:   Johnson Reprint Corp.,
        1970; New York:   Arno Press, 1971.

1139.   Levering, C.   "Locating the Government Wagon Road
        from Niobrara, Nebraska, to Virginia City, Mon-
        tana."   IHR, 2:3 (July 1886), 312-321; 2:4 (October
        1886), 361-370; 3:1 (January 1887), 422-428; 3:2
        (April 1887), 469-477; 3:3 (July 1887), 497-503.
        Some information about the Sioux.

1140.   Lowie, Robert H.   Indians of the Plains.   Garden
        City, NY:   The Natural History Press, 1963.   258
        pp.

1141.   Lowie, Robert H.   Plains Indian Age Societies:  His-
        torical and Comparative Summary.   New York:
        Published by Order of the Trustees, 1916; APAM,
        11:3 (1916).

1142.   Ludlow, William.   Report of a Reconnaissance of the
        Black Hills of Dakota Made in the Summer of 1874.
        Washington, DC:   Government Printing Office, 1875.
        The official report of the 1874 expedition by engi-
        neering officer Captain Ludlow.

1143.   Lynd, J. W.   "History of the Dakotas."   CMHS, 2
        (1889), 143-174.   Written by scholar-trader Lynd
        before his death during the Minnesota Sioux War;
        prepared for publication by Stephen Return Riggs.

1144.   McGee, W. J.   "The Siouan Indians:  A Preliminary
        Sketch."   ARBAE, 15 (1897), 153-204.

1145.   McKenzie, Fayette A.   The Indian in Relation to the
        White Population of the United States.   1908; rpt.
        New York:   Burt Franklin, Publisher, 1970.

1146.   McLaird, James D., and Lesta V. Turchen.   "Ex-
        ploring the Black Hills, 1855-1875:  Reports of the
        Government Expeditions.   Colonel William Ludlow
        and the Custer Expedition, 1874."   SDH, 4:3 (Sum-
        mer 1974), 280-319.   Prepared from the letters
        and diaries of various personnel on the expedition.

1147.   McLaird, James D., and Lesta V. Turchen.   "Ex-
        ploring the Black Hills, 1855-1875:  Report of the

Government Expeditions. The Dacota Explorations of Lieutenant Governeur Kemble Warren, 1855-1856-1857. " SDH, 3:4 (Fall 1973), 359-389.

1148.   McLaird, James D. , and Lesta V. Turchen. "Exploring the Black Hills, 1855-1875: Reports of the Government Expeditions. The Explorations of Captain William Franklin Raynolds, 1859-1860. " SDH, 4:1 (Winter 1973), 18-62. Material about Sioux leaders from the letters and journals of Raynolds, who served as topographical engineer.

1149.   McLaird, James D. , and Lesta V. Turchen. "Exploring the Black Hills, 1855-1875: Reports of the Government Expeditions. The Scientist in Western Explorations: Ferdinand Vandiveer Hayden. " SDH, 4:2 (Spring 1974), 161-197. A geologist, he made the expeditions to the Upper Missouri region in the period 1853-1866, and explored the Black Hills and the Badlands.

1150.   McNeely, John. History of Tribal Claims of Dakota Sioux Indians Against the United States. Washington, DC: Library of Congress Photoduplication Service, 1939.

1151.   Mallery, Garrick. A Calendar of the Dakota Nation. Washington, DC: Government Printing Office, 1877. 25 pp.

1152.   Manypenny, George W. Our Indian Wards. Cincinnati, OH: Robert Clarke and Co. , 1880. Recollection about the Sioux and other Indian people by a former treaty negotiator and Indian agent.

1153.   Marshall, Samuel L. A. Crimsoned Prairie: The Wars Between the United States and the Plains Indians During the Winning of the West. New York: Charles Scribner's Sons, 1972. Superficial treatment of several campaigns.

1154.   Mattes, Merrill J. "Under the Wide Missouri. " NDH, 21:4 (October 1954), 145-167. A survey of important sites along the Missouri River valley that were flooded following the completion of the mainstem dams, some of which related to Sioux history.

1155.  Mattison, Ray H.  "Report on Historic Sites in the
       Garrison Reservoir Area, Missouri River. "  NDH,
       22:1 (January 1955),  5-73.  Considerable informa-
       tion about the Sioux--battle sites, etc.

1156.  Mdewakanton and Wahpakoota (Sioux) Indians.  Wash-
       ington, DC:  Government Printing Office,  1912.
       8 pp.

1157.  "Mdawakanton Sioux in 1850. "  In School, Pt. III, pp.
       613-614.

1158.  Mekeel, Scudder.  "A Short History of the Teton Da-
       kota. "  NDH,  10:3 (1943),  137-199.  Deals largely
       with the years prior to the establishment of the
       reservations.  Contains a map.  Interpretations
       are dated.

1159.  Meyer, Roy W.  "The Prairie Island Community:  A
       Remnant of Minnesota Sioux. "  MiH,  37 (September
       1961),  271-282.  About a Mdewakanton community
       with a population of approximately 100.

1160.  Meyer, Roy W.  History of the Santee Sioux:  United
       States Indian Policy on Trial.  Lincoln:  University
       of Nebraska Press, 1967.  434 pp.  A general sur-
       vey of one segment of the Sioux federation prepared
       largely from public documents, with little informa-
       tion that reflects the Indian viewpoint.

1161.  Meyer, Roy W.  "The Santee Sioux, 1934-1965. "  In
       The Western American Indian:  Case Studies in
       Tribal History.  Ed. Richard N. Ellis.  Lincoln:
       University of Nebraska Press, 1972.  pp. 165-172.

1162.  Miles, C.  "Sioux. "  Hobbies,  67 (March 1962),  112.

1163.  Miles, C.  "South Dakota Research. "  Hobbies,  67
       (March 1962),  113.

1164.  Miller, Alfred Jacob.  Braves and Buffalo:  Plains
       Indian Life in 1837.  Toronto:  University of Toron-
       to Press, 1973.

1165.  Miller, Carl F.  "Reevaluation of the Eastern Siouan
       Problem, with Particular Emphasis on the Virginia
       Branches--the Occaneechi, the Saponi, and the Tu-
       telo. "  BBAE,  164 (1957),  115-212.

1166.   Milligan, Edward A.   Dakota Twilight: The Standing
        Rock Sioux, 1874-1890.   Hicksville, NY: Exposi-
        tion Press, 1976.   190 pp.   An amateurish book
        about conditions on Standing Rock Reservation in
        the last quarter of the nineteenth century that has
        value only because it contains Indian viewpoints
        recorded by the author.

1167.   Mooney, James.   The Siouan Tribes of the East.
        1894; rpt. American Indian History Series.   St.
        Clair Shores, MI: Scholarly Press, 1970; New
        York: Johnson Reprint Corp., 1971.

1168.   Moorehead, Warren K.   "Sioux Women at Home."
        Illustrated American, 5 (1891), 481-484.

1169.   Morris, Richard B., and Jack M. Sosin, eds.   The
        Opening of the West.   Harper Torchbook.   New
        York: Harper and Row, 1969.

1170.   Munkres, Robert L.   "The Arrival of Emigrants and
        Soldiers: Curiosity, Contempt, Confusion and Con-
        flict."   See entry no. 1250, pp. 63-91.

1171.   Murray, Robert A.   Pipestone: A History.   60 pp.
        An unpublished manuscript, available at the Office
        of the Chief Historian, National Park Service, on
        the management of the sacred site since it was ac-
        quired from the Yankton tribe by the United States
        in the 1930's.

1172.   Murray, Stanley Norman.   A Study of Indian Land Re-
        lations as Illustrated Through the History of the
        Lake Traverse Reservation Sioux.   Madison, WI:
        Dane County Title Co., 1960.

1173.   Neill, Edward D.   "Dakota Land and Dakota Life."
        CMHS, 1 (1872), 254-301.   Originally published in
        1853.   Contains ethnological information about the
        Sioux.

1174.   Neill, Edward D.   Dahkotah Land and Dahkotah Life,
        with the History of the Fur Traders of the Extreme
        Northwest During the French and British Dominions.
        Philadelphia: Lippincott, 1859.   239 pp.   Reprint
        of a portion of his History of Minnesota.

1175.   Neill, Edward D.   Footprints of Civilization in the

Valley of Upper Mississippi, with the History of
the Dahkotas and Fur Traders During the French
and British Dominion.    Philadelphia:    J.  B.  Lippincott and Co. ,  1873.    239 pp.

1176.   Neill,  Edward D.    "History of the Ojibways,  and
        Their Connection with Fur Traders,  Based upon
        Official and Other Records. "   CMHS,  5 (1885),
        395-510.

1177.   Neill,  Edward D.    Memoir of the Sioux--A Manuscript
        in the French Archives,  Now First Printed,  with
        Introduction and Notes.    Contributions of the De-
        partments of History,  Literature,  and Political Sci-
        ence.    First Series.    St. Paul,  MN:    Macalester
        College,  1890.

1178.   Neill,  Edward D.    The Relations of the Government
        to the Indian Tribes.    n. p. ,  1863.    4 pp.    A let-
        ter to Hon. James Doolittle,  U. S.  Senator from
        Wisconsin.

1179.   Neill,  Edward D.    Some Facts in the History of Min-
        nesota:    Address to Alexander Ramsey,  First
        Governor of Minnesota and First President of Its
        Historical Society.    St.  Paul:    The Pioneer Press
        Co. ,  1888.    7 pp.

1180.   Nelson,  Bruce.    Land of the Dacotahs.    1946; rpt.
        Lincoln:    University of Nebraska Press,  1964.
        354 pp.

1181.   Nesset,  Noralf.    Excerpts of Standing Rock History.
        Fort Yates,  ND:    Standing Rock Sioux Tribe,  1961.

1182.   Nichols,  David A.    Lincoln and the Indians.    Colum-
        bia:    University of Missouri Press,  1978.    256 pp.
        Argues that "The Indian Civil War" was more a
        cultural conflict than an armed confrontation.

1183.   Nichols,  Col. George W.    "The Indian:    What We
        Should Do with Him. "   H,  40 (1870),  732-739.    A
        recommendation that Indians be placed under the
        War Department,  not the Interior Department,  and
        that they should be forced to submit to controls.

1184.   Nicollet,  N. J.    "Notices of the Natural Caves in the

Sioux Country, on the Left Banks of the Upper Mississippi River. " In School, Pt. II, pp. 95-99. Information on the Sioux, who used the caves.

1185. Oliver, Symmes C. "The Plains Indians as Herders. " In Paths to the Symbolic Self: Essays in Honor of Walter Goldschmidt. Ed. James P. Loucky and Jeffrey R. Jones. Los Angeles: University of California, 1976. pp. 35-44.

1186. O'Meara, Walter A. The Sioux Are Coming. Boston: Houghton Mifflin, 1971.

1187. "100 Years for the Sioux. " LD, 20 May 1933, p. 19.

1188. Pancoast, Henry Spackman. Impressions of the Sioux Tribes in 1882, with Some First Principles in the Indian Question. Philadelphia: Franklin Printing House, 1883. 27 pp.

1189. Parker, Donald D. "Surveying the South Dakota-Minnesota Boundary Line. " CHSSD, 32 (1964), 236-259. Contains observations about the Sioux.

1190. Parker, Watson. "The Majors and the Miners: The Role of the U. S. Army in the Black Hills Gold Rush. " JW, 11:1 (1972), 99-113. Discusses efforts by federal forces to prevent the entry of prospectors into the Black Hills region prior to the Great Sioux War and to remove those already there.

1191. Paulson, Howard W. "The Allotment of Land in Severalty to the Dakota Indians Before the Dawes Act. " SDH, 1:2 (Spring 1971), 132-153.

1192. Paulson, Howard W. "Federal Indian Policy and the Dakota Indians: 1800-1840. " SDH, 3:3 (Summer 1973), 285-309.

1193. Paxson, Frederick L. Last American Frontier. Boston: Houghton Mifflin, 1910. A general history that includes information about Indian affairs, including fraud in the Office of Indian Affairs.

1194. Peithmann, Irvin M. Broken Peace Pipes: A Four-Hundred-Year History of the American Indian. Springfield, IL: Charles C. Thomas, Publisher, 1964. 298 pp.

1195.   Petersen, William J.   "Indians and the Steamboats on
        the Upper Mississippi. " IJHP, 30 (1932), 155-181.
        Much on the Sioux and how they came to like cer-
        tain steamboats.

1196.   Pfaller, Fr. Louis.   "Indian Scare of 1890. "  NDH,
        39:2 (Spring 1972), 4-17, 36.   About the effects of
        the Ghost Dance on North Dakota Sioux.

1197.   Phillips, George H.   "The Indian Ring in Dakota Ter-
        ritory, 1870-1890. "  SDH, 2:4 (Fall 1972), 344-
        376.

1198.   The Plains Indians:   Their Origins, Migrations and
        Cultural Development.   New York:   T. Y. Crowell,
        1976.

1199.   Pond, Samuel William.   "The Dakotas or Sioux in
        Minnesota as They Were in 1834. " CMHS, 12 (1908),
        319-501.   One of the first Protestant missionaries
        to work among the Sioux, Pond had long experience
        among them.   This explains how he viewed their
        culture when he arrived in Minnesota.   A valuable
        source, but distorted by Pond's religious commit-
        ment.

1200.   Powers, William K.   The Indians of the Northern
        Plains.   New York:   G. P. Putnam's Sons, 1969.

1201.   Pratt, Richard H.   Battlefield and Classroom:   Four
        Decades with the American Indian, 1867-1904.   Ed.
        Robert M. Utley.   New Haven:   Yale University
        Press, 1964.   358 pp.   Written in 1920 by the
        founder of Carlisle Indian School, it contains much
        information about the Sioux.

1202.   Prescott, Philander.   "Contributions to the History,
        Customs, and Opinions of the Dacota Tribe. "  In
        School, Pt. II, pp. 168-199; continued as "The
        Dacotahs or Sioux of the Upper Mississippi. "
        School, Pt. III, pp. 225-46.

1203.   Prescott, Philander.   "Sioux Population of the Seven
        Mississippi Bands.   Returns of 1850. "  In School,
        Pt. V, pp. 701-702.

1204.   Priest, Loring B.   Uncle Sam's Stepchildren:   The

Reformation of United States Indian Policy, 1865-
1887. 1942; rpt. New York: Octagon Books, 1969.

1205. Prucha, Fr. Francis P. American Indian Policy in
Crisis: Christian Reformers and the Indian, 1865-
1900. Norman: University of Oklahoma Press,
1976. 456 pp. Excellent work that explains the
roles of reformers in the shaping of Indian policy
during the late nineteenth century. To illustrate
the actions of reformers, Prucha describes their
support of the reduction of the Great Sioux Reserve.

1206. Prucha, Fr. Francis P. The Indian in American
History. New York: Holt, Rinehart and Winston,
1970.

1207. Prucha, Fr. Francis P. Lewis Cass and American
Indian Policy. Detroit: Wayne State University
Press, 1967.

1208. Pumphrey, Stanley. Indian Civilization: A Lecture
by Stanley Pumphrey of England. Philadelphia:
The Bible and Tract Distributing Society, 1887.
52 pp. Describes Bishop Henry Whipple's views
on the Sioux.

1209. Putney, Effie Florence. In the South Dakota Country.
Mitchell, SD: Education Supply Co., 1924.

1210. Rachlis, Eugene, and John C. Ewers. The Indians
of the Plains. New York: Harper and Row,
1960.

1211. Relf, Francis H. "Removal of the Sioux Indians from
Minnesota." MiH, 2:6 (May 1918), 420-425. Includes the text of John P. Williamson's letter to
his mother on May 13, 1868, after he accompanied
eastern Sioux on their removal by steamboat to
Crow Creek on the Missouri.

1212. Richardson, James D., ed. A Compilation of the
Messages and Papers of the Presidents, 1789-1897.
10 vols. Washington, DC: Government Printing
Office, 1896-1899. A collection of messages and
papers that contains material on government relations with the Sioux.

1213.   Riggs, Stephen R.   "History of the Dakotas:   James
        W. Lynd's Manuscripts. "   CMHS, 2, Pt. 2 (1889),
        143-149.

1214.   Riggs, Stephen R.   "Mounds of Minnesota Valley. "
        CMHS, 1 (1872), 149-152.

1215.   Riggs, Thomas L.   "The Last Buffalo Hunt. "   CHSSD,
        11 (1922), 399-410.   Says the last hunt by the Sioux
        was in the winter of 1880-81.

1216.   Riggs, Thomas L.   "Sioux Memorials:   Biennial Ad-
        dress by President Thomas L. Riggs. "   CHSSD,
        2 (1904), 103-111.

1217.   Robinson, Doane.   "A History of the Dakota or Sioux
        Indians from Their Earliest Traditions and First
        Contact with White Men to the Final Settlement of
        the Last of Them upon Reservations and the Conse-
        quent Abandonment of the Old Tribal Life. "   CHSSD,
        2, Pt. 2 (1904), 523 pp. ; rpt. Aberdeen, SD:   New
        Printing Company, 1904; Minneapolis:   Ross and
        Haines, 1956, 1971.   The first significant attempt
        to survey the history of the Sioux.   It was an im-
        portant contribution, though it was deficient.   It
        dealt largely with the eastern tribes,  reflected
        nineteenth century anti-Indian bias,  and included
        little Indian viewpoint even though Robinson was in
        continuous contact with Sioux people.

1218.   Robinson, Doane.   "South Dakota and the War of
        1812. "   CHSSD, 12 (1924), 85-98.   Refers to the
        participation of eastern Sioux on the side of the
        British.

1219.   Robinson, Will G.   "Commissioner of Indian Affairs
        Reports as Pertain to the Sioux and Other Indians
        of Dakota Territory. "   CHSSD, 29 (1958), 307-500.

1220.   Robinson, Will G.   "Digest Indian Commissioner Re-
        port, 1876. "   CHSSD, 31 (1962), 1-73.

1221.   Robinson, Will G.   "Digest of the Report of the Com-
        missioner of Indian Affairs, 1877. "   CHSSD, 32
        (1964), 260-516.

1222.   Robinson, Will G.   "Digest of Reports of the Com-

missioner of Indian Affairs. " CHSSD, 26 (1952),
456-533. Covers the years 1815-1852.

1223. Robinson, Will G. "Digest of the Reports of the
Commissioner of Indian Affairs as Pertain to Dakota Indians--1869-1872. " CHSSD, 28 (1956), 179-
344.

1224. Robinson, Will G. "Digest of Reports of the Commissioner of Indian Affairs--1853-1869. " CHSSD, 27
(1954), 160-515.

1225. Robinson, Will G. "Our Indian Problem: Discussion
Before South Dakota Social Science Association, May
7, 1948. " CHSSD, 25 (1950), 350-368. Includes
a map.

1226. Roe, Frank Gilbert. The Indian and the Horse. Norman: University of Oklahoma Press, 1968. 434 pp.

1227. Roosa, Alma Carlson. "Homesteading in the 1880s:
The Anderson Carlson Families of Cherry County. "
NDH, 38:3 (Fall 1977), 371-394. Contains infor-
mation and photographs of the Sioux.

1228. Rosen, Peter. Pa-Ha-Sa-Pah or Black Hills of South
Dakota. St. Louis, MO: Nixon-Jones Printing Co. ,
1895. 645 pp.

1229. Rosenfelt, Willard. The Last Buffalo: Cultural Views
of the Great Plains; The Sioux or Dakota Nation.
Minneapolis: Denison, 1972. 119 pp. Contains information about the history and culture of the Sioux,
as well as information on some of their principal
leaders.

1230. Ruby, Robert H. The Oglala Sioux: Warriors in
Transition. New York: Vantage Press, 1955.
115 pp.

1231. Ruxton, George F. A. Life in the Far West. New
York: Harper and Bros. , 1849; rpt. Louisville,
KY: Last Cause Press, 1960. 239 pp.

1232. Sanders, W. E. "Trail of the Ancient Sioux: An Introduction to Their Ethnic History. " CHSSD, 26
(1952), 278-433. Contains information about several
Sioux tribes, and their migrations.

1233.   Schell, Herbert S.   History of South Dakota.   3rd ed.
        Lincoln:   University of Nebraska Press,   1975.
        444 pp.   Excellent state history that contains in-
        formation about the Sioux in the period 1900-1950.

1234.   Schulenberg, Raymond F.   "Indians of North Dakota. "
        NDH,  23:3 and 4 (July-October 1956),  119-236.
        Both information and photographs on the Sioux.

1235.   Schulenberg, Raymond F.   Indians of North Dakota.
        Bismarck, ND:   State Historical Society of North
        Dakota,  1956.   116 pp.   Reprinted from NDH,  23:
        3 and 4 (July-October 1956),  119-236,  entry no.
        1234 cited above.

1236.   Shumway, Grant L.   "First Settlement of the Scotts
        Bluff Country. "   PNSHS,  19 (1919),  103-113.   Ap-
        proximately half of the article is on the Sioux,  and
        the census of the several tribes.

1237.   Sievers, Michael A.   "The Administration of Indian
        Affairs on the Upper Missouri,  1858-1865. "   NDH,
        38:3 (Summer 1971),  366-394.   Contains informa-
        tion about the Sioux,  including photographs of their
        camp sites.

1238.   "The Sioux Nation and the United States. "   Washington,
        DC:   National Indian Defense Association,  1891.
        32 pp.

1239.   "Sioux Population in 1836. "   In School,  Pt. III,  p.
        612.

1240.   Sniffin, Matthew K.   Observations Among the Sioux.
        Philadelphia:   Indian Rights Association,  1906.
        35 pp.

1241.   Stewart, William J.   "Settler, Politician, and Specu-
        lator in the Sale of the Sioux Reserve. "   MiH,  39
        (Fall 1964),  85-92.   About events following the Min-
        nesota Sioux War of 1862-63.

1242.   Strong, William Duncan.   "From History to Prehistory
        in the Northern Great Plains. "   In Essays in His-
        torical Anthropology of North America published in
        honor of John R. Swanton.   Washington, DC:   Smith-
        sonian Institution,  1940, pp. 353-394; rpt. PlA,  17:
        57 (August 1972).

1243. Swanton, John R. "Siouan Tribes and the Ohio Valley." AA, 45:1 (January 1943), 49-66.

1244. Swanton, John R. "Some Neglected Data Bearing on Cheyenne, Chippewa, and Dakota History." AA, 32:1 (January-March 1930), 156-160.

1245. Swisher, Jacob A. "The Sioux." Palimpsest, 9:2 (February 1928), 49-52; rpt. in Palimpsest, 38:2 (February 1957), 51-54. Brief history.

1246. Tallent, Annie D. The Black Hills: Or, the Last Hunting Ground of the Dakotahs. 1889; rpt. Sioux Falls, DC: Brevet Press, 1974; New York: Arno Press, 1975.

1247. Terrell, John Upton. Sioux Trail. New York: McGraw-Hill, 1974. 213 pp. An unreliable book.

1248. Terrell, John Upton, and Donna M. Terrell. Indian Women of the Western Morning. Garden City, NY: Anchor Press, 1974. 194 pp. Not trustworthy.

1249. Textor, Lucy E. Official Relations Between the United States and the Sioux Indians. Palo Alto, CA: Leland Stanford Junior University Publications, 1896. 162 pp. An excellent summary of relationships between Sioux tribes and the U. S. government down to the end of the nineteenth century, based upon careful research.

1250. Tyler, Daniel, ed. Red Men and Hat-Wearers: Viewpoints in Indian History. Boulder, CO: Pruett Publishing Co., 1976. 171 pp. Papers presented at the Colorado state conference on the teaching and writing of Indian history in 1972, several of which were on the Sioux.

1251. U. S. Congress. House. Expenditures for Fulfilling the Treaty with the Sioux Indians. House Misc. Doc. 126. Serial 1702. 44th Cong., 1st Sess., 1876. Deals with rations and annuity goods.

1252. U. S. Congress. House. Hostile Indians in Dakota. House Misc. Doc. 65. Serial 1572. 44th Cong., 3rd Sess., 1873-1874.

1253. U. S. Congress. House. Legislative Assembly of

Dakota Territory. <u>Memorial in Reference to the</u>
<u>Black Hills Country Serving as a Retreat for Hos-</u>
<u>tile Indians.</u> House Misc. Doc. 65, Serial 1572,
42nd Cong., 3rd Sess., 1872-1873.

1254.  U. S. Congress. House. <u>The Removal of the Sioux</u>
<u>Indians.</u> House Exec. Doc. 10. Serial 1751. 44th
Cong., 2nd Sess., 1876-1877.

1255.  U. S. Congress. House. <u>Report on Indian Affairs in</u>
<u>Dakota Territory.</u> House Exec. Doc. 147. Serial
1267. 39th Cong., 1st Sess., 1866. Investigation
of corruption in the administration of Yankton
Agency.

1256.  U. S. Congress. House. <u>Support of Indians.</u> House
Rept. 29. Serial 1388.   40th Cong., 3rd Sess.,
1869-1870. Recommends paying General Harney's
indebtedness as a result of his participation in Indian affairs.

1257.  U. S. Congress. Senate. <u>Certain Concessions from</u>
<u>the Sioux Indians.</u> Senate Exec. Doc. 9. Serial
1718. 44th Cong., 2nd Sess., 1876-1877.

1258.  U. S. Department of the Interior, Office of Indian Af-
fairs. <u>Annual Report of the Commissioner of Indian</u>
<u>Affairs to the Secretary of the Interior 1890.</u>
Washington, DC: Government Printing Office, 1890.
Deals with a troublesome year for the Sioux.

1259.  United States Office of Indian Affairs. <u>Reports of the</u>
<u>Commissioner of Indian Affairs, 1835-1870.</u>  36
vols. Rpt. New York:  AMS Press, 1970.

1260.  Utley, Robert M.  "The Celebrated Peace Policy of
General Grant. "  <u>NDH</u>, 20:3 (July 1953), 121-142.
About federal Indian policy in the years 1869-1876,
particularly with the Sioux.

1261.  Utley, Robert M.  <u>The Last Days of the Sioux Nation.</u>
New Haven: Yale University Press, 1963.  314 pp.
Best account of events that led to the massacre at
Wounded Knee in 1890.

1262.  Ven Heuzen, George Harry.  <u>The United States Gov-</u>
<u>ernment and the Sioux Indians, 1878-1891.</u>  St.

Louis, MO: Washington University, 1950. 213 pp.
Based on his M. A. thesis at Washington University.

1263. Vestal, Stanley. New Sources of Indian History,
1850-1891. The Ghost Dance--The Prairie Sioux--
A Miscellany. Norman: University of Oklahoma
Press, 1934. Rpt. New York: Burt Franklin,
1971. 351 pp. Deals with Sioux history in general, but concentrates on the Ghost Dance and the
death of Sitting Bull and their respective histories.

1264. Vestal, Stanley. "Sailing the Prairies." SR, 33:4
(July 1938), 428-435. On the experiences of some
old Sioux warriors with covered wagons and rail-
roads.

1265. Vestal, Stanley. Warpath and Council Fire: The
Plains Indians. Struggle for Survival in War and
Diplomacy 1851-1891. New York: Random House,
1948. 338 pp.

1266. Warren, William W. "History of the Ojibways, Based
upon Traditions and Oral Statements." CMHS, 5
(1885), 23-394. Sioux history through Ojibway-
Sioux relationships.

1267. Welsh, Herbert. Report and Supplementary Report of
a Visit to Spotted Tail's Tribe of Brule Sioux Indians, the Yankton and Santee, Sioux, Poncas and
the Chippeways of Minnesota, October, 1870. Philadelphia: M'Calla and Stavely, Printers, 1870. 28
pp.

1268. Welsh, Herbert. Report of a Visit to the Great Sioux
Reserve, Dakota, Made During the Months of May
and June, 1883, in Behalf of the Indian Rights Association. Philadelphia: Indian Rights Association,
1883.

1269. Welsh, Herbert. Report of a Visit to Spotted Tail's
Tribe of Brule Sioux Indians, the Yankton and Santee Sioux, Poncas and the Chippewas of Minnesota,
in September, 1870. Philadelphia: M'Calla and
Stavely, Printers, 1870. 20 pp.

1270. Welsh, Herbert. Report of a Visit to the Sioux and
Ponka Indians on the Missouri River, July 1872.

Washington, DC:   Government Printing Office,
1872.   36 pp.

1271.   Welsh, Herbert.   Sioux and Ponca Indians.   In Reports to the Missionary Organization of the Protestant Episcopal Church and to the Secretary of the
Interior on Indian Civilization.   Philadelphia:
M'Calla and Stavely, Printers, 1870.   28 pp.

1272.   Welsh, William.   Civilization Among the Sioux Indians:   Report of a Visit to Some of the Sioux
Reservations of South Dakota and Nebraska.   Philadelphia:   Indian Rights Association, 1893.

1273.   Welsh, William.   Four Weeks Among Some of the
Sioux Tribes of Dakota and Nebraska.   Together
with a Brief Consideration of the Indian Problem.
Germantown, PA:   Horace F. McCann, Steam-Power
Printer, 1882.   31 pp.   Well-intentioned but con-
descending attitude toward Indian people.

1274.   Welsh, William.   Letter to the Forty-third Congress
in Regard to the Sale of Pine Timber Belonging to
the Chippewa Indians and the Contracts Supplying
Beef to the Agencies Among the Sioux Indians.
Philadelphia:   M'Calla and Stavely, Printers, 1874.
8 pp.

1275.   Welsh, William.   Taopi and His Friends, or the Indians' Wrongs and Rights.   Philadelphia:   Claxton,
Remsen, and Haffelfinger, 1869.   125 pp.

1276.   Welsh, William.   A Visit to the Sioux Indians.   New
York:   American Church Press Company, 1869.
11 pp.   Letter to the editor of the Spirit of Missions, November 1869.

1277.   Wemett, William M.   The Indians of North Dakota.
Fargo, ND:   The Northern School Supply Co.,
1927.   256 pp.

1278.   White, Richard.   "The Winning of the West:   The Ex-
pansion of the Western Sioux in the Eighteenth and
Nineteenth Centuries."   JAH, 65:2 (September 1978),
319-343.   A revisionist study that says Sioux tribes
"fought largely for the potential economic and social
benefits to be derived from furs, slaves, better

hunting grounds, and horses, " rather than for hon-
or and territorial rights.  Places Sioux in unfavor-
able light.

1279.  Williamson, John P.  Memoir of the Sioux.  Comment
on text from the archives department de la marine,
Paris.  n. p. , n. d.

1280.  Williamson, John P.  "Removal of the Sioux Indians
from Minnesota. "  MHB, 2 (1918), 420-425.  Letter from John P. Williamson to his mother, May
13, 1863, regarding the removal of eastern Sioux
by steamboat to Crow Creek on the Missouri.

1281.  Williamson, Thomas S.  "Dacotas of the Missisippi. "
In School, Pt. I, pp. 247-256.

1282.  Williamson, Thomas S.  "The Sioux or Dakotas.  A
Sketch of Our Intercourse with the Dakotahs on the
Missouri River, and Southwest of that Stream. "
CMHS, 3 (1870-1880), 283-294.

1283.  Williamson, Thomas.  "Who Were the First Men?"
CMHS, 1 (1872), 295-301; (1902), 241-246.  Sioux
in prehistoric times.

1284.  Winchell, Newton H.  The Aborigines of Minnesota:
A Report.  St. Paul:  Minnesota Historical Society, 1911.  761 pp.

1285.  Wissler, Clark.  North American Indians of the Plains.
1912; rpt. New York:  Burt Franklin, Pub. , 1970.


ILLNESSES AND HEALTH CARE

1286.  Allen, Thomas E. , and Patricia Allen.  Health Care
Crisis at Rosebud.  Vermillion:  University of
South Dakota, 1973.  44 pp.  About health care
delivery on Rosebud Reservation in the twentieth
century.

1287.  Andros, F.  "The Medicine and Surgery of the Winne-
bago and Dakota Indians. "  American Medical Association Journal, 1 (1883), 116-118.

1288.  Cassell, John, Etra Page, and Gaynelle Hogan.
       Economic and Social Resources Available for Indian
       Health Purposes:   A Study of Selected Reservations
       in the Aberdeen Area.  Chapel Hill:   University of
       North Carolina Press,  1956.

1289.  Dollar, Clyde C.  "The High Plains Smallpox Epidem-
       ic of 1837-38. "  WHQ,  8:1 (January 1977),  15-38.

1290.  Eastman, Charles A.  "The Indian's Health Problem. "
       PSM,  86 (January 1915),  49-54.   Dr. Eastman
       served as agency physician on Pine Ridge Reserva-
       tion during the Wounded Knee Massacre in 1890.

1291.  Fagan, Bernard D.  "Alcohol:   And Suggestions. "
       GPO,  February 1967,  p.  11.

1292.  Gregg, Elinor D.  The Indians and the Nurse.   Nor-
       man:   University of Oklahoma Press,  1965.   173
       pp.   By a public health nurse who spent many years
       on Rosebud and Pine Ridge Reservations.

1293.  Higheagle, Raymond.   "First Aid and Red Cross Ser-
       vice Among the Sioux, Yesterday and Today. "  IW,
       1 December 1936, pp.  44-45.   Traditional health
       care by Sioux medicine men and Mini Aku (field
       nurses).

1294.  Holzhueter, Ann M. , John B.  Gregg,  and Sylvester
       Clifford.   "A Search for Stapes Footplate Fixation
       in an Indian Population Prehistoric and Historic. "
       AJPA,  23:1 (March 1965),  35-40.   Chiefly on the
       Sioux of South Dakota.

1295.  Hoover, Herbert T. , proj. dir.   "Health Care Crisis
       at Rosebud. "   Film dir. Sanford Gray.   Twenty-
       two-minute color film on contemporary health care
       problems on Rosebud Reservation.   Vermillion:
       University of South Dakota,  1973.   Available on
       loan, Educational Media Department,  University of
       South Dakota.

1296.  Hurt, Wesley R. ,  and Richard M. Brown.   "Social
       Drinking Patterns of the Yankton Sioux. "   HO,  24
       (Fall 1965),  222-230.

1297.  Kemnitzer, Luis S.   "Adjustment and Value Conflict

in Urbanizing Dakota Indians, Measured by Q-Sort Technique. " AA, 75 (June 1973), 687-707.

1298. Kemnitzer, Luis S. "The Structure of Country Drinking Parties on Pine Ridge Reservation, South Dakota. " PlA, 17 (May 1972), 134-142.

1299. Krush. Thaddeus P. , and John Bjork. "Mental Health Factors in an Indian Boarding School. " MH, 49 (January 1965), 94-103. About Flandreau Indian School in South Dakota.

1300. Krush, Thaddeus P. , and John Bjork, et aL "Some Thoughts on the Formation of Personality Disorder: Study of an Indian Boarding School Population. " MH, 50 (February 1966), 868-876. About Flandreau Indian school.

1301. Kuttner, R. , and A. Lorinez. "Alcohol and Addiction in Urbanized Sioux Indians. " MH, 51 (1967), 530-542.

1302. Levy, Louis. "Tuberculosis Among Indians. " Sioux San Sun, February 1956, pp. 2-3. From Sioux Sanatorium, Rapid City, S. D.

1303. Lewis, Thomas H. "A Syndrome of Depression and Mutism in the Oglala Sioux. " AJPs, 132:7 (1975), 753-755.

1304. McCone, R. Clyde. "Death and Persistence of Basic Personality Structure among the Lakota. " PlA, 13:Pt. 1 (1968), 305-309.

1305. McKinney, Wayne R. "The Sioux Lookout Medical Problem. " B (Spring 1973), pp. 52-57. On health care.

1306. "Medicine Among the American Indians. " Ciba Symposia, 1:1 (April 1939), 1-34. About Indian medical problems and traditional treatments.

1307. Query, William T. , and Joy M. Query. "Aggressive Responses to the Holtzman Inkblot Technique by Indian and White Alcoholics. " JCP, 3:4 (December 1972), 413-416. Sioux and Chippewa Indians of North Dakota.

1308.   Robinson, Doane.  "Tuberculosis Among the Sioux In-
        dians. "  RR, 33 (March 1906), 340-341.

1309.   Stearn, Esther W. , and Allen E. Stearn.  Effects of
        Smallpox on the Destiny of the Amerindian.  Deer
        Park, NY:  Brown Book Co. , 1971.

1310.   Tessendorf, K. C.  "Red Death on the Missouri. "
        AW, 14:1 (1977), 48-53.  On the smallpox epidemic
        of 1837, which killed an estimated 17, 000 Indians.

1311.   Treon, Frederick.  "Surgery Among the Sioux Indians. "
        The Journal Lancet, N. S. , 53:7 (September 1933),
        464-465, 474.

1312.   United States.  Bureau of Indian Affairs.  Survey of
        Health Facilities:  Cheyenne River Reservation,
        South Dakota, and Vicinity.  Billings, MT:  Mis-
        souri River Basin Investigations Project, 1952.
        8 pp.

1313.   Wallis, Ruth Sawtell, and Wilson D. Wallis.  "The
        Sins of the Fathers:  Concept of Disease Among the
        Canadian Dakota. "  SJA, 9 (1953), 431-435.  Re-
        counts belief among traditional Sioux that illness
        and death results from ill-behavior of a close rela-
        tive, as punishment by the Great Spirit.

1314.   The White Plague at Fort Totten. "  IW, 1 January
        1935, pp. 15-18.  Tuberculosis on the reservation
        --50 active cases and 184 positive reactors.

1315.   Williamson, Thomas S.  "The Diseases of the Dakota
        Indians. "  NMSJ, 16:12 (June 1874), 410-419.

1316.   Wissler, Clark.  "Measurements of Dakota Indian
        Children. "  Annals of the New York Academy of
        Sciences, 20 (1911), 355-364.

## INDIAN AUTHORS

1317.   Allen, Paula Gunn.  The Blind Lion.  Berkeley, CA:
        Thorp Springs Press, 1974.  Poems by Laguna-
        Lakota author.

1318.   Allen, Paula Gunn. A Cannon Between the Knees.
        New York: Strawberry Press, 1978. Poetry.

1319.   Allen, Paula Gunn. Coyote's Daylight Trip. Albu-
        querque: La Confluencia, 1978.

1320.   Allen, Paula Gunn. "Dine." SDR, 12:4 (Winter 1974-
        75), 111. A one-page poem.

1321.   Allen, Paula Gunn. "Lament of My Father, Lakota."
        SDR, 11:1 (Spring 1973), 3. A one-page poem.

1322.   Allen, Paula Gunn. "Lost Breed." Sun Tracks, 2:2
        (Spring 1976), 9. A poem.

1323.   Beatty, Willard W. "Melvin Leo McBride of Rose-
        bud." IW, May-June, 1944, pp. 15-16. The Di-
        rector of the Office of Indian Education pays tribute
        to a Sioux war hero killed on the Tunisian front in
        1943.

1324.   Black Elk, Benjamin. "Black Elk's Notes on Teton
        Sioux Culture." USDMN, 23:3 (1962), 1-6, 8.

1325.   Black Elk, Benjamin. "Red Is the Knowledge." SDR,
        11:3 (Autumn 1973), 23-26; rpt. in The Literature
        of South Dakota. Ed. John Milton. Vermillion,
        SD: Dakota Press, 1976, pp. 321-324. A poetic
        statement of what a Sioux is and his beliefs.

1326.   Bordeaux, G. Jake. "The Name I Carved into Bleed-
        ing Stone." BCQ, 24:1 (1978), unpaged. Twenty-
        two pages of poems by a young Lakota, who wrote
        while he was in the South Dakota State Penitentiary.

1327.   Bordeaux, William J. Custer's Conqueror. Sioux
        Falls, SD: Smith and Co., 1951. 98 pp.

1328.   Burnette, L. Sharon. "Entanglement." Sun Tracks,
        1:3 (Winter 1971-72), 25. A short poem.

1329.   Burnette, Robert. The Tortured Americans. Engle-
        wood Cliffs, NJ: Prentice-Hall, 1971. 155 pp.
        Indictment of non-Indian Society and Rosebud tribal
        politics.

1330.   Burnette, Robert, and John Koster. The Road to

Wounded Knee. New York: Bantam Books, 1974.
332 pp. Criticism of non-Indian society by a
former Rosebud tribal chairman.

1331. Charger, Samuel. "Biography of Martin Charger. "
CHSSD, 22 (1946), 1-26. Martin Charger was a
leader of the Fool Soldiers, who rescued non-
Indian prisoners from Sioux captors.

1332. Chief Eagle, Dallas. Winter Count. Boulder, CO:
Johnson Publishing Co. , 1967. 211 pp. A novel
of the old times, ending with Wounded Knee.

1333. Cook, Elizabeth. "Authentic Pictures of the Sioux?"
GPO, March 1971, pp. 5-7. Criticism of Frederick Manfred's Scarlet Plume.

1334. Cook, Elizabeth. "A Child's Story. " PM, 7 (1976),
225-226.

1335. Cook, Elizabeth. "Some of My Best Friends. " SDR,
14:1 (Spring 1976), 68. A short poem.

1336. Cook-Lynn, Elizabeth. Then Badger Said This.
New York: Vantage Press, 1977. 42 pp. Poetry
and stories, by Elizabeth Cook, under married
name.

1337. Cook-Lynn, Elizabeth. "Three. " PS, 50 (Summer
1976), 148-150.

1338. Cook, Violet. "Camala. " InH, 9:2 (Spring 1976),
7. A short poem by a Hunkpapa Sioux, from Crow
Creek Reservation.

1339. Cook, Violet. "Dream. " InH, 9:2 (Spring 1976), 21.
A short poem.

1340. Cook, Violet. "Memories. " InH, 9:2 (Spring 1976),
16. Short poem.

1341. Cook, Violet. "Songs. " InH, 9:2 (Spring 1976), 6.
Short poem.

1342. Cook, Violet. "A Wave. " InH, 9:2 (Spring 1976), 29.
Short poem.

1343.   Davids, Dorothy W.  "The Melting Pot and the Amer-
        ican Indian. "  GPO, May 1969, pp. 8-13.  Materi-
        al on the Sioux, by a Stockbridge-Munsee Indian.

1344.   Deloria, Ella C.  "Dakota Treatment of Murderers. "
        PAPS, 88:5 (November 1944), 368-371.  Describes
        three methods.

1345.   Deloria, Ella C.  "The Indian in Wartime (1944). "
        In No. 1936, pp. 314-318.

1346.   Deloria, Ella C.  "Some Notes on the Santee. "
        USDMN, 28:5-6 (1967), 1-21.

1347.   Deloria, Ella C.  "Some Notes on the Yankton. "
        USDMN, 28:3-4 (1967), 1-30.

1348.   Deloria, Ella C.  Speaking of Indians.  New York:
        Friendship Press, 1944; rpt. Vermillion, SD:  Da-
        kota Press, 1979.

1349.   Deloria, Sam.  "Move to City Slums?"  GPO, Febru-
        ary 1967, pp. 8-9.

1350.   Deloria, Vine, Jr.  "The American Indian and His
        Commitments, Goals, and Programs:  A Need to
        Reconsider. "  InH, 5:1 (Spring 1972), 5-10.

1351.   Deloria, Vine, Jr.  "The Basis of Indian Law. "  In
        Look to the Mountain Top.  Ed. Charles Jones.
        San Jose, CA:  Gousha Publishers, 1972, pp. 75-
        82.

1352.   Deloria, Vine, Jr.  Behind the Trail of Broken
        Treaties.  New York:  Dell Publishing Co. , 1974.
        263 pp.  About the history of Indian-government
        relations; advocates independence for reservation
        Indians as residents of enclaves within the U. S.

1353.   Deloria, Vine, Jr.  A Better Day for Indians.  New
        York:  The Field Foundation, 1977.  35 pp.  De-
        scribes seven main concerns of contemporary In-
        dian people.

1354.   Deloria, Vine, Jr.  "The Cheyenne Experience. "  NHi,
        81:9 (November 1972), 96-100.  Flattering review
        of Hyemeyohst Storm's Seven Arrows.

1355.  Deloria, Vine, Jr.  "Civilization and Isolation. "  NAR,
       263:2 (Summer 1978),  11-14.

1356.  Deloria, Vine, Jr.  "Consolidating Indian Efforts
       (1970). "  See entry no. 1936, pp. 380-384.

1357.  Deloria, Vine, Jr.  Custer Died for Your Sins:  An
       Indian Manifesto.  New York:  Macmillan, 1969;
       rpt. New York:  Avon Books, 1970.  279 pp.  An
       influential book covering all aspects of Indian-White
       relationships.

1358.  Deloria, Vine, Jr.  God Is Red.  New York:  Gros-
       set and Dunlap, 1973.  376 pp.

1359.  Deloria, Vine, Jr.  "Implications of the 1968 Civil
       Rights Act in Tribal Autonomy. "  See entry no.
       1893, pp. 85-92.

1360.  Deloria, Vine, Jr.  The Indian Affair.  New York:
       Friendship Press, 1974.  95 pp.  Series of short
       papers.

1361.  Deloria, Vine, Jr.  Indians of the Pacific Northwest.
       New York:  Doubleday, 1977.

1362.  Deloria, Vine, Jr.  "Largest Collection of Indian
       Items Is Put on Display. "  Smithsonian, 9:5 (Au-
       gust 1978), 58-65.  About the opening of "Echoes
       of Drums, " material from the Museum of the
       American Indian, in New York.

1363.  Deloria, Vine, Jr.  "The Next Three Years:  A
       Time of Change. "  InH, 7:No. 2 (Spring 1974), 25-
       27, 53.

1364.  Deloria, Vine, Jr.  Of Utmost Good Faith.  San
       Francisco, CA:  Straight Arrow Books, 1971.
       462 pp.  Documents on Indian treaties and court
       cases.

1365.  Deloria, Vine, Jr.  "Rev. of The Sacred Scrolls of
       the Southern Ojibway.  By Selwyn Dewdney. "  JES,
       4:2 (Summer 1976), 95-97.  Praises the book.

1366.  Deloria, Vine, Jr.  "The Rise and Fall of the First
       Indian Movement. "  The Historian, 33:4 (August

1971), 656-664. A review of Hazel W. Hertzberg's The Search for an American Indian Identity (Modern Pan-Indian Movements), a fairly good book according to Deloria.

1367. Deloria, Vine, Jr. "The Theological Dimension of the Indian Protest Movement." In Three Perspectives on Ethnicity: Blacks, Chicanos, and Native Americans. Ed. Carlos E. Cortes, et al. New York: G. P. Putnam's Sons, 1976, pp. 364-368. Appeared originally in The Christian Century, 21 September 1973, pp. 912-914.

1368. Deloria, Vine, Jr. "This Country Was a Lot Better Off When the Indians Were Running It." In Native Americans Today: Sociological Perspectives. Ed. Howard M. Bahr, Bruce A. Chadwick, and Robert C. Day. New York: Harper and Row, 1972, pp. 498-506; and in Alvin M. Josephy, ed. Red Power: The American Indians' Fight for Freedom. New York: American Heritage Press, 1971, pp. 247-259, and in Three Perspectives (No. 1367), pp. 319-328.

1369. Deloria, Vine, Jr. "The Twentieth Century." See entry no. 1250, pp. 155-166.

1370. Deloria, Vine, Jr. "The Urban Scene and the American Indian." See entry no. 1893, pp. 333-355.

1371. Deloria, Vine Jr. "The War Between the Redskins and the Feds." In The Indian in American History. Ed. Francis P. Prucha. New York: Holt, Rinehart and Winston, 1971, pp. 116-122. From New York Times Magazine, 7 December 1969.

1372. Deloria, Vine, Jr. We Talk, You Listen. New York: Macmillan Co., 1970. 227 pp. Indians cope better with modern conditions than do other groups because Indian ways endure.

1373. Deloria, Vine, Jr., and Jennings C. Wise. Red Man in the New World Drama. New York: Macmillan Co., 1971.

1374. DeLorme, J. M. "The Golden Prey." SDR, 13:2 (Summer 1975), 96-102. A short story in a reservation setting.

1375. Ducheneaux, Frank. "The Cheyenne River Sioux."
       AIn, 7:3 (Spring 1956), 20-30.   By the late Tribal
       Chairman on Cheyenne River Reservation.

1376. Eastman, Charles A.   "Camping with Indians."   TB,
       1:9 (September 1915), 223-230.   On camping and
       fishing at Rainy Lake on the U. S. -Canadian border.

1377. Eastman, Charles A.   "The Great Cat's Nursery."
       H, 107 (November 1903), 939-946.

1378. Eastman, Charles A.   "A Half-Forgotten Lincoln
       Story."   Rotarian, 76 (February 1950), 34.

1379. Eastman, Charles A.   Indian Scout Talks.   A Guide
       for Boy Scouts and Camp Fire Girls.   Boston:
       Little, Brown and Co., 1914.   190 pp.   Contains
       camping, hunting and wood-lore information that
       might be useful to Boy Scouts and Camp Fire Girls.

1380. Eastman, Charles A.   The Indian To-Day: The Past
       and Future of the First American.   1915; rpt.
       Garden City, NY; rpt. Detroit:  Gale Research Co.,
       1971, New York:  AMS Press, 1975.   185 pp.

1381. Eastman, Charles A.   "The Indian's Gift to the Na-
       tion."   QJSAI, January-March 1915, pp. 17-23.

1382. Eastman, Charles A.   "The Indian's Plea for Free-
       dom."   AIM, Winter 1919, p. 164.

1383. Eastman, Charles A.   "Justice for the Sioux."   AIM,
       Summer 1919, p. 80.

1384. Eastman, Charles A.   "The Mustering of the Herds."
       Out West, 2 (1904), 439-445.

1385. Eastman, Charles A.   "The Sioux Mythology."   PSM,
       46 (November 1894), 88-91.

1386. Eastman, Charles A.   "The Sioux of Yesterday and
       Today."   AIM, Winter 1917, pp. 235-237.

1387. Eastman, Charles A.   "The Song of the Birch Canoe."
       Craftsman, 23 (October 1912), 3-11.

1388. Eastman, Charles A.   "The War Maiden of the Sioux."
       LHJ, 23 (August 1906), 14.

1389.  Giago, Tim A.  The Aboriginal Sin.  San Francisco,
       CA:  Indian Historian Press, 1978.  About the ex-
       periences of Indian children at Holy Rosary Mission
       on Pine Ridge Reservation in the period 1930s to
       1960s.

1390.  Hairy Shirt, LeRoy, et al.  Lakota Woonspe Wawapi.
       Rosebud, SD:  Sinte Gleska College Center, 1973.
       202 pp.

1391.  Hare, DeWitt.  "The Yankton Indians."  CHSSD, 6
       (1912), 320-328.

1392.  Herman, Jake.  "Pine Ridge."  In The American In-
       dian Reader.  Ed. Jeannette Henry.  San Francisco:
       Indian Historian Press, 1973, pp. 130-147.  Auto-
       biography, poetry and material he wrote for a
       column.

1393.  Howe, Oscar.  "Theories and Beliefs--Dakota."  In
       The American Indian Speaks, I. Ed. John R. Milton.
       Vermillion, SD:  Dakota Press, 1969, pp. 69-79.
       Theories about art and life by an artist.

1394.  Kickingbird, Kirke, and Karen Ducheneaux.  One
       Hundred Million Acres.  New York:  The Macmil-
       lan Co., 1973.  Contends that the Indians have a
       legitimate claim to that much land.

1395.  LaBuff, Thomas G. (Crazy Eagle).  "I Keep Wonder-
       ing How Many of My People."  GPO, March 1970,
       p. 3.

1396.  LaBuff, Thomas G. (Crazy Eagle).  "A Prayer."
       GPO, January 1970, p. 5.

1397.  LaBuff, Thomas G. (Crazy Eagle).  "To Rule or
       Renew?"  GPO, October 1970, p. 3.

1398.  LaBuff, Thomas G. (Crazy Eagle).  "The 70's--Sur-
       vival or Not?"  GPO, April 1970, p. 6.

1399.  LaBuff, Thomas G. (Crazy Eagle).  "Treaty--Weapon
       of White Power."  GPO, August 1971, p. 7.

1400.  LaBuff, Thomas G. (Crazy Eagle).  "We Have to Be
       Willing to Lay Our Lives on the Line."  GPO, Jan-
       uary 1970, p. 4.

1401.  LaPointe, Frank. "The Legend of Bear Butte. " WT,
       1:2 (January 1972), 4-6.

1402.  LaPointe, Frank. "Millie's Gift. " In An American
       Indian Anthology. Ed. Fr. Benet Tvedten. Mar-
       vin, SD: Blue Cloud Abbey, 1971, pp. 14-17.

1403.  McGaa, Ed. "Indian Legal Rights Legal Training and
       Qualified Lawyers Are Sorely Needed. " GPO,
       February 1969, pp. 6-7.

1404.  McGaa, Ed. "Indian Legal Rights Suddenly Subject to
       New Laws. " GPO, January 1969, pp. 12-14.

1405.  McGaa, Ed. "Rights. " BCQ, 15:2 (1969), [2]-[8].

1406.  McGaa, Ed. "To End Indian Poverty and Teach
       Tourists. " GPO, May 1970, p. 9.

1407.  McNickle, D'Arcy. "Rescuing Sisseton. " AIn, 3:2
       (Spring 1946), 21-27.   Relates what happened to
       Sisseton after Congressman Karl Mundt introduced
       H. R. 2947 "to authorize the consolidation of lands
       on the Sisseton Indian Reservation. "

1408.  Marshall, Joe. "Hambliciyapi:  The Vision. " GPO,
       May 1970, p. 7.  A poem in Lakota, with transla-
       tion.

1409.  Marshall, Joe. "White Goal--Tame the Land, Ex-
       terminate the Varmints. " GPO, May 1970, pp. 4-
       6; rpt. November 1970, pp. 10-11.  About the
       mistreatment of Indians.

1410.  Maynard, Eileen, and Gayla Twiss.  Hechel Lena
       Oyate Kin Nipi Kte:  That These People May Live.
       Pine Ridge, SD:  U. S. Public Health Service, 1969.
       183 pp.  A report on modern history and condi-
       tions at Pine Ridge Reservation.

1411.  Medicine, Bea. "The American Indian in Modern
       Society. " SDR, 7:2 (Summer 1969), 189-191.  An
       essay.

1412.  Medicine, Bea. "The Big Foot Trail to Wounded
       Knee. " InH, 6:4 (Fall 1973), 23-25.  A poem.

1413. Medicine, Bea. The Native American Woman: A Perspective. Austin, TX: National Educational Lab, 1978.

1414. Medicine, Bea. "Red Power: Real or Potential." See entry no. 1893, pp. 299-332.

1415. Medicine, Bea. "Responsibilities of Foundations in Native American Programs." See entry no. 1893, pp. 357-364.

1416. Medicine, Bea. "The Role of Women in Native American Societies." InH, 8:3 (Summer 1975), 50-53.

1417. Milk, Albert R. "Self-Image." In "Ten Poems." BCQ, 15:3 (1969), 1.

1418. Milton, John, ed. Four Indian Poets. Vermillion: University of South Dakota Press, 1974.

1419. Morey, Sylvester M., ed. Can the Red Man Help the White Man? New York: Gilbert Church, Publisher, 1970. 113 pp. A Denver conference with Indian elders.

1420. Palaneapape. "How the Indians Are Victimized by Government Agents and Soldiers." See entry no. 1936, pp. 195-203. Taken from Senate Report No. 156, 39th Cong., 2nd Sess., pp. 366-372. Statement by Yankton Head Chief Struck-by-the-Ree.

1421. Penn, Robert. "Art and Self." SDR, 7:2 (Summer 1969), 95-96. About his own paintings.

1422. Red Cloud. "Reasons for the Trouble Between the Indians and the Government During the Ghost Dance Excitement of 1890." See entry no. 1936, pp. 263-266. By the foremost Oglala Sioux Chief.

1423. Red Cloud. "Speech at Cooper Union, New York, July 16, 1870." See entry no. 1936, pp. 211-213. An extract from the New York Times, July 17, 1870.

1424. Red Horse. "The Battle on the Little Big Horn." TB, 2 (June 1916), 587-592. By a Sioux participant.

1425.  Red Iron.  "An Interview with Governor Alexander
       Ramsey of Minnesota, December, 1852. "  See en-
       try no. 1936, pp. 163-165.  Governor refused to
       pay for Indian land, and rebuked this Sisseton chief.

1426.  Reifel, Benjamin.  "Organizing the Sioux. "  IW, June
       1939, pp. 29-30.  While a field agent explaining
       the Indian Reorganization Act to plains tribes, Reifel
       describes intra-tribal dissension over this legisla-
       tion.

1427.  Renville, Grady.  "Race. "  BCQ, 15:2 (1969), [1].
       A short poem on the meaning of Indian Power.

1428.  [Roubideau, Ramon. ]  "Bureau of Indian Affairs' Most
       Vicious Bureaucracy in History. "  GPO, March
       1969, p. 7.

1429.  Roubideau, Ramon.  "'Shake the Shackles of the BIA. ' "
       GPO, August 1969, pp. 11-13.

1430.  Shearer, Tony.  Lord of the Dawn:  Quetzalcoatl, the
       Plumed Serpent of Mexico.  Healdsburg, CA:  Na-
       turegraph, 1971.  By a Sioux author.

1431.  Shunk, Harold W.  "Reminiscing About the Dakota. "
       KQ, 3:4 (Fall 1971), 116-123.  Former teacher,
       B. I. A. Superintendent; a Yankton Sioux.

1432.  Sitting Bull.  "Keeping Treaties. "  See entry no.
       1936, p. 201.

1433.  Sitting Bull.  "A Message for the President of the
       United States, 1881. "  See entry no. 1936, 252-
       253.

1434.  Snana.  "Narration of a Friendly Sioux.  By Snana,
       the Rescuer of Mary Schwandt. "  CMHS, 9 (1901),
       427-430.  A brief autobiography by a Sioux, who
       became Mrs. Maggie Brass.

1435.  Sneve, Virginia Driving Hawk.  Betrayed.  New York:
       Holiday House, 1974.  Juvenile literature about the
       experiences of non-Indian women and children who
       fell captive to Sioux in the nineteenth century, and
       their rescue.

1436.  Sneve, Virginia Driving Hawk.  "Commentary: Some
       Thoughts on South Dakota. "  InH, 8:1 (Spring 1975),
       49.

1437.  Sneve, Virginia Driving Hawk.  Dakota's Heritage. . . .
       Sioux Falls, SD:  Brevet Press, 1973.

1438.  Sneve, Virginia Driving Hawk.  High Elk's Treasure.
       New York:  Holiday House, 1972.  96 pp.  Juvenile
       literature.

1439.  Sneve, Virginia Driving Hawk.  Jimmy Yellow Hawk.
       New York:  Holiday House, 1972.  76 pp.

1440.  Sneve, Virginia Driving Hawk.  That They May Have
       Life:  The Episcopal Church in South Dakota, 1859-
       1976.  New York:  Seabury Press, 1977.  224 pp.

1441.  Sneve, Virginia Driving Hawk.  When Thunders Spoke.
       New York:  Holiday House, 1973.

1442.  Standing Bear, Luther.  "Indian Family Life. "  See
       entry no. 1936, pp. 41-45.  From Land of the
       Spotted Eagle, pp. 84-93.

1443.  Standing Bear, Luther.  "The Tragedy of the Sioux. "
       AMe, 24 (November 1931), 273-278.  Expresses re-
       sentment for the bondage of the Sioux in 1931.

1444.  Standing Bear, Luther.  "What the Indian Means to
       America (1933). "  See entry no. 1936, pp. 306-
       308.

1445.  Stroud, David H.  We Wore Our Feathers High.
       Pine Ridge, SD:  n. p. , 1958.  25 pp.

1446.  "Taoyateduta Is Not a Coward!"  MiH, 38 (September
       1962), 115.  The speech of Chief Little Crow de-
       livered on August 18, 1862, to a group of Sioux
       who called him a coward.  This version was given
       to H. L. Gordon by Wowinapa, Chief Little Crow's
       son.

1447.  Taylor, Colin.  The Warriors of the Plains.  New
       York:  Arco Publishing Co. , 1975.  Deals with
       many Great Plains tribes, including the Sioux.

1148.   Track, Sage.  "The Clearing in the Valley. "  SDR,
        7:2 (Summer 1969), 153-170.  A story, by a Sioux-
        Pueblo from Taos.

1449.   Track, Sage.  "Indian Love Letter. "  SDR, 7:2 (Sum-
        mer 1969), 136.  A poem, by a Sioux-Pueblo from
        Taos.

1450.   Turning Hawk, Captain Sword, Spotted Horse, and
        American Horse.  "The Massacre at Wounded Knee,
        South Dakota, on December 29, 1890. "  ARBAE
        14:Pt. 2 (1896), 884-886; rpt. in entry no. 1936,
        pp. 267-271.

1451.   Twiss, Gayla.  "A Short History of Pine Ridge. "
        InH, 11:1 (Winter 1978), 36-39.

1452.   Vizenor, Gerald R.  "South Dakota:  God Have Mercy
        on You. "  GPO, October 1968, pp. 5-7.  On Thomas
        White Hawk's sentence to die.

1453.   Vizenor, Gerald R.  Thomas James White Hawk.
        Mound, MN:  The Four Winds, 1968.  A Chippewa
        writes about Thomas White Hawk, a Sioux student,
        who was convicted of murder and rape.

1454.   Volborth, J. Ivaloo.  "Lakota Group Sound Chant. "
        Alcheringa, N. S. 3:1 (1977), 100.  By an Apache-
        Comanche.

1455.   Walsh, Marnie.  The Taste of the Knife.  Boise, ID:
        Ahsahta Press, 1976.  A collection of poetry by a
        Sioux.

1456.   Wana Khun Shni (Vince Pratt).  "To Take Another
        Look. "  GPO, May 1969, p. 14.

1457.   Warcloud, Paul.  "A Description of Unity Through the
        Great Spirit. "  SDH, 2:4 (Fall 1972), 377-383.

1458.   White Buffalo Man, Frank.  "Sioux. "  IW, 1 July
        1936, p. 25.  Poem by a great-grandson of Sitting
        Bull.

1459.   White Buffalo Man, Frank.  "Two Survivors of the
        Battle of the Little Big Horn. "  IW, 15 October
        1937, pp. 41-42.  About Henry Oscar One Bull and
        Joseph White Bull.

1460. White Hawk, Thomas J. "Dream: Culture?" GPO,
      September 1970, p. 6. A poem by a young Sioux
      sentenced to die.

1461. White Hawk, Thomas J. "A Letter from the State
      Pen." GPO, September 1970, p. 7. A letter to
      a girl with scholastic problems.

1462. White Swan. "Recollections of a Famous Fight."
      TB, 1:10 (November-December 1915), 308-311. On
      the Battle of the Little Bighorn, in English transla-
      tion.

1463. White Wing, Donna. "August 24, 1963--1:00 A. M. --
      Omaha." SDR, 7:2 (Summer 1969), 106. A short
      poem.

1464. Yellow Robe. An Album of the American Indian.
      New York: Franklin Watts, Inc., 1969. 96 pp.


JUDICIAL CLAIMS, LAWS, AND TREATIES

1465. Abernathy, Alonzo. "Early Iowa Indian Treaties and
      Boundaries." AIo, 11:4 (January 1914), 241-259;
      AIo, 11:5 (April 1914), 358-380. On treaties be-
      tween Sioux and Sac and Fox.

1466. Abourezk, James. "South Dakota Indian Jurisdiction."
      SDLR, 11:1 (Winter 1966), 101-118.

1467. Anderson, Grant K. "The Black Hills Exclusion Poli-
      cy: Judicial Challenges." NH, 58:1 (Spring 1977),
      1-24. About attempts by U.S. Army to keep min-
      ers out of the Black Hills after George Custer dis-
      covered gold there.

1468. Anderson, Harry. "The Controversial Sioux Amend-
      ment to the Fort Laramie Treaty of 1851." NHM,
      37 (1956), 201-220.

1469. Baker, Daniel W. Reuben Quick Bear, Ralph Eagle
      Feather, and Charles Talkett, on Behalf of Them-
      selves and Other Members of the Rosebud Reserva-
      tion Agency. Complaints against Commissioner
      Leupp. Washington, DC: Government Printing Of-
      fice, 1906.

1470.  Baker, James H.  "Address at Fort Snelling in the
       Celebration of the Centennial Anniversary of the
       Treaty of Pike with the Sioux. "  CMHS, 12 (1908),
       291-301.  On Pike's treaty, 1805.

1471.  Bielefeld, Alvin E.  "Navigability in the Missouri
       River Basin. "  LWLR, 4:1 (1969), 97-119.  About
       Indian water rights.

1472.  Case, Francis H.  The Sioux Indians Are Entitled to
       Settlement of Their Claims.  Washington, DC:
       Government Printing Office, 1939.  A senator from
       South Dakota on Indian claims.

1473.  Case, Ralph H.  Golconda to the Whites, Golgotha to
       the Sioux!  The Treaty of Fort Laramie, Septem-
       ber, 1851.  Cheyenne River Agency, SD:  Cheyenne
       River Sioux Tribal Council, 1951.  20 pp.

1474.  Clayton, William F.  "Indian Jurisdiction and Related
       Double Jeopardy Questions. "  SDLR, 17:2 (Spring
       1972), 341-349.

1475.  Clow, Richmond L.  "General Philip Sheridan's Leg-
       acy:  The Sioux Pony Claims of 1876. "  NH, 57:4
       (Winter 1976), 461-477.

1476.  Clowser, Don C.  Dakota Indian Treaties:  The Da-
       kota Indians from Nomad to Reservation.  Dead-
       wood, SD:  Don C. Clowser, 1974.

1477.  Cragun, John W.  Petitioner's Proposed Findings of
       Fact and Brief for Yankton Sioux Tribe of Indians
       v. United States of America.  Washington, DC:
       Wilkinson, Cragun and Barker, Attorneys, 1968.

1478.  Daughters of the American Revolution.  Minnesota
       Chapter.  A Brief Sketch and History of the Sign-
       ing of the Treaty of Traverse des Sioux.  St.
       Peter:  Captain Richard Somers Chapter, D. A. R. ,
       1914.  39 pp.  On the negotiations.

1479.  Fay, George E. , ed.  Charters, Constitutions and By-
       Laws of the Indian Tribes of North America.  Part
       I.  The Sioux Tribes of South Dakota.  Greeley,
       CO:  Colorado State University, 1967.  120 pp.
       Compendium of documentation of U. S. -Sioux re-
       lationships, June 18, 1934, to April 24, 1963.

1480.  Fay, George E. , ed.  Charters, Constitutions and
       By-Laws of the Indian Tribes of North America.
       Part IIa.  The Northern Plains.  Greeley, CO:
       Colorado State University, 1967.  141 pp.  Com-
       pendium of documentation on U. S. -Indian relation-
       ships including those of North Dakota and Mon-
       tana.

1481.  Fay, George E. , ed.  A Grand Compendium of U. S.
       Congressional Documentation of Relationships be-
       tween the Bands of the Sioux and the United States.
       Greeley, CO:  University of Northern Colorado,
       1975.  Covers the period 1805 to 1854.

1482.  Fay, George E. , ed.  Treaties, and Land Cessions,
       Between the Bands of the Sioux and the United
       States of America, 1805-1906.  3 vols.  Greeley,
       CO:  Colorado State University, 1972.  323 pp.

1483.  Fisher, Robert L.  "Treaties of Portage Des Sioux. "
       MVHR, 19 (March 1933), 495-508.  In the years
       1815, 1816 and 1817.

1484.  Grass, John.  "Indian Conditions for Treaty Renewal,
       October 11, 1876. "  See entry no. 1936, pp. 232-
       234.  From Senate Exec. Doc. No. 9, 44th Cong. ,
       2nd Sess. , pp. 47-48.

1485.  Hacker, Patrick E. , Dennis C. Meier, and Dan J.
       Pauli.  "State Jurisdiction Over Indian Land Use:
       An Interpretation of the 'Encumbrance' Savings
       Clause of Public Law 280. "  LWLR, 9:1 (1974),
       421-456.

1486.  Heilbron, Bertha L.  "Frank B. Mayer and the
       Treaties of 1851. "  MiH, 22:2 (1941), 133-156.

1487.  Hoover, Herbert T.  "Yankton Sioux Tribal Claims
       Against the United States, 1917-1975. "  WHQ, 7
       (April 1976), 125-142.

1488.  Hughes, Thomas.  "The Treaty of Traverse Des Sioux
       in 1851, Under Governor Alexander Ramsey, with
       Notes of the Former Treaty There, in 1841, under
       Governor James D. Doty, of Wisconsin. "  CMHS,
       10: Pt. 1 (1905), 101-129.

1489.  Indian Claims Commission.  Sioux Indians.  Vol. 4.

Findings of Fact and Opinion. American Indian
Ethnohistory Series: The Plains Indians. New
York: Garland Publishers, 1974.

1490.   Indian Rights Association. Opposition to the Sioux
        Agreement. Philadelphia: Indian Rights Associa-
        tion, 1888. 2 pp.

1491.   Indian Rights Association. Popular Statement and Ab-
        stract of "An Act to Divide a Portion of the Reser-
        vation of the Sioux Nation of Indians, in Dakota,
        into Separate Reservations, and to Secure the Re-
        linquishment of the Indian Title to the Remainder,"
        Commonly Known as Senator Dawes' Sioux Bill.
        Philadelphia: Indian Rights Association, 1866. 7
        pp.

1492.   Indian Rights Association. The Sioux Bill. Philadel-
        phia: Indian Rights Association, 1884. 4 pp.

1493.   Indian Rights Association. The Sisseton Indians. Phil-
        adelphia: Indian Rights Association, 1891. 2 pp.

1494.   Indian Rights Association. Synopsis of the Three In-
        dian Bills Advocated. Philadelphia: Indian Rights
        Association, 1866. 7 pp.

1495.   Indian Rights Association, Executive Committee. Pro-
        test by the Executive Committee ... Against the Pas-
        sage of Senator Pettigrew's Bill for the Removal of
        the Lower Brule Indians to the Rosebud Reserve.
        Philadelphia: Indian Rights Association, 1893. 4
        pp.

1496.   Jackson, Leroy F. "Sioux Land Treaties." CHSND,
        3 (1910), 498-528. On various treaties to the year
        1859.

1497.   Johnston, Sr. Mary Antonio. Federal Relations with
        the Great Sioux Indians of South Dakota, 1887-1933,
        with Particular Reference to Land Policy under the
        Dawes Act. Washington, DC: Catholic University
        of America Press, 1948. 137 pp.

1498.   Jones, Douglas C. The Treaty of Medicine Lodge:
        The Story of the Great Treaty Council as Told by
        Eyewitnesses. Norman: University of Oklahoma

Press, 1966.  237 pp.  Deals with circumstances surrounding the negotiation of the Treaty of Fort Laramie 1868.

1499.  Kane, Lucille M.  "The Sioux Treaties and the Traders."  MiH, 32 (June 1951), 65-80.

1500.  Kappler, Charles J., ed.  Indian Affairs, Laws and Treaties.  4 vols.  Washington, DC:  Government Printing Office, 1904-1909; rpt.  2 vols.  New York: Burt Franklin, Publishers, 1967; 5 vols.  1904-1941.  New York:  AMS Press, 1971.

1501.  Kappler, Charles J.  Indian Treaties, 1778-1883.  1904; rpt.  New York:  Interland, 1975.

1502.  LeDuc, W. G.  Minnesota Year Book for 1852.  St. Paul:  W. G. LeDuc, [1852].  98 pp.  On the treaties of Traverse des Sioux and Mendota, June 3, August 5, 1851.

1503.  "Lo!  The Poor Sioux:  Claims Settled."  Time, 16 July 1945, p. 16.

1504.  McCurdy, James R.  "Federal Income Taxation and the Great Sioux Nation."  SDLR, 22:2 (Spring 1977), 296-321.  Cheyenne River attorney explains that Indians are exempted from federal taxation.

1505.  Mayer, Frank B.  With Pen and Pencil on the Frontier in 1851:  The Diary and Sketches of Frank B. Mayer.  Ed. and intro. Bertha L. Heilbron.  St. Paul:  Minnesota Historical Society, 1932.  214 pp. Dakota life, and the Treaty of Traverse des Sioux.

1506.  Morris, A.  Treaties of Canada with the Indians of Manitoba and the Northwest Territories.  Toronto: Belsfords & Clarke, 1880.

1507.  Museum of Anthropology.  Charters, Constitutions and By-Laws of the Indian Tribes of North America.  Pt. 13.  Midwestern Tribes.  Greeley:  University of Northern Colorado, 1971.  106 pp.  Includes Santee Sioux.

1508.  Museum of Anthropology.  Treaties, Land Cessions, and Other U. S. Congressional Documents Relative

to the American Tribes. No. 24. Treaties and
Land Cessions Between the Bands of the Sioux and
the United States of America, 1805-1906. In two
parts: Part 1a (1972); Part 1b (1974). Greeley:
University of North Colorado, 1978.

1509.  National Indian Defense Association. The Sioux Nation and the United States. A Brief History of the
Treaties of 1868, 1876, and 1889, Between That
Nation and the United States. Washington, DC:
n. p. , 1891. 32 pp.

1510.  Newcombe, Barbara T. "'A Portion of the American
People': The Sioux Sign a Treaty in Washington in
1858. " MiH, 45:3 (Fall 1976), 82-96.

1511.  Ogborn, Michael J. "Constitutional Implications of
an Indian Defendant's Right to a Lesser-Included
Offense Instruction. " SDLR, 16:2 (Spring 1971),
468-480. Case of U. S. vs. Antelope.

1512.  Raismes, Joseph de. "The Indian Civil Rights Act
of 1968 and the Pursuit of Responsible Tribal Self-
Government. " SDLR, 20:1 (Winter 1975), 59-105.

1513.  Richard, Clinton G. "Federal Jurisdiction over Crim-
inal Matters Involving Indians. " SDLR, 2:2 (Spring
1957), 48-58. About South Dakota Sioux.

1514.  Robinson, Will G. "Dakota Courts. " SDBJ, 30:3
(January 1962), 11-27. Important article on the
history of Sioux court cases.

1515.  Sanborn, John B. "Bishop Whipple as a Mediator for
the Rights of the Indians in Treaties. " CMHS, 10:
Pt. 2 (1905), 713-715.

1516.  Schifter, Richard. "Trends in Federal Indian Administration. " SDLR, 15:1 (Winter 1970), 1-21. Observations by a counsel to the Oglala who believes
the Indians should have freedom to develop.

1517.  Simonin, Louis Laurent. Fort Russell and Fort Laramie Peace Commission in 1867. Ed. Wilson O.
Clough. Missoula, MT: n. p. , 1931. 12 pp. An
account of Simonin's visit to Ft. Russell and his
journey to Ft. Laramie with the Peace Commission
of 1867.

1518.  "Sioux Treaty of 1868." InH, 3:1 (Winter 1970), 13-
       17.

1519.  The Sioux Tribe of Indians v. The United States. No.
       C-531-(7) Black Hills. Plaintiff's Statement of fact,
       request for special findings of fact, and brief. 2
       vols. Washington, DC: Government Printing Of-
       fice, 1937-41. Black Hills case before the U.S.
       Court of Claims.

1520.  Statement of the Claim of the State of Minnesota
       against the United States for a Part of the Expense
       Incurred in Suppressing the Indian War of 1862.
       St. Paul, MN: n.p., 1906. 11 pp.

1521.  Thayer, James B. "A People Without Law." Atlan-
       tic, 68 (1891), 540-551, 676-687. About U.S.
       treaties with Indians.

1522.  The Treaty of Traverse des Sioux with the Sioux In-
       dians on the Minnesota River, July 23, 1851. Man-
       kato, MN: Hubbard Milling Co., 1924. 19 pp.

1523.  United States. Commission Appointed to Treat with
       the Sioux Indians for the Relinquishment of the
       Black Hills. Report of the Commission Appointed
       to Treat with the Sioux Indians for the Relinquish-
       ment of the Black Hills. Washington, DC: Govern-
       ment Printing Office, 1875. 20 pp. The Commis-
       sion of Alfred H. Terry, A. Comingo, Samuel D.
       Hinman, G. P. Beauvais, A. G. Lawrence, William
       H. Ashby and J. S. Collins.

1524.  United States Congress. House. Indian Claims Com-
       mission Act. Amendment: Hearing Before the Sub-
       committee on Interior and Insular Affairs, House of
       Representatives, 49th Cong., 2nd Sess., on H.R.
       14629, September 10, 1976. Washington, DC:
       Government Printing Office, 1976. 147 pp. On
       Sioux and Wichita claims.

1525.  United States Congress. House. Committee on In-
       dian Affairs. Claims for Depredations by Sioux In-
       dians. Washington, DC: Government Printing Of-
       fice, 1864. 13 pp. Report of the Sioux Commis-
       sion of 1863, in H.R. No. 42, 38th Cong., 1st
       Sess.

1526.    United States Congress.    House.    Committee on In-
         dian Affairs.    Complaint of the Pine Ridge Sioux.
         Washington, DC:   Government Printing Office, 1920.
         61 pp.    Hearings before the Committee on Indian
         Affairs.    House of Representatives 66th Cong.,
         2nd Sess., April 6, 1920.

1527.    United States Congress.    House.    Committee on In-
         dian Affairs.    Providing for the Inclusion of Cer-
         tain Additional Names in the Roll of the Yankton
         Sioux Tribe of Indians.    Washington, DC:   Govern-
         ment Printing Office, 1932.    13 pp.    Hearings on
         H. R.  8089.

1528.    United States Congress.    House.    Committee on In-
         terior and Insular Affairs.    Authorizing the Nego-
         tiation and Ratification of Separate Settlement Con-
         tracts with the Sioux Indians of the Lower Brule
         and the Crow Creek Reservations in South Dakota
         for Indian Lands and Rights Acquired by the United
         States for the Fort Randall Dam and Reservoir,
         Missouri River Development; and to Authorize an
         Appropriation for the Removal and Reestablishment
         of the Indians of the Yankton Indian Reservation in
         South Dakota; A Report to Accompany H. R.  2231.
         Washington, DC:   Government Printing Office, 1953.
         4 pp.

1529.    United States Congress.    House.    Committee on In-
         terior and Insular Affairs.    Sioux Indian Tribes,
         North and South Dakota.    Hearings Before the Sub-
         committee on Indian Affairs Pursuant to H. Res.
         30, to ...  Make Investigations into any Matter with
         in its Jurisdiction, and for Other Purposes.  Septem-
         ber 9, 10 and 12, 1955.    Washington, DC:   Govern-
         ment Printing Office, 1956.    147 pp.

1530.    United States Congress.    Senate.    Committee on In-
         dian Affairs.    Agreement with the Yankton Sioux
         Indians of South Dakota.    Report to accompany S.
         2993.    Washington, DC:   Government Printing Of-
         fice, 1906.    19 pp.    59th Cong., 1st Sess., S. R.
         No.  2369.

1531.    United States Congress.    Senate.    Committee on In-
         dian Affairs.    Claims of Certain Sioux Indians.
         Washington, DC:   Government Printing Office, 1912.
         31 pp.    62nd Cong., 2nd Sess., S. R.  No.  449.

1532.   United States Congress.  Senate.  Committee on In-
        dian Affairs.   Petitions of Members of the Santee
        Sioux Tribe of Indians of Nebraska Praying for Pay-
        ment of Annuities Withheld from them by Reason of
        Alleged Participation in the Outbreak at Redwood
        Agency in the Year 1862.  Washington, DC:  Gov-
        ernment Printing Office, 1896.  15 pp.   54th Cong.,
        1st Sess., S. D. No. 85.

1533.   United States Congress.  Senate.  Committee on In-
        dian Affairs.  Mdewakanton and Wahpakoota (Santee)
        Sioux Indians.  Washington, DC:  Government Print-
        ing Office, 1908.  10 pp.   60th Cong., 1st Sess.,
        S. R. 468.

1534.   United States Congress.  Senate.  Committee on In-
        dian Affairs.  Mdewakanton and Wahpakoota (Santee)
        Sioux Indians.  Washington, DC:  Government Print-
        ing Office, 1910.  9 pp.   61st Cong., 2nd Sess.,
        S. R. No. 304.

1535.   United States Congress.  Senate.  Committee on Indian
        Affairs.  Payment to Sisseton and Wahpeton Bands
        of Sioux Indians for Certain Lands.  Washington,
        DC:  Government Printing Office, 1939.  9 pp.
        Hearing on S. No. 2085, for land ceded, July 23,
        1851.

1536.   United States Congress.  Senate.  Committee on In-
        dian Affairs.  Restoration of Forfeited Annuities
        to the Santee Sioux Indians.  Washington, DC:
        Government Printing Office, 1902.  8 pp.   57th
        Cong., 1st Sess., Sen. Doc. No. 243.

1537.   United States Court of Claims.  Mdewakanton and Wah-
        pakoota Bands of Sioux Indians, Otherwise Known as
        Santee Sioux Indians, Plaintiffs v. The United
        States ... March 6, 1917-June 5, 1922.  Washing-
        ton, DC:  Government Printing Office, 1917-1922.
        Court of Claims No. 33728.

1538.   United States Court of Claims.  The Sioux Tribe of
        Indians v. the United States.  No. C-531-(7).
        Black Hills Plaintiff's Statement of Fact, Request
        for Special Findings of Facts, and Brief.  2 vols.
        Washington, DC:  Government Printing Office, 1937-
        41.

1539.   United States Court of Claims.  The United States v.
        the Sisseton and Wahpeton Bands of Sioux Indians.
        Appeals from the Court of Claims.  Washington,
        DC:  Government Printing Office,  1907-08.  Claims
        for annuities granted by treaty in 1851 but declared
        forfeited by Act of February 16, 1863 (12 Stat. 652);
        includes opinion of the court and brief, for the im-
        portant "Santee Claim. "

1540.   United States Department of the Interior.  Instructions
        to the Special Commission Appointed to Visit the
        Indian Country in the Neighborhood of Fort Phil
        Kearney.  Washington, DC:  Government Printing
        Office,  1867.  3 pp.

1541.   United States Department of the Interior.  Readjudica-
        tion of Special Individual Sioux Personal Property
        Claims.  2 vols.  Washington, DC:  Government
        Printing Office, 1944.  Texts and summary of pay-
        ment on claims under Act of May 3, 1938 (45
        Stat. 484); Pony Claims, etc.

1542.   United States Department of the Interior.  Report of
        the Secretary of the Interior ...  Relative to the
        Allegations of Fraud by Alexander Ramsey, Super-
        intendent of Indian Affairs, in the Disbursement of
        Money Appropriated for the Fulfillment of Treaties
        with the Sioux Indians.  Washington, DC:  Govern-
        ment Printing Office,  1853.  32nd Cong. , 2nd
        Sess. , Sen. Ex. Doc. no. 29, Ser. no. 660.

1543.   United States Office of Indian Affairs.  Encounter Be-
        tween Sioux Indians of the Pine Ridge Agency, S.
        Dak. , and a Sheriff's Posse of Wyoming.  Washing-
        ton, DC:  Government Printing Office, 1904.  134
        pp.

1544.   Veeder, William H.  "Confiscation of Indian Water
        Rights in the Upper Missouri River Basin. "  SDLR,
        21:2 (Spring 1976), 282-309.  Continued violation of
        Indian rights.

1545.   Waggoner, Alvin.  "The Sioux Shortage Cases. "
        SDBJ, 8:3 (January 1940), 46-50.  Shortage of
        money given the Sioux for claims against the United
        States.

1546.   Welsh, Herbert. The Action of the Interior Depart-
        ment in Forcing the Standing Rock Indians to Lease
        Their Lands to Cattle Syndicates.    Philadelphia:
        Indian Rights Association, 1902.   27 pp.

1547.   Ziontz, Alvin J.   "In Defense of Tribal Sovereignty:
        An Analysis of Judicial Error in Construction of
        the Indian Civil Rights Act."   SDLR, 20:1 (Winter
        1975),  1-58.


                        LANGUAGE

1548.   Allen, Louis.  "Siouan and Iroquoian."  IJAL,  6
        (1931), 185-193.   Suggests a genetic connection be-
        tween Siouan and Iroquoian languages.

1549.   Allison, Edward H.  "Sioux Proper Names."  CHSSD,
        6 (1912),  275-278.

1550.   Amon, Aline.  Talking Hands:  Indian Sign Language.
        Garden City,  NY:   Doubleday and Co. ,  1968.   Ju-
        venile literature.

1551.   Axtell, Juliet L.   The Indian Sign Language and the
        Invention of Mr.  Lewis F.  Hadley, as Applied to the
        Speedy Christian Civilization and Education of the
        Wild Adult Indians.   Chicago:   Western Label Co. ,
        1891.

1552.   Bailey, J. B.   J. B. Bailey's Price List.   Yankton,
        Dakota Territory:   n. p. ,  1888.   A broadside, ap-
        parently translated by John P.  Williamson.

1553.   Berthel, Mary Elizabeth (Whellhouse).   "Indian Names
        on Our State Map."   GH,  6:2 (1941),  4.

1554.   Berthel, Mary Elizabeth (Whellhouse).   "Place Names
        of the Mille Lacs Region. "   MiH,  21 (December
        1940),  345-352.   Names from both Chippewa and
        Sioux.

1555.   Binford, Lewis R.   " Comments on the 'Siouan Prob-
        lem. ' "   E,  6 (1959),  28.   A linguistic problem, on
        whether Occaneechie, Saponi, and Tutelo are Siouan
        or Algonquian.

1556.   Boas, Franz, ed. Handbook of American Indian Lan-
        guages. 2 parts. 1922; rpt. New York: Human-
        ities Press, Inc. , 1969. 1069 pp. /903 pp.

1557.   Boas, Franz. Race, Language and Culture. 1940;
        rpt. New York: Free Press, 1966. 647 pp.

1558.   Boas, Franz. "Some Traits of the Dakota Language. "
        Language, 13 (1937), 137-141; rpt. in No. 1557,
        pp. 226-231. With reference to the work of Ella
        C. Deloria on language.

1559.   Boas, Franz, and Ella Deloria. "Dakota Grammar. "
        MNAS, 23:2 (1941), 1-183; rpt. Vermillion, SD:
        Dakota Press, 1979.

1560.   Boas, Franz, and Ella Deloria. "Notes on the Da-
        kota, Teton Dialect. " IJAL, 7 (1932), 97-121.

1561.   Boas, Franz, and John R. Swanton. "Siouan Dakota
        (Teton and Santee Dialects): With Remarks on the
        Ponca and Winnebago. " In Handbook of American
        Indian Languages. Part I. Washington, DC: Gov-
        ernment Printing Office, 1911, pp. 875-965.

1562.   Boas, Franz, and John R. Swanton. Siouan--Teton
        and Santee Dialects--Dakota. 1911; rpt. Seattle,
        WA: Shorey Publications, 1970.

1563.   Buechel, Fr. Eugene. A Dictionary of the Teton
        Dakota Sioux Language. Ed. Paul Manhart.
        Pine Ridge, SD: Red Cloud Indian School, 1970.
        852 pp. Lakota-English: English-Lakota, with
        considerations given to Yankton and Santee.

1564.   Buechel, Fr. Eugene. A Grammar of Lakota. St.
        Louis: John S. Swift, Co. , 1939. 374 pp.

1565.   Buechel, Fr. Eugene. Wowapi Wakan Wicowayake
        Yuptecelapi Kin. New York: Benziger Bros. ,
        1924. 349 pp. Bible history in Lakota dialect.

1566.   Burman, William Alfred. The Sioux Language.
        Winnipeg, Manitoba: Free Press Print, 1883. 4
        pp.

1567.   Cassidy, Frederic G. "The Names of Green Bay,

Wisconsin. " Names, 21:3 (September 1973), 168-
178. Includes Siouan.

1568.  Chafe, Wallace. "Another Look at Siouan and Iroquoian. " AA, 66:4 (August 1964), 852-862.

1569.  Chafe, Wallace. "Language and Linguistics. " In
Introduction to Cultural Anthropology. Ed. James
A. Clifton. Boston: Houghton Mifflin, 1968, pp.
49-75. Most examples are from Dakota.

1570.  Chafe, Wallace. "Siouan, Iroquoian, and Caddoan. "
In Current Trends in Linguistics. Vol. 10. Linguistics in North America. Ed. William Bright, et
al. The Hague: Mouton, 1973, pp. 1164-1209.

1571.  Chamberlain, Alexander F. "Acquisition of Written
Languages by Primitive Peoples. " AJP, 17:1 (January 1906), 69-80. Includes Siouan.

1572.  Clark, Ann (Nolan). About the Slim Butte Raccoon.
Paha zizipela wic'iteglega kin. Lawrence, KS:
Haskell Institute Printing Department, 1942. 81
pp. A reader.

1573.  Clark, Ann (Nolan). Brave Against the Enemy: A
Story of Three Generations. Toka wan itkokip
ohitike kin he. Lawrence, KS: Haskell Institute
Printing Department, 1944. 215 pp. ; rpt. Lawrence, KS: Publications Service, Haskell Institute,
1963. 94 pp.

1574.  Clark, Ann (Nolan). The Grass Mountain Mouse.
Illus. Andrew Standing Soldier. Lawrence, KS:
Haskell Institute, U. S. Bureau of Indian Affairs,
1954. 108 pp. In Sioux language with English
translation.

1575.  Clark, Ann (Nolan). The Hen of Wahpeton. Ill.
Andrew Standing Soldier. Lawrence, KS: Haskell
Institute, U. S. Bureau of Indian Affairs, 1954.
97 pp. In Sioux language with English translation.

1576.  Clark, Ann (Nolan). The Pine Ridge Porcupine.
Wazi ahanhan p'ahin k'un he. Lawrence, KS:
Haskell Institute Printing Department, 1941. 73
pp.

1577.    Clark, Ann (Nolan).  Singing Sioux Cowboy Reader.
         Drawings Andrew Standing Soldier, text Emil Afraid-
         of-Hawk.  Lawrence, KS:  U. S.  Indian Service,
         1947.  114 pp.

1578.    Clark, Ann (Nolan).  There Are Still Buffalo.  Na-
         hanhio pte yuk onpi.  Lawrence, KS:  Haskell In-
         stitute Printing Department, 1942.  96 pp.

1579.    Cleveland, William Joshua, comp.  Original Sioux
         Letters with English Translations.  Madison, SD:
         The Daily Leader Print, 1894.  32 pp.  Taken
         from Daybreak (Anpaokin).

1580.    Congregational Winyan ptaya omniciye.  Woiciconze
         qa Woope.  Constitution and by-laws, general so-
         ciety.  Santee, NB:  Santee Normal Training School
         Press, 1897.  6 pp.  Printed in both Sioux and
         English languages.

1581.    Darnell, Regna.  "The Powell Classification of Amer-
         ican Indian Languages. "  PIL, 4 (July 1971), 71-98.
         A survey of Powell's classification method.

1582.    Darnell, Regna.  "The Revision of the Powell Classi-
         fication. "  PIL, 4 (October 1971), 233-257.

1583.    Darnell, Regna, and Joel Sherzer.  "Areal Linguistic
         Studies in North America:  A Historical Perspec-
         tive. "  IJAL, 37 (1971), 20-28.

1584.    Davis, Irvine.  "The Native Languages of America:
         A Survey of Recent Studies. "  Phonetica, 7:1 (1961),
         40-63.

1585.    Dorsey, James Owen.  "Indian Personal Names. "
         AA, 3:3 (July 1890), 263-268.

1586.    Dorsey, James Owen.  "On the Comparative Phonol-
         ogy of Four Siouan Languages. "  ARSI (1883), pp.
         919-929.  On the four Siouan dialects:  Dakota,
         Çegiha, Tchiwere, and Tutelo.

1587.    Dorsey, James Owen.  "Siouan Onomatopes. "  AA,
         5:1 (January 1892), 1-8.  A word formed to re-
         semble the sound made by the thing signified.

1588.  Dorsey, James Owen, A. S. Gatschet, and S. R.
       Riggs. "Illustration of the Method of Recording
       Indian Languages. " ARBAE, 1 (1881), 579-587.

1589.  Driver, Harold E. , and William C. Massey. "Lin-
       guistic Classification" and "Linguistic Families. "
       In Indian Tribes of North America. Baltimore:
       Waverly Press, 1953, pp. 8-14.

1590.  Dunbar, William. "On the Language of Signs Among
       Certain North American Indians. " TAPS, 6 (1801),
       1-3.  On the use of sign language by trans-
       Mississippi Indian tribes.

1591.  Elmendorf, William W. "Item and Set Comparison of
       Yuchi, Siouan, and Yukian. " IJAL, 30 (1964), 328-
       340.

1592.  Elmendorf, William W. "Yukian-Siouan Lexical Simi-
       larities. " IJAL, 29 (1963), 300-309.

1593.  An English-Dakota Dictionary.  Compiled by Working
       Indians Civil Association, Inc.  Ft. Pierre, SD:
       Working Indian Civil Association, Inc. , 1969.  264
       pp.  Includes grammar.

1594.  Finlay, James A.  Price List.  Pine Ridge, SD:
       Pine Ridge Agency, 1891.  8 pp.

1595.  Gabelentz, Hans C.  Grammatik der Dakota-Sprache.
       Leipzig:  F. A.  Brockhaus, 1852.  64 pp.

1596.  Gilmore, Melvin R.  "Meaning of the Word 'dakota. ' "
       AA, 24 (1922), 242-245.

1597.  Gilmore, Melvin R.  "Some Indian Place Names in
       Nebraska. "  PNSHS, 19 (1919), 130-139.  Many
       names in Sioux.

1598.  Goddard, Pliny Earle.  "The Present Condition of Our
       Knowledge of North American Languages. "  AA, 16
       (1914),  555-601.

1599.  Goshe, Frederick.  Sioux Indian Language, Grammar
       and Vocabulary.  Rev. ed.  1964; rpt. Palo Alto,
       CA:  n. p. , 1967.  86 pp.

1600.  Haas, Mary R.  "Athapascan, Tlingit, Uchi, and
       Siouan. "  ICA, 35:Vol. 2 (1962), 495-500.

1601.  Haas, Mary R.  "The Proto-Gulf Word for Water
       (With Notes on Siouan-Yucki). "  IJAL, 17 (1951),
       71-79.

1602.  Hayden, Ferdinand V.  Contributions to the Ethnogra-
       phy and Philology of the Indian Tribes of the Mis-
       souri Valley.  Philadelphia:  C. Sherman and Son,
       1862.  461 pp.  Includes Sioux vocabulary.

1603.  Hinman, Samuel D.  Calvary Wiwicawangupi Wowapi,
       &c. (Calvary Catechism in the Dakota Language).
       Faribault, MN:  Central Republican Office, 1864.
       50 pp.

1604.  Hinman, Samuel D.  Ikce Wocekiye Wowapi  Qa
       Isantanka Makoce.  Kin en Token Wohduze, qa
       Okodakiciye Wakan en Tonakiya Woccon kin, hena
       de he Wowapi kin ee.  St. Paul, MN:  Pioneer
       Printing Co. , 1865.  321 pp.  Translation of The
       Book of Common Prayer.

1605.  Hinman, Samuel D.  Hymns in Dakota.  n. p. :  Indian
       Commission of the Protestant Episcopal Church,
       1881.  127 pp.

1606.  Hoijer, Harry.  "Anthropological Linguistics. "  In
       Trends in European and American Linguistics 1930-
       1960.  Ed. Christine Mohrmann, Alf Sommerfelt,
       and Joshua Whatmough.  Utrecht, Netherlands:
       Spectrum Publishers, 1961, pp. 110-127.  A gen-
       eral review of linguistics' theories about Indian lan-
       guages.

1607.  Hoijer, Harry.  "History of American Indian Linguis-
       tics. "  In Current Trends in Linguistics.  Vol. 10.
       Ed. Thomas A. Sebeok.  The Hague:  Mouton, 1973,
       pp. 657-677.

1608.  Hoijer, Harry.  "Some Problems of American Indian
       Linguistic Research. "  UCPL, 10: No. 1 (1954), 3-
       12.  Addresses the existence of linguistic families.

1609.  Holmer, Nils M.  "Lexical and Morphological Contacts
       Between Siouan and Algonquian. "  Lunds Universitet

Arsskrift, 1919; rpt. Lund: C. W. K. Gleerup, 1949. 39 pp.

1610. Huggins, Eliza Eilson, comp. Dakota Text-Book, Waniyetu, Modoketu iyahna anpetu otoiyohi on oehde wanjidan wowapi wakan etanhan. New York: American Tract Society, 1872.

1611. Hyer, Joseph D., and Charles Guerreu. Dictionary of the Sioux Language. 1866; rpt. New York: Printed Privately for F. D. Potter, [1931]. 34 pp. Words collected in 1866.

1612. Karol, Joseph S., and Stephen L. Rozman, eds. Everyday Lakota: An English-Sioux Dictionary for Beginners. Lincoln: Nebraska Curriculum Development Center, University of Nebraska, 1971. 122 pp.

1613. Katolik Wocekiye. Sioux Falls, SD: Brown and Saenger, 1890. 44 pp. A Dakota prayer book.

1614. Kinkade, M. Dale. "Indian Languages at Haskell Institute." IJAL, 36 (1970), 46-52.

1615. Kroeber, Alfred J. "On Typological Indices I: Ranking of Languages." IJAL, 26:3 (1960), 171-177.

1616. Lakota Wocekiye na olowan wowapi. St. Louis: Central Bureau of the Catholic Central Verein of America, 1927. 386 pp. Sioux prayer and hymn book with an appendix of English prayers and hymns by Jesuit Fathers at St. Francis Mission on Rosebud Reservation.

1617. Levin, Norman Balfour. "Problems in the Linguistic Description of Nakota." ICA, 36: Vol. 2 (1964), 213-215. A dialect of Siouan.

1618. Ljung, Magnus. "Principles of a Stratificational Analysis of the Plains Indian Sign Language." IJAL, 31 (1965), 119-127.

1619. Lord, Mary P. Sunkawakan Wicayuhapi. Santee, NB: Santee Normal Training School Press, 1894. 8 pp.

1620.   McGillycuddy, Valentine T.   "Black Hills Names. "
        CHSSD, 6 (1912), 273-274.   Included many names
        in Sioux.

1621.   Mallery, Garrick.   "Sign Language Among North
        American Indians Compared with that Among Other
        Peoples and Deaf Mutes. "   ARBAE, 1 (1881), 263-
        552; rpt. The Hague:   Mouton, 1972.

1622.   Mallery, Garrick.   "The Sign Language of the Indians
        of the Upper Missouri, in 1832. "   AAOJ, 2 (1879),
        218-228.

1623.   Matteson, Esther, et al.   Comparate Studies in Amer-
        indian Languages.   The Hague:   Mouton, 1972.
        251 pp.

1624.   Matthews, G. Hubert.   "A phonemic Analysis of A
        Dakota Dialect. "   IJAL, 21 (1955), 56-59.   From
        Reuben Jacobs, a Yankton-Teton Sioux.

1625.   Matthews, G. Hubert.   "Proto-Siouan Kinship Termin-
        ology. "   AA, 61:2 (April 1959), 252-278.   Divides
        Siouan languages into groups, and includes linguis-
        tic notes.

1626.   Matthews, G. Hubert.   "Some Notes on the Proto-
        Siouan Continuants. "   IJAL, 36 (1970), 98-109.

1627.   Meagher, Tom.   "Proper Classification of Indian
        Tribes of North America. "   AIn, 3:No. 11 (August
        1929), 14-15; No. 12 (September 1929), 14-15.   In-
        cludes 58 linguistic families.

1628.   Newton, Richard.   The King's Highway.   Yankton
        Agency, Dakota Territory:   St. Paul's School Press,
        1879.   429 pp.   Translated by Daniel Hemans,
        edited by Joseph Cook; in Santee Sioux dialect.

1629.   Peterson, Karen D. , ed.   "Ojibway and Dakota Place
        Names in Minnesota. "   MA, 15:1 (1963), 5-40.

1630.   Plaut, W. Gunther.   "A Hebrew-Dakota Dictionary. "
        American Jewish Historical Society Publication, 42
        (June 1953), 361-370.   The work of Samuel W.
        Pond, 1842.

1631.  Pond, Gideon H.  The Dakota Friend (Dakota Tawaxit-
       ka kin).  St. Paul, MN:  The Dakota Mission, 1850-
       1852.  A bilingual monthly paper edited by Gideon
       Pond and published in twenty numbers.

1632.  Pond, Gideon H. , and Samuel W. Pond.  Joseph
       Oyakapi Kin.  The story of Joseph and His Brethren,
       translated from Genesis by Revs. Gideon H. and
       Samuel W. Pond.  Cincinnati, OH:  Kendall and
       Henry, 1839.  40 pp.

1633.  Pond, Gideon H. , and Stephen R. Riggs.  The Dakota
       First Reading Book.  Cincinnati, OH:  Kendall and
       Henry, 1839.  50 pp.

1634.  Pond, Samuel W.  Dakota Wangapi Wowapi.  Cate-
       chism in the Dakota or Sioux Language.  New Haven,
       CT:  Hitchcock and Stafford, 1844.  12 pp.

1635.  Pond, Samuel W.  Legends of the Dakotas, and Other
       Selections from the Poetical Works of Reverend
       Samuel Pond.  Minneapolis:  K. C. Holter Publish-
       ing Co. , 1911.  152 pp.

1636.  Pond, Samuel W.  Wowapi Inonpa.  The Second Da-
       kota Reading Book, consisting of Bible stories from
       the Old Testament.  Boston:  Crocker and Brew-
       ster, 1842.  54 pp.

1637.  Ravoux, Fr. A.  Wakantanka Ti Ki Canku.  [Path to
       Heaven].  2nd ed.  St. Paul, MN:  Pioneer Printing
       Co. , 1863.  88 pp.

1638.  Renville, John B.  Woonspe Itakihna Ihakeun Okaga.
       "Precept Upon Precept. "  Translated into Dakota,
       by Stephen Return Riggs.  Boston:  American Tract
       Society, 1864.  228 pp.

1639.  Renville, Joseph.  Dakota Dowanpi kin.  Hymns in
       the Dakota or Sioux Language.  Trans. Alfred L.
       Riggs.  Boston:  Printed for the American Board
       of Commissioners for Foreign Missions, by Crocker
       and Brewster, 1842.  97 pp.

1640.  Renville, Joseph, trans.  Extracts from Genesis and
       the Psalms:  With the Third Chapter of Proverbs,
       and the Third Chapter of Daniel, In the Dakota

Language. Cincinnati, OH: Kendall and Henry,
1839. 72 pp. The first significant efforts to write
Sioux language were accomplished by trader Joseph
Renville and Presbyterian missionary Thomas S.
Williamson. Renville translated French Biblical
text into Dakota while Williamson wrote for publication.

1641. Renville, Joseph, and Thomas S. Williamson. Extracts from the Gospels of Matthew, Luke, and
John, from the Acts of the Apostles, and from the
First Epistle of John, in the Language of the Dakota or Sioux Indians. Cincinnati, OH: Kendall
and Henry, 1839. 48 pp.

1642. Renville, Joseph, and Thomas S. Williamson. Wiconi
Owihanke Wanin Tanin Kin. Boston: Crocker and
Brewster, 1837. 23 pp. Contains Dr. Watts'
Second Catechism for children, translated into Da-
kota dialect.

1643. Renville, Joseph, and Thomas S. Williamson. Wo-
tanin Waxte Markus Owa Kin. The Gospel According to Mark, in the Language of the Dakotas.
Cincinnati, OH: Kendall and Henry, 1839. 96 pp.

1644. Riggs, Alfred L. Congregational Tacanku kin Hunka-
wanjinkiciyapi Okadakiciye. The Congregational
Way. Santee, NB: Santee Normal Training School
Press, 1910. 7 pp.

1645. Riggs, Alfred R. Wicoie Wowapi Kin. The Word
Book. New York: American Tract Society, 1881.
49 pp.

1646. Riggs, Frederick B. Tukten Wayawapi Kte He. Santee, NB: Santee Normal Training School Press,
n. d. Broadside in Dakota dialect about education
for Indians.

1647. Riggs, Mary Ann Clare. Eliza Marpi-cokawin, Rara-
tonwan Oyato en Wapiye Sa: qa Sara Warpanica
qon. A Narrative of Pious Indian Women. Boston:
Crocker and Brewster, 1842. 12 pp.

1648. Riggs, Mary Ann Clare. An English and Dakota Vocabulary. New York: R. Craighead, 1852. 120 pp.

1649.   Riggs, Stephen R.   The Book of Psalms.   Trans.
        from Hebrew into Dakota language.   New York:
        American Bible Society, 1869.   133 pp.

1650.   Riggs, Stephen R. , trans.   Cante teca.   The Pil-
        grim's Progress.   New York:   American Tract
        Society, 1892.

1651.   Riggs, Stephen R.   The Constitution of Minnesota,
        in the Dakota Language.   Boston:   Press of T. R.
        Marvin and Son, 1856.   36 pp.

1652.   Riggs, Stephen R.   Dakota ABC.   Wowapi kin.   Tam-
        akoce Kaga.   Chicago:   Dean and Ottaway, Steam
        Printers, 1866; rpt.   Santee, NB:   Santee Normal
        Training School Press, 1929.   40 pp.

1653.   Riggs, Stephen R.   The Dakota First Reading Book.
        Cincinnati,  OH:   Kendall and Henry,  Printers,
        1839.   56 pp.

1654.   Riggs, Stephen R.   Dakota Grammar, Texts, and
        Ethnography.   Ed.  James Owen Dorsey,  CNAE,  9
        (1893); rpt.  Marvin,  SD:   Blue Cloud Abbey, 1977.
        239 pp.

1655.   Riggs, Stephen R.   "The Dakota Language. "   CMHS,
        1 (1872), 89-107.   Written in 1850.

1656.   Riggs, Stephen R.   Dakota Odowan.   Hymns in Da-
        kota language with tunes.   New York:   American
        Tract Society, 1855.   127 pp.

1657.   Riggs, Stephen R.   Dakota Sioux-English Dictionary.
        1890; Rpt. facsimile ed.   Minneapolis:   Ross and
        Haines, 1968.   664 pp.

1658.   Riggs, Stephen R.   Dakota Tawoonspe.   Wowapi I.
        Tamakoce Kaga.   Dakota Lessons.   Book I.
        Louisville, KY:   Morton and Griswold, 1850.   48
        pp.

1659.   Riggs, Stephen R.   Dakota Tawoonspe.   Wowapi II.
        Dakota Lessons.   Book II.   Louisville,  KY:   Mor-
        ton and Griswold, 1850.   48 pp.

1660.   Riggs, Stephen R.   Dakota Wiwicawangapi Kin.   Dakota catechism. New York: American Tract Society, 1864. 36 pp.

1661. Riggs, Stephen R. Dakota Wowapi Wakan Kin. The New Testament in the Dakota Language; trans. from the original Greek. New York: American Bible Society, 1865; rpt. New York: American Bible Society, 1913. 408 pp. Contains Genesis and Proverbs, also, in Dakota dialect.

1662. Riggs, Stephen R. Grammar and Dictionary of the Dakota Language. SCK, 4 (1852); rpt. Barrington, IL: Peter Wolff, 1976. 338 pp.

1663. Riggs, Stephen R. Jesus Ohnihdewicaye Cin Aranyanpi Qon: Qa Palos Wowapi Kagi ciqon; nakun, Jan Woyake ciqon dena cepi. Tamakoce Okaga. The Acts of the Apostles, and the Epistles of Paul; with the Revelation of John; in the Dakota language, translated from Greek. Cincinnati, OH: Kendall and Barnard, 1843. 228 pp.

1664. Riggs, Stephen R. Model First Reader. Wayawa Tokaheya. Chicago: G. Sherwood and Co., 1873. 112 pp. In English and Santee dialect.

1665. Riggs, Stephen R. Woonspe Itakihna. Ehakeun okaga. "Precept upon Precept" in Dakota dialect. Boston: American Tract Society, n. d. 228 pp.

1666. Riggs, Stephen R. Wowapi Mitawa: Tamakoce kaga. Boston: Crocker and Brewster, 1842. 64 pp. Prepared in Dakota language from "Mother's Primer" and "Child's Picture Defining and Reading Book."

1667. Riggs, Stephen R. Wowapi Nitawa. Your Own Book. A Dakota Primer for schools. Minneapolis: n. p., 1862. 32 pp.

1668. Riggs, Stephen R., and Gideon H. Pond. The Dakota First Reading Book. Cincinnati: Kendall and Henry, 1839. 39 pp.

1669. Riggs, Stephen R., and Alfred R. Riggs, trans. Makaoyakapi. [Arnold Henry] Guyot's Elementary Geography, in Dakota dialect. New York: Scribner, Armstrong and Co., 1876.

1670.   Riggs, Stephen R., and John P. Williamson, eds.
        Dakota Odowan.   Hymns in the Dakota Language.
        New York:   American Tract Society, 1863.   162
        pp.

1671.   Riggs, Theodore F.   Woyazanska.   Tuberculosis.
        Santee, NB:   Santee Normal Training School Press,
        1908.   11 pp.

1672.   Roehrig, Frederic Louis Otto.   "On the Language of
        the Dakota or Sioux Indians."   ARSI (1871), pp.
        434-450; rpt. Washington, DC:   Government Print-
        ing Office, 1872.   19 pp.   Taken from Sioux living
        in the north, near Fort Wadsworth.

1673.   Roth, David D.   "Lakota Sioux Terms for White and
        Negro."   PlA, 20:68 (May 1975), 117-120.

1674.   Rudes, Blair A.   "Sound Changes Separating Siouan-
        Yuchi from Iroquois-Caddoan."   IJAL, 40 (April
        1974), 117-119.

1675.   Rydjord, John.   Indian Place-Names; Their Origin,
        Evolution, and Meanings, Collected in Kansas from
        the Siouan, Algonquian, Shoshonean, Caddoan, Iro-
        quoian, and Other Tongues.   Norman:   University
        of Oklahoma Press, 1968.

1676.   Sapir, Edward.   "A Bird's-Eye View of American
        Languages North of Mexico."   S, n. s. 54 (October
        1921), 408.   Identifies six great groups of lan-
        guages, including Hokan-Siouan.

1677.   Sherzer, Joel, and Richard Bauman.   "Areal Studies
        and Culture History:   Language as a Key to the
        Historical Study of Culture Contact."   SJA, 28
        (1972), 131-152.

1678.   "Sioux Proper Names."   CHSSD, 6 (1912), 275-278.

1679.   Stark, Donald S.   "Boundary Markers in Dakota."
        IJAL, 28 (1962), 19-35.

1680.   Stevens, Jedidiah D.   Sioux Spelling Book, Designed
        for the Use of Native Learners.   Boston:   Crocker
        and Brewster, 1836.   22 pp.

1681.   Stuart, C. L. J. M. "American Indian Languages at
        Haskell Institute. " IJAL, 28 (1962), 151.

1682.   Swadesh, Morris. "Toward a Satisfactory Genetic
        Classification of Amerindian Languages. " ICA, 31
        (1954), 1001-1012.

1683.   Swadesh, Morris, et al. "Symposium:   Time Depths
        of American Linguistic Groupings. " AA, 56 (1954),
        361-377.

1684.   Taylor, Allan R. "Note Concerning Lakota Sioux
        Terms for White and Negro. " PlA, 21:71 (Febru-
        ary 1976), 63-65.   A comment on David Roth's
        article, No. 1673.

1685.   Tomkins, William.   Universal Indian Sign Language
        of the Plains Indians of North America.   18th ed.
        San Diego, CA: Neyenesch Printers, 1970.   106 pp.

1686.   Tooker, William Wallace. "The Algonquian Appella-
        tives of the Siouan Tribes of Virginia. " AA, 8:4
        (October 1895), 376-392.

1687.   Tooker, William Wallace.   The Algonquian Names of
        the Siouan Tribes of Virginia:   With Historical and
        Ethnological Notes.   New York: F. P. Harper,
        1901.   83 pp.

1688.   Trumbull, J. Hammond.   "On Numerals in American
        Indian Languages, and the Indian Mode of Counting. "
        TAPA, 5 (1874), 41-76.   Interesting article with
        examples from many tribes.

1689.   United Society of Christian Endeavor.   Jesus Htakini-
        wacinskanpi Okodakiciye Woope Kin.   Santee, NB:
        Santee Normal Training School Press, 1890.   16
        pp.   Constitution and by-laws in Dakota-English;
        text by Alfred Riggs.

1690.   United States en Woicicage kin (Ieska Owapi).   Santee,
        NB:   Santee Normal Training School Press, 1888.
        47 pp.   The U. S. Constitution translated into Da-
        kota dialect by James W. Garvie.

1691.   Voegelin, C. F. "Influence of Area in American In-
        dian Linguistics. " Word, 1 (1945), 54-58; rpt. in

Language in Culture and Society. Ed. Dell Hymes.
New York: Harper and Row, 1964, pp. 638-641.
On how the area affected the study of Siouan and
four other linguistic families.

1692. Voegelin, C. F. "Internal Relationships of Siouan
Languages." AA, 43 (1941), 246-249.

1693. Voegelin, C. F., and Dell H. Hymes. "A Sample of
North American Indian Dictionaries with Reference
to Acculturation." PAPS, 97:5 (October 1953),
634-644.

1694. Voegelin, C. F., and F. M. Voegelin. "Languages
of the World: Native American Fascicle One."
AnL, 6:No. 6 (June 1964), 1-149; "Native American
Fascicle Two." 7:No. 7 (October 1965), 1-150.
Listing of linguistic families.

1695. Voegelin, C. F., et al. "Obtaining an Index of
Phonological Differentiation from the Construction
of Non-Existent Minimax Systems." IJAL, 29
(1963), 4-28.

1696. Walker, James R. "Oglala Kinship Terms." AA,
16:1 (January-March 1914), 96-109. An extensive
text in Sioux language.

1697. Walker, Jerell R. "The Sign Language of the Plains
Indians of North America." CO, 31 (1953), 168-
177.

1698. Warcloud, Paul. Sioux Dictionary: Over 4,000 Words.
Pronunciation-at-a-Glance. Pierre, SD: State Publishing Co., 1971. 172 pp.

1699. Watts, Isaac. Wiconi Owihanke Wannin Tanin Kin.
Boston: Crocker and Brewster, 1837. 23 pp.
Dr. Watt's second catechism for children, trans-
lated into Dakota by Joseph Renville and Thomas
Williamson.

1700. Williamson, Andrew W. "The Dakotah an Indo-
European Language." AAOJ, 11 (1889), 246-248.
A letter to the editor on language.

1701. Williamson, Andrew W. "The Dakotan Languages, and

Their Relations to Other Languages. " AAOJ, 4
(1882), 110-128. Important early article.

1702. Williamson, Andrew W. Minnesota Geographical
Names Derived from the Dakota Language, with
Some That Are Obsolete. St. Paul: The Pioneer
Press Co., 1885. 8 pp. Extracted from the Thir-
teenth Annual Report of the Geological and Natural
History Survey of Minnesota, 1884.

1703. Williamson, John P. An English-Dakota Dictionary.
Wasicun ka Dakota Ieska Wowapi. New York:
American Tract Society, 1902. 264 pp.

1704. Williamson, John P. An English-Dakota School Dictionary. Yankton Agency, Dakota Territory: Iapi
Oaye Press, 1886. 144 pp.

1705. Williamson, John P. English-Dakota Vocabulary.
Wasicun ka Iapi Ieska Wowapi. Santee, NB: Santee Agency, 1871. 137 pp.

1706. Williamson, John P. "The Letters of John P. Williamson. " MA, 20 (January 1956), 1-21.

1707. Williamson, John P. Oowa Wowapi. The Book of
Letters; an illustrated School Book. New York:
American Tract Society, 1864. 84 pp.

1708. Williamson, John P. "The Outlook for Dakota. "
CHSSD, 3 (1906), 49-58. In this address, the
eminent missionary bared his feelings about Sioux
religion and culture.

1709. Williamson, John P. Yankton Primer. Santee, NB:
Santee Agency, 1869. 16 pp. "The first work
printed in the Yankton dialect.

1710. Williamson, John P., and Alfred L. Riggs, eds.
Odowan: Dakota Hymns. New York: American
Tract Society, 1893. 222 pp.

1711. Williamson, Thomas, trans. Bible O. T. Dakota.
Dakota iapi en, Pejuta wicasta kaga: Exodus, the
Second Book of Moses, in the Dakota lang., trans.
from Original Hebrew by Thomas Williamson. Lewi
toape, wowapi, Mowis Owa iyamni kin, Dakota iapi

en, Pejuta wicasta kaga: Leviticus, the Third
Book of Moses, in Dakota lang., trans. by Thomas
Williamson from original Hebrew. New York:
American Bible Society, 1869. 47 pp.

1712. Williamson, Thomas. The Books of Exodus and Leviticus, trans. from the Hebrew into the Dakota
Language. New York: American Bible Society,
1869. 112 pp.

1713. Williamson, Thomas S., trans. Josuwa, Qa Wayacopi
Kin, Qa Pute, Ohanyanpi Qon Oyakapi Wowapi Kin:
The Books of Josua, Judges and Ruth. New York:
American Bible Society, 1875. 85 pp.

1714. Williamson, Thomas S. Wicoicage Wowapi, Mowis
Owa: qa Wicoie Wakan kin, Solomon Kaga. Peji-
huta Wicashta Dakota Iapi en Kaga. The Book of
Genesis and Proverbs in the Dakota Language;
translated from the original Hebrew. New York:
American Bible Society, 1865. 115 pp.

1715. Williamson, Thomas S., and Stephen R. Riggs, trans.
Dakota Wowapi Wakan. The Holy Bible. New
York: American Bible Society, 1914.

1716. Williamson, Thomas S., et al. Wicoicage Wowapi
Qa Odowan Wakan.... The Book of Genesis, a
Part of the Psalms, and the Gospels of Luke and
John. Cincinnati, OH: Kendall and Barnard, 1842.
295 pp.

1717. Wolff, Hans. "Comparative Siouan L " IJAL, 16
(1950), 61-66, II, pp. 113-121; III, pp. 168-178;
IV, IJAL, 17 (1951), 197-204.

1718. Young Men's Christian Associations. Dakota Kristian
Koska Okodakiciye Woicicage woo pe kin ga woecon
woope. Constitution and by-laws of the Dakota
Young Men's Christian Association. Santee, NB:
Santee Normal Training School Press, 1890. 16 pp.

1719. Zisa, Charles A. American Indian Languages: Classification and List. Washington: Clearinghouse
for Linguistics, 1970. 74 pp.

LEADERS AND HEROES

1720.  Ackermann, Gertrude W.  "Joseph Renville of Lac
       Qui Parle. "  MiH, 12:3 (September 1931), 231-
       246.

1721.  Adams, Alexander B.  Sitting Bull:  An Epic of the
       Plains.  New York:  G. P. Putnam's, 1973.  446
       pp.  An unreliable, melodramatic biography.

1722.  Agogina, George.  Oscar Howe, Sioux Artist.  Occa-
       sional Papers, No. 1.  Vermillion, SD:  Institute
       of Indian Studies, 1959.

1723.  Allen, Charles W.  "Red Cloud and the U. S. Flag. "
       NH, 22 (1941), 77-88.

1724.  Allison, Edwin H.  The Surrender of Sitting Bull,
       Being a Full and Complete History of the Negotia-
       tions Which Resulted in the Surrender of Sitting
       Bull and His Entire Band of Hostile Sioux in 1881.
       Dayton, OH:  Walker Litho and Printing Co. , 1891;
       rpt. as "Surrender of Sitting Bull. "  CHSSD, 6
       (1912), 231-270.  Allison claimed credit for nego-
       tiating the surrender of Sitting Bull's followers in
       1881, and for bringing the Hunkpapa leader into
       Fort Buford.

1725.  Allison, Edwin H.  "Sitting Bull's Birthplace. "
       CHSSD, 6 (1912), 270-272.

1726.  Ambrose, Stephen E.  Crazy Horse and Custer:  The
       Parallel Lives of Two American Warriors.  Garden
       City, NY:  Doubleday, 1975.  486 pp.  An inter-
       esting account that traces the activities of the two
       men through the years prior to their meeting at the
       Battle of the Little Big Horn in 1876.  Assessments
       of the two men fit white better than Indian sensibil-
       ities.

1727.  Anderson, Grant K.  "The Prairie Paul Revere. "
       SDH, 8:1 (Winter 1977), 24-33.  An account of the
       ride of mixed-blood Samuel J. Brown on the night
       of April 19, 1866 to warn people that the Sioux he
       had reported as hostile were peaceable.

1728.  Anderson, LaVere.  Sitting Bull:  Great Sioux Chief.

Ed. Elizabeth M. Graves. Champaign, IL: Garrard Publishing Co. , 1970.

1729. Andrews, Ralph W. Indian Leaders Who Helped Shape America, 1620-1900. Seattle: Superior Publishing Co. , 1970.

1730. Barry, David F. "What Has Become of the Sitting Bull Family?" TD, n. d. , 19-21. A photographer from Superior, Wisconsin, who claimed to have known Sitting Bull published this piece of questionable reliability shortly after World War L

1731. Bordeaux, William J. Sitting Bull, Tanka-Iyotaka. Grand Rapids, MI: Custer Ephemera Society, 1974. Small pamphlet. 12 pp.

1732. Brady, Cyrus. "Captain Yates' Capture of Rain-in-the-Face. " TB, 2 (June 1916), 562-66.

1733. Brininstool, Earl A. "Chief Crazy Horse, His Career and Death. " NH, 12:1 (January-March 1929), 4-78. Material from Indian, military, and newspaper sources.

1734. Brininstool, Earl A. , ed. Crazy Horse: The Invincible Oglalla Sioux Chief, The "Inside Stories" by Actual Observers of a Treacherous Deed Against a Great Indian Leader. Los Angeles: Wetzel Publishing Co. , 1949. 87 pp. The story of the murder of Crazy Horse at old Fort Robinson in Nebraska on September 5, 1877 by men who witnessed the event: Gen. Jesse M. Lee, Dr. V. T. McGillycuddy, and others.

1735. Brininstool, Earl A. "The Wisdom of Chief Red Cloud. " OTT, 1:4 (November-December 1940), 19-21.

1736. Brown, Samuel J. "Biographic Sketch of Chief Gabriel Renville. " CMHS, 10: Pt. 2 (1905), 614-618.

1737. Brown, Vinson. Great Upon the Mountain: Crazy Horse of America. Healdsburg, CA: Naturegraph Publishers, 1971. 146 pp. A biography illustrated with photographs and drawings.

1738.   Buel, James W.   Heroes of the Plains:   ...  Custer's
        Famous "Last Fight" on the Little Big Horn, with
        Sitting Bull.   St. Louis, MO:   N. D. Thompson
        and Co., 1881.

1739.   Burdick, Usher L.   The Last Days of Sitting Bull:
        Sioux Medicine Chief.   Baltimore:   Wirth Brothers,
        1941.   A biography that contains questionable inter-
        pretations, though it is based largely upon the
        papers of James McLaughlin.

1740.   Butler, William Francis.   Red Cloud, the Solitary
        Sioux:   A Story of the Great Prairie.   Boston:
        Roberts Brothers, 1882.   327 pp.   A romanticized
        account of questionable value by Lt. Col. Butler.

1741.   Clark, Robert A., ed.   The Killing of Chief Crazy
        Horse:   Three Eyewitness Views by the Indian Chief
        He Dog, the Indian-White William Garnett, the
        White Doctor Valentine McGillycuddy.   Glendale,
        CA:   A. H. Clarke Co., 1976.   152 pp.

1742.   Clarke, Robert Dunlap.   The Works of Sitting Bull in
        the Original French and Latin.   Chicago:   Knight
        and Leonard, Printers, 1878.   Spurious.   See en-
        try no. 1872.

1743.   Clough, Wilson O.   "Mini-Aku, Daughter of Spotted
        Tail."   AWy, 39 (1967), 187-216.

1744.   Collins, Dabney O.   "The Fight for Sitting Bull's
        Bones."   AW, 3:1 (1966), 72-78.

1745.   Creelman, James.   On the Great Highway:   The Wan-
        derings and Adventures of a Special Correspondent.
        Boston:   Lothrop Publishing Co., 1901.   Includes
        Creelman's recollections of an interview with Sit-
        ting Bull through interpreter-scout Allison while the
        Hunkpapa leader was imprisoned at Fort Randall;
        portrays Sitting Bull as champion of liberty.

1746.   Curtin, L. J.   "By Order of Rain-in-the-Face."   OL,
        116 (December 1955), 12.

1747.   "Dakota Images:   Ella C. Deloria."   SDH, 6:4 (Fall
        1976), back cover inside, with photograph.   A short
        biographical sketch of Ella Deloria, who died Febru-
        ary 12, 1972.

1748.   DeBarthe, Joe.   The Life and Adventures of Frank
        Grouard.  Ed. Edgar I. Stewart.  Norman:  Uni-
        versity of Oklahoma Press, 1958.   Contains im-
        pressions of Sitting Bull by Grouard, who lived
        with the Hunkpapa leader, 1870-1872.

1749.   Dempsey, Hugh A.   Crowfoot: Chief of the Blackfeet.
        Norman:  University of Oklahoma Press, 1972.
        226 pp.   The biography of a Blood Indian that con-
        tains many references to Sitting Bull and other
        Sioux.

1750.   DePeyster, Arent S.   "Salute to the Sioux."   MiH,
        40 (Spring 1966), 21.   A narrative by Colonel De-
        Peyster, published originally in 1813, that includes
        a salute to Chief Wabasha.

1751.   Dines, Charles.   Crazy Horse.   New York:  G. P.
        Putnam's Sons, 1966.   Juvenile literature.

1752.   "Dr. Charles A. Eastman, Prominent Sioux, Dies."
        IW, May 1939, p. 44.   Describes highlights of his
        career.

1753.   Dykshorn, Jan M.   "Heritage Profile:  Chief John
        Grass."   DW, 2:3 (Fall 1976), 20-21.

1754.   Dykshorn, Jan M.   "Heritage Profile:  Chief Red
        Cloud."   DW, 2:4 (Winter 1976), 10-11.

1755.   Dykshorn, Jan M.   "Heritage Profile:  Chief Spotted
        Tail."   DW, 2:2 (Summer 1976), 20-21.

1756.   Dykshorn, Jan M.   "Leaders of the Sioux Indian Na-
        tion."   Dakota Highlights, 3 (1975), 1-8.   Contains
        brief biographies of Spotted Tail, Sitting Bull,
        Crazy Horse, Red Cloud, Gall, Charging Bear (John
        Grass), Hump, Big Foot, Young-Man-Afarid-of-
        His-Horses, Struck-by-the-Ree, and American
        Horse.

1757.   Eastman, Charles A.   "The Gray Chieftain."   H,
        108 (May 1904), 882-887.

1758.   Eastman, Charles A.   Indian Heroes and Great Chief-
        tains.   Boston:  Little, Brown and Co., 1918.   241
        pp.   About fifteen important Indian leaders, including

Crazy Horse, Sitting Bull, Chief Joseph, Gall, and
Dull Knife.

1759.  Eastman, Charles A.  "Rain-in-the-Face, the Story
of a Sioux Warrior. "  Out, 26 October 1906, pp.
507-512.

1760.  Eastman, Charles A.  "Rain-in-the-Face, the Story
of a Sioux Warrior. "  TB, 2 (June 1916), 577-578,
645-647.

1761.  Ewers, John C.  "Five Strings to His Bow:  The Remarkable Career of William (Lone Star) Dietz,
artist-athlete-actor-teacher-football coach. "  Montana, 27:1 (January 1977), 2-13.  Artist William
Dietz had a mixed-blood Sioux mother.

1762.  Farrell, R. C.  "The Burial of Sitting Bull. "
USDMN, 15:1 (1954), 1-2.

1763.  Fechet, Edmund Gustav.  "The Capture of Sitting
Bull. "  CHSSD, 4 (1908), 185-193.  After serving
as commander at Fort Yates in the summer of
1890, Colonel Fechet led a support unit to Grand
River when Indian Policeman Bullhead went out to
arrest Sitting Bull.  Describes events that led to
the death of the Hunkpapa leader.

1764.  Fechet, Edmund Gustav.  "True Story of the Death
of Sitting Bull. "  Cosmopolitan, 20 (1898), 493.

1765.  Fechet, Edmund Gustav.  "The True Story of the
Death of Sitting Bull. "  PNSHS, 2:2nd Ser. (1898),
179-190.  Includes Colonel Fechet's impressions of
the sequence of events that led to the death of Sitting Bull.

1766.  Fielder, Mildred.  Sioux Indian Leaders.  Seattle,
WA:  Superior Publishing Co. , 1975.  160 pp.  Contains biographies of Crazy Horse, Spotted Tail, Sitting Bull, Gall, Martin Charger, Red Cloud, Chauncey Yellow Robe and Ben Reifel.  Based upon secondary sources, it is not very reliable.

1767.  Fiske, Frank Bennett.  Life and Death of Sitting Bull.
Fort Yates, ND:  Pioneer-Arrow Print. , 1933.  72
pp.  Fiske was a youngster at Fort Yates when

Sitting Bull was killed. His account is valuable, however, because it is based upon an interview with John M. Carignon, who operated a day school 1 1/2 miles from Sitting Bull's cabin on Grande River in 1890.

1768.  Fitzgerald, John D. Brave Buffalo Fighter (Waditaka Tatanka Kisisohitika). Independence, MO: Independence Press, 1973. 188 pp.

1769.  Florin, Lambert. Tales of Western Tombstones. Seattle, WA: Superior Publishing Co., 1967. 191 pp. Includes information about Sitting Bull.

1770.  Flynn, Darline. "A Tribute to Our Great Chief Crazy Horse." Quetzal, 2 (Winter-Spring 1972), 39. Poem by a Sioux author.

1771.  Frackelton, William. "Sitting Bull." OTT, 1:6 (March-April 1941), 25-27; rpt., pp. 143-145.

1772.  Frink, Maurice Mahurin. "Lakota Letters." Outing, 67 (1915), 302-305. Includes information about High Hawk, George Breast and Tom Brown Eyes.

1773.  Garnett, William. Story of the Death of Crazy Horse. Pine Ridge, SD: Pine Ridge Agency, 1920.

1774.  Garst, Doris Shannon. Crazy Horse. Eau Claire, WI: E. M. Hale and Co., 1950. Juvenile literature, written as a novel.

1775.  Garst, Doris Shannon. Sitting Bull: Champion of His People. New York: Julian Messner, Inc., 1946. 189 pp. A fictionalized biography that contains faulty information. Yet it was based upon fairly sound scholarship for the development of general themes.

1776.  "Gertrude Simmons Bonnin Dies." IW, March 1938, p. 23. Zitkala Ša dies at age 62. She had taught at Carlisle, was a writer, was a founder and president of the National Council of American Indians.

1777.  Gibbon, John. "Hunting Sitting Bull." ACQR, 2 (October 1899), 665-694. Describes Colonel Gibbon's expedition against Sitting Bull and the Sioux in 1877.

1778.   Giese, Paula. "Free Sarah Bad Heart Bull (and the Other Custer Defendants)." NCA, No. 13 (October-November 1974), pp. 64-71. Deals with Sioux leaders arrested for an incident at Custer, South Dakota.

1779.   Gilbert, Alfred B. The Way of the Indian. Portland, OR: F. E. Gotshall, 1908. Romanticized, brief biography of Sitting Bull.

1780.   Hart, Irving H., ed. "The Story of Beengwa, Daughter of a Chippewa Warrior." MiH, 9:4 (December 1928), 319-330. A Chippewa who recalled Sioux-Chippewa skirmishes, when she was age 90 in 1927.

1781.   Henderson, H. "Sitting Bull Was an Artist Too." Collier's, 18 July 1953, pp. 36-39.

1782.   Hilger, Sr. Mary Ione. The First Sioux Nun: Sister Marie-Josephine Nebraska, S. G. M., 1859-1894. Milwaukee, WI: Bruce, 1963. 157 pp. A romanticized biography about a Grey Nun--Sister of Charity of the Montreal Motherhouse--who entered the Order after her father was killed by Saulteaux.

1783.   Hines, Thomas Walter. Life and Death of Sitting Bull. Seattle, WA: N. P. Bank Note Co., 1944. Collection of 24 plates of paintings and photographs.

1784.   Hinman, Eleanor H. The Eleanor H. Hinman Interviews on the Life and Death of Crazy Horse. New Brunswick, NJ: Garry Owen Press, 1976. 48 pp.

1785.   Hinman, Eleanor H. "Oglala Sources on the Life of Crazy Horse." NH, 67:1 (Spring 1976), 1-51. Mari Sandoz prepared her biography from material given her by Hinman.

1786.   Hirsch, E. Carl. Famous American Indians of the Plains. Chicago: Rand McNally and Co., 1973. 93 pp. Includes biographical and cultural information about many Great Plains tribal leaders, including Sioux.

1787.   Howard, O. O. "Sitting Bull, The Great Dakota Leader." StN, 35 (October 1908), 1094-1097.

1788.  Hughes, Thomas.  Indian Chiefs of Southern Min-
       nesota.  Containing Sketches of the Prominent
       Chieftains of the Dakota and Winnebago Tribes
       from 1825 to 1865.  Mankato, MN:  Free Press
       Co., 1927; rpt.  Minneapolis:  Ross and Haines,
       1969.  133 pp.  Largely about Sioux chiefs from
       the eastern tribes.

1789.  Johnson, Dorothy M.  "The Hanging of the Chiefs."
       Montana, 20:3 (July 1970), 60-70.  Three Sioux
       chiefs were hanged in May of 1865 at Fort Lara-
       mie after bringing in two female captives:  Sarah
       Larimer and Lucinda Ewbanks.

1790.  Johnson, Dorothy M.  Warrior for a Lost Nation:
       A Biography of Sitting Bull.  Philadelphia:  West-
       minster Press, 1963.  173 pp.  A readable biogra-
       phy based upon limited research.

1791.  Johnson, Roy P.  "Sitting Bull:  Hero or Monster?"
       NDH, 29:1 and 2 (January-April 1962), 215-221.
       A corrected version of narratives that appeared in
       the Fargo Forum, September 4 and 5, 1962; con-
       tains material reported as Sitting Bull's own state-
       ments.

1792.  Johnson, Willis Fletcher.  The Red Record of the
       Sioux:  Life of Sitting Bull and History of the In-
       dian War of 1890-91....  Story of the Sioux Na-
       tion; Their Manners and Customs, Ghost Dances
       and Messiah Craze.  Philadelphia:  Edgewood Pub-
       lishing Co., 1891.  544 pp.  The first biography
       published on Sitting Bull, which reflects strong anti-
       Indian bias and contains questionable information.

1793.  Josephy, Alvin M.  "Crazy Horse, Patriot of the
       Plains."  In The Patriot Chiefs:  A Chronicle of
       American Indian Resistance.  New York:  The Vik-
       ing Press, 1969, pp. 257-309.

1794.  Joyner, Christopher C.  "The Hegira of Sitting Bull
       to Canada:  Diplomatic Realpolitik."  JW, 13:3
       (1974), 6-18.

1795.  Kitchen, Dick.  "Fifth Face on the Mountain."  DW,
       1:3 (Winter 1975), 8-10.  About Ben Black Elk,
       with photographs.

1796.   Knight, Oliver.  "War of Peace:  The Anxious Wait
        for Crazy Horse."  NH, 54:4 (Winter 1973), 521-
        544.

1797.   Kurth, Godefroid Joseph François.  Sitting Bull.
        Brussels:  Administration de la Revue Generale,
        1879.  305 pp.

1798.   Lange, Dietrich.  The Threat of Sitting Bull, A
        Story of the Time of Custer.  Boston:  Lothrop,
        Lee and Shepard, 1920.  370 pp.  Fictionalized his-
        tory.

1799.   Larkin, Georgia.  "Chief Blue Cloud, Biography of
        the Yankton Sioux Chief."  BCQ, 10:2 (1964), 33 pp.
        Mixed-blood selected by an Indian agent to replace
        Pretty Boy as clan chief in the Yankton tribe.
        When he died in 1918, he was the last man recog-
        nized as a chief in the Yankton tribe.  His non-
        Indian name was William Bean.

1800.   Lee, Jesse Matlock.  "The Capture and Death of
        Chief 'Crazy Horse'."  n. p. , 1924.  An unpublished
        manuscript by a military officer who accompanied
        Crazy Horse just prior to his death.  A copy is
        preserved in the Ayer collection at the Newberry
        Library in Chicago.

1801.   [Leonard, Jean D.]  "After Words."  GPO, June 1970,
        pp. 13-15.  On Chief Red Cloud.

1802.   MacEwan, John Walter Grant.  Sitting Bull:  The
        Years in Canada.  Edmonton, Alberta:  Hurtig Pub-
        lishers, 1973.  221 pp.  An interesting, journalis-
        tic account of Sitting Bull's exile in Canada during
        the period 1877-1881.

1803.   McGaa, Ed.  Red Cloud:  The Story of an American
        Indian.  Minneapolis:  Dillon Press, 1971.  By a
        Sioux author.

1804.   McKenney, Thomas L. , and James Hall.  History of
        the Indian Tribes of North America, with Biograph-
        ical Sketches and Anecdotes of the Principal Chiefs,
        Embellished with One Hundred and Twenty Portraits
        from the Indian Gallery in the Department of War,
        in Washington.  3 vols.  Philadelphia:  Frederick W.

Greenough, 1838; rpt. 1934, St. Clair Shores, MI:
Scholarly Press, 1972. A classic that has appeared in many editions, under several titles.

1805.  McLaughlin, James.  An Account of the Death of Sitting Bull and of the Circumstances Attending It.
Philadelphia:  Indian Rights Association, 1891.

1806.  McLaughlin, James.  My Friend the Indian:  Or,
Three Heretofore Unpublished Chapters of the Book
I Published under the Title of My Friend the Indian.  Baltimore:  The Proof Press, 1936.  The
agent's views about Sitting Bull's last years.

1807.  McLaughlin, James.  The Superior Edition of My
Friend the Indian.  Preface and epilogue Fr. Louis
L. Pfaller.  Seattle, WA:  Superior Publishing Co.,
1970.  107 pp.  The complete works of Agent Mc-
Laughlin by his principal biographer.

1808.  McNichols, Charles L.  Crazy Weather.  1944; rpt.
Lincoln:  University of Nebraska Press, 1967.
195 pp.

1809.  McNicol, Donald Monroe.  Amerindians:  From Acuera
to Sitting Bull, From Donnacona to Big Bear.  New
York:  Stokes, 1937.  341 pp.

1810.  Malm, Einar.  Sitting Bull:  och Kampen om vilda
Vastern.  Stockholm:  H. Geber, 1946.  295 pp.

1811.  Marquis, Thomas Bailey.  Sitting Bull and Gall, the
Warrior.  Hardin, MT:  Custer Battle Museum,
1934.  An unobjective source that appraises the
leadership careers of Sitting Bull and Gall, to cor-
rect "propagandistic falsehoods."

1812.  "Mary Crawler."  IW, 1 December 1935, p. 47.
Also called Moving Robe, she was the only woman to
fight at the Battle of the Little Bighorn.

1813.  May, Julian.  Sitting Bull:  Chief of the Sioux.  Mankato, MN:  Creative Educational Society, 1973.
38 pp.  Juvenile literature.

1814.  Meadowcroft, Enid L.  Crazy Horse:  Sioux Warrior.
Champaign, IL:  Garrard Publishing Co., 1965.
Juvenile literature.

1815.   Meadowcroft, Enid L. Story of Crazy Horse. New
        York: Grosset and Dunlap, 1954. 181 pp. Ju-
        venile literature.

1816.   Mears, David Y. "Campaigning Against Crazy
        Horse. " PNSHS, 2nd Ser. , 10 (1907), 68-77.

1817.   Melander, Richard. Nybyggarne vid Missouri; andra
        omarbetade upplagan av i Sitting Bulls land.  Stock-
        holm: Aktiebolaget Ljus, 1913. 258 pp.

1818.   Miller, David H. "Sitting Bull's White Squaw: The
        Overdressed Zealot from Brooklyn who Braved Dis-
        honor to Befriend the Recalcitrant Old Chief. "
        Montana, 14:2 (April 1964), 55-71.

1819.   Milroy, Thomas W. "A Physician by the Name of
        Ohiyesa: Charles Alexander Eastman, M. D. "
        Minnesota Medicine, 54 (1971), 569-572.

1820.   Milton, John. Oscar Howe: The Story of an Ameri-
        can Indian. Minneapolis: Dillon Press, Inc. , 1971.
        56 pp.

1821.   Moorehead, Warren K. "The Passing of Red Cloud. "
        TKHS, 10 (1908), 295-311.

1822.   Neill, Edward D. "A Sketch of Joseph Renville A
        'Bois Brule, ' and Early Trader of Minnesota. "
        CMHS, 1 (1872), 196-206.

1823.   Newell, Cicero. The History of Sitting Bull and His
        Sioux Indians. Milwaukee, WI: F. Trayser, 1884.
        15 pp.

1824.   O'Connor, Richard. Sitting Bull: War Chief of the
        Sioux. New York: McGraw-Hill, 1970.

1825.   Olden, Sarah E. The People of Tipi Sapa (The Da-
        kotas): Tipi Sapa Mitaoyate kin. Milwaukee:
        Morehouse Publishing Co. , 1918. 158 pp. In-
        cludes the story of Philip J. Deloria, as he de-
        scribed his life himself.

1826.   Olsen, Louise P. "Ben Bear. " NDH, 18:1 (January
        1951), 25-29. About a Sioux who worked in Pierre,
        SD, then in New Mexico, until he died in 1948.

1827.  Olson, James C.  Red Cloud and the Sioux Problem.
       Lincoln:  University of Nebraska Press, 1965.
       357 pp.  A scholarly appraisal of relationships be-
       tween the Oglalas and the Indian Field Service in
       post-Civil War years.

1828.  Olson, James C.  "Red Cloud vs. McGillycuddy."
       In The Western American Indian:  Case Studies in
       Tribal History.  Ed. Richard N. Ellis.  Lincoln:
       University of Nebraska Press, 1972, pp. 97-116.

1829.  Parker, Donald Dean.  Gabriel Renville, Young Sioux
       Warrior:  The Adventures of an Indian Boy in Ear-
       ly Minnesota.  New York:  Exposition Press, 1973.
       173 pp.  Semi-fictional story.

1830.  Pearman, Robert.  "Sitting Bull Murdered."  AI, 1:
       1 (1963), 30.

1831.  Pennanen, Gary.  "Sitting Bull:  Indian Without a
       Country."  CHR, 51 (June 1970), 123-140.

1832.  Peterson, Harold D.  "Wahkonsa."  Palimpsest, 23:
       4 (April 1942), 121-135.  About a Sioux who be-
       friended a white youngster in 1851, then surrendered
       at the time of the Spirit Lake Affair in 1857.

1833.  Pfaller, Fr. Louis.  "The Brave Bear Murder Case."
       NDH, 36:2 (Spring 1969), 120-139.  About a Yank-
       tonnai who led a terrorist group in the period 1874-
       1882.

1834.  Pfaller, Fr. Louis.  "Enemies in '76, Friends in
       '85--Sitting Bull and Buffalo Bill."  Prologue, 1:2
       (Fall 1969), 17-31.

1835.  Phillips, David G.  "Sioux Chiefs Before the Secre-
       tary."  HW, 12 February 1891, p. 142.

1836.  Pruitt, O. J.  "Smutty Bear Tribe."  AI, 31:7 (Janu-
       ary 1953), 544-547.  Yankton clan chief who occu-
       pied the region between Yankton and Springfield and
       resisted the concentration of his tribe on the reser-
       vation under the terms of the Treaty of Washington,
       1858.

1837.  Riggs, Frederick B.  "The Death of Sitting Bull."

IW, November 1935, pp. 39-40.  Describes conditions surrounding killing and burial of Sitting Bull
and seven supporters in 1890.

1838.   Riggs, Stephen R.  "Dakota Portraits. "  Ed. Willoughby M. Babcock.  MiH, 2:8 (November 1918), 481-
568.  Contains biographical sketches of Sioux leaders and others, including Mrs. Joseph Renville.

1839.   Robinson, Doane.  "The Divine Right of Princes. "
CHSSD, 12 (1924), 186.  Sitting Bull's statement to
the negotiating commission of 1883 at Standing Rock,
as he and other Indian leaders withdrew because
the commission members had been drinking.

1840.   Robinson, Doane.  "The Education of Red Cloud. "
CHSSD, 12 (1924), 156-178.

1841.   Robinson, Doane, ed.  "A Sioux Indian View of the
Last War with England. "  CHSSD, 5 (1910), 397-
401.  From an interview with Rev. John B. Renville, Presbyterian clergyman and son of Joseph
Renville and a Sioux woman.

1842.   Robinson, Doane.  "Sioux of the Dakotas:  Interview
with Red Cloud. "  HGM, 2 (November 1932), 7-12.

1843.   Robinson, Doane.  "Some Sidelights on the Character
of Sitting Bull. "  CHSSD, 5 (1910), 391-396.

1844.   Robinson, Doane.  "Some Sidelights on the Character
of Sitting Bull. "  PNSHS, 16 (1911), 187-192.

1845.   Robinson, Doane.  "Wounded Knee. "  CHSSD, 12
(1924), 180-181.  About a Sioux who got this name
as a result of a wound in his youth.

1846.   Robinson, Will G.  "Educated Sioux. "  CHSSD, 22
(1946), 28-61.  Biographies of Sioux who have been
prominent in the twentieth century.

1847.   Rosenberg, Marvin, and Dorothy Rosenberg.  "There
Are No Indians Left Now But Me. "  AH, 15:4
(June 1964), 18-23.  About Sitting Bull and his
bitterness regarding the reduction of the Great
Sioux Reservation.

1848.    Sandoz, Mari. Crazy Horse. Lincoln: University
         of Nebraska Press, 1961. 428 pp. The standard
         biography.

1849.    Seagle, William. "The Murder of Spotted Tail."
         InH, 3:4 (Fall 1970), 10-22.

1850.    Sibley, Henry H. Iron Face: The Adventures of
         Jack Frazer, Frontier Warrior, Scout, and Hunter.
         Chicago: The Caxton Club, 1950. 206 pp. Gen-
         eral Sibley's impressions of a mixed-blood, of Scotch
         and Mdewakanton extraction, whom he knew well
         during the period of the Minnesota Sioux War.

1851.    Sibley, Henry H. "Sketch of John Other Day." CMHS,
         3 (1870-1880), 99-102. About a man who was fam-
         ous for his efforts to save non-Indians during the
         Minnesota Sioux War.

1852.    "Sioux Indian Woman Awarded Achievement Medal."
         IW, September-October 1943, pp. 25-26. Ella
         Deloria awarded the 1943 medal in Chicago.

1853.    "Sioux Physician, George F. Frazier, Wins 1939 In-
         dian Achievement Medal." IW, December 1939, p.
         20.

1854.    Smith, Cornelius C. "Crook and Crazy Horse."
         Montana, 16:2 ( Spring 1966), 14-26.

1855.    Smith, J. L. "Interview with Robert Holy Dance."
         USDMN, 26:9/10 (1965), 5-8.

1856.    Sneve, Virginia Driving Hawk. They Led the Nation.
         Ed. Jane Hunt; portraits Loren Zephier. Sioux
         Falls, SD: Brevet Press, 1975. 46 pp. Contains
         biographies of twenty Sioux leaders.

1857.    Soladay, Mildred. Oscar Howe, Artist Laureate of
         the Middle Border. Mitchell, SD: Mitchell Print-
         ing Co., 1968. Small pamphlet. 20 pp.

1858.    Stambaugh, Samuel C. A Statement and Explanation
         of the Origin and Present Condition of the Claim of
         Pelagie Ferribault, a Half-breed Woman of the
         Sioux Tribe, for the Value of an Island at the Con-
         fluence of St. Peter's and Mississippi Rivers, Re-

served to Her by the Sioux Chiefs from a Tract of
Land Conveyed to the U. S. for Military Purposes,
at the Establishment of Fort Snelling, Aug. 9, 1820.
Washington, DC:   Union Office, 1856.   36 pp.

1859.  Steel, M. F.   "Buffalo Bill's Bluff. "   CHSSD,  9 (1918),
       475-485.   An account of the arrest and death of
       Sitting Bull on December 15, 1890, after the gov-
       ernment rejected Buffalo Bill's offer to bring the
       Hunkpapa leader in.

1860.  Stenholt, Lars A.   Sitting Bull.   Minneapolis:   W.
       Kriedt, 1891; rpt. St. Paul:   Capitol Publishing Co. ,
       1917.   162 pp.

1861.  Stevenson, Augusta.   Sitting Bull:   Dakota Boy.   In-
       dianapolis:   Bobbs-Merrill Co. , 1956.   189 pp.

1862.  Stirling, Matthew W.   Three Pictographic Autobi-
       ographies of Sitting Bull.   Washington, DC:   Smith-
       sonian Institution, 1938.   Contains three of four
       pictographic autobiographies created by Sitting Bull.
       See also entry no. 407.

1863.  Swisher, Jacob A.   "War Eagle. "   Palimpsest,  30:2
       (February 1949), 33-41.   An eastern Sioux who be-
       came chief for a mixed group of Yanktons and oth-
       ers who lived near the mouth of the Big Sioux River
       until his death in the 1850s.

1864.  Taylor, Joseph H.   "Bloody Knife and Gall. "   NDHQ,
       4:3 (April 1930), 165-173.   Bloody Knife was a
       mixed-blood Sioux-Arikara who served as a scout
       for Custer; Gall was a war leader of Hunkpapa.

1865.  Taylor, Joseph H.   "A Romantic Encounter. "   NDHQ,
       4:4 (July 1930), 207-219.   About Sioux and Arikara
       warriors.

1866.  Terry, Alfred.   "The Commission Appointed by the
       Direction of the President of the United States,
       Under Instructions of the Honorables the Secretary
       of War and the Secretary of the Interior, to Meet
       the Sioux Indian Chief, Sitting Bull, with a View
       to Avert Incursions into the Territory of the United
       States from the Dominion of Canada. "   In Report of
       the Secretary of the Interior for 1877; rpt. Wash-

ington, DC: Government Printing Office, 1877. General Alfred Terry, A. G. Lawrence and H. C. Corbin met Sitting Bull at Fort Walsh, in the presence of Col. McLeod, to try to get him to return to the United States, but the Hunkpapa leader refused.

1867.  "Three Noted Chiefs of the Sioux: Sitting Bull, John Grass and Chief Gall. " HW, 20 December 1890, pp. 995-996.

1868.  Turner, C. Frank. Across the Medicine Line. Toronto: McClelland and Stewart, 1973. 269 pp. About Sitting Bull and his followers.

1869.  Utley, Robert M. "Ordeal of Plenty Horses. " AH, 26 (December 1974), 15-19.

1870.  Vestal, Stanley. Sitting Bull: Champion of the Sioux. Boston: Houghton-Mifflin Co. , 1932; rpt. Norman: University of Oklahoma Press, 1969. 380 pp. The most reliable biography on Sitting Bull, based upon careful oral and documentary research, and written as literary history.

1871.  Vestal, Stanley. Warpath: The True Story of the Fighting Sioux Told in a Biography of Chief White Bull. Boston: Houghton-Mifflin, 1924. 291 pp. By the nephew of Sitting Bull.

1872.  Vestal, Stanley. "The Works of Sitting Bull: Real and Imaginary. " SR, 19:3 (April 1934), 265-278. On spurious works published by R. D. Clarke in 1878. See entry no. 1742.

1873.  Victor, Mrs. Francis Auretta. Eleven Years in the Rocky Mountains and Life on the Frontier. Hartford, CT: Columbian Book Co. , 1877; rpt. Hartford, CT: Bliss and Co. , 1881. Contains information about Sitting Bull and his confrontation with George Custer.

1874.  Wade, F. C. "Surrender of Sitting Bull. " CM, 24 (February 1905), 335-344.

1875.  Wade, Mary H. "Sitting Bull: Great Medicine Chief of the Sioux. " Ten Little Indians; Stories of How

Indian Children Lived and Played. Boston: W. A.
Wilde Co., 1904, pp. 219-240. Children's literature.

1876.   Watson, Elmo Scott. "Orlando Scott Goff, Pioneer
        Dakota Photographer." NDH, 29:1 and 2 (January-
        April 1962), 210-215. The first to photograph
        Sitting Bull; relates the story of his experience.

1877.   Whittaker, Jane. Patriots of the Plains: Sitting Bull,
        Crazy Horse, Chief Joseph. New York: Scholas-
        tic Book Services, 1973. 128 pp. Juvenile litera-
        ture.

1878.   Williamson, Thomas S. "Napehshneedoota: The First
        Male Dakota Convert to Christianity." CMHS, 3
        (1880), 188-191. About the son of Mrs. Joe Ren-
        ville's sister, named Joseph Napeshnee.

1879.   Willson, Charles C. "The Successive Chiefs Named
        Wabasha." CMHS, 12 (1908), 502-512.

1880.   Worcester, Donald E. "Spotted Tail: Warrior, Diplo-
        mat." AW, 1:4 (Fall 1964), 39-46, 87.

1881.   Yarbough, Leroy. "Sitting Bull: Truth and Legend."
        AI, 1:1 (1963), 26.

1882.   Yarbough, Leroy. "The Tragedy of Crazy Horse."
        AI, 1:1 (1963), 22.


## LITERATURE--COLLECTIONS AND STORIES

1883.   Abrahall, John Hoskyns. Western Woods and Waters:
        Poems and Illustrative Notes. London: Longman,
        Roberts and Green, 1864. 419 pp.

1884.   Armstrong, Virginia I. I Have Spoken: American
        History Through the Voices of the Indians. Chi-
        cago: Swallow Press, 1971. 206 pp. Contains
        statements by nineteenth-century Sioux leaders.

1885.   Beckwith, Martha W. "Mythology of the Oglala Da-
        kota." JAFL, 43 (October-December 1930), 339-
        367. Stories collected on Pine Ridge Reservation

in 1926 from Tetons, on Crow Creek Reservation
from Yanktonai, and on Yankton Reservation from
Yanktons.  Some forty stories.

1886.  Bessaignet, Pierre.  "Histoires Sioux. " JSAP, 44
(1955), 49-54.  Collected at Pine Ridge in 1954, it
includes both stories and historical accounts.

1887.  Brennan, Mary R.  "The Legend of Minnewaukan--
Mysterious Water. " CHSND, 1 (1906), 476-478.
A Dakota legend.

1888.  Brown, Dorothy M.  "Indian Tree Myths and Legends. "
WA, N. S. 19: No. 2 (1938), 30-36.

1889.  Buechel, Eugene.  Lakota Tales and Texts.  Ed. Paul
Manhart.  Pine Ridge, SD:  Holy Rosary Mission,
1978.

1890.  Burgum, Jessamine (Slaughter).  Stars over the
Prairies:  A Book of Verse of Indian Legends,
Myths and Episodes of the Land of the Dacotahs.
Minneapolis:  Colwell Press, 1947.  72 pp.

1891.  Bushotter, George.  "A Teton Dakota Ghost Story. "
JAFL, 1 (1888), 68-72.

1892.  Colby, L. W.  "Wanagi Olowan Kin (The Ghost Songs
of the Dakotas. )" PNSHS, 6 (1895), 131-150.  Original texts and translations by a Brigadier General.

1893.  Costo, Rupert, ed.  Indian Voices:  The First Convocation of American Indian Scholars.  San Francisco:
Indian Historian Press, 1970.  Articles by various
Indian scholars, including Sioux.  Latter are entered individually herein.

1894.  Cropp, Richard.  Dacotah Tales.  Mitchell, SD:
Mitchell Printing Co. , 1968.  38 pp.  Four Iktomi
and five other legends.

1895.  Dale, Edward E.  Tales of the Teepee.  Boston:
D. C. Heath and Co. , 1920.  119 pp.

1896.  Deloria, Ella.  Dakota Texts.  New York:  G. E.
Stechert and Co. , 1932; rpt.  Ed. Agnes Picotte and
Paul Pavich.  Vermillion, SD: Dakota Press, 1978.

279 pp.   An excellent, large collection of Sioux legends.

1897.   Deloria, Ella.   "Short Dakota Texts, Including Conversation. "   IJAL, 20 (1954), 17-22.

1898.   Dorsey, George A.   "Legend of the Teton Sioux Medicine Pipe. "   JAFL, 19 (1906), 326-329.   From the delivery of the Peacepipe to the Sioux by the White Buffalo Calf Girl to its modern preservation by the Pipe Keeper.

1899.   Dorsey, James Owen.   "Dakota Legend of the Head of Gold. "   JAFL, 13 (October 1900), 294-296.

1900.   Dorsey, James Owen.   "The Myths of the Raccoon and the Crawfish Among the Dakotah Tribes. "   AAOJ, 6 (1884), 237-240.

1901.   Dorsey, James Owen.   "Nanibozhu in Siouan Mythology. "   JAFL, 5 (1892), 293-304.   Re-telling eight tales.

1902.   Dorsey, James Owen.   "Siouan Folk-Lore and Mythologic Notes. "   AAOJ, 6 (1884), 174-176; 7 (1885), 105-108.

1903.   Dorsey, James Owen.   "Teton Folk-Lore. "   AA, 2:2 (April 1889), 143-158.   Some short legends.

1904.   Dorsey, James Owen.   "Teton Folk-Lore Notes. "   JAFL, 2 (1889), 133-139.

1905.   Eastman, Charles A.   Red Hunters and the Animal People.   New York:   Harper and Brothers, 1904, 249 pp. ; rpt. New York: AMS Press, 1976.   A dozen stories that relate the associations between Sioux and animals.

1906.   Eastman, Charles A. , and Elaine Goodale Eastman.   Smoky Day's Wigwam Evenings:   Indian Stories Re-Told.   Boston:   Little, Brown and Co. , 1924.   148 pp.   Short tales, focusing on animals, each of which ends with a moral in italics.

1907.   Eastman, Charles A. , and Elaine Goodale Eastman.   Wigwam Evenings:   Animal Tales.   Boston:   Little, Brown and Co. , 1930.   250 pp.

1908.   Eastman, Charles A. , and Elaine Goodale Eastman.
        Wigwam Evenings: Sioux Folk Tales Retold.   Bos-
        ton:   Little, Brown and Co. , 1909; rpt. Eau Claire,
        WI:   E. M. Hale, 1937.   253 pp.

1909.   Eastman, Elaine Goodale.   Indian Legends Retold.
        Boston:   Little, Brown and Co. , 1919.   161 pp.

1910.   Eastman, Mary H.   Dahcotah; Or, Life and Legends
        of the Sioux Around Fort Snelling.   1849; rpt.
        Minneapolis, MN:   Ross and Haines, Inc. , 1962;
        New York:   Arno Press, 1975.   268 pp.

1911.   Emch, Lucille B.   "An Indian Tale by William J.
        Snelling. "   MiH, 26 (1945), 211-221.   Yankton tale:
        "The Last of the Iron Hearts. "

1912.   Erdoes, Richard, ed.   The Sound of Flutes and Other
        Indian Legends.   New York:   Pantheon Books, 1976.
        137 pp.   Thirty short legends, told by Lame Deer,
        Jenny Leading Cloud, Leonard Crow Dog and others.

1913.   Gilmore, Melvin R.   "The Dakota Story of the Bean
        Mouse. "   IN, 2 (1925), 183-184.

1914.   Gilmore, Melvin R.   Prairie Smoke.   Bismarck, ND:
        Bismarck Tribune Print, 1922; rpt. New York:
        Columbia University Press, 1929.   208 pp.

1915.   Gordon, Hanford L.   Indian Legends, and Other Poems.
        Salem, MA:   Salem Press Co. , 1910.   405 pp.

1916.   Gordon, Hanford L.   Legends of the Northwest.   St.
        Paul, MN:   Book and Stationery Co. , 1881.   143 pp.

1917.   Heilbron, Bertha L.   "Some Sioux Legends in Pictures. "
        MiH, 36 (March 1958), 18-23.   Pictures of places
        associated with history and legend.

1918.   Herman, Jake.   Stories and Legends of the Oglala
        Sioux from Pine Ridge Reservation, South Dakota.
        Pine Ridge, SD:   n. p. , n. d.

1919.   Higheagle, Robert.   "The Legend of the Standing Rock. "
        IW, 1 December 1935, pp. 30-31.   Relates one of
        the several versions of this story.

1920.   Highwater, Jamake.   Ritual of the Wing:   North Amer-

ican Ceremonies, Music, and Dances. New York:
The Viking Press, 1977. 192 pp. A narrative
taken partly from Sioux tradition blends ceremonies,
music and dances with legend.

1921. Huggins, Eli Lundy. Winona: A Dakota Legend, and
Other Poems. New York: G. P. Putnam's Sons,
1890. 176 pp.

1922. Jerome, Father. "Story of Howastena (Beautiful
Voice), Fort Totten, N. D. " CHSND, 1 (1906), 478.
A Dakota myth.

1923. Jones, Hettie, ed. Coyote Tales. New York: Holt,
Rinehart and Winston, Co. , 1974. Four stories
about Coyote.

1924. Judson, Katharine B. Myths and Legends of the Great
Plains. Chicago: A. C. McClurg and Co. , 1913.
205 pp. Numerous Sioux legends and stories from
other tribal literatures.

1925. Judson, Katharine J. Myths and Legends of the Mississippi Valley and the Great Lakes. Chicago:
A. C. McClurg and Co. , 1914. 215 pp.

1926. Katz, Jane B. , ed. I Am the Fire of Time: The
Voices of Native American Women. New York:
E. P. Dutton, 1977. 201 pp. An anthology of
Indian women's autobiographical and other writing;
many Sioux included.

1927. Kunike, Hugh D. W. Prairie-Indianer Marchen.
Berlin: A. Juncker, n. d. 166 pp.

1928. Lanman, Charles. Adventures in the Wilds of the
United States and British American Provinces.
Philadelphia: J. W. Moore, 1856.

1929. LaPointe, James. Legends of the Lakota. San Francisco: Indian Historian Press, 1976. 160 pp.
Twenty tales.

1930. Legends of the Mighty Sioux. Comp. by Workers of
the South Dakota Writers Project Work Projects
Administration. Chicago: Labert Whitman Co. ,
1941; rpt. Sioux Falls, SD: Fantab, Inc. [1970].
158 pp. Approximately forty short tales.

1931.   Long, James L.   "Indian Hunting Story. "  IW, 15
        May 1936, pp. 44-45.   "Fish story" about a bear
        who tried to shoot a hunter with his own gun.

1932.   McLaughlin, Marie L.   Myths and Legends of the
        Sioux.   Bismarck, ND:   Bismarck Tribune Co.,
        1916; rpt.   Bismarck, ND:   Tumbleweed Press,
        1974.   198 pp.   Mixed-blood Mdewakanton, wife of
        Agent James McLaughlin, recorded stories she
        heard growing up around Wabasha, Minnesota, in
        the nineteenth century.

1933.   Marriot, Alice, and Carol K. Rachlin.   Plains In-
        dian Mythology.   New York:   Thomas Y. Crowell,
        1975.   194 pp.

1934.   Meeker, Louis L.   "Siouan Mythological Tales. "
        JAFL, 14 (1901), 161-164; JAFL, 15 (1902), 84-87.

1935.   Meeker, Louis L.   "White Man:   A Siouan Myth. "
        JAFL, 15 (1902), 84-87.

1936.   Moquin, Wayne, and Charles Van Doren, eds.   Great
        Documents in American Indian History.   New York:
        Praeger Publishers, 1973.   416 pp.   All selections
        are by Indians; those by the Sioux appear as indi-
        vidual citations elsewhere in this text.

1937.   Morris, H. S.   Historical Stories, Legends and Tradi-
        tions:   Northeastern South Dakota.   Sisseton, SD:
        The Sisseton Courier, n. d.   156 pp.

1938.   Nabokov, Peter, ed.   Native American Testimony:
        An Anthology of Indian and White Relations, First
        Encounter to Dispossession.   New York:   Thomas
        Y. Crowell, 1978.   242 pp.   Some Sioux autobio-
        graphical statements.

1939.   Nebraska Writers' Project.   "Indian Place Legends. "
        NFP, 2 (1957), 1-15.

1940.   Nebraska Writers' Project.   "Santee-Sioux Indian
        Legends. "   NFP, 21 (1937), 1-15; 23 (1937), 1-14.

1941.   Neihardt, John G.   "Red Hail and the Two Suitors. "
        IW, May-June 1945, pp. 6-10.   Retelling of an old
        Sioux story celebrating the genius of woman.

1942.  Newell, Cicero.  Indian Stories.  New York:  Silver,
       Burdett & Co. , 1912.  191 pp.

1943.  Pidgeon, William.  Traditions of De-coo-dah.  New
       York:  H. Thayer, 1958.

1944.  Pond, Samuel W.  Legends of the Dakotas and Other
       Selections from the Poetical Works.  Minneapolis,
       MN:  K. Holter Publishing Co. , 1911.  Pond's own
       poetic works, including the retelling of some Sioux
       legends.

1945.  Price, S. Goodale.  Black Hills:  The Land of Legend.
       Los Angeles, CA:  DeVorss and Co. , 1935.  Four-
       teen short tales.

1946.  Prucha, Fr. Francis Paul, ed.  Americanizing the
       Indians:  Writings by the "Friends of the Indian"
       1880-1900.  Cambridge, MA:  Harvard University
       Press, 1973.  358 pp.  A number contain informa-
       tion on the Sioux.

1947.  R[obinson], D[oane].  "The Legend of Medicine Knoll. "
       CHSSD, 12 (1924), 179.

1948.  Robinson, Doane.  "Tales of the Dakota:  One Hun-
       dred Anecdotes Illustrative of Sioux Life and Think-
       ing. "  CHSSD, 14 (1928), 485-537.

1949.  Searls, Mrs. L  Legend of St. Anthony Falls:  Sioux
       Legends.  St. Paul, MN:  Published Privately,
       1921.  11 pp.

1950.  Severance, Mary Frances (Harriman).  Indian Legends
       of Minnesota.  New York:  D. D. Merrill Co. ,
       1893.  184 pp.

1951.  Snelling, William J.  William Joseph Snelling's Tales
       of the Northwest.  1830; rpt. Minneapolis:  Univer-
       sity of Minnesota Press, 1936.  254 pp.

1952.  Sneve, Virginia Driving Hawk.  The Chichi Hoohoo
       Bogeyman.  New York:  Holiday House, 1975.  63
       pp.  Juvenile literature.

1953.  The Souvenir:  A Token of Remembrance.  London:
       T. Nelson and Sons, 1859.  28 pp.  Contains songs
       with music.

1954.   Spence, Lewis.   The Myths of North American In-
        dians.   London:   G. G. Harrap and Co. , 1914;
        rpt. New York:   Kraus Reprint, 1972.   393 pp.
        Contains a section of thirty-five pages of short
        Sioux stories.

1955.   Standing Bear, Luther.   Stories of the Sioux.   Bos-
        ton:  Houghton Mifflin Co. , 1934.   79 pp.

1956.   Theisz, R. D.   Buckskin Tokens:   Contemporary Oral
        Narratives of the Lakota.   Aberdeen, SD:   North
        Plains Press, 1975.   72 pp.   Told by four con-
        temporary Lakota storytellers.

1957.   Thorson, Alice O.   The Tribe of Pezhakee:   A Legend
        of Minnesota.   Minneapolis:   Heywood Manufacturing
        Co. , 1901.   232 pp.

1958.   Tvedten, Benet, comp.   An American Indian Anthol-
        ogy.   Marvin, SD:   Blue Cloud Abbey, 1971.

1959.   Wallis, Wilson D.   "Beliefs and Tales of the Canadi-
        an Dakota. "   JAFL, 36 (1923), 36-101.   Told by
        Sioux at Portage la Prairie and Griswold, Manitoba,
        in 1914.

1960.   Washburn, Wilcomb E.   Narratives of North Ameri-
        can Indian Captivities.   111 vols.   New York:   Gar-
        land Publishing, Inc. , 1977-  .   Facsimile reprints
        devoted to narratives of Indian captivity from 1542
        through 1955.   Thirteen volumes contain Sioux ma-
        terial, some of which pertains to legend.

1961.   Wilson, Gilbert L.   "The Iktomi Myth. "   CHSND, 1
        (1906), 474-475.   Told by a Santee and a Yankton
        Sioux.

1962.   Wissler, Clark.   "Some Dakota Myths.  L "   JAFL,
        20 (1907), 121-131; II, 195-206.   Five myths from
        Pine Ridge Reservation.

1963.   Zitkala-S̊a (Gertrude Bonnin).   American Indian
        Stories.   Washington, DC:   Hayworth Publishing
        House, 1921.   195 pp.   Autobiography, essays,
        and legends.

1964.   Zitkala-S̊a.   Old Indian Legends.   Boston:  Ginn and Co. ,
        1901.   165 pp.   Fourteen legends, largely about Iktomi.

## THE MINNESOTA SIOUX WAR

1965.   Adams, Moses N.  "The Sioux Outbreak in the Year
        1862, with Notes of Missionary Work Among the
        Sioux. "  CMHS, 9 (1901), 431-452.  Adams served
        as a missionary, then as an agent.

1966.   Anderson, Harry H.  "A Challenge to Brown's Sioux
        Indian War Thesis. "  Montana, 12:1 (January 1962),
        40-49.  Brown blamed the War on Sioux renegades.

1967.   Andrist, Ralph D.  "Massacre!  Minnesota's Sioux
        Uprising. "  AH, 13 (April 1962), 8-17.

1968.   Babcock, Willoughby M.  "Minnesota's Frontier:  A
        Neglected Sector of the Civil War. "  MiH, 38 (June
        1963), 274-286.

1969.   Babcock, Willoughby M.  "Minnesota's Indian War. "
        MiH, 38 (September 1962), 93-98.

1970.   Babcock, Willoughby M.  "The Sioux Outbreak of
        1857 and 1862. "  WM, 18 (1921), 142-146.

1971.   Big Eagle.  "The Great Sioux Uprising of 1862. "
        See entry no. 1936, pp. 173-185.  Big Eagle was
        a Santee Sioux, writing from personal experience.

1972.   "Big Eagle's Story of the War. "  CMHS, 6 (1894),
        382-400.

1973.   Block, Herman A.  Two Young Ministers of the Wis-
        consin Conference of the Now Known Evangelical
        United Brethren Church Who Were Killed by Indians
        in Minnesota in 1862.  Milwaukee:  Ken Cook Co. ,
        1959.   12 pp.

1974.   Boyd, Robert K.  "The Birch Cooley Monuments. "
        MiH, 12:3 (September 1931), 297-301.

1975.   Brill, Ethel C.  Rupahu's Warning, A Story of the
        Great Sioux Outbreak.  Philadelphia:  Macrae Smith
        Co. , 1931.   286 pp.

1976.   Brown, Samuel J.  "Night Ride of Samuel J. Brown:
        To My Friends and Comrades This Little Edition Is
        Dedicated. "  n. p. , n. d. , 18 pp.   Extracted from
        Senate Doc. No. 23, 56 Cong. , 2nd Sess.

1977.   Buck, Daniel. Indian Outbreaks. Minneapolis: Ross
        and Haines, Inc., 1965. 284 pp. Buck witnessed
        many events during the Minnesota Sioux War.

1978.   Buell, Salmon A. "Judge Flandrau in the Defense of
        New Ulm During the Sioux Outbreak of 1862."
        CMHS, 10:Pt. 2 (1905), 782-818.

1979.   Burleigh, Walter A. Indian Massacre in Minnesota:
        Removal of the Sioux Indians. Washington, DC:
        n.p., 14 pp. Correspondence of Congressional
        Delegate Burleigh with the Secretary of the Interior
        and the Commissioner of Indian Affairs about the
        possibility of the removal of eastern Sioux who were
        engaged in the Minnesota War to Nebraska.

1980.   Calkins, Franklin W. "Cut-Face--A Historical Sketch
        by F. W. Calkins." MM, 5 (1896), 249-253.

1981.   Carley, Kenneth, ed. "As Red Men Viewed It:
        Three Indian Accounts of the Uprising." MiH, 38
        (1962), 126-149. The stories of Chief Big Eagle,
        Lightning Blanket, and George Quinn.

1982.   Carley, Kenneth. "The Sioux Campaign of 1862:
        Sibley's Letters to His Wife." MiH, 38 (Septem-
        ber 1962), 99-114.

1983.   Carley, Kenneth. The Sioux Uprising of 1862. St.
        Paul: Minnesota Historical Society, 1961. 80 pp.
        A pictorial history of thirty-eight days.

1984.   Connolly, Alonzo P. Minneapolis and the G. A. R.
        with a Vivid Account of the Battle of Birch Coulee,
        Sept. 2 and 3, the Battle of Wood Lake, Sept. 23,
        the Release of the Women and Children Captives at
        Camp Release, Sept. 26, 1862. Minneapolis:
        George N. Morgan Post, A. P. Connolly, 1906.
        56 pp.

1985.   Connolly, Alonzo P. A Thrilling Narrative of the
        Minnesota Massacre and the Sioux War of 1862-63:
        Graphic Accounts of Siege of Fort Ridgley; Battles
        of Birch Coulie, Wood Lake, Big Mound, Stony
        Lake, Dead Buffalo Lake and Missouri River.
        Chicago: A. P. Connolly, 1896. 273 pp.

1986.   Connors, Joseph. "The Elusive Hero of Redwood

Ferry. " MiH, 34 (Summer 1955), 233-238. On a
Ferryman killed during the Minnesota Sioux War
after ferrying others to safety.

1987.   Crooker, George A. S.   "A Letter to Lincoln on the
        Sioux Outbreak. "  MA, 19:3 (July 1954), 3-17.
        Dated October 7, 1862.

1988.   Dakota Indians, Defendants.  The Court Proceedings
        in the Trial of Dakota Indians Following the Mas-
        sacre in Minnesota in August, 1862.  Minneapolis:
        Satterlee Printing Co. , 1927.   79 pp.

1989.   Daniels, Asa W.   "Reminiscences of Little Crow. "
        CMHS, 12 (1908), 513-530.   Daniels, a physician
        among the eastern Sioux before the War,  said of
        the causes:   "There is good reason to believe that
        had the treatment been just, humane and generous,
        the outbreak of 1863 would never have occurred. "

1990.   Daniels, Asa W.   "Reminiscences of the Little Crow
        Uprising. "  CMHS, 15 (1915), 323-336.   Differs
        somewhat from the above, yet Daniels concludes:
        "Had the government faithfully carried out the treaty
        obligations and dealt with the Sioux justly and hu-
        manely,  the outbreak would not have occurred. "

1991.   Davis, Jane S.   "Two Sioux War Orders:  A Mystery
        Unraveled. "  MiH, 41:3 (Fall 1968),  117-125.
        About Abraham Lincoln's hand written order,  the
        copy that went to Sibley was not in the President's
        hand.   See also "Lincoln's Sioux War Order, " en-
        try no. 2028.

1992.   Davis, LeRoy G.   "Ambushed by Indians.   The New
        Ulm Massacre--A Thrilling Chapter in Minnesota's
        History. "  MM, 5 (1896), 64-66.

1993.   Davis, Samuel M.   "The Sioux Massacre of 1862. "
        MWH, 16 (1892), 660-664.

1994.   Davis, Samuel M.   "Sioux Massacre, 1862. "  NMa,
        16 (1891), 660.

1995.   Dietz, Charlton.   "Henry Behnke:  New Ulm's Paul
        Revere. "  MiH, 45:3 (Fall 1976),  111-115.

1996. "The Doud Diary." CHSSD, 9 (1918), 471-474. Excerpts from the journal of George W. Doud, a Private in Company F, 5th Regiment of the Minnesota Volunteers during the 1862 War.

1997. Earle, Ezmon W. Reminiscences of the Sioux Indian Massacre in 1862. Fairfax, MN: A. M. Wallace, 1908. 45 pp.

1998. Eastlick, Lavina (Dat). "Revolt of the Sioux." In Scalps and Tomahawks: Narratives of Indian Captivity. Ed. Frederick Drimmer. New York: Coward-McCann, 1961. pp. 314-329.

1999. Ebell, Adrian N. "The Indian Massacres and the War of 1862." H, 27 (June 1863), 1-24. After consulting with Albert Colgrave, Alfred L. Riggs and J. E. Whitney, Ebell wrote a fairly objective account.

2000. Eckman, Jeannette, ed. The Kinkeads of Delaware as Pioneers in Minnesota, 1856-1863. Wilmington, DE: G. W. Butz, Jr., 1949. Contemporary accounts of experiences in the Sioux war of 1862. 95 pp.

2001. Egan, James Joseph. The Battle of Birch Cooley as Described by Two of the Participants--J. J. Eagan and Robert Boyd. Olivia, MN: The Olivia Times Publishing Co., 1926. 32 pp.

2002. "Ending the Outbreak." CHSSD, 9 (1918), 409-469. Valuable article, which includes a report on the journey up the Missouri by the Peace Commission of 1866, a speech by Yanktonai Bone Necklace, a report on a Sun Dance, etc.

2003. Endreson, Mrs. Guri. "Guri Endreson, Frontier Heroine." MiH, 10 (1929), 425-430. A letter from Guri of Harrison, Minnesota to her daughter in Norway, dated December 2, 1866, in which she describes her experiences during the Minnesota Sioux War.

2004. "Execution of Thirty-eight Sioux Indians at Mankato, Minnesota, December 26, 1862." Mankato Daily Review, December 26, 1896.

2005.  Fearing, Jerome W.  The Picture Story of the Min-
       nesota Sioux Uprising.  St. Paul, MN:  N. W. Pub-
       lications, 1962.  31 pp.

2006.  Fort, Solomon R.  "The Sioux Indian War."  IHR, 10:
       3 (July 1894), 132-137; 11:3 (July 1895), 323-329.
       Personal recollections about the Minnesota Sioux
       War.

2007.  Fort Ridgley State Park and Historical Society.  Mem-
       orial of the Sioux Indian Outbreak.  Fairfax, MN:
       Fairfax Standard Print, n. d.  20 pp.

2008.  French, John C.  The Heroine of Lake Shetek in Min-
       nesota:  A Western Historical Fragment Interwoven
       with Pennsylvania.  Altoona, PA:  Tribune Press,
       1923.  10 pp.

2009.  Fridley, Russell W.  "Charles E. Flandrau:  Attor-
       ney at War."  MiH, 38 (September 1962), 116-125.
       About Flandrau's role in the War.

2010.  Fridley, Russell W. , et al. , eds.  Charles E. Flan-
       drau and the Defense of New Ulm.  New Ulm, MN:
       Brown County Historical Society, 1962.  62 pp.  A
       biography of Flandrau is followed by a description
       of the Battle of New Ulm and his recollections about
       it.

2011.  Furness, Marion R.  "Governor Ramsey and Frontier
       Minnesota:  Impressions from His Diary and Let-
       ters."  MiH, 28:4 (December 1947), 309-328.  Com-
       ments on the Minnesota Sioux War.

2012.  Gluek, Alvin C.  "The Sioux Uprising:  A Problem in
       International Relations."  MiH, 34 (Winter 1955),
       317-324.  Canadian fears of a possible invasion by
       Sioux.

2013.  Goff, Lyman Bullock.  An 1862 Trip to the West.
       Pawtucket, RI:  Pawtucket Boy's Club Press,  1926.
       158 pp.

2014.  Gray, John S.  "The Santee Sioux and the Settlers at
       Lake Shetek."  Montana, 25:1 (January 1975), 42-
       54.

2015. H. H. A. "Official Correspondence Pertaining to the War of the Outbreak, 1862-1865." CHSSD, 31 (1962), 469-563.

2016. Hachin-Wakanda (Lightning Blanket). Story of the Battle of Fort Ridgley, Minn., August 20 and 22, 1862. Morton, MN: O. S. Smith, 1908. 5 pp.

2017. Hagadorn, Henry J. "On the March with Sibley in 1863: The Diary of Private Henry J. Hagadorn." Ed. John P. Pritchett. NDHQ, 5 (January 1931), 103-129.

2018. Henig, Gerald S. "A Neglected Cause of the Sioux Uprising." MiH, 54:3 (Fall 1976), 107-110.

2019. Hoover, Herbert T. "Little Crow Was a Peacemaker." NCA, No. 2 (October 1972), pp. 79-80.

2020. Howard, John R. "The Sioux War Stockades." MiH, 12 (1931), 301-303.

2021. Hummel, August. 1922 Souvenir: 60th Anniversary of the Indian Wars, New Ulm, August 18-25, 1862, Fort Ridgley, August 18-27, 1862. New Ulm, MN: n.p., 1922. 4 pp. Also published on the 75th anniversary in 1937.

2022. Humphrey, John Ames. "Boyhood Remembrances of Life Among the Dakotas and the Massacre in 1862." CMHS, 15 (1915), 337-348. Places the Sioux in very bad light.

2023. Ingham, William H. "The Iowa Northern Border Brigade of 1862-3." AIo, 5:7 (October 1902), 481-523. Participated in defense of New Ulm. Contains military correspondence, roster of men, etc.

2024. Jones, Robert H. "The Northwestern Frontier and the Impact of the Sioux War, 1862." Mid, 41 (1959), 131-153.

2025. Ketchem, Roule, and Tracy H. Marsh. The Sioux Uprising of 1862 in Meeker County. Grove City, MN: Grove City Women's Club, 1962. 44 pp.

2026. Laut, Agnes Christina. "Heroines of Lake Shetek,

Minnesota. " OM, 51 (March 1908), 686-698; OM, 52 (June 1908), 271-286.

2027.  Leonhart, Rudolph.  Erinnerungen an Neu Ulm. Erlebnisse aus dem Indianer-gemetzel in Minnesota 1862.  Pittsburg, KS:  n. p. , 1880.  46 pp.

2028.  "Lincoln's Sioux War Order. "  MiH, 33 (Summer 1952), 77-79.  A facsimile of Lincoln's hand-written order that gives the names of thirty-nine Indians and mixed-bloods sentenced to be hanged for "crimes" in the Minnesota Sioux War.

2029.  Little Crow.  "Speech to Council of War on the Eve of the Sioux Uprising in Minnesota, August 18, 1862. "  See entry no. 1936, pp. 171-172.  Taken from "Taoyateduta Is Not a Coward. "

2030.  McKusick, Marshall.  "Major William Williams at Iowa Lake in 1862. "  AIo, 42:8 (Spring 1975), 569-582.  About military affairs in the Minnesota Sioux War.

2031.  Malmros, Oscar.  "The Sioux War. "  In Minnesota Adjutant-General Office Report, 1862.  St. Paul, MN:  n. p. , 1863, pp. 23-133.

2032.  Mason, August L.  "The Tragedy of Minnesota. "  In The Pioneer History of America.  Boston:  N. Wilson & Co. , 1891, pp. 794-835.

2033.  Minnesota.  Legislature.  "Civil War and the Sioux Uprising Centennial Commission. "  Newsletter, October 27, 1960-October 19, 1961.

2034.  Minnesota State Commissioner for the Distribution of the Refugee Fund.  Report of the State Commissioner for the Distribution of the Refugee Fund, February 28th, 1863.  St. Paul:  F. Driscoll, Printer, 1863.  14 pp.

2035.  Minnesota State Fair, August 31-September 5, 1908. Souvenir Libretto:  The Great Spectacular Production of Fort Ridgley in 1862, 1000 People Including 300 Indians.  n. p. , 1908.  8 pp.

2036.  Minnesota Territorial Legislative Assembly.  Com-

The Minnesota Sioux War                                    199

mittee on Memorializing Congress for Expenses of
Expedition Against Indians. St. Paul, MN: The
Assembly, 1857. 4 pp.

2037. Minnesota Valley Historical Society. Sketches, Historical and Descriptive, of the Monuments and Tab-
lets, Erected by the Minnesota Valley Historical
Society in Renville and Redwood Counties, Minnesota. Morton: Minnesota Valley Historical Society,
1902. 79 pp. To commemorate incidents, and to
honor certain Indians and non-Indians who participated in the Minnesota Sioux War.

2038. Moncrieff, Ascott Robert Hope. The Sioux Rebellion
in Minnesota. Stuttgart: E. Klett Verlag, 1956.
40 pp. Story of an immigrant boy.

2039. Neill, Edward D. History of Fillmore County, Including Explorers and Pioneers of Minnesota; ...
and Charles S. Bryant. Sioux Massacre of 1862
and State Education. Minneapolis: Minnesota Historical Company, 1882. 626 pp. Also included in
his History of Freeborn County, History of Houston
County, and History of Rice County, each of which
were published in 1882.

2040. Nicolay, John George. Lincoln's Secretary Goes West:
Two Reports by John G. Nicolay on Frontier Indian
Troubles 1862. Ed. Theodore C. Blegen. La-
Crosse, WI: Sumac Press, 1965. 69 pp.

2041. Nyberg, Sigfrid. Svenskerne i Minnesota: An Episod
ur det Amerikanska Inbordeskriget, 1862-63. Gote-
borg, Sweden: O. L. Lamms Forlag, 1863. 88
pp. Apparently a fictionalized account of an episode in the Minnesota Sioux War.

2042. Nziramasanga, Caiaphas T. "Minnesota: First State
to Send Troops." JW, 14:1 (June 1975), 42-59.
Considerable information about the Minnesota Sioux
War.

2043. Oehler, Charles M. The Great Sioux Uprising. New
York: Oxford University Press, 1959. 272 pp.
Accompanied by a war chronology and maps, this
readable narrative is based largely upon published
and secondary sources. It explains the origins, the

beginning, the progress, and the results of the Minnesota Sioux War. Reliable and balanced, though somewhat romanticized.

2044. "Official Correspondence Pertaining to the War of the Outbreak, 1862-1865." CHSSD, 8 (1916), 100-588. Deals largely with military affairs during and immediately following the Minnesota Sioux War. Contains a statement by I-Ha-O-Jan-Jan, a Sisseton Chief at Lac Traverse.

2045. Oman, A. P. "The Monson Lake Massacre." My Church, 21 (1935), 37-46. Report on a massacre in 1862, as told to Victor E. Lawson by A. P. Oman.

2046. Oviatt, Charles J. "The 'Sibley Scout.'" OTT, 1:3 (September-October, 1940), 5-11, 22; rpt. pp. 51-57, 68.

2047. Painter, Charles C. How We Punish Our Allies. Philadelphia: Indian Rights Association, 1888. 7 pp. Information about Sisseton and Wahpeton soldiers and scouts.

2048. Patten, F. J. The Great Sioux Uprising, 1862. Marshall, MI: n. p. , 1862. 12 pp. Personal narratives by soldiers of Company H, 6th Minnesota Infantry.

2049. Peterson, Clarence Stewart. Known Military and Civilian Dead During the Minnesota Sioux Indian Massacre in 1862. Known Dead During the Great Blizzard in Minnesota in January 1873. Baltimore, n. p. , 1958.

2050. Peterson, O. A. "I Was in Sioux Uprising." Rotarian, 76 (April 1950), 1.

2051. Pierce, Parker L. The Adventures of "Antelope Bill" in the Indian War of 1862. 1898; rpt. as Antelope Bill. Minneapolis, MN: Ross and Haines, 1962. 203 pp.

2052. Pio, Louis. "The Sioux War of 1862: A Leaf from the History of Scandinavian Settlers in Minnesota, 1884." Scandinavia, 1:5-6 (March-April, 1884), 141-145, 177-178.

2053.  Ramsey, Alexander, Governor of Minnesota. Message
       of Governor Ramsey to the Legislature of Minnesota.
       St. Paul, MN: W. R. Marshall, State Printer,
       1862.  24 pp.  Delivered during an extra session,
       September 9, 1862.

2054.  Renville, Gabriel.  "A Sioux Narrative of the Out-
       break in 1862, and of Sibley's Expedition in 1863."
       CMHS, 10: Pt. 2 (1905), 595-613.

2055.  Renville, Victor.  "A Sketch of the Minnesota Mas-
       sacre."  CHSND, 5 (1923), 251-272.  Includes a
       genealogy of Victor Renville.

2056.  Ronnenberg, H. A.  "America's Greatest Mass Exe-
       cution."  AMe, 67 (November 1948), 565-571.

2057.  Russo, Priscilla Ann.  "The Time to Speak Is Over:
       The Onset of the Sioux Uprising."  MiH, 45:3 (Fall
       1976), 97-106.

2058.  Satterlee, Marion P.  The Court Proceedings in the
       Trial of Dakota Indians Following the Massacre in
       Minnesota in August 1862.  Minneapolis, MN:  Sat-
       terlee Printing Co., 1927.  16 pp.

2059.  Satterlee, Marion P.  A Description of the Massacre
       by Sioux Indians, in Renville County, Minnesota,
       August 18-19, 1862.  Minneapolis, MN:  The Fish-
       er Paper Box Company, 1916.  18 pp.  Compila-
       tion of names of victims and the circumstances
       surrounding their deaths.

2060.  Satterlee, Marion P.  A Detailed Account of the Mas-
       sacre by the Dakota Indians of Minnesota in 1862.
       Minneapolis, MN:  Marion P. Satterlee, 1923.
       136 pp.  Lists casualties, prisoners, and Indians
       killed, hanged and pardoned.

2061.  Satterlee, Marion P.  "Narratives of the Sioux War."
       CMHS, 15 (1915), 348-370.  His account of the
       killing of Little Crow on July 3, 1863.  Blames the
       War on the failure of the federal government to re-
       lease payments and food on time.

2062.  Satterlee, Marion P.  The Story of Capt. Richard
       Strout and Company, Who Fought the Sioux Indians
       at the Battle of Kelly's Bluff, at Action, Minn., on

Wednesday, September 3rd, 1862.    Minneapolis,
MN:   Marion P. Satterlee, 1909.   9 pp.

2063.   Scanthebury, Thomas.    Wanderings in Minnesota Dur-
        ing the Indian Troubles of 1862.    Chicago:   F.  C.  S.
        Calhoun,  Printer, 1867.   32 pp.    Valuable account
        by a contemporary observer.

2064.   Schmahl, Julius August.    Address at New Ulm, Min-
        nesota, August 20, 1919, and Kimball, Minnesota,
        Sept. 27, 1919, on the Occasion of a Home-coming
        of Soldiers of the World War, and of the Fifty-
        seventh Anniversary of the Repulse of the Sioux In-
        dians.    Minneapolis:   Syndicate Printing Co. , 1919.
        21 pp.

2065.   Seymour, C. G. , and J. C. Gresham.    "Sioux Re-
        bellion. "   HW, 7 February 1891, pp.  106,  108-09.

2066.   "Sioux War of 1862 at Superior. "   WMH, 3:4 (June
        1920), 473-477.    Letters by Thomas Bardon.

2067.   "Sioux War in Minnesota, 1862-1863. "   Winners of
        the West, 13:10 (September 1936), 16 pp.

2068.   Smith, R. A.    "A Risk That Cost Two Lives. "   AIo,
        11:6 (July 1914), 425-428.

2069.   "Der Aufstand der Sioux im Jahre 1862. "   Katholi-
        schen Missionen (1876), pp.  133-138, 182-186, 201-
        203.

2070.   Sweet, George W.    "Incidents of the Threatened Out-
        break of Hole-in-the-Day and Other Ojibways at
        Time of the Sioux Massacre of 1862. "   CMHS, 6
        (1894), 401-408.

2071.   Sweet, Mrs. Sarah.    The Massacre of 1862:   A
        Memoriam of Early Frontier Life in Minnesota.
        Hopkins, MN:   n. p. , 1863.    Poetry.

2072.   Trenerry, Walter N.    "The Shooting of Little Crow:
        Heroism or Murder?"   MiH, 38 (September 1962),
        150-153.    The shooting occurred July 3, 1863.

2073.   U. S.  Office of Indian Affairs.    Letter of the Secre-
        tary of the Interior, Communicating ... Information

in relation to the Conditions of the Indians Now Lo-
cated in the Vicinity of Lake Traverse and Fort
Wadsworth, Dakota Territory, at the Outbreak in
Minnesota in 1862, the Part They Took in Con-
nection with the Outbreak, and the Cause of Their
Being Permitted to Remain Near the Minnesota
Frontier. Washington, DC: Government Printing
Office, 1867. 12 pp. Senate Exec. Doc. No. 22,
39 Cong., 2nd Sess.

2074. U. S. President. Message of the President of the
United States in Answer to a Resolution of the Senate of the 5th Instant in Relation to the Indian Bar-
barities in Minnesota. Washington, DC: Government Printing Office, 1862. 9 pp. Senate Exec.
Doc. No. 7, 37 Cong., 3rd Sess.

2075. U. S. Quartermaster Corps. "List of Scouts Em-
ployed in Sibley's Campaign Against the Sioux Indians." n. p., n. d. 51 pp. A copy with the W. R.
Marshall Journal, Minnesota Historical Society.

2076. U. S. Sioux Commissioners. Claims for Depredations
by Sioux Indians. Washington, DC: Government
Printing Office, 1864. 23 pp. House Exec. Doc.
No. 58, 38 Cong., 1st Sess.

2077. U. S. War Department. "Official Correspondence Pertaining to the War of the Outbreak, 1862-1865."
CHSSD, 8 (1916), 100-588.

2078. U. S. War Department. Inspector General's Office.
Dakota Indian War Claims of 1862: Letter from the
Chief Clerk of the War Department, Transmitting a
Report of Inspector General James A. Hardie.
Washington, DC: Government Printing Office, 1874.
House Exec. Doc. No. 286, 43 Cong., 1st Sess.

2079. Wall, Oscar G. Recollections of the Sioux Massacre:
An Authentic History of the Yellow Medicine Inci-
dent, of the Fate of Marsh and His Man, of the
Sieges and Battles of Fort Ridgely, and of Other
Important Battles and Experiences, Together with a
Historical Sketch of the Sibley Expedition of 1863.
Lake City, MN: The Home Printery, 1908. 282
pp. An early attempt to condense eyewitness ac-
counts and to prepare from them a general history

of the Minnesota Sioux War.   Hailed by Mark
Twain for its "literary excellence," it makes good
reading, although it lacks objectivity.

2080.   Warner, Charles E., and Charles M. Foote.   History
of the Minnesota Valley, Including the Explorers and
Pioneers of Minnesota ... and History of the Sioux
Massacre.   Minneapolis, MN:   North Star Publishing Co., 1882.

2081.   Webb, Wayne E.   The Great Sioux Uprising:   A Tour-
ist Guide to the Area Swept by the Uprising of the
Sioux Indians of Minnesota.   Redwood Falls, MN:
n. p., 1962.   24 pp.

2082.   Webb, Wayne E.   Uprising:   A Newspaper Story of
the Sioux Uprising of 1862.   Redwood Falls, MN:
n. p., 1962.   27 pp.   First appeared in the Redwood
Gazette.

2083.   Welsh, Herbert.   "The Meaning of the Sioux Outbreak."
SMa, 9 (April 1891), 439-452.   Says Indians were
responsible for Wounded Knee 1890; proposes ways
to help Indians.

2084.   West, Nathaniel.   The Ancestry, Life, and Times of
Hon. Henry Hastings Sibley.   St. Paul, MN:   Pioneer Press Publishing Co., 1889.   596 pp.   Considerable information about the Minnesota Sioux War
in this apologetic biography.

2085.   Weston, Leonard C.   "The Intrepid Hero of the Battle of Fort Ridgely, 1862."   NAM, 5:1 (Spring 1967),
34-46.

2086.   Wilson, Horace B.   Reminiscences of the Indian War
of 1862.   Red Wing, MN:   Red Wing Printing Co.,
1886.   15 pp.

2087.   Winks, Robin W.   "The British North American West
and the Civil War."   NDH, 24:3 (July 1957), 139-
152.   Contains information about the Minnesota
Sioux War and its effects upon Canada, and the
dispatch of American cavalry under Major Edwin
Hatch to combat the Sioux in that area.

2088.   Woolworth, Nancy Louise.   "Marshall's Expedition,
1862."   Wi-iyohi, 16:4 (1962), 1-7.

MISSIONARIES

2089.   Aldrich, Vernice M. "Father George Antoine Bel-
        court, Red River Missionary. " NDHQ, 2:1 (Octo-
        ber 1927), 30-52.   Information about a hunting ex-
        pedition with the Sioux in 1845, and other observa-
        tions.

2090.   Allis, Samuel.  "Forty Years Among the Indians on
        the Eastern Borders of Nebraska. " PNSHS, 2
        (1887), 133-166.   On a missionary's work with the
        Sioux.

2091.   Anderson, Rufus.  Memorial Volume of the First
        Fifty Years of the American Board of Commis-
        sioners for Foreign Missions.   Boston: The Board,
        1861.   642 pp.   Includes information about the
        work of Congregational and Presbyterian mission-
        aries among the Sioux under the American Board.

2092.   Annual Report of the Board of Missions of Protestant
        Episcopal Church.   New York:  Sanford Narroun
        and Co. , 1865-69.   Supplies information about the
        early work of Episcopal missionaries among the
        Sioux.

2093.   Barnds, William Joseph. "The Ministry of the Rever-
        end Samuel Dutton Hinman Among the Sioux. "  His-
        torical Magazine of the Protestant Episcopal Church,
        38:4 (December 1969), 393-401.   After traveling to
        Crow Creek with the eastern Sioux, the controver-
        sial Hinman became principal Episcopal missionary
        among Sioux in Dakota Territory.

2094.   Barraghen, Gilbert J.   Father DeSmet's Sioux Peace
        Mission of 1868 and the Journals of Charles Gal-
        pin.   Chicago:  Illinois Catholic Historical Society,
        1930.

2095.   Bartlett, Samuel Colcord.   Historical Sketch of the
        Missions of the American Board Among the North
        American Indians.   Boston:  The Board, 1876.   47
        pp.   Contains information about Congregationalists
        and Presbyterians among the Sioux.

2096.   Barton, Winifred.   John P. Williamson:  A Brother to
        the Sioux.   New York:   Fleming H. Revell Co. ,

1919. With more emotion than objectivity, the
daughter of Williamson describes his remarkable
life as a Presbyterian missionary among the Sioux.

2097.  Beard, Augustus Field.  A Crusade of Brotherhood:
A History of the American Missionary Association.
Boston:  The Pilgrim Press, 1909.  334 pp.  Cov-
ers Indian missions, pp. 63-93.

2098.  Betschart, Ildefons.  Der Apostel der Siouxindianer:
Bischof Martinus Marty, O. S. B. ,  1834-1896.
Einsiedeln, Switzerland:  Stift Einsiedeln, 1934.
132 pp.  The only complete biography of Bishop
Marty, who established Benedictine missions among
the Sioux, has been translated by Rev. Joseph
Eisenbarth as "The Apostle of the Sioux Indians. "
American Catholic Historical Society of Philadel-
phia Records,  49 (1838), 97-134, 214-48; 50 (1839),
33-64.

2099.  The Blackrobe in the Land of the Wigwam.  St. Francis, SD:  St. Francis Mission, 1920.  31 pp.  About
the work of Jesuits on Rosebud Reservation in the
days of Father Digmann.

2100.  Blegen, Theodore C.  "The Pond Brothers. "  MiH,
15 (September 1934), 273-281.  First Protestant
missionaries among the Sioux, arrived at Lake
Calhoun in 1834.

2101.  Blegen, Theodore C.  "Two Missionaries in the Sioux
Country:  The Narrative of Samuel W. Pond. "
MiH,  21:1 (March 1940), 15-32; 21:3 (June 1940),
158-175; 21:4 (September 1940), 272-283.

2102.  Brain, Belle M.  The Redemption of the Red Man.
New York:  Board of Home Missions of the Presbyterian Church U. S. A. ,  1904.  Describes Presbyterian work among the Sioux; some on the Minnesota Sioux War.

2103.  [Burleson, Hugh L.]  "Bishop Hare as a Citizen. "
CHSSD, 10 (1920), 13-24.  Address by Bishop
Burleson at the presentation of an oil painting in
Pierre, January 15, 1919.

2104.  Carson, Charles.  "The Indians as They Are. "  The

*Catholic World,* November, 1898, pp. 146-160.
Praises the work of Catholic missionaries and com-
plains about government discrimination against this
denomination, with some justification.

2105.  Chittenden, Hiram M. , and Alfred T. Richardson.
        The Life, Letters and Travels of Father Pierre
        Jean De Smet, S. J. 1801-1873:  Missionary Labors
        and Adventures Among the Wild Tribes of the North
        American Indians.  4 vols.  1905; rpt. New York:
        Arno Press, 1969.  From his initial appearance
        among Yanktons in 1839 to his final efforts just be-
        fore his death in 1873, Father DeSmet worked often
        among the Sioux, both as an evangelist and as
        spokesman for the U. S. government.  This is the
        most complete work on his efforts.

2106.  Clark, Alden H.  1835 Speaks to 1935.  n. p. , n. d.
        11 pp.  Address preserved by the Minnesota His-
        torical Society delivered at Fort Snelling June 11,
        1935, about the founding of the first Protestant
        mission in Minnesota among the Sioux.

2107.  Clements, Fr. David J. , comp.  "Built on a Firm
        Foundation":  Standing Rock Centenary, 1873-1973.
        Fort Yates, SD:  Catholic Indian Mission, 1973.
        Brief history of the first Catholic mission station
        among the Sioux in the Dakotas that grew into a
        permanent facility.

2108.  Collins, Mary C.  How I Became a Missionary.  New
        York:  American Missionary Association, n. d.
        Founded a mission and hospital facility on Standing
        Rock Reservation, became religious adviser to
        Sitting Bull.  See entry no. 2178.

2109.  Collins, Mary C.  The Story of Elizabeth Winyan, A
        Dakota Woman.  Chicago:  American Missionary
        Association, 1886.  8 pp.

2110.  Committee for Indian Missions.  Annual Report of
        Committee for Indian Missions.  New York:  Bible
        House, 1878.

2111.  Connolly, James B.  "Father DeSmet in North Dakota. "
        NDH,  27:1 (Winter 1960), 4-24.  About the work of
        DeSmet with Sioux.

2112.   Cook, Joseph Witherspoon.   Form for Making Cate-
        chists in the Missionary Jurisdiction of Niobrara.
        Yankton Agency:   St. Paul's School Press, 1878.
        5 pp.   In Dakota language.

2113.   Cox, Ignatius Loyola.   "The Mission in Long Prairie. "
        AD,  3 (July 1914),  276-282.

2114.   Creswell, Robert J.   Among the Sioux:   A Story of
        the Twin Cities and the Two Dakotas.   Intro.  David
        R. Breed.   Minneapolis:   University of Minnesota
        Press, 1906.

2115.   Cutler, F. Sanford.   "An Evaluation of Documents
        Useful to the Ethnohistorian:   The Writings of
        Father Hennepin. "   PMAS,  23 (1955),  23-28.

2116.   Dakota Congregational Winyan Okadikiciye ... Woici-
        conae qa Woope.   Constitution and By-laws.   San-
        tee, NB:   Santee Normal Training School, 1897.
        11 pp.   Dakota text followed by English.

2117.   Daniels, R.   "Fierce-Fighting Sioux Turned Christian. "
        The Mentor,  12 (March 1924),  43-45.

2118.   Davis, Samuel M.   "Hennepin as Discoverer and Au-
        thor. "   CMHS,  9 (1901),  223-240.   Hennepin spent
        some three months among the Sioux in 1680.

2119.   Deming, Wilbur Stone.   The Church on the Green:
        The First Two Centuries of the First Congrega-
        tional Church at Washington, Connecticut, 1741-
        1841.   Hartford, CT:   Brentano's, 1941.   235 pp.
        Includes information about the work of Samuel and
        Gideon Pond in Minnesota among the Sioux.

2120.   DeSmet, Fr. Pierre Jean.   The Indian Missions in
        the United States of America,  Under the Care of
        the Missouri Province of the Society of Jesus.
        Philadelphia:   King and Baird, Printers, 1841.

2121.   DeSmet, Fr. Pierre Jean.   Life, Letters and Travels,
        Eighteen Hundred One to Eighteen Seventy Three.
        4 vols.   1905; rpt. New York:   Kraus Reprint
        Corp. , 1971.   Listed also under entry no. 2105.

2122.   DeSmet, Fr. Pierre Jean.   New Indian Sketches.
        1904; rpt. Seattle:   Shorey Publications, 1970.

2123.   DeSmet, Fr. Pierre Jean. Western Missions and
        Missionaries. 1863; rpt. White Plains, NY: Irish
        University Press, Inc. , 1970.

2124.   Donnelly, W. Patrick. "Father Pierre-Jean DeSmet:
        United States Ambassador to the Indians." HRS,
        29 (1954), 7-142.

2125.   Drury, Clifford M. Presbyterian Panorama: One
        Hundred and Fifty Years of National Missions His-
        tory. Philadelphia: Board of Christian Education,
        Presbyterian Church, 1952.

2126.   Duratschek, Sr. Mary Claudia. Beginnings of Cathol-
        icism in South Dakota. Washington, DC: Catholic
        University of America Press, 1943.

2127.   Duratschek, Sr. Mary Claudia. Crusading Along Sioux
        Trails: A History of the Catholic Indian Missions of
        South Dakota. St. Meinrad, IN: Grail Publisher,
        1947. 334 pp.

2128.   Duratschek, Sr. Mary Claudia. Under the Shadow of
        His Wings: History of Sacred Heart Convent of
        Benedictine Sisters. Aberdeen, SD: North Plains
        Press, 1971. 368 pp.

2129.   Father Eugene Buechel, S. J. Memorial Museum. St.
        Francis, SD: St. Francis Indian Mission, 1973.
        60 pp. History of St. Francis Mission 1885-1973;
        lists Sioux artifacts held by the Museum at St.
        Francis.

2130.   Fitzgerald, Sr. Mary Clement. "Bishop Marty and
        His Sioux Missions, 1876-1896." CHSSD, 20 (1940),
        528-558.

2131.   Flandrau, Charles E. "The Work of Bishop Whipple
        in Missions for the Indians." CMHS, 10: Pt. 2
        (1905), 688-696.

2132.   Forbes, Bruce D. "Presbyterian Beginnings in South
        Dakota, 1840-1900. " SDH, 7:2 (Spring 1977), 115-
        153. Presbyterian work began in Minnesota with
        Dr. Thomas Williamson, Dr. Stephen R. Riggs,
        Joseph B. Renville.

2133.   Frackelton, William. "The Story of Father De-

Smet. "  OTT,  1:2  (July-August 1940),  5-6,  14-
16,  18-19.

2134.    Gates,  Charles  M.  "The  Lac  Qui  Parle  Indian  Mission. "  MiH,  16:2  (June 1935),  133-151.  Mission
station  founded  in  July  1835  along  the  Minnesota
River  by  Thomas  S.  Williamson  and  Alexander  Huggins.

2135.    Gerhardt,  Alfred  C.  P.  1665-1965:  Three  Hundred
Years  of  Missionary  Work  Among  the  Sioux  Indians:
A  Research  Project  in  Chronological  Order  on  the
History  of  the  Missionary  Work  that  Was  Done
Among  the  Sioux  Indians.  Dunmore,  PA:  Frank
Pane  Offset  Printing  Co. ,  1969.  103 pp.

2136.    Gesner,  Anthon  Temple.  The  Sioux  of  South  Dakota.
Hartford,  CT:  Junior  Auxiliary  Publishing  Co. ,
1898.  17 pp.

2137.    Gilman,  Samuel  C.  The  Conquest  of  the  Sioux.  Indianapolis,  IN:  The  Hollenbeck  Press,  1900.  86
pp.

2138.    Gmeiner,  John.  The  Last  Sioux  of  Minnesota.  St.
Paul,  MN:  D.  D.  Merrill  Co. ,  1893.  7 pp.
Extr.  from  Literary  Northwest,  3:3  (June  1893),
156-163.

2139.    Goll,  Fr.  Louis  J.  Jesuit  Missions  Among  the  Sioux.
St.  Francis,  SD:  St.  Francis  Mission,  1940.  70
pp.

2140.    Graber,  Kay,  ed.  Sister  to  the  Sioux:  The  Mem-
oirs  of  Elaine  Goodale  Eastman,  1885-91.  Lincoln:
University  of  Nebraska  Press,  1978.  175 pp.
Based  on  Eastman's  diary  while  a  teacher  on  the
Sioux  reservation.

2141.    Graham,  Hugh.  "Catholic  Missionary  Schools  Among
the  Indians  of  Minnesota. "  13:3  (January  1931),
199-206.

2142.    Grandjean,  A.  La  Mission  remande.  Ses  Racines
dans  le  sol  suisse  romand.  Son  epanouissement
dans  la  race  thonga. ...  Paris:  Librarie  Fisch-
bacher,  1917.  328 pp.  On  missions  among  the
Sioux.

2143.   Gruwe, Luke.   "Rt. Rev. Martin Marty. "   LM,   2
        (April 1917),   120-122.

2144.   Hancock, Joseph W.   "Missionary Work at Red Wing,
        1849 to 1852. "   CMHS,   10: Pt. 1 (1905),   165-178.

2145.   Hare, William Hobart.   An Address Delivered by
        William Hobart Hare, Missionary Bishop of South
        Dakota, in Calvary Cathedral, Sioux Falls, January
        10, 1888.   Sioux Falls, SD:   Dakota Bell Publishing
        Co. , 1888.

2146.   Hare, William Hobart.   Annual Report of Missionary
        Bishop of Niobrara.   New York:   Bible House,
        1873-1893.

2147.   Hare, William Hobart.   A Statement from Bishop
        Hare Concerning the Sioux Indians of Dakota.   Phil-
        adelphia:   Indian Rights Association, 1890.   3 pp.

2148.   Hare, William Hobart.   Who Shall Be the Victims?
        Philadelphia:   Office of Indian Rights Association,
        1891.   7 pp.

2149.   Hennepin, Fr. Louis.   A New Discovery of the Vast
        Country in America . . .   Reprinted for the Second
        London Issue in 1698, with Facsimiles of Original
        Title-Pages, Maps, and Illustrations.   2 vols.   In-
        tro. , notes by Reuben G. Thwaites.   Chicago:
        A. C. McClurg Co. , 1903.

2150.   Hertz, Rudolf.   The Most Successful Mission of the
        American Board.   Santee, NB:   Santee Normal
        Training School, 1934.   11 pp.

2151.   Hinman, Samuel Dutton.   The Dakota Mission. . . .
        Report to the Minnesota Convention for the Year
        Ending June 1864.   The Mission of St. John to the
        Dakota Indians, Now Located at Fort Thompson, on
        the Upper Missouri.   Faribault, MN:   n. p. , 1864.

2152.   Hinman, Samuel Dutton.   Journal of the Rev. S. D.
        Hinman, Missionary to the Santee Sioux Indians,
        and Taopi, by Bishop Whipple.   Philadelphia:
        McCalla and Stavely, 1869.   89 pp.

2153.   Hinman, Samuel Dutton.   Protestant Episcopal Church
        in the U. S. A.   Book of Common Prayer.   Dakota.

Ikce Wocekiye Wowapi.   St. Paul, MN:   Pioneer
Printing Co., 1865.   321 pp.

2154.   Historical Records Survey.   Minnesota.   Report of
        the Chippewa Mission Archaeological Investigation.
        St. Paul:   The Minnesota Historical Records Survey
        Projects, 1941.   On Lac Qui Parle Mission.

2155.   Hoover, Herbert T., and Sr. Patricia Mylott.   Marty
        Mission:   A Brief History.   Marty, SD:   Marty
        Indian School, 1975.   16 pp.   Brief history pub-
        lished for distribution at the 50th anniversary of the
        Mission, just before the boarding school was turned
        over to the Yankton Sioux Tribe by the Benedictine
        Order.

2156.   Howe, Mark A. Dewolf.   "Apostle to the Sioux:
        Bishop Hare of South Dakota."   AMo, 108 (Septem-
        ber 1911), 359-370.

2157.   Howe, Mark A. Dewolf.   The Life and Labors of
        Bishop Hare, Apostle to the Sioux.   New York:
        Sturgis, 1911.   417 pp.   Principal leader of Sioux
        missions operated by Episcopalians in the Dakotas;
        the standard biography.

2158.   Humphreys, Mary Gay, ed.   Missionary Explorers
        Among the American Indians.   New York:   C.
        Scribner's Sons, 1913.

2159.   Humphreys, Mary Gay.   "Stephen Riggs Forty Years
        with the Sioux."   Missionary Explorers Among the
        American Indians.   New York:   C. Scribner's Sons,
        1913, pp. 187-227.

2160.   Hunt, Elizabeth H., ed.   "Two Letters From Pine
        Ridge Mission."   CO, 50 (Summer 1972), 219-225.

2161.   Kenton, Edna, ed.   Jesuit Relations.   New York:
        Vanguard Press, 1970.

2162.   Kenton, Edna.   With Hearts Courageous.   New York:
        Liveright, 1971.   On missions in churches for Indi-
        ans.

2163.   Kleber, Fr. Albert.   History of St. Meinrad Arch-
        abbey, 1854-1954.   St. Meinrad, IN:   Grail Press,

1954. Includes the history of the establishment of Benedictine Missions among the Sioux by Martin Marty.

2164. Landon, Raymond Horace, ed. "Letters of Early Missionary Days." MA, 26 (1964), 55-63. Mainly letters to Gideon Pond.

2165. "Louis Hennepin, the Franciscan, First Explorer of the Upper Mississippi River." CMHS, I (1872), 302-313.

2166. McCoy, Mary Ann, and LeRoy Paulson. Takoo Wakan to Christian Faith: 126 Years' Mission to the Dakota Indians; A Pageant to Be Presented at Lac Qui Parle Mission Park, July 15-16, 1961. n. p., 1961. 21 pp.

2167. Maiers, Sr. Marmson. The History of Immaculate Conception Indian Mission, Stephan, South Dakota, 1886-1961. Watertown, SD: n. p., 1961.

2168. Mattingly, Fr. Ambrose. "The Sioux." IS, 1 (April 1919), 6-8.

2169. Mattison, Ray H. "Indian Missions and Missionaries on the Upper Missouri to 1900." NH, 38:2 (June 1957), 127-154. Brief survey of missionary efforts from the establishment of the first "civilization fund" in 1819 to the year 1900, by a National Park Service historian.

2170. Merrill, Frank W. The Church and the Dakota Indians. Being Some Account of the Convocation of the Indian Congregations in the Missionary District of South Dakota. New York: n. p., 1905. Reprinted from Spirit of Missions, 69 (1904).

2171. Neill, Edward D. Early Days of the Presbyterian Branch of the Holy Catholic Church in the State of Minnesota. Minneapolis, MN: Johnson and Smith, Printers, 1873. 27 pp. Address delivered at First Presbyterian Church before the Synod of Minnesota, September 26, 1873.

2172. Neill, Edward D. "A Memorial to the Brothers Pond, the First Resident Missionaries Among the Dakotas."

In Macalester College Contributions, 2:8 (1892), 159-198.

2173.  North, Sr. Aquinas.  Catholic Missionary Activities in the Northwest 1818-1864.  Washington, DC: Catholic University of America, 1930.  154 pp.

2174.  North, Sr. Aquinas.  "Missionary Activity in the Northwest Under the French Regime 1640-1740. " AC, 6 (October, 1934), 141-160.

2175.  Norton, Sr. Mary Aquinas.  "Catholic Missions and Missionaries Among the Indians of Dakota. "  NDHQ, 5:3 (April 1931), 149-165.

2176.  Nute, Grace L. , ed.  Documents Relating to Northwest Missions, 1815-1827.  St. Paul:  Minnesota Historical Society for the Clarence W. Alvord Memorial Commission, 1942.  469 pp.

2177.  O'Hara, Edwin Vincent.  "Father De Smet in the Ecclesiastical Province of St. Paul. "  AD, 3 (July 1914), 290-305.

2178.  Olsen, Louise P.  "Mary Clementine Collins Dacotah Missionary. "  NDH, 18:4 (October 1951), 59-81.  Missionary from 1875 to 1905; supported Indian causes before the public and the federal government.

2179.  Parker, Donald D.  Denomination Histories of South Dakota.  Brookings, SD:  Published Privately, 1964.

2180.  Parker, Donald D.  Founding of the Church in South Dakota.  Brookings, SD:  Published Privately, 1962.

2181.  Parker, Donald D.  Founding Presbyterianism in South Dakota.  Brookings, SD:  Synod of South Dakota, 1963.

2182.  Parker, Donald D.  Lac qui Parle:  Its Missionaries, Traders and Indians.  Brookings, SD:  Published Privately, 1964.  286 pp.

2183.  Peabody, Mary B.  Zitkana Duzahan--Swift Bird:  A Life of Rt. Rev. William Hobart Hare.  Hartford,

CT:  Church Missions Publishing Co. ,  (1910?).
94 pp.

2184.  Pfaller, Fr.  Louis.  Father De Smet in Dakota.
Richardton, ND:  Assumption Abbey Press, 1962.
64 pp.

2185.  Pond, Gideon H.  "Life Among the Sioux at Lake Calhoun. "  Minnesota Historical Society Transactions
(1879),  pp.  5-9.

2186.  Pond, Samuel W.  Two Voluntary Missionaries Among
the Dakota,  Or the Labors of Samuel W.  and Gideon
H.  Pond.  Boston:  Congregational Sunday School
and Publishing Society, 1893.  Memoir on Sioux
mission work from the arrival of the Ponds in 1834
to the late nineteenth century.

2187.  Protestant Episcopal Church.  Book of Common Prayer.
Dakota.  Archdeaconry of the Niobrara.  Santee,
NB:  Mission Press, 1871.  16 pp.  Contains chants
and hymns of morning and evening prayer, in Dakota dialect.

2188.  Protestant Episcopal Church.  Book of Common Prayer.
Dakota.  South Dakota Obaspe:  Niobrara Deanery,
1947.  368 pp.  Reprint of the Book of Common
Prayer of 1929, with English and Dakota in parallel
columns.

2189.  Protestant Episcopal Church.  Catechism.  Dakota.
Santee, NB:  Mission Press, 1871.  28 pp.

2190.  Protestant Episcopal Church.  Liturgy and Ritual.
English and Dakota Service Book from the Book of
Common Prayer.  Philadelphia:  The Bishop White
Prayer Book Society, 1918.  519 pp.

2191.  Protestant Episcopal Church, Niobrara Missionary
District.  Annual Report of the Missionary Bishop
of Niobrara.  Philadelphia:  Board of Christian Education, 1873-  .

2192.  Rahill, Peter J.  The Catholic Indian Missions and
Grant's Peace Policy, 1870-1884.  Washington, DC:
Catholic University of America Press, 1953.  396
pp.  Much on the Sioux, especially Standing Rock
and Devil's Lake Reservations.

2193.  Ravoux, Fr. Augustin.  The Labors of Mgr. A.
       Ravoux Among the Sioux or Dakota Indians:  From
       the Fall of the Year 1841 to the Spring of 1844.
       St. Paul, MN:  Pioneer Press Company Printers,
       1897.  10 pp.  Includes the work of Mgr. J. Cretin,
       Bishop of the Diocese of St. Paul, which Ravoux
       continued until 1859.

2194.  Ravoux, Fr. Augustin.  Memoirs, Reminiscences et
       Conferences de Monseigneur A. Ravoux.  St. Paul,
       MN:  Ledoux et Le Vasseur, 1892.  257 pp.

2195.  Ravoux, Fr. Augustin.  Missionary Excursion in Iowa.
       Baltimore:  n. p. , 1848.  Letters to Bishop of Du-
       buque, Rt. Rev. Mathias Loras.

2196.  Ravoux, Fr. Augustin.  Reminiscences, Memoirs and
       Lectures of Monsignor A. Ravoux.  St. Paul, MN:
       Brown, Treacy and Co. , 1890.  223 pp.  Experi-
       ences among the Dakota in Minnesota.

2197.  "Rev. Mary Clementine Collins. "  CHSSD, 10 (1920),
       388-395.  Mary Collins served as missionary to the
       Sioux.  See entry no. 2178.

2198.  Riggs, Alfred Longley.  United Society of Christian
       Endeavor.  n. p. , 1890.  16 pp.  Constitution and
       by-laws in English and Dakota text.

2199.  Riggs, Mary B.  Early Days at Santee:  The Begin-
       nings of the Santee Normal Training School Founded
       by Dr. and Mrs. A. L. Riggs in 1870.  Santee,
       NB:  Santee Normal Training School Press, 1928.
       70 pp.

2200.  Riggs, Stephen R.  "The Dakota Mission. "  CMHS, 3
       (1880), 114-128.

2201.  Riggs, Stephen R.  "Journal of a Tour from Lac-Qui-
       Parle to the Missouri River. "  CHSSD, 13 (1926),
       330-344.  Tour in the year 1840.

2202.  Riggs, Stephen R.  "In Memory of Rev. Thos. S.
       Williamson, M. D. from a Sketch by Rev. Stephen
       R. Riggs, D. D. , in the New York Evangelist, July
       17, 1879. "  CMHS, 3 (1870-1880), 372-385.

2203.  Riggs, Stephen R.   Mary and I: Forty Years with the
       Sioux. Chicago: W. G. Holmes, 1880; rpt. Boston:
       Congregational House, 1887; Minneapolis, MN: Ross
       and Haines, 1969; Williamstown, MA: Carver
       House, 1971.  437 pp.  Autobiography of a mis-
       sionary.

2204.  Riggs, Stephen R.  "Memoir of Hon. Jas. W. Lynd. "
       CMHS, 3 (1880), 107-114.

2205.  Riggs, Stephen R.  "Protestant Missions in the North-
       west. "  CMHS, 6 (1894), 117-188.  Deals mainly
       with missions among the Sioux and Chippewa.

2206.  Riggs, Stephen R.  "Rev. T. S. Williamson, M. D. :
       His Long Career as Missionary Among the Sioux. "
       Minnesota Historical Society Transactions, 1879,
       pp. 135-144.

2207.  Riggs, Stephen R.  "Sketch of Mr. Pond's Life, by
       Rev. S. R. Riggs: Published in the Iapi Oaye
       (Word-Carrier) April, 1878. "  CMHS, 3 (1870-1880),
       358-364.

2208.  Riggs, Stephen R.  Sketches of the Dakota Mission.
       n. p. , 1873.  19 pp.  Published first in Iapi Oaye
       and Word Carrier, at Santee Normal Institute.

2209.  Riggs, Stephen R.  Tah-Koo Wah-Kan; Or, The Gos-
       pel Among the Dakotas.  Boston: Congregational
       Sabbath-School and Publishing Co. , 1869; rpt.
       Chicago: Library Resources, 1971; New York:
       Arno Press, 1972.  491 pp.

2210.  Riggs, Stephen R. , Thomas S. Williamson, and H. H.
       Sibley.  "Memorial Notices of Rev. Gideon H.
       Pond. "  CMHS, 3 (1889), 356-371.

2211.  Riggs, Theodore F.  A Log House Was Home: South
       Dakota Stories for My Two Boys.  Fwd. Louis P.
       Good.  New York: Exposition Press, 1961.  208
       pp.

2212.  Riggs, Thomas L. , and Margaret Kellog Howard.
       "Sunset to Sunset: A Lifetime with My Brothers
       the Dakotas. "  CHSSD, 29 (1958), 87-306.  Told
       by Riggs to his niece, Margaret Howard, this ac-

count contains considerable information about the
Sioux and their culture.

2213.  Ring, Nancy.  "The First Sioux Mission. "  14:4
(April 1932), 344-351.  The Mission of St. Michael
the Archangel, Fort Beauharnois.

2214.  Roden, Eugene J.  Augustin Ravoux, Pioneer Priest.
Minneapolis, MN:  Printed Privately, 1954.  160
pp.

2215.  Scott, John M.  High Eagle and His Sioux.  St. Louis,
MO:  Central Bureau Press, 1963.  96 pp.  The
story of a Jesuit missionary in the Dakotas.

2216.  Shea, John D. G.  History of the Catholic Missions
Among the Tribes of the United States, 1529-1854.
New York:  P. J. Kennedy, 1854.  514 pp.  Reis-
sued many times.

2217.  Sibley, Henry H.  "Tribute to Mr. Pond by Gen.
H. H. Sibley, in the Pioneer Press, Jan. 26,
1878. "  CMHS, 3 (1870-1880), 364-366.

2218.  Staffelbach, Georg I.  Schweizer als Glaubensboten
und Kulturtrager in Nordamerika.  (Luzern) Druck
and Verlag:  Buchdruckerei Schupfheim, a. g. , 1940.
78 pp.  Contains information about Martin Marty,
Bishop of Dakota.

2219.  Sterling, Everett W.  "Moses N. Adams:  A Missionary as Indian Agent. "  MiH, 35 (1956), 167-177.

2220.  The Story of Harriet Woodbridge Gilfillan:  Told by
Her Children.  n. p. , 1931.  29 pp.

2221.  Strong, William E.  The Story of the American Board:
An Account of the First Hundred Years of the Amer-
ican Board of Commissioners for Foreign Missions.
Boston:  Pilgrim Press, 1910.  523 pp.

2222.  Tanner, George C.  "History of Fort Ripley, 1849 to
1859, Based on the Diary of Rev. Solon W. Manney,
D. D. , Chaplain of this Post from 1851 to 1859. "
CMHS, 10: Pt. 1 (1905), 178-202.  Much information
about the Sioux, written by a minister.

2223.  Taylor, M. R. "Among the Sioux." Messenger of
       the Sacred Heart. 33 (1898), 1113-1120.  Begin-
       ning with Louis Hennepin, he traced missionary ef-
       forts by Catholic priests among the Sioux to the
       time of publication.

2224.  Terrell, John U. Black Robe: The Life of Pierre-
       Jean De Smet, Missionary, Explorer, Pioneer.
       New York: Doubleday, 1964. 381 pp.

2225.  Tuttle, Sarah. History of the Sioux or Dakota Mis-
       sion. Boston: Massachusetts Sabbath School Soci-
       ety, 1841. 94 pp.

2226.  Upham, Warren. "Obituary of Edward D. Neill."
       CMHS, 8 (1898), 497-501. Neill lived 1823-1893.

2227.  Virtue, Ethel B. "The Pond Papers." MHB, 3 (May
       1919), 82-86.

2228.  Welch, William, ed. Journal of the Rev. S. D. Hin-
       man, Missionary to the Santee Sioux Indians. And
       Taopi, by Bishop Whipple. Philadelphia: McCalla
       and Stavely Printers, 1869. 87 pp. Taopi was a
       Sioux chief who died in 1869.

2229.  Westropp, Fr. Henry L In the Land of the Wigwam:
       Missionary Notes from the Pine Ridge Mission.
       Pine Ridge, SD: Holy Rosary Mission, 1915. 14
       pp.

2230.  Whipple, Henry. Lights and Shadows of a Long Epis-
       copate: Being Reminiscences and Recollections of
       the Right Reverend Henry Whipple, Bishop of Min-
       nesota. New York: Macmillan, 1902.

2231.  Whipple, Henry. "Recollections of Persons and Events
       in the History of Minnesota." CMHS, 9 (1901), 576-
       586.

2232.  Whipple, Henry. Report of Bishop Whipple to the
       Board of Missions on the Indian Question and the
       Cause of the War. New York: M. B. Brown and
       Co., Printers and Stationers, 1869. 28 pp.

2233.  White, Fr. Robert A. "Church Imposed Uniformity."
       GPO, August 1969, pp. 13-14.

2234.  Willand, Jon. Lac Qui Parle, and the Dakota Mis-
       sion. Madison, MN: Lac Qui Parle County His-
       torical Society, 1964. 304 pp.

2235.  Williamson, Andrew W. "From a Memoir [of Thomas
       S. Williamson] in The Herald and Presbyter, July
       1879." CMHS, 3 (1889), 384-385.

2236.  Williamson, Jesse P. "Stephen Return Riggs."
       CHSSD, 13 (1926), 324-329. Presented at the dedi-
       cation of the bridge between Ft. Pierre and Pierre,
       South Dakota, to Riggs.

2237.  Williamson, John P. The Dakota Mission: Past and
       Present. Minneapolis, MN: Tribune Job Printing
       Co., 1886. 27 pp.

2238.  Williamson, Thomas S. "Tribute to Mr. Pond, by
       Rev. Thos. S. Williamson, Published in the 'Herald
       and Presbyter,' March 20, 1878." CMHS, 3 (1870-
       1880), 367-371.

2239.  Wolff, Gerald W. "Father Sylvester Eisenman and
       Marty Mission." SDH, 5:4 (Fall 1975), 360-389.
       On the founder of Marty Mission on the Yankton
       Reservation.

2240.  Woodruff, K. Brent. "The Episcopal Mission to the
       Dakotas, 1860-1898." CHSSD, 17 (1934), 553-603.

2241.  Young, Gertrude Stickney. "The Correspondence of a
       Niobrara Archdeacon." Historical Magazine of the
       Protestant Episcopal Church, 32 (1963), 3-15.

2242.  Young, Gertrude Stickney. "The Journal of a Mis-
       sionary to the Yankton Sioux: 1875-1902." CHSSD,
       29 (1958), 63-86. On Joseph Witherspoon Cook's
       mission work among the Yankton Sioux.

2243.  Zens, Sr. M. Serena. "The Educational Work of the
       Catholic Church Among the Indians of South Dakota,
       From the Beginning to 1935." CHSSD, 20 (1940),
       299-356.

RELIGION

2244.  Aberle, David F. "The Sun Dance and Reservation
       Underdevelopment." JES, 1:2 (Summer 1973), 66-
       73. See also entry no. 2337.

2245.  Albers, P., and S. Parker. "The Plains Vision Ex-
       perience: A Study of Power and Privilege." SJA,
       27:3 (1971), 203-233.

2246.  Aquila, Richard. "Plains Indian War Medicine." JW,
       13:3 (1974), 19-43.

2247.  Benedict, Ruth F. The Concept of Guardian Spirit in
       North America. 1923; rpt. New York: Kraus Re-
       print Corp., 1970.

2248.  Benedict, Ruth F. "The Vision in Plains Culture."
       AA, 24:1 (January-March 1922), 1-23. How Sioux
       sought visions by lacerating themselves.

2249.  Bennett, John. "The Development of Ethnological
       Theory as Illustrated by Studies of the Plains Sun
       Dance." AA, 46:2 (April-June 1944), 162-181.

2250.  Bible Society Record, 32:10 (1887). 147 pp. This
       pertains to a ban on the Dakota translation of the
       Bible by the Indian Office, and the Sioux response
       to it.

2251.  Blacksmith, May. "The Peace Pipe." IW, 1 August
       1936, pp. 35-36. Relates the origin of the peace
       pipe and the power it retains in modern times. By
       an Oglala Sioux.

2252.  Blish, Helen H. "The Ceremony of the Sacred Bow
       of the Oglala Dakota." AA, 36:2 (April-June 1934),
       180-187. Sometimes called "Medicine Bow," used
       by Medicineman Black Road, who used snake sym-
       bolism to cure snake bites.

2253.  Blish, Helen H. "The Drama of the Sioux Sun Dance."
       TAM, 17 (1933), 629-634.

2254.  Blish, Helen H. "Ethical Conceptions of the Oglala
       Dakota." University of Nebraska-University Studies,
       26:3-4 (July-October 1926), 79-123. Includes de-
       scriptions of several ceremonies.

2255.   Blumensohn, Jules.   "The Fast Among the North
        American Indians. "   AA, 35:3 (July-September
        1933), 451-469.

2256.   Brown, Joseph Epes.   "The Roots of Renewal. "   In
        Walter W. Capps, ed.   Seeing with a Native Eye.
        New York:   Harper and Row, 1976, pp. 25-34.

2257.   Brown, Joseph Epes.   The Sacred Pipe.   Norman:
        University of Oklahoma Press, 1953.   144 pp. ;
        Baltimore:   Penguin Books, Inc. , 1971.   The seven
        rites of the sacred pipe, as told to Brown by Black
        Elk.

2258.   Brown, Joseph Epes.   The Spiritual Legacy of the
        American Indian.   Lebanon, PA:   Sowers Printing
        Co. , 1970.   32 pp.   Pendle Hill Pamphlet No. 135.

2259.   Brown, Joseph Epes.   "The Unlikely Associates:   A
        Study in Oglala Sioux Magic and Metaphysic. "
        Ethnos, 35 (1970), 5-15.

2260.   Bryde, John.   "Indian Heritage:   No Other People So
        Naturally and Deeply Religious. "   GPO, December
        1968, pp.  10-14.

2261.   Bryde, John.   "The Indian Would Seek to Find His
        Place in Life by Vision Quest. "   GPO, November
        1970, pp.  6-7.

2262.   Bushnell, David Ives.   "Burials of the Algonquian,
        Siouan and Caddoan Tribes West of the Mississippi. "
        BBAE, 83 (1927); rpt. St. Clair Shores, MI:   Schol-
        arly Press, 1976.

2263.   Bushotter, George.   "Oath-Taking Among the Dakota. "
        IN, 4 (1927), 81-83.

2264.   Carrington, Henry B.   The Dacotah Tribes:   Their
        Beliefs, and Our Duty to Them Outlined.   Salem,
        MA:   The Salem Press, 1881.   From PAAAS, Vol.
        29.

2265.   Clements, F.   "Plains Indian Tribal Correlations with
        Sun Dance Data. "   AA, 33:2 (April-June 1931), 216-
        227.

2266.   Collier, Donald. "The Sun Dance of the Plains In-
        dians." IW, April 1940, pp. 46-50. It all but
        disappeared late in the nineteenth century but was
        revived in altered form in the 1930's.

2267.   Collins, M. C. "Religion of the Sioux Indians."
        MRW, 24 (November 1907), 827-831.

2268.   Corbett, William P. "The Red Pipestone Quarry:
        The Yanktons Defend a Sacred Tradition, 1858-
        1929." SDH, 8:2 (Spring 1978), 99-116. Yanktons
        reserved rights to the Pipestone Quarry site in the
        Treaty of Washington, 1858, and surrendered claim
        in return for payment from the U. S. government,
        1929.

2269.   Corum, Charles Ronald. "A Teton Tipi Cover Depic-
        tion of the Sacred Pipe Myth." SDH, 5:2 (Summer
        1975), 229-244. A buffalo hide tipi cover prepared
        in the period 1770-1820, now in the Königlichen
        Museum für Völkerkunde in Berlin.

2270.   Dance, R. H. "The Seven Pipes of the Dakota Sioux."
        PlA, 15:48 (1970), 81-82.

2271.   Daugherty, George H. "Mysticism and Associative
        Symbols of Thought Revealed in Indian Compositions."
        OC, 40 (August 1926), 449-468. Belief that there
        is psychological unity among all Indian tribes.

2272.   Deloria, Ella. "The Sun Dance of the Oglala Sioux."
        JAFL, 42 (October-December 1929), 354-413. In-
        cludes song lyrics in Sioux language, with English
        translations.

2273.   Densmore, Frances. "The Sun Dance of the Teton
        Sioux." Nature, 104 (January 1920), 437-440.

2274.   Devereux, George. Reality and Dream: Psychothera-
        py of a Plains Indian. 1951; rpt. New York: New
        York University Press, 1969; Anchor Books. New
        York: Doubleday Doran Co., 1969.

2275.   Dorsey, George A. "Legend of the Teton Sioux Medi-
        cine Pipe." JAFL, 19 (October-December 1906),
        326-329. Given by full-blood Percy Phillips, of
        Cheyenne River Reservation.

2276.   Dorsey, James Owen.  "A Study of Siouan Cults. "
        ARBAE,  11  (1894),  351-544;  rpt. in microfiche by
        NCR Microcard, 1968.   George Bushotter's recol-
        lections.

2277.   DuBois,  C.   "The 1870 Ghost Dance. "   UCPAR,  3:1
        (1939).

2278.   Eastman, Elaine Goodale.  "American Indian and His
        Religion. "   MRW,  60 (March 1937),  128-130.

2279.   Eastman, Elaine Goodale.  "The Ghost Dance and the
        Wounded Knee Massacre of 1890-91. "   NH,  26
        (1945),  26-42.

2280.   Eastman, Seth.   "Demoniacal and Superstitious Ob-
        servances of the Tribes in Minnesota, on the Upper
        Mississippi. "  In School,  Pt.  IV,  pp.  495-497.

2281.   Eastman, Seth.   "The Giant's Feast and Dance. "   In
        School,  Pt.  III,  pp.  487-488.   The giant is Heyoka.

2282.   Eastman, Seth.   "Gods of the Dacotahs. "  In School,
        Pt.  III,  pp.  485-487.

2283.   Feraca, Stephen E.   "The Teton Sioux Eagle Medicine
        Cult. "   AIT,  8:5 (1962),  195-196.

2284.   Feraca, Stephen E.   "Wakinyan:  Contemporary Teton
        Dakota Religion Museum of the Plains Indian. "   In
        Studies in Plains Anthropology and History.   Brown-
        ing, MT:   Museum of the Plains Indian, 1963.   No.
        2.   Discusses Sun Dance, vision quest, etc.

2285.   Feraca, Stephen E.   "The Yuwipi Cult of the Oglala
        and Sicanger Teton Sioux. "   PlA,  6:13 (August
        1961),  155-163.

2286.   Fletcher, Alice C.   "The Elk Mystery or Festival:
        Ogallala Sioux. "   PMR,  3 (1882),  276-288.

2287.   Fletcher, Alice C.   "The Emblematic Use of the Tree
        in the Dakotan Group. "   PAAAS,  45 (1896).   21 pp.

2288.   Fletcher, Alice C.   " Emblematic Use of the Tree in
        the Dakotan Group. "   Science,  2 October 1896, pp.
        475-487.

2289.   Fletcher, Alice C.   Indian Ceremonies.   Salem, MA:
        Salem Press, 1884.  73 pp.   Excellent book.

2290.   Fletcher, Alice C.   "Notes on Certain Beliefs Con-
        cerning Will Power Among the Siouan Tribes. "
        Science,  26 February 1897, pp.  331-334.

2291.   Fletcher, Alice C.   "The Religious Ceremony of the
        Four Winds or Quarters, as Observed by the San-
        tee Sioux. "  PMR,  3 (1882),  289-307.

2292.   Fletcher, Alice C.   "The Shadow or Ghost Lodge:  A
        Ceremony of the Ogallala Sioux. "  PMP,  3:3 and 4
        (1882).

2293.   Fletcher, Alice C.   "The Sun Dance of the Oglala
        Sioux. "  PAAAS,  31:Part 2 (1882),  580-584.

2294.   Fletcher, Alice C.   "The White Buffalo Festival of
        the Uncpapas. "  PMR,  3 (1882),  260-275.   A per-
        son who kills a non-Indian is considered to receive
        a blessing from the Great Spirit.

2295.   Franks, Kenny A.   "'The Sun-Dance of the Sioux':
        Written and Illustrated by Frederic Remington. "
        SDH,  6:4 (Fall 1976),  421-432.   Rpt. with notes
        of Frederic Remington.   See entry no. 2385.

2296.   Fugle, Eugene.   "The Nature and Function of the
        Lakota Night Cults. "  USDMN,  27:3/4 (1966), 1-
        38.

2297.   Gauvreau, Emile.   "Les Dakotas:  Religion, Moeurs,
        Coutumes. "  ICA,  15, Vol. I (1906),  311-313.   A
        résumé.

2298.   Gillette, J. M.   "The Medicine Society of the Dakota
        Indians. "  CHSND,  1 (1906),  459-474.

2299.   Gilmore, Melvin R.   "The Dakota Ceremony of Hunka. "
        IN,  6 (1929),  75-79.

2300.   Gilmore, Melvin R.   "The Dakota Ceremony of Pre-
        senting a Pipe. "  PMA,  18 (1932),  295-296.

2301.   Gilmore, Melvin R.   "Oath-taking Among the Dakota. "
        IN,  4 (1927),  81-83.

2302.   Goddard, Pliny Earl.   Notes on the Sun Dance of the
        Sarsi.   New York:   The Trustees, 1919.   On the
        Sun Dance among the Cree, but contains material
        on the same practice among Sissetons.

2303.   Greenway, John.   "The Ghost Dance: Some Reflec-
        tions with Evidence on a Cult of Despair Among the
        Indians of North America. "   AW,  6:4 (1969), 42-
        47.   Contains a photograph taken in 1891 near Pine
        Ridge.

2304.   Grobsmith, Elizabeth S.   "Wakunza:  Uses of Yuwipi
        Medicine Power in Contemporary Teton Dakota Cul-
        ture. "   PlA,  19:64 (May 1974), 129-133.   Wakunza
        means supernatural retribution, and is a mechanism
        for social control.

2305.   Hadjo, Masse.   "A Defense of the Ghost Dance Re-
        ligion. "   See entry no. 1936, pp. 90-91; from
        The Chicago Tribune, 3 December 1890.   Author
        was Sioux.

2306.   Haeckel, Joseph.   "Totemismus and Zweiklassensys-
        tem bei den Sioux-Indianern. "   Anthropos, 32
        (1937),  210-238,  450-501.

2307.   Hallam, John.   "A Sioux Vision-Thick-Headed-Horse
        Dream. "   In William W.  Beach's Indian Miscel-
        lany....   Albany, NY:   J. Munsell, 1897, pp.
        127-144.

2308.   Hallowell, A. Irving.   "Bear Ceremonialism in the
        Northern Hemisphere. "   AA,  28 (1926), 1-175.
        Very informative.

2309.   Hanson, James.   "The Oglala Sioux Sun Dance. "
        Museum of the Fur Trade Quarterly, 1:3 (1965),
        3-5.

2310.   Heath, Virginia S.   The Dramatic Elements in Amer-
        ican Indian Ceremonials.   Americana Series, No.
        37.   Rpt. New York:  Haskell House Publishers,
        1970.

2311.   Herman, Jake.   Oglala-Sioux Sun Dance.   n. p. , 1961.

2312.   Herman, Jake.   "The Sacred Pole. "   Masterkey, 37:1
        (January-March 1963), 35-57.   About the Sun Dance.

2313.   Hollinshead, Ellen Rice.  "A Sioux Medicine Dance
        and a Perilous Journey."  RCH, 3:2 (Fall 1966),
        12-16.  Reminiscences near St. Paul.

2314.   Holm, James.  "Aristocrats in the Happy Hunting
        Grounds."  CHSSD, 12 (1924), 182-183.  Overheard
        a death prayer by an elderly Sioux woman.

2315.   Holy Dance, Robert.  "The Seven Pipes of the Dakota
        Sioux."  PlA, 15:48 (May 1970), 81-82.  From St.
        Francis on Rosebud Reservation, writes about the
        seven rites of the Peacepipe.

2316.   Hood, Flora M.  Something for the Medicine Man.
        Chicago:  Melmont Publishers, Inc., 1962.  Juven-
        ile literature.

2317.   Hoover, Herbert T., ed.  "Interview:  Noah White."
        SDR, 8:3 (Autumn 1970), 171-177.  White, a Winne-
        bago, is married to an eastern Sioux and lives at
        Prairie Island Reservation in Minnesota, where he
        is a leader in the Native American (Peyote) Church.
        Explains the meaning of Peyote.

2318.   Hovey, H. C.  "Eyah Shah."  AA, 1 (January 1887),
        35-36.

2319.   Howard, James H.  "The Dakota Heyoka Cult."  SM,
        78 (April 1954), 254-258.  About a "contrary cult"
        with special powers.

2320.   Howard, James H.  "A Note on the Dakota Water
        Drinking Society."  AIT, 7:3 (1961), 96.

2321.   Howard, James H.  "Notes on Two Dakota 'Holy
        Dance' Medicines and Their Uses."  AA, 55 (Octo-
        ber 1953), 608-609.

2322.   Howard, James H.  "The Tree Dweller Cults of the
        Dakota."  JAFL, 68 (1955), 169-174.  A folk-
        character of the eastern Sioux is the tree dweller;
        emphasizes the religious elements.  No story
        given.

2323.   Howard, James H.  "Yanktonai Dakota Eagle Trap-
        ping."  SJA, 10 (1954), 69-74.

2324.   Howard, James H.   "A Yanktonai Dakota Mide Bun-
        dle. "   NDH,  19:2 (April 1952),  133-139.

2325.   Howard, James H. , and Wesley R. Hurt, Jr.   "A
        Dakota Conjuring Ceremony. "   SJA,  8 (Autumn
        1952),  286-296.   See entry no.  2334.

2326.   Hultkrantz, Ake.   Conceptions of the Soul Among
        North American Indians:  A Study of Religious
        Ethnology.   Stockholm:  The Ethnographical Museum
        of Sweden,  1953.

2327.   Hultkrantz, Ake.   "North American Indian Religion in
        the History of Research:  A General Survey,  Part
        I. "   HR,  6:2 (November 1966),  91-107; "Part II. "
        HR,  6:3 (February 1967),  183-207; "Part III. "  HR,
        7:1 (August 1967),  13-34; "Part IV. "   HR,  7:2
        (November 1967),  112-148.

2328.   Hultkrantz, Ake.   "Prairie and Plains Indians. "
        Iconography of Religions,  10:3 (1973).

2329.   Hultkrantz, Ake.   "The Structure of Theistic Beliefs
        Among North American Plains Indians. "   Temenos,
        7 (1971),  66-74.

2330.   Hunt, Jerome.   Catholic Wocekiye Wowapi.   Fort
        Totten, ND:  Printed at the Catholic Indian Mission,
        1907.   154 pp.   Prayer book and hymnal in Sioux
        language.

2331.   Hurt, Wesley R.   "Factors in the Persistence of
        Peyote in the Northern Plains. "   PlA,  5:9 (May
        1960),  16-27.   Focuses attention upon the Sioux.

2332.   Hurt, Wesley R.   "The Yankton Dakota Church:  A
        Nationalistic Movement of the Northern Plains In-
        dians. "   In Essays in the Science of Culture in
        Honor of Leslie A. White.   Ed.  G. E. Dole and
        R. L. Carneiro.   New York:  T. Y. Crowell,
        1960,  pp.  269-287.

2333.   Hurt, Wesley R.   "A Yuwipi Ceremony at Pine
        Ridge. "   PlA,  5:10 (November 1960),  48-52.

2334.   Hurt, Wesley R. , and James H. Howard.   "A Dakota
        Conjuring Ceremony. "   SJA,  8 (1952),  286-296.
        On the Yuwipi,  a "doctoring ceremony. "

2335.  Jennings, Dana C. "Commandments of the Sioux."
       GPO, February 1967, p. 15.

2336.  Johnson, Dorothy M. "Ghost Dance: Last Hope of
       the Sioux." Montana, 6:3 (July 1956), 42-50.

2337.  Jorgensen, Joseph G. The Sun Dance Religion:
       Power for the Powerless. Chicago: University
       of Chicago Press, 1974. Very little on the Sioux.

2338.  Josephy, Alvin M. "Freedom for the American In-
       dian." The Critic, 32:1 (September-October 1973),
       18-27. Mentions the Sioux in particular.

2339.  Kehoe, Alice B. "The Ghost Dance Religion in Sas-
       katchewan, Canada." PlA, 13:42, Pt. 1 (Novem-
       ber 1968), 296-304. On the Sioux at Round Plain
       Reserve, near Prince Albert.

2340.  Kemnitzer, Luis S. "Yuwipi." InH, 11:2 (Spring
       1978), 2-5. Description of a Yuwipi ceremony,
       and comments on its meaning.

2341.  Kitchen, Dick. "Prayer Rock." DW, 2:1 (Spring
       1976), 26-27. Large boulder near Britton, SD,
       with markings.

2342.  Knickeberg, Walter. "The Indian Sweat Bath." Ciba
       Symposia, 1:1 (April 1939), 19-26.

2343.  LaBarre, Weston. The Ghost Dance--Origins of Re-
       ligion. Garden City, NY: Doubleday, 1970.

2344.  Laubin, Reginald, and Gladys Laubin. "Story of the
       Peace Pipe." Norman: University of Oklahoma
       Press, 1977. A 16mm color movie in the Plains
       Indian Culture Series, available by purchase only.
       Addresses the traditions and importance of the
       Peacepipe in Sioux religion.

2345.  Lewis, Thomas H. "The Heyoka Cult in Historical
       and Contemporary Oglala Sioux Society." Anthro-
       pos, 69:1 (1974), 17-32. By a psychiatrist.

2346.  Lewis, Thomas H. "Notes on the Heyoka, Teton
       Dakota 'Contrary Cult.'" PRRB, No. 11 (January
       1970, pp. 7-19.

2347.  Lewis, Thomas H.  "The Oglala (Teton Dakota) Sun
       Dance:  Vicissitudes of Its Structures and Func-
       tions. "  PlA, 17:55 (1972), 44-49.

2348.  Lewis, Thomas H., and Levi Mesteth, Jr.  "The
       Oglala Sun Dance 1968. "  PRRB, No. 5 (1968), pp.
       52-64.

2349.  Lynd, James W.  "The Religion of the Dakotas. "
       CMHS, 2: Pt. 2 (1889), 150-174.  Edited for publi-
       cation by Stephen Return Riggs, the observations
       of an educated trader among the eastern Sioux who
       "for a number of years may be said to have lived
       in a wigwam. "  Though not completed before his
       death in 1863, Lynd's manuscript is quoted often
       for its insights into Sioux religious philosophy.
       Contains perhaps the first written description of the
       Yuwipi ceremony.

2350.  McAllester, David P.  Peyote Music.  New York:
       Johnson Reprint Corp. , 1949.

2351.  McCann, Frank D.  "Ghost Dance:  Last Hope of
       Western Tribes. "  Montana, 16 (January 1966), 25-
       34.

2352.  McLeod, William C.  "Self-Sacrifice in Mortuary and
       non-Mortuary Ritual in North America. "  Anthro-
       pos, 33 (1938), 349-400.  Some information about
       the Sioux.

2353.  Mails, Thomas E.  Dog Soldiers, Bear Men, and
       Buffalo Women:  A Study of the Societies and Cults
       of the Plains Indians.  Englewood Cliffs, NJ:
       Prentice-Hall, 1973.  384 pp.

2354.  Mails, Thomas E.  Sundancing at Rosebud and Pine
       Ridge.  Sioux Falls, SD:  Center for Western
       Studies, 1978.  408 pp.  Emphasizes religious life
       in the context of Indian culture.

2355.  Malan, Vernon D. , and Clinton J. Jesser.  The Da-
       kota Indian Religion.  South Dakota Experiment Sta-
       tion Bulletin No. 473.  Brookings, SD:  South Da-
       kota State College, 1959.  Explains differences in
       Sioux and non-Indian value systems.

2356.   Marriott, Alice, and Carol K. Rachlin. Peyote.
        New York:   T. W. Crowell Co. ,  1971.

2357.   Masakutemani, Paul. "Narrative of Paul Masakute-
        mani. "  Trans.  Stephen Return Riggs.   CMHS, 3
        (1880),  82-90.

2358.   Masakutemani, Paul.  Testimony to the Love of Jesus:
        The Last Words of His Friend.  n. p. ,  1874.  29
        pp.

2359.   Melody, Michael E.  "The Lakota Sun Dance:  A
        Composite View and Analysis. "  SDH,  6:4  (Fall
        1976),  433-455.   Contains a summary of scholar-
        ship on the Sun Dance.

2360.   Melody, Michael E.  "Maka's Story:  A Study of a
        Lakota Cosmogony. "  JAFL,  90 (April-June 1977),
        149-167.   An Oglala creation story,  from the
        J. R. Walker manuscripts.

2361.   Meyers, John F.   "The Ghosts Danced in Blood. "
        AI,  1:1 (1963),  38-43.

2362.   Miller, David H.  Ghost Dance.  New York:  Duell,
        Sloan, 1959.  318 pp.   Based upon interviews with
        persons who participated in the Ghost Dance and
        survived the Wounded Knee Massacre.

2363.   Milligan, Edward A.  Sun Dance of the Sioux.  Bot-
        tineau, ND:   Privately Printed, 1969.  25 pp.

2364.   Mitchell, J. A.   "The Pipestone Quarry or Restoring
        an Ancient Indian Shrine. "  IW,  1 December 1934,
        pp. 25-29.   Describes work to restore this shrine.

2365.   Mooney, James.  "The Doctrine of the Ghost Dance. "
        In Teachings from the American Earth:  Indian Re-
        ligion and Philosophy.   Ed.  Dennis Tedlock and
        Barbara Tedlock.  New York:  Liveright, 1975, pp.
        75-95.

2366.   Mooney, James.  The Ghost Dance Religion and the
        Sioux Outbreak of 1890.   ARBAE, 14: Pt.  2 (1892-
        93),  641-1136;  rpt.  New York:   Dover, Inc. ,  1973.

2367.   Mooney, James.  The Ghost Dance Religion and the

Sioux Outbreak of 1890. Ed. F. C. Wallace. Chicago: University of Chicago Press, 1965. An abridged edition of entry no. 2366, the classic on the Ghost Dance, which Mooney wrote from careful research in documents at the National Archives.

2368. Mooney, James. "The Indian Ghost Dance." PNSHS, 16 (1911), 168-186.

2369. Moorehead, Warren K. "The Indian Messiah and the Ghost Dance." AAOJ, 13 (1891), 161-167. Primarily on the Sioux.

2370. Müller, Werner. Glauben und Denken der Sioux. Zur Gestalt Archaisen Weltbilker. Berlin: Von Dietrich Reimer, 1970. 413 pp.

2371. Muntsch, Albert. "The Relations Between Religion and Morality Among the Plains Indians." PrM, 4:1 and 2 (January-April 1931), 22-29. Contains material on the Sioux.

2372. Nephew, Allen. "American Indian: Must His Gift Be Lost?" GPO, December 1967, pp. 4-5.

2373. Neuman, Robert W. "Historic Burials, Fort Thompson, South Dakota." PlA, 7:16 (June 1962), 95.

2374. Nurge, Ethel. "The Sioux Sun Dance in 1962." ICA, 3 (1964), 105-114. On the piercing of Bill Schweigman, Lakota.

2375. O-Jan-Jan-Win (Harriette Westbrook). "Interesting Sioux Legend of the White Buffalo Calf Pipe." AI, 4:No. 6 (March 1930), 8. The story of the presentation of the Peacepipe to the Sioux by the White Buffalo Calf Girl.

2376. Overholt, Thomas W. "The Ghost Dance of 1890 and the Nature of the Prophetic Process." E, 21:1 (Winter 1974), 37-63.

2377. Pond, Gideon H. "Dakota Superstitions." CMHS, 2: Pt. 2 (1889), 215-255. Mostly on eastern Dakota (Santee) religion, by a knowledgeable but dogmatic Christian observer.

2378.   Pond, Gideon H.  Paganism, A Demon Worship:  A
        Discourse Delivered Before the Synod of Minnesota,
        September, 1860.  Philadelphia:  W. S. Young
        Book and Job Printer, 1861.  30 pp.  Appeared
        originally in Presbyterian Quarterly Review, Janu-
        ary, 1861.

2379.   Pond, Gideon H.  "Power and Influence of Dakota
        Medicine-Men. "  In School, Pt. IV, pp. 641-651.

2380.   Pond, Samuel W.  "The Dakotas or Sioux in Minne-
        sota as They Were in 1834. "  CMHS, 12 (1908),
        319-501.  Observations on eastern Sioux religion.

2381.   Powers, William K.  Oglala Religion.  1975; rpt.
        Lincoln:  University of Nebraska Press, 1977.
        233 pp.  Sound perceptions of Oglala religion, but
        presented in terms that few laymen will understand.

2382.   "Prayer for Rain. "  SEP, 4 September 1937, pp. 18-
        19.

2383.   Radin, Paul.  "Monotheism Among American Indians. "
        In Teachings from the American Earth.  Ed. Den-
        nis and Barbara Tedlock.  New York:  Liveright,
        1975, pp. 219-247.

2384.   Red Owl, Edward M.  "Religion. "  BCQ, 15:2 (1969),
        9-14.  The author is Sisseton Sioux.

2385.   Remington, Frederic.  "The Sun-Dance of the Sioux. "
        Century, 39:5 (March 1890), 753-759.  Witnessed
        the Sun Dance while visiting Spotted Tail Agency on
        Beaver Creek in Nebraska.

2386.   Ricketts, Mac Linscott.  "J. G. Jorgenson.  The Sun
        Dance Religion. "  JAAR, 41:2 (1973), 256-259.  Re-
        view of Jorgenson's book, entry no. 2337.

2387.   Riegert, Wilbur A.  Quest for the Pipe of the Sioux:
        As Viewed from Wounded Knee.  Rapid City, SD:
        Printing, Inc. , 1975.  164 pp.  A Chippewa writes
        about Sioux religion.

2388.   Riggs, Stephen R.  "The Dakota Mission. "  CMHS, 3
        (1870-1880), 115-128.

2389.   Riggs, Stephen R.   "The Theogony of the Sioux."
        AAOJ, 2 (1880), 265-270.

2390.   Ruby, Robert H.   "Yuwipi Ancient Rite of the Sioux."
        Montana, 16:4 (October 1966), 74-79; rpt. PRRB,
        No. 11 (January 1970), pp. 20-29.

2391.   Schusky, Ernest L.   "Political and Religious Systems
        in Dakota Culture."   See entry no. 528, pp. 140-
        147.

2392.   Schusky, Ernest L.   The Right to Be Indian.   Vermil-
        lion, SD:   Board of Missions of the United Presby-
        terian Church and Institute of Indian Studies, 1965.
        92 pp.

2393.   Schuster, Sr. M. Teresa, ed.   "Documents: Letters
        from the Dakota Frontier: I."   ABR, 11:3 and 4
        (September-December 1960), 302-326; "II."  ABR,
        12:1 (March 1961), 97-130.   Letters of Sr. M.
        Mattilda Cattani, O.S.B., written to her family in
        the period 1882-1905, containing information about
        the Sioux.

2394.   Schwatka, Frederick.   "The Sun Dance of the Sioux."
        CMag, 39 (1889-1890), 753-759.

2395.   Sidoff, Phillip G.   "An Ethnological Investigation of
        the Medicine Bundle Complex Among Selected Tribes
        of the Great Plains."   WA, 58:3 (September 1977),
        173-204.   Contains material on western Sioux and
        Assiniboines, as well as on other tribes.

2396.   Sioux Indian Prayer and Hymn Book.   Cincinnati, OH:
        J. Berning Printing Co., 1918.   A Catholic liturgy
        and ritual guide.

2397.   Skinner, Alanson.   "Medicine Ceremony of the Menom-
        ini, Iowa, and Wahpeton Dakota, with Notes on the
        Ceremony Among the Ponca, Bungi Ojibwas and
        Potawatomi Indians."   INM, 4 (1920), 357 pp.   Con-
        tains various belief-summaries.

2398.   Smith, J. L.   "A Ceremony for the Preparation of
        the Offering Cloths for Presentation to the Sacred
        Calf Pipe of the Teton Sioux."   PlA, 9:25 (August
        1964), 190-196.   Includes prayers in English transla-
        tion, and preparation of offerings.

2399.   Smith, J. L.  "The Sacred Calf Pipe Bundle:  It's
        [sic] Effect on the Present Teton Dakota. "  PlA,
        15:48 (May 1970), 87-93.  Contains legends.

2400.   Smith, J. L.  "A Short History of the Sacred Calf
        Pipe Bundle of the Teton Dakota. "  USDMN,  28:7
        and 8 (1967).

2401.   Spier, Leslie.  "The Sun Dance of the Plains Indians:
        Its Development and Diffusion. "  APAM,  16:Pt. 7
        (1921), 449-527.

2402.   Steinmetz, Fr. Paul B.  "The Relationship Between
        Plains Indian Religion and Christianity:  A Priest's
        Viewpoint. "  PlA,  15:48 (May 1970), 83-86.

2403.   Stewart, Omer C.  "The Peyote Religion and the
        Ghost Dance. "  InH,  5:4 (Winter 1972), 27-30.

2404.   Tedlock, Barbara.  "The Clown's Way. "  In Teach-
        ings from the American Earth.  Ed. Dennis Ted-
        lock and Barbara Tedlock.  New York:  Liveright,
        1975, pp. 105-118.

2405.   Thomas, Sidney J.  "A Sioux Medicine Bundle. "  AA,
        43:4 (1941), 605-609.  About the Buffalo Calf Pipe
        bundle on the Cheyenne River Reservation, in the
        possession of the Looking Horse family.

2406.   Upham, Warren.  "Mounds Built by the Sioux in Min-
        nesota. "  AAOJ,  27 (1905), 217-223.

2407.   Walker, James R.  "Oglala Metaphysics. "  In Teach-
        ings from the American Earth.  Ed. Dennis Ted-
        lock and Barbara Tedlock.  New York:  Liveright,
        1975, pp. 205-218.

2408.   Walker, James R.  "The Sun Dance and Other Cere-
        monies of the Oglala Division of the Teton Dakota. "
        APAM,  16:Pt. 2 (1917), 51-221; rpt. New York:
        AMS Press, 1977.

2409.   Walker, James R.  "The Sun Dance of the Oglala. "
        In The Golden Age of American Anthropology.  Ed.
        Margaret Mead and Ruth L. Bunzel.  New York:
        G. Braziller, 1960, pp. 377-391.

2410.   Wallis, Ruth S.  "The Changed Status of Twins Among

the Eastern Dakota. "  AnQ, 3:3 (July 1955), 116-
120.  Twinship connotes supernatural power among
the traditional Canadian Sioux.

2411.   Wanica, Anpetu Olhanke.  "The Lakota Sun Dance. "
Expedition, 13:1 (Fall 1970), 17-23.  A participant
describes the seven steps from preparation to fin-
ish.

2412.   Wassell, William H.  "The Religion of the Sioux. "
H, 89 (November 1894), 945-952.  Useful only as
an example of materials published by non-Indian
bigots with little knowledge.

2413.   West, George A.  Tobacco, Pipes and the Smoking
Customs of the American Indians.  1934; rpt.
Westport, CT:  Greenwood Press, Inc. , 1970.

2414.   [Whirlwind Soldier, Clement. ]  "Naming the Child. "
CHSSD, 9 (1918), 403-408.  Ceremony performed
in 1915 by High Pipe, for the son of Rosebud
Superintendent John H. Scriven.

2415.   Wilford, Lloyd A. , et al.  Burial Mounds of Central
Minnesota:  Excavation Reports.  St. Paul:  Minnesota Historical Society, 1969.

2416.   Williams, Mrs. W. K.  "Sun Dance of the Teton Dakota Was Very Trying Ordeal. "  AmI, 5:1 (November 1930), 10-11, 15.

2417.   Williamson, Andrew W.  "The Dakotas and Their
Traditions. "  AAOJ, 13 (1891), 54-55.

2418.   Wolcott, Peter Clarke.  The Religion of the Dakotas:
A Sermon Preached by Special Appointment, Before
the Convention of the Diocese of Iowa, in Davenport
Cathedral ...  May 15, 1888.  Davenport, IA:  Ed
Borcherat, 1888.  Although he erred in saying the
Sioux prayed to "many gods, " and in interpreting
other points of the religion, he obviously had observed Sioux religious practices and knew some
fundamentals.

2419.   Yarrow, Henry Crecy.  "A Further Contribution to
the Study of the Mortuary Customs of the North
American Indians. "  In ARBAE, 1 (1881).  On

burial customs of the Brules, and a description of
the "spirit keeper" tradition.

2420. Yarrow, Henry Crecy. "Some Superstitions of the
Live Indians. " AAOJ, 4 (1882), 136-144. Second-
hand information about burial customs and religious
practices among the Sioux.

2421. Zimmerly, David W. "When the People Gather:
Notes on the Teton Dakota Sun Dance. " InH, 11:1
(Winter 1978), 40-42 and PRRB, No. 6 (1968).
Comments on the ceremony, and identifies some of
the dancers.


RESERVATION AFFAIRS

2422. "The Action of the Interior Department in Forcing the
Standing Rock Indians to Lease Their Lands to Cattle Syndicates. " Indian Rights Association Publication. 2nd Series, No. 61. Philadelphia: Indian
Rights Association, May 12, 1902. 27 pp.

2423. Alberts, George B. "I. E. C. W. on the Fort Totten
Reservation. " IW, 1 March 1936, p. 25.

2424. Allen, Helen N. "Community Canning Kitchens at
Fort Peck. " IW, 1 January 1936, pp. 41-43.

2425. Anderson, Fred. "Wakpala's Subsistence Garden Suc-
cessful-- Thanks to Dam Built by CCC-ID. " IW, 15
October 1937, pp. 27-29. A community garden.

2426. Asbury, F. A. "Live Stock Activities of Pine Ridge
Indians. " IW, 15 January 1936, pp. 37-40. On
efforts to revive the cattle industry there.

2427. Bagby, Ralph. Indian Life and Adventures: Life and
Early Experiences on the Cheyenne and Standing
Rock Reservation. Pierre, SD: Hipple Printing
Co. , 1910.

2428. Baird, W. David. "The Quest for a Red-Faced White
Man: Reservation Whites View Their Indian Wars. "
See entry no. 1250, pp. 113-131.

2429.   Baumhoff, Richard G.   The Dammed Missouri Valley.
        New York:   Alfred A. Knopf, 1951.   On the main-
        stem dams and taking areas from the Indians.

2430.   Blakeslee, Clement.   "Some Observations on the In-
        dians of Crow Creek Reservation, South Dakota. "
        PlA, No. 5 (December 1955), 31-35.

2431.   Brosius, S. M.   "Rosebud Indians of South Dakota. "
        Indian Rights Association Publications, 2nd Series,
        from Senate Document No. 158, U. S. Senate. 58th
        Cong. , 2nd Sess.

2432.   "Buffalo Herds Return to Indian Ranges. "   IW, 1
        February 1935, p. 25.   Fifty buffalo were placed
        on Pine Ridge as part of a wildlife restocking plan.
        Some were taken to the Crow Reservation.

2433.   Bureau of Indian Affairs.   Rules and Regulations Re-
        lating to the Issuance of Patents in Fee and Cer-
        tificates of Competency and the Sale of Allotted
        and Inherited Indian Lands.   Washington, DC:
        Government Printing Office, 1910.

2434.   Burton, Henrietta K.   "Reinstating an Ancient Tribal
        Craft on the Pine Ridge Indian Reservation. "   IW,
        15 May 1935, pp. 21-25.   Oldtimers assemble to
        teach young people the ancient art of drying meat.

2435.   Byrnes, Philip S.   "Red Shirt Table Development. "
        IW, April 1939, pp. 16-19.   Describes a commun-
        ity development on the Pine Ridge Reservation dur-
        ing the 1930's.

2436.   Cash, Joseph H.   "The Reservation Indian Meets the
        White Man (1860-1914). "   See entry no. 1250, pp.
        93-111.

2437.   Champe, John L.   Yankton Chronology.   Indian
        Claims Commission Report for Docket 332-C.   New
        York:   Garland, 1974.

2438.   Coe, Auburn.   "Rodent Eradication, Fort Peck Reser-
        vation. "   IW, 1 November 1934, pp. 22-23.   IECW
        employed up to 100 men to poison ground squirrels
        on 230, 000 acres to provide employment and elim-
        inate an obstacle to agricultural production.

2439.  Collier, John. "Sioux Indian Rehabilitation and Re-
       lief:  The Facts of the Past Five Years. " IW, 1
       April 1936, pp. 15-17.  Collier defends his poli-
       cies in response to criticism from Marty Mission
       and elsewhere that he failed to protect the Sioux
       during depression years.

2440.  "Commissioner Collier Visits South Dakota Reserva-
       tions:  Reorganization's Purposes Told Sioux at
       Series of Meetings. " IW, 1 January 1935, pp. 23-
       24.  On his second visit to Sioux country, he went
       to Pine Ridge, Rosebud, Yankton, Lower Brule,
       Crow Creek, Cheyenne River, and Standing Rock
       reservations to explain the Wheeler-Howard Act.

2441.  Danziger, Edmund J.  "The Crow Creek Experiment:
       An Aftermath of the Sioux War of 1862. " NDH, 37:
       2 (Spring 1970), 104-123.  About the removal of
       eastern Sioux from Ft. Snelling to Crow Creek after
       the Minnesota Sioux War; a tragic event.

2442.  Danziger, Edmund J.  Indians and Bureaucrats:  Ad-
       ministering the Reservation Policy During the Civil
       War.  Urbana:  University of Illinois Press, 1974.
       240 pp.  Contains considerable information about the
       Sioux, including the Santee Uprising in 1862.

2443.  Decory, George.  "Grass Mountain Indian Dance Hall. "
       IW, 1 July 1935, pp. 32-33.  A typical dance hall
       used as a community facility.

2444.  De Mallie, Raymond.  "Pine Ridge Economy:  Cultural
       and Historical Perspectives. " In American Indian
       Economic Development.  Ed. Sam Stanley.  The
       Hague:  Mouton, 1978, pp. 237-312.

2445.  Dennett, Fred.  "Information Relative to the Opening
       of the Rosebud on Tripp County Lands. " CHSSD,
       11 (1922), 535-539.  A letter from the Indian Com-
       missioner dated August 25, 1908.

2446.  Dennett, Fred.  "Regulations, Opening Pine Ridge
       and Rosebud Lands. " CHSSD, 11 (1922), 551-555.

2447.  Department of the Interior.  "Report from Pine Ridge:
       Conditions on the Oglala Sioux Reservation. " CRD,
       7 (Summer 1975), 28-38.

2448.   Dollar, Clyde D.   "Renaissance on the Reservation."
        AW, 11:1 (1974), 6-9, 58-62.   About Rosebud
        Reservation.

2449.   Dollar, Clyde D.   Tribal Government Viewed Histor-
        ically:   Brief Remarks on the Brule Sioux's Con-
        cept of Tribal Government.   Vermillion, SD:   Da-
        kota Press, 1968.

2450.   Donnelly, Ignatius.   The Sale of the Sioux Reserva-
        tion.   Washington, DC:   Congressional Globe Office,
        1868.   8 pp.   A letter from Donnelly in reply to
        an editorial in the Winona Republican.

2451.   Eicher, Karl K.   Constraints on Economic Progress
        on the Rosebud Sioux Indian Reservation.   Cam-
        bridge:   Harvard University Press, 1960.   266 pp.

2452.   Eicher, Karl K.   "Income Improvement on the Rose-
        bud Reservation."   HO, 20 (Winter 1961-62), 191-
        196.   Gives reasons for lack of economic progress
        on Rosebud Reservation in the 1950's.

2453.   "The Emergency Employment Programs and the Sioux."
        IW, 1 February 1934, pp. 27-28.   Description of
        work relief available to Sioux people early in the
        New Deal period.

2454.   Estes, George C., and Richard R. Loder.   Kul-
        Wicasa-Oyate:   Lower Brule Sioux Tribe.   Lower
        Brule, SD:   Lower Brule Sioux Tribe, 1971.

2455.   Executive Orders Relating to the Indian Reservations,
        from May 14, 1855 to July 1, 1912.   Washington,
        DC:   Government Printing Office, 1912.

2456.   "Extension at Standing Rock Agency, North Dakota."
        IW, 1 June 1935, p. 24.   Describes home extension
        efforts that accompanied the Indian New Deal.

2457.   F. E. L.   "Taking Indians' Land:   Dealing of Con-
        gress with the Rosebud Sioux."   Philadelphia:   In-
        dian Rights Association, n.d.

2458.   Flood, H. J.   "Flandreau Rehabilitation."   IW, June
        1939, pp. 26-27.   Flandreau Reservation economy
        revived and grew through the expenditure of Indian
        relief and rehabilitation funds during the 1930's.

2459.  Foley, Michael F.   Yankton Tribal Lands:   An His-
       torical Analysis of the Opening and Development
       from 1849 to 1869.   New York:   Clearwater Pub-
       lishers, 1976.

2460.  Gilbert, Luke.   "Three Years of Emergency Work at
       the Cheyenne River Agency in South Dakota. "  IW,
       15 July 1936, pp. 36-37.   Tribal chairman de-
       scribes achievements.

2461.  "Grass Mountain Colony. "  IW, June 1939, pp. 28-29.

2462.  Green, Charles L.   "The Indian Reservation System
       of the Dakotas in 1889. "  CHSSD, 14 (1928), 307-
       417.

2463.  Haas, Theodore H.   Ten Years of Tribal Government
       Under IRA.   Chicago:   U. S. Indian Service, 1957.

2464.  Harrison, Jonathan Baster.   The Latest Studies on In-
       dian Reservations.   Philadelphia:   Indian Rights
       Association, 1887.

2465.  Hartle, Donald D.   The Dance Hall of the Santee Bot-
       toms on the Fort Berthold Reservation,  Garrison
       Reservoir.   BBAE,  185 (1963),  123-132.

2466.  Harwood, W. S.   "Opening the Yankton Reservation
       to Settlement. "  HW, 20 April 1895, p. 381.   In-
       cludes photographs.

2467.  Hawkinson, E. G.   "IECW on Lower Brule Indian
       Reservation. "  IW, 15 September 1935, pp. 37-38.

2468.  Hoover, Herbert T.   "Yankton Sioux Tribal Claims
       Against the United States, 1917-1975. "  WHQ, 7
       (April 1976), 125-142.

2469.  "An IECW Report from Rosebud Made at the Request
       of the Indian Workers. "  IW, 1 October 1934, p.
       22.   Progress on dams, fire breaks, truck trails,
       wells, etc.

2470.  Indian Rights Association.   Crow Creek Reservation,
       Dakota.   Philadelphia:   Office of the Indian Rights
       Association, 1885.   45 pp.   About the management
       of Crow Creek land.

2471.  Jackson, Thomas J.  The Indians and the Agriculture
       of the Crow Creek Reservation,  S. D.  Brookings:
       South Dakota State College, 1960.  66 pp.

2472.  Jennings, Dana C.  "Rosebud Revisited:  Progress
       with a Great Big 'P'."  GPO, February 1967, pp.
       13-14.

2473.  "Just Bad Indians:  State Jurisdiction over Indian Af-
       fairs."  NR, 30 March 1963, p.  8.

2474.  Kennan, George.  "Indian Lands and Fair Play."
       Out, 27 February 1904.  7 pp.

2475.  Lawson, Michael J.  "The Oahe Dam and the Standing
       Rock Sioux."  SDH,  6:2 (Spring 1976), 203-228.

2476.  Lawson, Michael J.  "Reservoir and Reservation:
       The Oahe Dam and the Cheyenne River Sioux."
       CHSSD, 37 (1974),  102-233.

2477.  Laymon, Oliver E.  Tribal Law for Oglala Sioux.
       Vermillion:  University of South Dakota, 1955.

2478.  Leasure, Daniel.  "A Visit to the Standing Rock
       Agency."  In William W. Beach.  The Indian Mis-
       cellany.  Albany, NY:  J. Munsell, 1877, pp.  387-
       395.

2479.  Lemley, Vernon.  "Sioux Indians of Pine Ridge."
       AI,  4: No.  12 (September-October 1930),  11.

2480.  Leonard, Jean D.  "A Proud People Can Have the
       Best of Both Worlds."  GPO, February 1967, pp.
       5-6.

2481.  Lippert, Lorenz C.  "Opportunity Knocks for Standing
       Rock Young Men."  IW, 1 August 1936, pp.  30-31.
       Occupational training for young men.

2482.  Lower Brule Sioux Tribe.  Make Way for Brules.
       Lower Brule, SD:  Lower Brule Sioux Tribal Coun-
       cil, 1963.  62 pp.

2483.  Macgregor, Gordon.  "Changing Society:  The Teton
       Dakotas."  See entry no. 528, pp. 92-106.

2484. Macgregor, Gordon. Warriors Without Weapons: A Study of the Society and Personality Development of the Pine Ridge Sioux. Chicago: University of Chicago Press, 1946. Subject of attack by Vine Deloria, Jr. in Custer Died for Your Sins.

2485. McPartland, Thomas S. A Preliminary Socio-Economic Study of the Sisseton-Wahpeton Sioux. Vermillion, SD: Institute of Indian Studies, 1955. A review of social and economic conditions and recommendations for improvements.

2486. Malan, Vernon. The Dakota Indian Economy: Factors Associated with Success in Ranching. Bulletin 509. Agriculture Experiment Station. Brookings, SD: Rural Sociology Department, 1963. 56 pp. On Pine Ridge Reservation.

2487. Malan, Vernon D. The Dakota Indian Family: Community Studies on the Pine Ridge Reservation. Bulletin 470. Brookings, SD: Rural Sociology Department, 1958. 70 pp.

2488. Malan, Vernon D. The Social System of the Dakota Indians. Extension Circular 606. Cooperative Extension Service. Brookings: South Dakota State College, 1962.

2489. Malan, Vernon D., and Clyde McCone. "Time Concept, Perspective, and Premise in the Socio-Cultural Order of the Dakota Indians." PlA, 5 (1960), 12-15.

2490. Malan, Vernon D., and Joseph P. Powers. The Crow Creek Indian Family. Bulletin No. 487. Agriculture Experiment Station. Brookings: South Dakota State College, 1960. Published to assist in the formation of programs to help families improve their social and economic conditions.

2491. Malan, Vernon, and Ernest L. Schusky. The Dakota Indian Community: An Analysis of the Non-Ranching Population of the Pine Ridge Reservation. Bulletin 505. Rural Sociology Department. Brookings: South Dakota State College, [1962]. 47 pp.

2492. Marsh, Othniel Charles. A Statement of Affairs at

Red Cloud Agency, Made to the President of the
United States.    n. p. ,   1875.    38 pp.

2493.    Marshall, Robert.    "Four Days with the Sioux. "    IW,
         1 January 1934, pp.  17-18.    Report of a 4-day in-
         spection tour by the Indian Service Director of For-
         estry on Pine Ridge and Rosebud.

2494.    Mattison, Ray H.    "The Indian Reservation System on
         the Upper Missouri, 1865-1890. "    NH, 36:3 (Sep-
         tember 1955),  141-174.

2495.    Maynard, Eileen.    "Community Portrait No. 4--
         Manderson Community. "    PRRB, No.  11 (January
         1970), pp.  30-49.

2496.    Mekeel, H. Scudder.    "A Discussion of Culture
         Change as Illustrated by Material from a Teton-
         Dakota Community. "    AA,  34:2 (March 1932),  274-
         285.    Concerning 950 Indians on the Pine Ridge
         Reservation in 1930.

2497.    Mekeel, H. Scudder.    "The Economy of a Modern
         Teton Dakota Community. "    YUPA,  6 (1936).

2498.    Meyer, Roy W.    "The Establishment of the Santee
         Reservation, 1866-1869. "    NH,  45 (March, 1964),
         59-97.

2499.    Morgan, Arthur E.    Dams and Other Disasters:    A
         Century of the Army Corps of Engineers in Public
         Works.    Boston:    Porter Sargent, 1971.    On the
         mainstem dams and taking areas along the Mis-
         souri River.

2500.    Museum of Anthropology.    Minutes of Indian Tribal
         Council Meetings of the Indian Tribes of the United
         States.    No.  25, Part I:    The Sioux Tribes of South
         Dakota.    Greeley:    University of Northern Colorado,
         1978.

2501.    Newell, Sylvia C.    "A Useful Club Member. "    IW, 1
         September 1935, pp.  15-16.    About a home exten-
         sion project typical of the New Deal era.

2502.    "Notes and Comment:    Visit to the Pine Ridge Indian
         Reservation. "    New Yorker,  24 March 1973, pp. 29-
         30.

2503.    "Opening of the Rosebud Reservation, S. D. , 1904. "
         CHSSD, 11 (1922), 519-530.  Includes the proclama-
         tion of President Theodore Roosevelt, and explana-
         tion.

2504.    "Opening of the Rosebud Reservation, 1908. "  CHSSD,
         11 (1922), 531-534.  The Proclamation of President
         Theodore Roosevelt on August 24, 1908.

2505.    Opland, David V.  "Marriage and Divorce for the
         Devil's Lake Indian Reservation. "  NDLR, (Winter
         1971), pp. 317-334.

2506.    Pancost, Henry Spackman.  Facts Regarding the Re-
         cent Opening to White Settlement of Crow Creek
         Reservation in Dakota.  Philadelphia:  Indian Rights
         Association, 1885.  12 pp.

2507.    Pennington, Robert.  "An Analysis of the Political
         Structure of the Teton-Dakota Indian Tribe of North
         America. "  NDH, 20:3 (July 1953), 143-156.  Con-
         tains an organization chart.

2508.    Pine Ridge Reservation, Tribal Council.  Pine Ridge
         Tribal Court and Code of Offenses.  Martin, SD:
         Martin Messenger Print, 1937.

2509.    Pommersheim, Frank.  Broken Ground and Flowing
         Waters.  Aberdeen, SD:  North Plains Press, 1977.
         176 pp.  An introductory text with materials on
         Rosebud Sioux Tribal Government.

2510.    Raabe, Evelyn.  "On the Pine Ridge Reservation. "
         Way-Catholic Viewpoint, 26:6 (July-August 1970),
         50-55.

2511.    Ridgeway, James F.  "More Lost Indians:  Pine
         Ridge Reservation. "  NR, 11 December 1965, pp.
         19-22.

2512.    Roberts, William O.  "Dakota Indians:  Successful
         Agriculture Within the Reservation Framework. "
         ApA, 11 (1943), 37-44.

2513.    Roberts, William O.  "The Pine Ridge Reservation
         Land Program. "  IW, May 1937, pp. 8-11.  The
         Reservation Superintendent describes a plan to re-
         cover land and revive the cattle industry.

2514.   Robinson, Doane. "Sioux Indian Courts." CHSSD, 5
        (1910), 402-414. Address before South Dakota Bar
        Association, at Pierre, January 21, 1909.

2515.   Roosevelt, Theodore. Report Made to the United
        States Civil Service Commission, Upon a Visit to
        Certain Indian Reservations and Indian Schools in
        South Dakota, Nebraska, and Kansas. Philadelphia:
        Indian Rights Association, 1893. 23 pp.

2516.   "Rosebud Sioux Council Speaks Out About Problems
        Ahead of Their People." IW, 15 November 1936,
        pp. 34-36. Tribal Chairman Antoine Roubideaux
        appeals for cooperation with tribal reorganization
        under the Wheeler-Howard Act.

2517.   Rosebud Sioux Tribe. Rosebud Tribal Court and Code
        of Offenses: Adopted by the Rosebud Sioux Tribal
        Council April 8, 1937. Rosebud, SD: Rosebud
        Sioux Tribe, 1939.

2518.   Rosebud to Dallas: The Reservation Indian Relocates
        to the Urban Environment. Dallas: Southern Re-
        source Center, 1977. 31 pp. Six articles that
        describe experiences of Rosebud tribal members
        on removal to Dallas since 1950.

2519.   Schusky, Ernest L. "Contemporary Migration and
        Culture Change on Two Dakota Reservation." PIA,
        7:17 (1962), 178-183. On Lower Brule and Pine
        Ridge Reservations.

2520.   Schusky, Ernest L. "Culture Change and Continuity
        in the Lower Brule Community." See entry no.
        528, pp. 107-122.

2521.   Schusky, Ernest L. "Development by Grantsmanship:
        Economic Planning on the Lower Brule Reserva-
        tion." HO, 34 (Fall 1975), 227-236.

2522.   Schusky, Ernest L. The Forgotten Sioux: An Ethno-
        history of the Lower Brule Sioux Reservation.
        Chicago: Nelson-Hall, 1975. 272 pp. A survey
        of reservation history since 1890. He argues that
        Indians can adapt their culture to new situations
        and it can survive on the Lower Brule Reservation.

2523.   Schusky, Ernest L. "The Lower Brule Sioux Reservation: A Century of Misunderstanding. " SDH, 7: 4 (Fall 1977), 422-437.

2524. Schusky, Ernest L. "Mission and Government Policy in Dakota Indian Communities. " PA, 10 (May-June 1963), 109-114.

2525. Schusky, Ernest L. Politics and Planning in a Dakota Indian Community: A Case Study of Views on Termination and Plans for Rehabilitation on the Lower Brule Reservation in South Dakota. Vermillion, SD: Institute of Indian Studies, 1959. 89 pp. Deals with social and economic planning through the use of funds paid for areas taken for the construction of Fort Randall Dam.

2526. Schusky, Ernest, and Vernon D. Malan. Social and Economic Factors in the Development of the Pine Ridge Reservation. Brookings: South Dakota State College, 1962.

2527. Sisseton-Wahpeton Sioux Tribe of the Lake Traverse Reservation. Sisseton, SD: n. p. , 1974. 7 pp.

2528. Sniffen, Matthew K. Indian Trust Funds for Sectarian Schools. The Statute Prohibiting Application of the Public Moneys for Support of Sectarian Schools Ignored by the Government in Expending Indian Trust Funds, Therefore the Indians Protest. Philadelphia: Indian Rights Association, 1905. 8 pp. The protest came from Rosebud Reservation. See entry no. 626, by Viken on Quick Bear v. Leupp.

2529. Sterling, Everett W. "Temporizing, Transitional Compromise: The Indian Reservation System on the North Central Plains. " Montana, 14 (April 1964), 92-100.

2530. Sweeney, Marian Hopkins. "Indian Land Policy Since 1887, with Special Reference to South Dakota. " CHSSD, 13 (1926), 250-283.

2531. Taft, William H. "Opening of Pine Ridge and Rosebud Lands, 1911: A Proclamation-- By the President of the United States. " CHSSD, 11 (1922), 548-551.

2532. Thompson, Samuel H. "Rosebud Community Gardens. "

IW, 1 September 1935, p. 46. About community
gardens to encourage self-sufficiency.

2533.  "25,000 Sioux Ask $700,000,000." LD, 19 May 1923,
p. 13.

2534.  Umber, Harold. "Interdepartmental Conflict Between
Fort Yates and Standing Rock: Problems of Indian
Administration, 1870-1881." NDH, 39:3 (Summer
1972), 4-13, 34.

2535.  United States. Bureau of Indian Affairs. Planning
Support Group. Irrigation Potential on the Stand-
ing Rock Reservation. Billings, MT: Bureau of
Indian Affairs, 1972.

2536.  United States. Bureau of Indian Affairs. Planning
Support Group. Livestock Production Alternatives
on the Standing Rock Reservation. Billings, MT:
Bureau of Indian Affairs, 1972. 42 pp.

2537.  United States. Bureau of Indian Affairs. Planning
Support Group. The Standing Rock Reservation--
Its Resources and Development Potential. Billings,
MT: Bureau of Indian Affairs, 1973. 118 pp.

2538.  United States. House. To Provide for the Acquisi-
tion by the United States of Lands Required for the
Reservoir to Be Created by the Construction of
Oahe Dam on the Missouri River, and to Provide
for Rehabilitation of the Sioux Indians of Standing
Rock Reservation in South and North Dakota. H. R.
No. 9533, 83rd Cong., 2nd Sess., 1954.

2539.  U. S. Congress. House. To Provide that Certain
Lands Shall Be Held in Trust for the Standing Rock
Sioux Tribe in North and South Dakota. H. R. No.
6827. 85th Cong., 1st Sess., 1957.

2540.  U. S. Congress. House. Committee on Indian Affairs. Conditions on Sioux Reservations. Washington, DC: Government Printing Office, 1937. 26
pp. Hearings on H. R. No. 5753, April 21, 1937.

2541.  U. S. Congress. House. Committee on Interior and
Insular Affairs. Acquisition of Lands for Reservoir
Created by Construction of Oahe Dam on the Mis-

souri River and Rehabilitation of Standing Rock
Sioux Indians, South Dakota and North Dakota.
H. R. No. 1888. 85th Cong., 2nd Sess., 1958.

2542. U. S. Congress. House. Committee on Interior and
Insular Affairs. Federal Indian Policy, Hearings
Before the House Subcommittee on Indian Affairs.
85th Cong., 1st Sess., 1957.

2543. U. S. Congress. House. Committee on Interior and
Insular Affairs. Providing for the Acquisition of
Lands by the United States Required for the Reser-
voir Created by the Construction of Oahe Dam on
the Missouri River and the Rehabilitation of the In-
dians of the Standing Rock Sioux Reservation in
South and North Dakota. H. R. No. 2498. 84th
Cong., 2nd Sess., 1956.

2544. U. S. Congress. House. Committee of the Whole
House on the State of the Union. Authorizing the
Transfer of the Brown Unit of the Fort Belknap In-
dian Irrigation Project on the Fort Belknap Indian
Reservation, Montana, to the Landowners within the
Unit. Report No. 91-1020. 91st Cong., 2nd Sess.,
1970.

2545. U. S. Congress. Senate. An Act to Declare that Certain Federally Owned Land Is Held by the United
States in Trust for the Fort Belknap Indian Community. H. R. No. 10702. 92nd Cong., 1st Sess.,
1971.

2546. U. S. Congress. Senate. An Act to Provide for the
Disposition of Funds to Pay a Judgment in Favor of
the Yankton Sioux Tribe in Indian Claims Commission Docket Numbered 332-A. H. R. No. 7742.
92nd Cong., 1st Sess., 1971.

2547. U. S. Congress. Senate. A Bill Authorizing the
Standing Rock and Cheyenne River Indian Tribes to
Participate in Clearing Oahe Reservoir Area. S.
No. 340. 87th Cong., 1st Sess., 1961.

2548. U. S. Congress. Senate. Investigation of the Sioux
Land-Buying Commission. S. R. No. 283. Serial
2174. 48th Cong., 1st Sess., 1884. Senator Dawes
investigated the activities of the Newton Edmunds

commission to negotiate the reduction of the Great
Sioux Reservation, claiming he acquired Indian
signatures through threats and deceit.

2549.   U. S. Congress.   Senate.   Reports Relative to the Pro-
posed Division of the Great Sioux Reservation and
Recommending Certain Legislation.   S. D.  No.  51.
Serial 2682.   51st Cong., 1st Sess., 1889-90.

2550.   U. S. Congress.   Senate.   Review of Plans of Engineer
Corps, Army, and Reclamation Bureau for Development of Missouri River Basin.   S. Exec. Doc. No.
247.   78th Cong., 2nd Sess., 1944.

2551.   U. S. Congress.   Senate.   Committee on Commerce.
Authorizing the Negotiation for Contracts with In-
dians in Connection with the Construction of the
Oahe Dam, South Dakota.   S. R. No. 1737.   81st
Cong., 2nd Sess., 1950.

2552.   U. S. Congress.   Senate.   Committee on Interior and
Insular Affairs.   Providing for the Payment of Individual Indian and Tribal Lands of the Lower
Brule Sioux Reservation in South Dakota, Required
by the United States for the Big Bend Dam and
Reservoir Project on the Missouri River, and for
the Rehabilitation, Social, and Economic Development of the Members of the Tribe.   Washington,
DC:   Government Printing Office, 1962.   35 pp.
Report to accompany H. R. No. 5144, 87th Cong.,
2nd Sess.  S. R. No. 1636.

2553.   U. S. Congress.   Senate.   Committee on Interior and
Insular Affairs.   Sub-Committee on Indian Affairs.
Tribal Judicial Reform:   Hearing Before the Sub-
committee on Indian Affairs of the Committee on
Interior and Insular Affairs ...   On the Need for
Indian Law Enforcement and Judicial Reform on In-
dian Reservations, February 24, 1975.   Washington,
DC:   Government Printing Office, 1975.   65 pp.

2554.   U. S. Department of the Interior.   Bureau of Indian
Affairs.   Cultural and Economic Status of the Sioux
People, 1955, Standing Rock Reservation, North
and South Dakota.   Report No. 151.   Billings, MT:
Missouri River Basin Investigations Project, 1957.

2555.    U. S. Department of the Interior.    Bureau of Indian
         Affairs.    Effects of the Oahe Reservation Project
         on the Cheyenne River and Standing Rock Reserva-
         tions.    Report No. 29.    Billings, MT:    Missouri
         River Basin Investigations Project, 1947.

2556.    U. S. Department of the Interior.    Bureau of Indian
         Affairs.    Fact Sheet on Standing Rock Reservation.
         Aberdeen,  SD:    Area Office, Bureau of Indian Af-
         fairs, 1970.

2557.    U. S. Department of the Interior.    Bureau of Indian
         Affairs.    The Fort Belknap Reservation Area.    Its
         Resources and Development Potential.    Report No.
         198.    Billings, MT:    Missouri River Basin Investi-
         gations Project, 1972.

2558.    U. S. Department of the Interior.    Bureau of Indian
         Affairs.    Oglala Irrigation Project-- Cattle Enter-
         prise.    Pine Ridge Reservation, South Dakota.
         Billings, MT:    Missouri River Basin Investigations
         Project, 1969.

2559.    U. S. Department of the Interior.    Bureau of Indian
         Affairs.    Report of Socio-Economic Survey, 1951,
         Standing Rock Indian Reservation, North and South
         Dakota.    Report No. 124.    Billings, MT:    Missouri
         River Basin Investigations Project, 1951.

2560.    U. S. Department of the Interior.    Bureau of Indian
         Affairs.    Resources of Sisseton Reservation Area--
         (Lake Traverse Reservation).    History-- Present--
         Potential.    Billings, MT:    Missouri River Basin In-
         vestigations Project, 1969.

2561.    U. S. Department of the Interior.    Bureau of Indian
         Affairs.    Rosebud Reservation Program.    Rosebud,
         SD:    Rosebud Indian Agency, January 24, 1950.

2562.    U. S. Department of the Interior.    Bureau of Indian
         Affairs.    The Sisseton Reservation Area.    Its Re-
         sources and Development Potential.    Planning Sup-
         port Group Report No. 204.    Aberdeen, SD:    Area
         Office, Bureau of Indian Affairs, 1972.

2563.    U. S. Department of the Interior.    Bureau of Indian
         Affairs.    The Social and Economic Effects of

Reservation Industrial Employment on Indian Em-
ployees and Their Families.    Pine Ridge Reservation, South Dakota.    Billings, MT:   Missouri Basin
Investigations Project, 1968.

2564.   U. S. Department of the Interior.    Bureau of Indian
        Affairs.    The Standing Rock Reservation.    Its Re-
        sources and Development Potential.    Billings, MT:
        Planning Support Group, 1973.

2565.   U. S. Department of the Interior.    Bureau of Indian
        Affairs.    Suggested Program for Use of Oahe Funds
        for Economic and Social Betterment, Standing Rock
        Reservation, North and South Dakota.    Report No.
        153.    Billings, MT:   Missouri River Basin Investi-
        gations Project, 1957.

2566.   "Uprising."    Time, 14 December 1959, p. 18.    An
        account of Cheyenne River Sioux under Chairman
        Anthony Rivers buying up land in their area.

2567.   Useem, John, Ruth Useem, and Gordon Macgregor.
        "Wartime Employment and Cultural Adjustment of
        the Rosebud Sioux."    ApA, 2 (January-March 1943),
        1-9.

2568.   Useem, Ruth.    The Aftermath of Defeat:   A Study of
        Acculturation among the Rosebud Sioux of South
        Dakota.    Madison:   University of Wisconsin, 1947.
        Microfilm publication.

2569.   Useem, Ruth, and Carl K. Eicher.    "Rosebud Reser-
        vation Economy."    See entry no. 528, pp. 3-34.

2570.   "The Visit of Commissioner Collier to the Pine Ridge
        Reservation."    IW, 15 January 1934, pp. 13-14.
        Description of ceremonies honoring Collier.

2571.   Vorse, Mary Heaton.    "There Is Hope in South Dakota."
        IW, 1 September 1935, pp. 11-14.    On how New
        Deal programs reinforced the community spirit of
        Sioux tradition on the Rosebud and Pine Ridge
        Reservations.

2572.   Voyat, Gilbert, and Stephen Silk.    "Cross-Cultural
        Study of Cognitive Development on the Pine Ridge
        Reservation."    PRRB, No. 11 (January 1970), pp.
        50-73.

2573.   Wax, Murray L.   "Poverty and Interdependency. "
        In The Culture of Poverty: A Critique.   Ed. E. B.
        Leacock.   New York:   Simon and Schuster, 1971,
        pp. 338-344.   About the Oglalas of Pine Ridge.

2574.   White Hawk.   "E. C. W. --1885. "   IW, 1 August
        1935, p. 25.   Seventy-one year old Fort Peck resi-
        dent describes an irrigation project established in
        1885.

2575.   Whitebull, James.   "The IECW on Pine Ridge Reserva-
        tion, South Dakota. "   IW, 1 November 1934, pp.
        18-19.   Report on work given by the camp manager.

2576.   Williams, Eleanor.   "Rosebud's Tribal Land Enter-
        prise. "   IW, March-April 1944, pp. 14-17.   De-
        scribes the origin and purpose of the land consoli-
        dation program.

2577.   Williamson, Ralph L.   The Lower Brule and Crow
        Creek Indian Reservations on the Missouri River,
        South Dakota.   Mitchell, SD:   Dakota Wesleyan
        University, 1955.

2578.   Wilson, Jesse E.   "Regulations, Opening Rosebud In-
        dian Lands in South Dakota (Tripp County). "   CHSSD,
        11 (1922), 540-547.   Letter from the Secretary of
        the Interior dated August 25, 1908.

2579.   Witten, James E.   "Information Relative to the Open-
        ing of the Pine Ridge and Rosebud Indian Reserva-
        tions, in South Dakota. "   CHSSD, 11 (1922), 555-
        563.   By the Superintendent at the opening.

2580.   Woolworth, Alan R.   Ethnohistorical Report on the
        Yankton Sioux.   The Sioux Indians.   Vol. III.   Amer-
        ican Indian Ethnohistory Series:   The Plains Indians.
        New York:   Garland Publishers, 1974.

2581.   Woolworth, Alan R.   Yankton Sioux:   Ethnohistorical
        Report on the Indian Occupancy of Royce Area 410.
        New York:   Clearwater, 1973.

2582.   "Yankton Women's Club Makes Fine Record. "   IW,
        January 1938, p. 34.   Women make starquilts and
        other objects for sale.

2583.   Youngkin, S. Douglas.   "'Hostile and Friendly':   The

Pygmalion Effect at Cheyenne River Agency, 1873-
1877." SDH, 7:4 (Fall 1977), 402-421. Indians
friendly to the United States during this period became acculturated; Indians hostile to the U. S. became enemies to the U. S. Army.


## SETTLERS AND AGENTS

2584.   Andrews, Ralph. Indians as the Westerner Saw Them.
        New York: Superior Publishing Co., 1962. 176 pp.
        Material from manuscripts and photographs of pio-
        neers, traders, army wives, and others.

2585.   Armstrong, Thomas R. My First and Last Buffalo
        Hunt. n. p., 1918, 48 pp.

2586.   "Auto-biography of Maj. Lawrence Taliaferro Written
        in 1864." CMHS, 6 (1894), 189-255. He was In-
        dian agent at Fort Snelling, 1819-1840.

2587.   Babcock, Willoughby M. "Major Lawrence Taliaferro:
        Indian Agent." MVHR, 11:3 (December 1924), 358-
        375. Deals extensively with his attempts to main-
        tain peace between Sioux and Chippewas.

2588.   Babcock, Willoughby M. "The Taliaferro Map of the
        St. Peter's Indian Agency." MA, 11 (1945), 115-
        147.

2589.   Belden, George P. Belden, the White Chief: Or,
        Twelve Years Among the Wild Indians of the Plains,
        From the Diaries and Manuscripts of George P.
        Belden. Ed. James S. Brisbin. 1872, 1875; rpt.
        Athens: Ohio University Press, 1974. 513 pp.

2590.   Berg, Lillie Clara. Early Pioneers and Indians of
        Minnesota and Rice County. San Leandro, CA:
        Privately Printed, 1959. 220 pp.

2591.   Best, J. J. "Letters from Dakota; Or Life and
        Scenes Among the Indians, Fort Berthold Agency,
        1889-1890." Ed. Stuart E. Brown, Jr. NDH, 43:1
        (Winter 1976), 4-31. Best wrote letters to his wife
        and other relatives.

2592.   "Biography of Old Settlers." CHSND, 1 (1906), 339-
        355. Contains biographies of six settlers, and their
        impressions of the Sioux.

2593.   Blackburn, George M. "George Johnston and the
        Sioux-Chippewa Boundary Survey." Michigan His-
        tory, 51 (Winter 1967), 313-322.

2594.   Bliss, John H. "Reminiscences of Fort Snelling."
        CMHS, 6 (1894), 335-353. As an army Colonel
        remembered the Sioux.

2595.   Briggs, Harold E. "The Settlement and Development
        of the Territory of Dakota, 1860-70." NDHQ, 7:2
        and 3 (1933), 114-149. Much on the Sioux and
        their military activities.

2596.   Bronson, Edgar B. Reminiscences of a Ranchman.
        1908; rpt. Lincoln: University of Nebraska Press,
        1972 under the title Cowboy Life on the Western
        Plains. About the Sioux around Pine Ridge agency.

2597.   Brower, Jacob V., and D. I. Bushnell, Jr. Memoirs
        of Explorations in the Basin of the Mississippi.
        Vol. 3. Mille Lac. St. Paul: Minnesota Histor-
        ical Society, 1900. 140 pp.

2598.   Burdick, Usher L. "Recollections and Reminiscences
        of Graham Island." NDH, 16:1 (January 1949), 5-
        29; 16:2 (April 1949), 101-130; 16:3 (July 1949),
        165-191. Autobiography beginning in 1904.

2599.   Case, John H. "Historical Notes of Grey Cloud Is-
        land and Its Vicinity." CMHS, 15 (1915), 371-378.
        Contains information about numerous Sioux leaders.

2600.   Chapman, William. Remember the Wind: A Prairie
        Memoir. New York: J. B. Lippincott Co., 1965.
        240 pp. Recollections from three years at St.
        Elizabeth's (Episcopal) School on Standing Rock
        Reservation.

2601.   Chittick, Douglas. "A Recipe for Nationality Stew."
        See entry no. 1115, pp. 88-145.

2602.   Clark, Greenleaf. "The Life and Influence of Judge
        Flandrau." CMHS, 10:Pt. 2 (1905), 771-782. In-

fluential attorney and Indian agent was knowledgeable on the Sioux, especially the Minnesota Sioux
War.

2603.   Cox, Mary McHenry.   Indians at Home.   Philadelphia:
        n. p. , 1890.   19 pp.   Visited two large reservations
        in South Dakota.

2604.   Dale, Edward E.   The Range Cattle Industry:   Ranch-
        ing on the Great Plains from 1865 to 1925.   1930;
        rpt. Norman:   University of Oklahoma Press, 1969.

2605.   Dally, Nathan (Nate).   Tracks and Trails:   Or, Inci-
        dents in the Life of a Minnesota Territorial Pioneer.
        Walker, MN:   The Cass County Pioneer, 1931.
        138 pp.

2606.   De Girardin, E.   "A Trip to the Bad Lands. "   Palimp-
        sest, 8:3 (March 1927), 98-101.   Observations on
        the Sioux from a trip to the vicinity of Pierre in
        1847.

2607.   DeLand, Charles E.   "Basil Clement (Claymore). "
        CHSSD, 11 (1922), 244-389.   Information about the
        period 1840-1900, including accounts of battles.

2608.   Drips, J. H.   Three Years Among the Indians in Da-
        kota.   Kimball, SD:   Brule Index Print. , 1894.
        Drips served as a sergeant with Company L, 6th
        Iowa Cavalry.

2609.   Eastman, Elaine Goodale.   Pratt:   The Red Man's
        Moses.   Norman:   University of Oklahoma Press,
        1935.   285 pp.   General Richard H. Pratt founded
        Carlisle Indian School in 1879, had considerable
        dealing with the Sioux.

2610.   Eastman, Mary H.   Romance of Indian Life.   1853;
        rpt. Upper Saddle River, NJ:   Literature House /
        The Gregg Press, 1971.   298 pp.   Observations
        by a soldier's wife.

2611.   "Expeditions of Capt. Jas. L. Fisk to the Gold Mines
        of Idaho and Montana, 1864-1866. "   CHSND, 2:1
        (1908), 421-461; 2:2 (1908), 34-85.   Includes Fanny
        Kelly's letters of July 1864 to Fisk asking rescue
        from the Uncpapas.

2612.   Flandrau, Charles E.   Recollections of the Past in
        Minnesota.   St. Paul:   St. Paul Pioneer Press Co.,
        1881.   30 pp.   A lecture before the St. Paul Li-
        brary Association, February 4, 1881.

2613.   Flandrau, Charles E.   "Reminiscences of Minnesota
        During the Territorial Period."   CMHS, 9 (1901),
        197-222.   Much on the Sioux, including an account
        of a Maiden's Feast.

2614.   Fletcher, Williams J., ed.   "Early Days at Red
        River Settlement and Fort Snelling:   Reminiscences
        of Mrs. Ann Adams."   CMHS, 6 (1894), 75-115.

2615.   Forsyth, Thomas.   "Fort Snelling:   Col. Leavenworth's
        Expedition to Establish It, in 1819."   CMHS, 3
        (1890), 139-167.   Forsyth was U. S. Indian Agent.

2616.   Gallaher, Ruth A.   "The Indian Agent in the United
        States Since 1850."   IJHP, 14:2 (April 1916), 173-
        238.   Information on the Sioux in a general article.

2617.   Gilbert, Benjamin F.   "The Black Hills Mining Rush."
        JW, 3 (1964), 313-317.

2618.   Goodrich, Albert Moses.   "Early Dakota Trails and
        Settlements at Centerville, Minn."   CMHS, 15
        (1915), 315-322.

2619.   Graber, Kay, ed.   Sister to the Sioux:   The Memoirs
        of Elaine Goodale Eastman, 1885-91.   Lincoln:
        University of Nebraska Press, 1978.   Elaine
        Goodale came to Dakota to serve as a day school
        teacher among western Sioux before she married
        Charles Eastman and became an author.

2620.   Hackett, Charles F.   "Along the Upper Missouri in
        the '70s."   CHSSD, 8 (1916), 27-55.   Published
        originally in the Sioux Falls Argus-Leader, in 1913,
        about a newsman who traveled along the Missouri
        in the 1870s and observed military posts and Sioux.

2621.   Hoopes, Alban W.   "Thomas S. Twiss, Indian Agent
        on the Upper Platte, 1855-1861."   MVHR, 20:3
        (December 1933), 353-364.   Deals with battles and
        other Sioux affairs.

2622.  J. A. W. "Memoir of Joseph R. Brown [1805-1871]. "
       CMHS, 3 (1870-1880), 201-212.  Brown was U. S.
       Indian Agent, and married to a Sioux.

2623.  Jacobsen, Ethel C.  "Life in an Indian Village. "
       NDH, 26:2 ( Spring 1959), 45-92.  The village of
       Running Antelope, on the Grand River in Standing
       Rock Reservation.

2624.  Johnson, Ben H.  "Hum-Pa-Zee. "  Montana, 18:1
       (January 1978), 56-64.  On Major Charles B. Loh-
       miller, Superintendent at Fort Peck Agency, 1893-
       1917.

2625.  Jones, Douglas C.  "Teresa Dean:  Lady Corres-
       pondent Among the Sioux Indians. "  JQ, 49 (Win-
       ter 1972).

2626.  Jorgensen, Gladys Whitehorn.  Before Homesteads,
       in Tripp County and the Rosebud.  Freeman, SD:
       Pine Hill Press, 1974.  138 pp.

2627.  Kelsey, D. M.  History of Our Wild West and Stories
       of Pioneer Life from Experiences of Buffalo Bill,
       Wild Bill, Kit Carson, David Crockett, Sam Houston,
       Generals Crook, Miles and Custer, Geronimo, Sit-
       ting Bull, Great Indian Chiefs, and Other Famous
       Frontiersmen and Indian Fighters.  New York:
       Willey Book Co. , 1928.

2628.  Lamare-Picquot, Augustin C.  "A French Naturalist
       in Minnesota, 1846. "  Trans. Anne H. Blegen.
       MiH, 6 (1925), 270-277.  Describes Little Crow's
       village.

2629.  Lamare-Picquot, Augustin C.  Une Scene Chez les
       Sioux.  Courier des Etats-Unis, 19 (1847), 1039-40.

2630.  Lanegraff, T. G.  Pioneering Among the Indians.
       Utica, NY:  N. T. Lewis, 1961.  20 pp.

2631.  Larsen, Arthur J. , ed.  "The Black Hills Gold Rush:
       Letters from Men Who Participated. "  NDHQ, 6:4
       (July 1932), 302-318.

2632.  Lightner, William H.  "Judge Flandrau as a Citizen
       and Jurist. "  CMHS, 10:Pt. 2 (1905), 819-828.

2633. McGillycuddy, Mrs. Julia (Blanchard). McGillycuddy,
      Agent: A Biography of Dr. Valentine T. McGilly-
      cuddy. Stanford, CA: Stanford University Press,
      1940. 291 pp. By the second wife of the U. S.
      Indian Agent who dealt with Red Cloud on Pine
      Ridge Reservation.

2634. McGuire, Henry N. The Black Hills and American
      Wonderland from Personal Explorations. Chicago:
      Donnelley, Loyd and Co., 1877.

2635. Mattison, Ray H. "An Army Wife on the Upper Mis-
      souri. The Diary of Sara E. Canfield, 1866-1868. "
      NDH, 20:4 (October 1953), 191-220. Traveled up
      the Missouri in the spring of 1867 to join her hus-
      band, Lt. Andrew Nahum.

2636. Mattison, Ray H., ed. "Journal of a Trip to, and
      Residence in, the Indian Country, by Henry A.
      Boller. " NDH, 33:3 (Summer 1966), 260-315.
      Journal dates September 1-December 31, 1857.

2637. Mattison, Ray H., ed. "The Letters of Henry A.
      Boller: Upper Missouri River Fur Trader. " NDH,
      33:2 (Spring 1966), 106-219.

2638. [Meyers, Augustus. ] "Dakota in the Fifties. " CHSSD,
      10 (1920), 130-194. Observations in the 1850s; in-
      cludes some vocabulary.

2639. Neill, Edward D. "Memoir of the Sioux--A Manu-
      script in the French Archives. " Macalester Col-
      lege Contributions, (1890), pp. 223-240. Uncertain
      authorship, written after 1719.

2640. Neill, Edward D. "Occurrences In and Around Fort
      Snelling, from 1819 to 1840. " CMHS, 2 (1889),
      102-142. Correspondence of Indian Agents contains
      information on the Sioux.

2641. Paine, Bayard Henry. Pioneers, Indians and Buf-
      faloes. Curtis, NB: Curtis Enterprise, 1935.

2642. Patton, Don. "The Legend of Ben Ash. " CHSSD,
      23 (1947), 185-211. Ash was a South Dakota pio-
      neer.

2643.   Paxson, Lewis C. "Diary Kept by Lewis C. Paxson,
        Stockton, N. J. (1862-64)." CHSND, 2:2 (1908),
        102-165. Was a member of the 8th Infantry at
        Fort Snelling during the Minnesota Sioux War.

2644.   Pfaller, Fr. Louis. "The Forging of an Indian Agent."
        NDH, 34:1 (Winter 1967), 62-76. About James Mc-
        Laughlin, Sioux agent at Devil's Lake in 1876; he
        later served at Standing Rock Reservation.

2645.   Pfaller, Fr. Louis L. James McLaughlin: The Man
        with an Indian Heart. New York: Vantage Press,
        1978. 439 pp. Biography of U. S. Agent among
        the Sioux, based upon archival research and oral
        history.

2646.   Pfaller, Fr. Louis. "James McLaughlin and the Rod-
        man Wanamaker Expedition of 1913." NDH, 44:2
        (Spring 1977), 4-11. McLaughlin and Joseph K.
        Dixon travelled for six months visiting 189 Indian
        tribes on seventy-five reservations. Contains some
        photographs of the Sioux.

2647.   Poole, DeWitt Clinton. Among the Sioux or Dakota:
        Eighteen Months Experience as an Indian Agent.
        New York: D. Van Nostrand, 1881. 235 pp.
        Served at Whetestone Agency, 1869.

2648.   Poole, John Hudson. American Cavalcade: A
        Memoir on the Life and Family of DeWitt Clinton
        Poole. Pasadena, CA: Ward Ritchie Press, 1939.
        350 pp.

2649.   Price, Archibald G. White Settlers and Native Peo-
        ples. 1949; rpt. Westport, CT: Greenwood Press,
        Inc., 1970.

2650.   Prickett, Robert C. "The Malfeasance of William
        Worth Belknap, Secretary of War, October 13,
        1869, to March 2, 1876." NDH, 17:1 (January
        1950), 5-51; 17:2 (April 1950), 97-134. Charged
        with mismanagement of reservation funds, but not
        convicted.

2651.   "Report of Lieutenant G. K. Warren, Topographical
        Engineer of the 'Sioux Expedition,' of Explorations
        in the Dacota Country, 1855." CHSSD, 11 (1922),

60-133. Warren spent several seasons in Dakota
country, wrote about the Sioux.

2652. Ritchey, Charles J. "Martin McLeod and the Minnesota Valley." MiH, 10:4 (December 1929), 387-
402. A man of great influence among Sioux along
the upper Minnesota River Valley through the
1830's-1850's.

2653. Roberts, Louisa J. Biographical Sketch of Louisa J.
Roberts with Extracts from Her Journal and Selections from Her Writings. Philadelphia: Press of
Alfred J. Ferris, 1895. 286 pp. About Nebraska
and Dakota reservations.

2654. Robinson, Will G. "Denny Moran's Reminiscenses
[sic] of Fort Randall." CHSSD, 23 (1947), 266-275;
24 (1949), 114-140. Moran spent ten years at Fort
Randall in the period 1870-1882, and observed Sioux
closely.

2655. Saum, Lewis O. "Frenchmen, Englishmen and the
Indian." AW, 1:4 (1964), 4-11, 87-89.

2656. Sibley, Henry Hastings. "Memoir of Jean Baptiste
Faribault." CMHS, 3 (1880), 168-179.

2657. Sibley, Henry Hastings. "Reminiscences of the Early
Days of Minnesota." CMHS, 3 (1880), 242-282.
Contains a section on the Sioux and their chiefs.

2658. Sibley, Henry Hastings. "Reminiscences: Historical
and Personal." CMHS, 1 (1872), 457-485. About
Sioux religion and culture.

2659. Slaughter, Linda W. "Leaves from Northwestern History." CHSND, 1 (1906), 200-292. Contains information on Sioux of North and South Dakota.

2660. Smith, De Cost. Indian Experiences. Caldwell, ID:
Caxton Printers, 1943. 387 pp. The artist left
information about Sitting Bull, Rain-In-The-Face
and others.

2661. Spring, Agnes Wright, ed. Tales of the 04 Ranch:
Recollections of Harold J. Cook, 1887-1909.
Lincoln: University of Nebraska Press, 1968.

While growing up on his father's ranch he knew
Red Cloud and other Sioux leaders who had participated in war against the United States. Recollections of a critical period in Sioux history.

2662.   Stevenson, C. Stanley. "Expeditions into Dakota."
        CHSSD, 9 (1918), 347-375. Information about the
        Sioux in the years 1844-1845.

2663.   Tarbell, Wright. "The Early and Territorial History
        of Codington County." CHSSD, 24 (1949), 276-469.
        Contains information about the campaign of 1864 and
        on Sisseton Reservation, and recounts several leg-
        ends: of Maiden Island, of Starvation Hill, and of
        Punished Woman's Lake.

2664.   Taylor, Joseph H. Sketches of Frontier and Indian
        Life on the Upper Missouri and Great Plains, Em-
        bracing the Author's Personal Recollections of Noted
        Frontier Characters, and Some Observations of Wild
        Indian Life During a Twenty-Five Years' Residence
        in the Two Dakotas and Other Territories, Between
        the Years 1864 and 1889. Pottstown, PA: Printed
        Privately, 1889. 200 pp.

2665.   Trudeau, Jean Baptiste. "Remarks on the Manners
        of Indians Living High up the Missouri." Medical
        Repository, 6 (1808), 52-56. On the education of
        young people by elders, the practice of smoking the
        Peacepipe, eating habits, religious beliefs, etc.

2666.   Van Cleve, Charlotte O. "A Reminiscence of Fort
        Snelling." CMHS, 3 (188), 76-81. About conflict
        between the Sioux and Chippewas.

2667.   Walters, Madge H. Early Days and Indian Ways.
        Los Angeles: Westernlore Press, 1964. An auto-
        biography that deals with the Sioux.

2668.   [Williams, J. Fletcher]. "Early Days at Fort Snell-
        ing." CMHS, 1 (1872), 420-438. Considerable in-
        formation about the Sioux, including their attack on
        the Chippewas in 1825.

2669.   Williams, J. Fletcher. "Henry Hastings Sibley, A
        Memoir." CMHS, 6 (1894), 257-310. Deals with
        the Minnesota Sioux War, and other Sioux affairs.

2670. Williamson, Thomas S. "The Sioux or Dakotas: A Sketch of Our Intercourse with the Dakotahs on the Missouri River, and Southwest of that Stream." CMHS, 3 (1889), 283-294.

2671. Woodall, Allan E. "William Joseph Snelling and the Early Northwest." MiH, 10:4 (December 1929), 367-385. Contains Snelling's experiences with the Sioux.

2672. Woolworth, Nancy L. "Captain Edwin V. Sumner's Expedition to Devil's Lake in the Summer of 1845." NDH, 28:2 and 3 (April-July 1961, 79-98. About dealings with the Sioux on an expedition through Iowa and southern Minnesota.

# TRAVELERS AND EXPLORERS

2673. Atwater, Caleb. Remarks Made on a Tour to Prairie du Chien: Thence to Washington City, in 1829. 1831; rpt. New York: Arno Press, 1975. 269 pp. One of three commissioners appointed to talk with Indians in the upper Mississippi valley in 1829 recorded rudiments of Sioux language.

2674. Beaver, Harold. "Parkman's Crack-up: A Bostonian on the Oregon Trail." NEQ, 48:1 (March 1975), 84-103. Material on the Sioux Sun Dance, etc.

2675. Bourne, Edward G. "The Travels of Jonathan Carver." AHR, 11 (January 1906), 287-302.

2676. Boutwell, William T. "Schoolcraft's Exploring Tour of 1832." CMHS, 1 (1902), 121-140.

2677. Bray, Edmund C. , and Martha C. Bray, trans. and eds. Joseph N. Nicollet on the Plains and Prairies: The Expeditions of 1838-39 with Journals, Letters, and Notes on the Dakota Indians. St. Paul: Minnesota Historical Press, 1976. 294 pp. Contains observations about Sioux language, life and culture.

2678. Bray, Martha C. "Joseph Nicolas Nicollet, Geographer." In Frenchmen and French Ways in the Mississippi Valley. Ed. John G. McDermott. Urbana: University of Illinois Press, 1969, pp. 29-42.

2679.   Bray, Martha C., ed.  The Journals of Joseph N.
        Nicollet.  Trans. Andre Ferty.  St. Paul:  Minne-
        sota Historical Society, 1970.

2680.   "Capt. Jonathan Carver and His Explorations.  From
        the 'Materials for Minnesota History'--1856."
        CMHS, 1 (1872), 349-367.  Much information on the
        Sioux, such as burial customs.

2681.   Carver, Jonathan.  Journals of Jonathan Carver and
        Related Documents 1766-1770.  Ed. John Parker.
        St. Paul:  Minnesota Historical Society Press,
        1976.  244 pp.

2682.   Carver, Jonathan.  Travels Through the Interior
        Parts of North America, in the Years 1766, 1767
        and 1768.  3rd ed.  Includes information about the
        author.  London:  C. Dilly, 1781; Minneapolis:
        Ross and Haines, 1956.  543 pp.  Since its initial
        publication in 1778, Travels has appeared in more
        than fifty editions.  Some scholars have called it
        the work of Dr. John Coakley Lettsom.  See AHR,
        11 (January 1906), 287-302.

2683.   Catlin, George.  Illustrations of the Manners, Cus-
        toms, and Conditions of the North American In-
        dians with Letters and Notes.  London:  Chatto
        and Windus, 1876; rpt. Chicago:  Library Re-
        sources, 1971.

2684.   Catlin, George.  Letters and Notes on the Manners,
        Customs, and Conditions on the North American
        Indians.  Written During the Eight Years' Travel
        Among the Wildest Tribes of Indians on North
        America:  With 150 Illustrations on Steeland Wood.
        Philadelphia:  J. W. Bradley, 1859.

2685.   Catlin, George.  Letters and Notes on the North
        American Indians.  Ed. Michael Macdonald Mooney.
        New York:  Crown Publishers, 1975.  Condensed
        version of the longer work, which first appeared
        in 1841.

2686.   Catlin, George.  Life Amongst the Indians.  London:
        Sampson, Low, Son and Marston, 1867.  339 pp.
        Juvenile literature, including stories about Indians
        and their lives and customs.

2687.  Coues, Elliott, ed. The Expeditions of Zebulon Mont-
       gomery Pike, to Headwaters of the Mississippi
       River, through Louisiana Territory, and in New
       Spain, during the years 1805-6-7. 3 vols. New
       York: Francis P. Harper, 1895; rpt. 2 vols.
       Minneapolis, MN: Ross and Haines, 1965. Also
       published as The Journals of Zebulon Montgomery
       Pike, with Letters and Related Documents. 2 vols.
       Ed. Donald Jackson. Norman: University of Okla-
       homa Press, 1966. Contains census estimates and
       observations on the Sioux.

2688.  Coues, Elliott. "Letters of William Clark and
       Nathaniel Pryor." AIo, 1:8 (January 1895), 613-
       620. Four letters, written June to October 1807,
       containing much information about the Sioux.

2689.  Cronau, Rudolph. "My Visit Among the Hostile Dakota
       Indians and How They Became My Friends." CHSSD,
       22 (1946), 410-425. A visit in 1881 to Fort Yates
       and other visits, including one to Sitting Bull at
       Fort Randall.

2690.  Culbertson, Thaddeus A. "Journal of an Expedition
       to the Mauvaises Terres and the Upper Missouri
       in 1850." ARSI (1850), pp. 84-132.

2691.  Culbertson, Thaddeus A. Journal of an Expedition to
       the Mauvaises Terres and the Upper Missouri in
       1850. Ed. John F. McDermott. BBAE, 147 (1952).
       164 pp. Information about the Sioux.

2692.  Dale, Edward E. Frontier Ways: Sketches of Life
       in the Old West. Rpt. Austin: University of
       Texas Press, 1959.

2693.  DeMallie, Raymond J. "Joseph N. Nicollet's Ac-
       count of the Sioux and Assiniboin in 1839." SDH,
       5:4 (Fall 1975), 343-59.

2694.  DePourtales, Albert Alexandre. On the Western Tour
       with Washington Irving: The Journal and Letters
       of Count De Pourtales. Ed. George F. Spaulding.
       Trans. Seymour Feiler. Norman: University of
       Oklahoma Press, 1968.

2695.  De Schweinitz, Edmund. The Life and Times of

David Zeisberger, The Western Pioneer and Apostle
of the Indians.  1870; rpt.  New York:  Arno Press,
1970.

2696.  Drannan, William F.  Thirty-one Years on the Plains
and in the Mountains, Or, the Last Voice from the
Plains.  Chicago:  Rhodes and McClure Publishing
Co., 1901; rpt. Chicago:  Library Resources, 1971.

2697.  Durrie, Daniel S.  "Jonathan Carver, and 'Carver's
Grant.'"  CWHS, 6 (1872), 220-270.  A grant from
the Sioux of land near the Falls of St. Anthony.

2698.  Ewers, John C.  "Plains Indian Reactions to the
Lewis and Clark Expedition."  Montana, 16:1 (January 1966), 2-12.

2699.  Farnham, Thomas.  Travels in the Great Western
Prairies.  2nd ed.  New York:  Plenim Publishing
Co., 1968.

2700.  Freemont, John C.  "Freemont's Story--1838-1839."
Ed. Doane Robinson.  CHSSD, 10 (1920), 71-97.
Joseph Renville, Jr., William Dickson, and Louison
Freniere guided John C. Freemont and Joseph
Nicollet through Sioux country in eastern South Da-
kota into Minnesota.  Contains information about the
Sioux.  See entry no. 2731.

2701.  Fridley, Russell W.  "An Evaluation of Documents
Useful to the Ethnohistorian:  The Papers of Jonathan Carver."  PMAS, 23 (1955), 9-14.

2702.  Goodrich, Albert M.  "The Prairie Island Case."
MiH, 12 (1932), 245-255.

2703.  Goodrich, Albert M.  "The Prairie Island Case
Again."  MiH, 13 (1932), 395-402.

2704.  Harmon, Daniel W.  Sixteen Years in the Indian
Country:  The Journal of Daniel William Harmon,
1800-1816.  Ed. and intro. W. Kaye Lamb.  Toronto:  Macmillan of Canada, 1957.  277 pp.

2705.  Hill, Alfred J.  "The Geography of Perrot; So Far as
It Relates to Minnesota and the Regions Immediately
Adjacent."  CMHS, 2 (1889), 200-214.  In French

with translation, contains information about the
Sioux and other tribes.

2706.  Hobart, Chauncey.  Recollections of My Life: Fifty
       Years of Itinerancy in the Northwest.  Red Wing,
       MN:  Red Wing Printing Co. , 1885.  409 pp.

2707.  Holand, Hjalmar R.  "Radisson's Two Western Jour-
       neys. "  MiH, 15 (June 1934), 157-180.

2708.  Howard, James H.  "John F. Lenger:  Music Man
       Among the Santee. "  NH, 53:2 (Summer 1972), 195-
       215.

2709.  Irving, Washington.  A Tour on the Prairies.  Ed.
       John F. McDermott.  1956; rpt.  Norman:  Univer-
       sity of Oklahoma Press, 1971.

2710.  Irving, Washington.  The Western Journals of Wash-
       ington Irving.  Ed. John F. McDermott.  1944;
       rpt. Norman:  University of Oklahoma Press, 1966.

2711.  James, Edwin, ed.  An Account of an Expedition from
       Pittsburgh to the Rocky Mountains under the Com-
       mand of Major Stephen H. Long.  2 vols.  March
       of America Series.  1822-1823; rpt. Ann Arbor,
       MI:  University Microfilms, 1966; Westport, CT:
       Greenwood Press, Inc. , 1968.

2712.  Jouan, Henri.  "Jean Nicolet:  Interpreter and Voya-
       guer in Canada, 1618-1642. "  Trans. Grace Clark.
       CWHS, 11 (1888), 1-22.  Nicolet was the first non-
       Indian to encounter the "Nadeussiu, " or Sioux, fed-
       eration in the woodlands.

2713.  LeRaye, Charles.  "The Journal of Charles LeRaye. "
       CHSSD, 4 (1908), 149-180.

2714.  "LeSueur, the Explorer of the Minnesota River. "
       CMHS, 1 (1872), 319-338.  Contains much informa-
       tion on Sioux, from his travels in the year 1700,
       when he recorded the first identification of the Yank-
       ton tribe in written records.

2715.  Lewis, Henry.  The Valley of the Mississippi Illus-
       trated.  Ed. Bertha L. Heilbron.  Trans. A. H.
       Postgieter.  St. Paul:  Minnesota Historical Society,
       1967.

2716.  Long, Stephen H.  "Voyage on a Six-oared Skill to
       the Falls of St. Anthony in 1817." CMHS, 2 (1889),
       7-88.  Contains both descriptions of and stories
       about the eastern Sioux.

2717.  Lossing, Benson John.  "Sketches on the Upper Mis-
       sissippi." H, 7 (July 1853), 177-190.

2718.  McCracken, Harold.  George Catlin and the Old Fron-
       tier.  New York:  Bonanza Books, 1959.  216 pp.
       Includes reproductions of many of Catlin's paintings.

2719.  Margry, Pierre.  "Daniel Greyselon du Lhut de son
       frère aux côtes du Lake Superieur; découverte du
       pays des Sioux et du Lac Alemipigon; Riviere Pere;
       Riviere à la Maune; Projet de découvrir la mer à
       l'ouest-nord-ouest."  In Vol. 6 of Découvertes et
       établissements de Français, 1886, pp. 17-52.

2720.  Margry, Pierre.  "Formation d'un établissement chez
       les Sioux sur les bords du Lac Pepin, sous les
       ordres du Sieur Boucher de la Perriere.  Ce Poste,
       ayant été abandonne est rétablir por le sieur de
       Linctat et abandonne de nouveau par Legardeur de
       Saint-Pierre (1723-1737)."  In Vol. 6 of Décou-
       vertes et établissements de Français, 1886, pp.
       539-580.

2721.  Margry, Pierre.  "Le Sueur commandant à Cha-
       gouamigon.  Il Amene des Sioux à Montreal.
       Etendue du commandment qu'il demande.  Il forme
       des établissements sur les bords du lac Pepin et
       a la Riviere Bleue.  Embarrass que lui suscite le
       Canada."  In Vol. 6 Découvertes et établissements
       des Français, 1886, pp. 53-92.

2722.  Marin, Joseph de la Margue.  Journal de Marin, fils,
       1753-1754, par ant. Champagne.  Quebec:  Provin-
       cial Archives, 1963.

2723.  Marks, Constant R., ed.  "Letellier's Autobiography."
       CHSSD, 4 (1908), 214-253.  Written in 1862 about
       his experiences in the Dakotas and the surrounding
       area.

2724.  Marryat, Frederick.  "Captain Marryat in Minnesota,
       1838."  MiH, 6 (1925), 168-184.  Published in Lon-
       don in 1839.

2725.   Marshall, Orasmus H.   The Historical Writings of
        Orasmus Holmes Marshall Relating to the Early
        History of the West.   1887; New York:   Burt
        Franklin, Pub., 1970.

2726.   Mattocks, John.   "The Life and Explorations of Jona-
        than Carver."   CMHS, 2 (1889), 266-284.   A mis-
        sionary's account of some of Carver's experiences.

2727.   Murray, C. A.   Travels in North America, Including
        a Summer Residence with the Pawnees.   2nd ed.
        Rpt. New York:   Plenum Publishing Corp., 1968.

2728.   Neill, Edward D.   "LeSueur's Explorations."   CMHS,
        1 (1872), 319-338; (1902), 261-277.   First published
        in 1856.

2729.   Neill, Edward D.   "Letter of Mesnard."   CMHS, 1
        (1872), 135-138; (1902), 105-108.   About the Sioux
        near Lake Superior.   First published in 1852 in
        the Annals of the Minnesota Historical Society.

2730.   Nelson, John W., and Harrington O'Reilly.   Fifty
        Years on the Trail, A True Story of Western Life:
        the Adventures of John Young Nelson, As Told to
        Harrington O'Reilly.   1963; rpt. Norman:   Univer-
        sity of Oklahoma Press, 1969.

2731.   [Nicollet, Joseph N.]   "Nicollet's Account, 1839."   Ed.
        Doane Robinson.   CHSSD, 10 (1920), 98-129.   See
        entry no. 2700.

2732.   North, Luther.   Man of the Plains:   Recollections of
        Luther North, 1856-1882.   Ed. Donald F. Danker.
        Lincoln:   University of Nebraska Press, 1961.

2733.   Nute, Grace L.   "Alexander Faribault."   MiH, 8
        (June 1927), 177-180.

2734.   Nute, Grace L.   "Border Chieftain."   B, March 1952,
        pp. 35-39.   On Dr. John McLoughlin.

2735.   Nute, Grace L.   Caesars of the Wilderness.   New
        York:   Appleton Century, 1943.

2736.   Nute, Grace L.   "James Dickson:   A Filibuster in Min-
        nesota in 1836."   MVHR, 10 (September 1923), 127-

140.   Documents related to Dickson's expedition
are printed on pp. 173-181 of the same issue.

2737.   Parker, Donald D.   "Penetration of a Western Wilderness. "  See entry no. 1122, pp. 40-71.   About
travelers and explorers with information about Indians.

2738.   Pike, Zebulon Montgomery.   An Important Visit.
Rpt. St. Paul, MN:  Great Northern Railway,  1925.
10 pp.   Deals with the origin of Fort Snelling,  the
itinerary of Zebulon Montgomery Pike,  and the
eastern Sioux during Pike's explorations early in
the nineteenth century.

2739.   "Pike's Explorations in Minnesota 1805-06. "  CMHS,
1 (1872),  368-416.   Contains information about the
Sioux,  including a copy of the agreement between
Sioux leaders and Zebulon Montgomery Pike.

2740.   Prescott, Philander.   "Autobiography and Reminiscenses of Philander Prescott. "  CMHS,  6 (1894),
475-491.   Prescott, who was killed during the Minnesota Sioux War of 1862,  wrote stories about Chief
Wabasha and other Sioux.

2741.   "Radisson and Groseilliers in Wisconsin. "  CWHS, 11
(1888),  65-96.   Contains the explorers' observations about the Sioux.

2742.   "Relation of M. Penicaut. '  Intro. Edward D. Neill.
Trans. A. J. Hill.  CMHS, 3 (1880), 1-12.   This
early explorer recorded considerable information
about the Sioux.

2743.   Robinson, Doane.   "Lewis and Clark in South Dakota. "
CHSSD, 9 (1918),  514-596.   Excerpts from their
journals that relate to the Sioux.

2744.   Schoolcraft, Henry Rowe.   Expedition to Lake Itaska:
The Discovery of the Source of the Mississippi.
Ed. Philip P. Mason.   East Lansing:   Michigan
State University Press, 1958.   390 pp.

2745.   Schoolcraft, Henry Rowe.   Narrative Journal of
Travels through the Northwestern Regions of the
United States,  Extending from Detroit through the

Great Chain of American Lakes, to the Sources of
the Mississippi River ... in the Year 1820.  Al-
bany, NY:  E. and E. Hosford, 1821; rpt.; New
York:  Arno Press, 1970.  424 pp.

2746.  Schoolcraft, Henry Rowe.  Narrative of an Expedition
Through the Upper Mississippi to Lake Itasca, the
Actual Source of This River; Embracing an Explora-
tory Trip Through the St. Croix and Burntwood (or
Broule) Rivers, in 1832.  New York:  Harper and
Brothers, 1834.  307 pp.

2747.  Scull, Gideon, ed.  Voyages of Pierre Esprit Radisson.  New York:  Peter Smith, 1943.

2748.  Tabeau, Pierre-Antoine.  Tabeau's Narrative of Loi-
sel's Expedition to the Upper Missouri.  1939; rpt.
Norman:  University of Oklahoma Press, 1968.

2749.  United States War Department.  Henry R. Schoolcraft:
Expedition into the Indian Country.  Letter from the
Secretary of War, transmitting ... information in
relation to an Expedition of Henry R. Schoolcraft
into the Indian Country.  March 7, 1832.  Washington, 1832.  St. Paul:  Minnesota Historical Society,
1967.  House Doc. No. 152.  22nd Congress.  1st
sess.

2750.  Upham, Warren.  "Explorations and Surveys of the
Minnesota and Red Rivers."  PMVHA, 7 (1913-
1914), 82-92.  On various explorers; much on the
Sioux.

2751.  Upham, Warren.  "Groseilliers and Radisson:  The
First White Men in Minnesota, 1655-56, and 1659-
60, and Their Discovery of the Upper Mississippi
River."  CMHS, 10: Pt. 2 (1905), 448-494.


TYPES OF LITERATURE AND CRITICISM

2752.  Abel, Midge B.  "American Indian Life as Portrayed
in Children's Literature."  EE, 50 (1973), 202-205.
Comments on books for elementary schools.

2753.  Alexander, Hartley.  "The Bad Heart Buffalo Manu-

script. " JAM, 16 (January 1932), 39-41. About
Blish's discovery of the manuscript, and its value.

2754.    Allen, Paula Gunn. "The Mythopoetic Vision in Native American Literature. " AICRJ, 1: No. 1 (1974),
3-13.

2755.    Allen, Paula Gunn. "The Sacred Hoop: A Contemporary Indian Perspective on American Indian Literature. " CC, 26: No. 2 (Summer 1976), 144-163;
See also entry no. 2769, pp. 111-135.

2756.    Allen, Paula Gunn. "Symbol and Structure in Native
American Literature: Some Basic Consideration. "
CCC, 24 (October 1973), 267-270.

2757.    Armstrong, Robert Plant. Patterns in the Stories
of the Dakota Indians and the Negroes of Paramari-
bo, Dutch Guiana. Ann Arbor, MI: Xerox University Microfilms, 1974. 263 pp.

2758.    Barbeau, Marius. "Indian Captivities. " PAPS, 94
(1950), 522-548. Bibliography and discussion of
Indian captivities.

2759.    Berkman, Brenda. "The Vanishing Race: Conflicting
Images of the American Indian in Children's Literature, 1880-1930. " NDQ, 44 (Spring 1976), 31-40.

2760.    Bissell, Benjamin H. American Indian in English
Literature of the Eighteenth Century. 1925; rpt.
Hamden, CT: Shoe String Press, Inc. , 1968.

2761.    Black, Nancy B. , and Bette S. Weidman, eds. White
on Red: Images of the American Indian. Port
Washington, NY: Kennikat Press, 1976. More than
forty views of Indians by non-Indians.

2762.    Blegen, Theodore C. "A Note on Schiller's Indian
Threnody. " MiH, 39 (Spring 1965), 198-200. On
the Sioux, with translation.

2763.    Byler, Mary Gloyne. "The Image of American Indians Projected by Non-Indian Writers. " LJ, 99
(February 1974), 546-549. By an eastern Cherokee. See entry no. 2828.

2764.   Campbell, Walter S.   "The Plains Indian in Litera-
        ture and in Life." In The Trans-Mississippi West:
        Papers Read at a Conference Held at the University
        of Colorado, June 18-June 21, 1929. Ed. James F.
        Willard and C. B. Goodykoontz.   Boulder:   Univer-
        sity of Colorado Press, 1930, pp. 175-194.

2765.   Cary, Elizabeth Luther.   "Recent Writings by Amer-
        ican Indians."   BB, N. S. 24 (1902), 21-25.   Re-
        views the writings of Charles Eastman, Francis La
        Flesche, and Zitkala-Ša.

2766.   Cawelti, John G.   "The West in Myth and Fantasy:
        Cowboys, Indians, Outlaws."   AW, 1 (Spring 1964),
        29-35.

2767.   Chamberlin, J. E.   The Harrowing of Eden:   White
        Attitudes Toward Native Americans.   New York:
        Seabury Press, 1975.   248 pp.

2768.   Chambers, Bradford.   "Interracial Books:   Background
        of a Challenge."   PW, 200 (October 1971), 23-29.

2769.   Chapman, Abraham, ed.   Literature of the American
        Indians:   Views and Interpretations.   New York:
        New American Library, 1975.   257 pp.

2770.   Clark, J. S.   "Delawares and Dakotas."   AAOJ, 13
        (1891), 234-236.

2771.   Clark, LaVerne Harrell.   "The Indian Writings of
        Mari Sandoz:   'A Lone One Left from the Old
        Times.'"   AIQ, 1:3 (Autumn 1974), 183-192.

2772.   Clark, Tim W.   "Some Relationships Between Prairie
        Dogs, Black-Footed Ferrets, Paleo-Indians, and
        Ethnographically Known Tribes."   PIA, 20:67 (Febru-
        ary 1978), 71-74.   Includes Sioux.

2773.   Clements, William M.   "Savage, Pastoral, Civilized:
        An Ecology Typology of American Frontier Heroes."
        JPC, 8:2 (Fall 1974), 254-266.

2774.   Cook-Lynn, Elizabeth.   "American Literature in Servi-
        tude."   InH, 10 (Winter 1977), 3-6.

2775.   Cook-Lynn, Elizabeth.   "Propulsives in Native Ameri-

can Literature. " CCC, 24 (October 1973), 271-
274. On the continuing richness of Native American literature.

2776.  Cracroft, Richard H.  "The American West of Karl
       May. " AQ, 19 (1967), 249-258.  About a noted
       German observer of the American Indian, who la-
       mented the degeneration of the "Indian nation. "

2777.  Daugherty, George H.  "Songs and Speeches of the
       Plains. " OC, 41 (1927), 338-357.  Quotations and
       comments about Native American literature.

2778.  Davis, Jack L.  "Hamlin Garland's Indians and the
       Quality of Civilized Life. " In Where the West Be-
       gins.  Ed. Arthur R. Huseboe and William Geyer.
       Sioux Falls, SD:  Center for Western Studies Press,
       1978, pp. 51-62.  On the Sioux, particularly Sitting
       Bull.

2779.  Dawes, H. L.  "Have We Failed with the Indians?"
       Atlantic, 84 (1899), 281-285.  He believed not;
       things seemed to be improving for the Indians.

2780.  Dillingham, Peter.  "The Literature of the American
       Indian. " EJ, 62 (January 1973), 37-41.  Praises
       The Magic World, Winter Count, House Made of
       Dawn, Miracle Hill, Black Elk Speaks, and other
       works.

2781.  Dollar, Clyde D.  "Historian Supports 'A Man Called
       Horse. ' " GPO, August 1970, pp. 8-9.

2782.  Dollar, Clyde D.  "Indians in Brief. " GPO, March
       1970, p. 7.  Review of Kopits' Indians.

2783.  Dorsey, James Owen.  "Folk-Lore and Mythology of
       the Sioux. " Antiquary, 7 (1889), 105.

2784.  Dorsey, James Owen.  "Indian Personal Names. "
       AA, 3:3 (July 1890), 263-268.

2785.  Dorsey, James Owen.  "Siouan Sociology:  A Posthu-
       mous Paper. " ARBAE, 15 (1897), pp. 205-244.

2786.  Dorsey, James Owen.  "The Social Organization of the
       Siouan Tribes. " JAFL, 4 (July-September 1891),
       257-266; 4 (October-December 1891), 331-342.

2787.   Dundes, Alan. "Oral Literature. " In Introduction to
        Cultural Anthropology. Ed. James A. Clifton.
        Boston:   Houghton Mifflin, 1968, pp. 117-129.

2788.   Dundes, Alan. "Structural Typology in North Ameri-
        can Indian Folktales. " SJA, 19 (1963), 121-129.

2789.   Evers, Lawrence J. "Further Survivals of Coyote. "
        NAL, 10:No. 3 (1976), 233-236.   The importance
        of the Coyote in American frontier tradition.

2790.   Fairchild, Hoxie N.   Noble Savage:   A Study in Ro-
        mantic Naturalism.   1928; rpt. New York:   Russell
        and Russell, 1961.

2791.   Fischer, J. L.   "The Sociopsychological Analysis of
        Folktales. "   CUA, 4 (June 1963), 235-295.   Com-
        ments by many scholars.

2792.   Fisher, Laura. "All Chiefs, No Indians:   What Chil-
        dren's Books Say About American Indians. "   EE,
        (1974), 185-189.   Discusses recent children's book
        on American Indians.

2793.   Flanagan, John T. "Folklore in Minnesota Literature. "
        MiH, 36 (September 1958), 73-83.

2794.   Flanagan, John T. "Some Sources for Northwest His-
        tory:   William Joseph Snelling's Western Narratives. "
        MiH, 17 (December 1936), 437-443.   Snelling wrote
        sketches on the Sioux.

2795.   Forbes-Lindsay, C. H. "Making Good Indians. "   HW,
        31 October 1908, pp. 12-13.

2796.   Friar, Ralph E. , and Natasha A. Friar.   The Only
        Good Indian ... The Hollywood Gospel.   New York:
        Drama Books, 1973.   346 pp.

2797.   Gilmore, Melvin R. "Folklore Concerning the Meadow
        Lark. "   AI, 3:2 (October 1921), 137.   On Sioux
        ideas about this bird.

2798.   Gilmore, Melvin R. "The Ground Bean and the Bean
        Mouse and Their Economic Relations. "   AI, 12:8
        (April 1921), 606-609.   Contains a Sioux legend.

2799.   Greenway, John. "Will the Indians Get Whitey?"

NaR, 21 (March 1969), 223-228. "Noble Savages" were not all noble.

2800.  Gurian, Jay. "Style in the Literary Desert: Little Big Man." WAL, 3 (Winter 1969), 285-296.

2801.  H. F. S. "Spider Myths of the American Indians." NHL, 21:4 (July-August 1921), 382-385. On many tribes, including the Sioux.

2802.  Hamilton, Wynette L. "The Correlation Between Societal Attitudes and Those of American Authors in the Depiction of American Indians, 1607-1860." AIQ, 1:1 (April 1974), 1-26.

2803.  Harrington, John. "Understanding Hollywood's Indian Rhetoric." CRAS, 8:1 (Spring 1977), 77-88.

2804.  Haslam, Gerald. "American Indians: Poets of the Cosmos." WAL, 5 (Spring 1970), 15-29.

2805.  Haslam, Gerald. "American Oral Literature: Our Forgotten Heritage." EJ, 60 (September 1971), 709-723.

2806.  Haslam, Gerald. "The Light That Fills the World: Native American Literature." SDR, 11 (Spring 1973), 27-41. About recent literature by and about Native Americans.

2807.  Hauptman, Laurence M. "Westward the Course of Empire: Geography Schoolbooks and Manifest Destiny, 1783-1893." The Historian, 40:3 (May 1978), 423-440. About historians and their attitudes about American Indians.

2808.  Hodge, F. W. "Indian Books for Children." SRe, August 8, 1931, p. 44.

2809.  Hough, Robert L. "Washington Irving, Indians, and the West." SDR, 6 (Winter 1968-69), 27-39.

2810.  Huseboe, Arthur R., and William Geyer, eds. Where the West Begins. Essays on Middle Border and Siouxland Writing, In Honor of Herbert Krause. Sioux Falls, SD: Center for Western Studies, 1978. Essays on the Sioux entered separately.

2811.  Hutton, P. A. "From Little Bighorn to Little Big
        Man: The Changing Image of a Western Hero in
        Popular Culture." WHQ, 7 (January 1976), 19-45.

2812.  Keiser, Albert. The Indian in American Literature.
        New York: Oxford Press, 1933; rpt. New York:
        Octagon Books, 1970. 312 pp.

2813.  Keshena, Rita. "The Role of American Indians in
        Motion Pictures." AICRJ, 1:No. 2 (1974), 25-28.
        Attacks Hollywood's portrayal of Indians. Keshena
        is Menominee.

2814.  Koster, John. "American Indians and the Media."
        CC, 26:2 (Summer 1976), 164-171.

2815.  Lane, Robert, and Barbara Lane. "On the Develop-
        ment of Dakota-Iroquois and Crow-Omaha Kinship
        Terminologies." SJA, 15:3 (Autumn 1959), 254-
        265.

2816.  Lincoln, Kenneth. "(Native) American Poetries."
        SR, 63:4 (Autumn 1978), 367-384. Contrasts In-
        dian and non-Indian poetry.

2817.  Lowie, Robert H. Studies in Plains Indian Folklore.
        Berkeley: University of California Press, 1932.

2818.  Lowie, Robert H. "The Test-Theme in North Ameri-
        can Mythology." JAFL, 21 (April 1908), 97-148.
        Discussion of principal themes in Indian mythology.

2819.  McClintock, W. "The Thunder Bird Myth." Master-
        key, 15 (1941), 164-168, 224-227; 16 (1942), 16-18.

2820.  McCluney, Eugene B. "LaCrosse: The Combat of
        Spirits." AIQ, 1:1 (Spring 1974), 34-42.

2821.  McCluskey, Sally. "Black Elk Speaks: And So Does
        John Neihardt." WAL, 6 (Winter 1972), 231-242.
        Credits Neihardt for making the book what it is.

2822.  McLaird, James D. "From the Deep Woods to Civi-
        lization: Charles Alexander Eastman, Dakota Au-
        thor." DBN, 3:1 (January 1968), 1-13.

2823.  Marken, Jack W. "Some Recent Resources in Indian
        Literature." AIQ, 2:3 (Autumn 1975), 282-289.

2824.  Marshall, Joe.  "'A Man Called Horse': Many Have
       Raised Harsh Criticisms. "  GPO, July 1970, p.
       13.  Marshall is Sioux.

2825.  Meyer, Roy W.  "Hamlin Garland and the American
       Indian. "  WAL, 2:2 (Summer 1967), 109-125.

2826.  Mickinock, Rey.  "The Plight of the Native Ameri-
       can. "  LJ, 96 (September 15, 1971), 2848-2851.
       Discusses good and bad books on Native Americans.

2827.  Monical, David G.  "Changes in American Attitudes
       Toward the Indian as Evidenced by Captive Litera-
       ture. "  PlA, 14:44, Pt. 1 (May 1969), 130-136.
       Whites shaped attitudes about Indians to justify be-
       havior toward them.

2828.  Monjo, F. N.  "Monjo's Manifest Destiny: Authors
       Can Claim Any Territory in Literature. "  LJ, 99
       (May 1974), 1454-1455.  Rejoinder against the be-
       lief that only Indians should write about Indians.
       See entry no. 2763.

2829.  Moore, L. Hugh.  "Francis Parkman on the Oregon
       Trail:  A Study in Cultural Prejudice. "  WAL, 12:
       2 (November 1977), 185-197.  Despite cultural pre-
       judice, Parkman recorded the best account of
       Oglala Sioux culture while it remained intact.

2830.  National Indian Education Association.  Native Ameri-
       can Evaluations of Media Materials.  2 vols.  Min-
       neapolis:  National Indian Education Assoc. , 1975.

2831.  Neihardt, John.  "The Book That Would Not Die. "
       WAL, 6 (Winter 1972), 227-230.  About Black Elk
       Speaks.  See entry no. 386.

2832.  Nichols, Roger L.  "Printer's Ink and Red Skins:
       Western Newspapermen and the Indians. "  KQ, 3:4
       (Fall 1971), 82-88.

2833.  O'Brien, Lynne Woods.  Plains Indian Autobiographies.
       WWS, 10 (1973).  48 pp.

2834.  Olivia, Leo E.  "Thomas Berger's Little Big Man as
       History. "  WAL, 7 (Spring and Summer, 1973), 33-
       54.

2835.   Pearce, Roy Harvey.  Savagism in Civilization:  A
        Study of the Indian and the American Mind.  Balti-
        more:  Johns Hopkins University Press, 1953.

2836.   Peet, Stephen D.  "Indian Myths and Effigy Mounds. "
        AAOJ, 11 (1889), 32-61.

2837.   Peet, Stephen D.  "The Indian Woman as She Was. "
        AAOJ, 27 (1905), 348-350.  Crude division of labor:
        he got the forest, she got the home.

2838.   Peet, Stephen D.  Myths and Symbols, or Aboriginal
        Religions in America.  1905; rpt. Kennebunkport,
        ME:  Longwood Press, 1976.

2839.   Peet, Stephen D.  "The Serpent Symbol in America. "
        AAOJ, 8 (1886), 197-221; 9 (1887), 133-163, 179-
        182.

2840.   Peet, Stephen D.  "The Serpent, A Symbol of the
        Rain Cloud. "  AAOJ, 16 (1894), 367-387.

2841.   Peet, Stephen D.  "The Snake Clan Among the Da-
        kotas. "  AAOJ, 12 (1890), 237-242.

2842.   "The Poetry of Indians. "  H, 57 (1878), 104-108.
        On the Sioux and other tribes.

2843.   Pope, Polly.  "Toward a Structural Analysis of North
        American Trickster Tales. "  SFQ, 31 (1967), 274-
        286.

2844.   Popp, James A.  "An Examination of Children's Books
        on the American Indian. "  BIA Education Research
        Bulletin, 3:1 (January 1975), 10-23.

2845.   Porter, Mark.  "Mysticism of the Land and the West-
        ern Novel. "  SDR, 11 (Spring 1973), 79-91.

2846.   Powell, J. W.  "Sketch of the Mythology of the North
        American Indians. "  ARBAE, 1 (1879-81), 19-56.

2847.   Price, John A.  "The Stereotyping of North American
        Indians in Motion Pictures. "  Ethnohistory, 20:2
        (Spring 1973), 153-171.

2848.   Prucha, Fr. Francis Paul, ed.  Americanizing the

American Indians: Writings by the "Friends of the
Indians," 1880-1900. Cambridge, MA: Harvard
University Press, 1973. 357 pp.

2849. Radin, Paul. Literary Aspects of North American
Mythology. Ottawa: Government Printing Office,
1915. 51 pp.

2850. Rans, Geoffrey. "Inaudible Man: The Indian in the
Theory and Practice of White Fiction." CRAS, 8:2
(Fall 1977), 103-115.

2851. Raymond, Art. "To Bill It as Authentic ... Is a
Lie." GPO, June 1970, p. 4; August 1970, p. 11.
About the film "A Man Called Horse." Raymond
is Sioux.

2852. Reichard, Gladys A. "Literary Types and Dissemina-
tion of Myths." JAFL, 34 (1921), 269-307. Important analysis of myth types.

2853. Reid, John T. Indian Influence in American Literature and Thought. Atlantic Highlands, NJ: Hu-
manities Press, 1965.

2854. Ridgley, Ronald. "The Gunfighter and the Student."
SS, 66 (March/April 1975), 69-71. Contains information on Indians in South Dakota.

2855. Riggs, Stephen R. "Mythology of the Dakotas."
AAOJ, 5 (1883), 147-149. Speaks respectfully of
Indian religion, but does not fully understand the
Sioux's perception of the Great Spirit.

2856. Roheim, Geza. "Culture Hero and Trickster in
North American Mythology." ICA, 29 (1949), 190-
194.

2857. Rooth, Anne Brigitta. "The Creation Myths of the
North American Indians." 52 (1957), 497-508.
Regards them as a traditional form of fiction.

2858. Roth, Russell. "The Inception of the Saga: Frederick Manfred's 'Buckskin Man.'" SDR, 7 (Winter
1969-70), 87-99. About Manfred's novels.

2859. Rourke, Constance. "The Indian Background of American Theatricals." In No. 2769, pp. 256-265.

2860.   Rucker, Mary E.   "Natural, Tribal, and Civil Law in
        Cooper's The Prairie. "  WAL, 12:2 (November
        1977),  215-222.

2861.   Russel, Jason A.   "Irving:   Recorder of Indian Life. "
        JAH,  25 (1931),  185-195.

2862.   Sandberg, Edwin T.   "A Course in the Literature and
        Music of the American Indian. "  JHE,  30 (1959),
        453-455.   No shortage of material available on vari-
        ous Indian cultures.

2863.   Sanders, Thomas E.   "Tribal Literature:   Individual
        Identity and the Collective Unconscious. "  CCC,  24
        (October 1973),  256-266.

2864.   Sargent, Epes.   "On Lake Pepin. "  The Knickerbocker
        Gallery (1855),  pp.  97-111.

2865.   Saum, Lewis O.   "The Fur Trader and the Noble
        Savage. "  AQ,  15 (1963),  554-571.

2866.   Sayre, Robert F.   "The Proper Study--Autobiographics
        in American Studies. "  AQ,  29:3 (1977),  241-262.
        On Black Elk Speaks and other books of that sort.

2867.   Schmerler, Henrietta.   "Trickster Marries His Daugh-
        ter. "  JAFL,  44 (1931),  196-207.

2868.   Skelton, William B.   "Army Officer's Attitudes To-
        ward Indians, 1830-1869. "  PNQ,  66 (July 1976),
        113-124.

2869.   Smith, G. Hubert.   "The Winona Legend. "  MiH,  13
        (December 1932),  367-376.

2870.   Sobosan, Jeffrey C.   "The Philosopher and the In-
        dian:   Correlations Between Plotinus and Black
        Elk. "  InH,  7:2 (Spring 1974),  47-48.

2871.   Stensland, Anna Lee.   "American Indian Culture and
        the Reading Program. "  JR,  15 (October 1971),  22-
        26.   Contains a bibliography of books that might be
        read.

2872.   Stensland, Anna Lee.   "American Indian Culture:
        Promises, Problems, and Possibilities. "  EJ,  60

(1971), 1195-1200. Suggestions for courses on Indian culture in curricula.

2873.  Stensland, Anna Lee. "Traditional Poetry of the
American Indian." EJ, 64 (September 1975), 41-
47.

2874.  Stipe, Claude E. "Eastern Dakota Clans: The Solu-
tion of a Problem." AA, 73:5 (October 1971),
1031-1035. Says clans never actually existed in
prehistory.

2875.  Swanson, Charles H. "The Treatment of the American Indian in High School History Texts." InH, 10:
2 (Spring 1977), 28-37.

2876.  Tedlock, Dennis. "On the Translation of Style in
Oral Literature." JAFL, 84 (1971), 114-133.

2877.  Ten Kate, Herman F. C. "The Indian in Literature."
ARSI (1921), pp. 507-528; and InH, 3 (Summer
(1970), 23-32.

2878.  Tilghman, Z. A. "Source of the Buffalo Origin
Legend." AA, N.S. 43 (1941), 487-488.

2879.  Troy, Anne. "The Indian in Adolescent Novels."
InH, 8:4 (Winter 1975), 32-35.

2880.  Underhill, Lonnie E., and Daniel F. Littlefield, eds.
Hamlin Garland and the American Indian. Tucson:
University of Arizona Press, 1974. Essays on
Garland.

2881.  Vestal, Stanley. "The Hollywooden Indian." SR, 21:
4 (July 1936), 418-423. Critical of Hollywood
treatment of Indians.

2882.  Wake, C. Staniland. "Asiatic Ideas Among the American Indians, Part I." AAOJ, 27 (1905), 153-62;
"Part II." AAOJ, 27 (1905), 189-97.

2883.  Wake, C. Staniland. "Mythology of the Plains'
[sic] Indians." AAOJ, 27 (1905), 9-16; "II--Nature
Deities," pp. 73-80; "III. Terrestrial Objects,"
pp. 323-328; "IV. Magical Animals." AAOJ, 28
(1906), 205-212.

2884.  Waterman, T. T.  "The Explanatory Element in the
       Folk-Tales of the North American Indians." JAFL,
       27 (1914), 1-54.

2885.  Watts, Harold H.  "Myth and Folk-Tale." ArQ, 11
       (1955), 293-311.

2886.  Weidman, Bette S.  "White Men's Red Man:  Peni-
       tential Reading of Four American Novels." MLS,
       4:2 (Fall 1974), 14-26.

2887.  Whitney, Blair.  "American Indian Literature of the
       Great Plains." GPR, 2:2 (Winter 1976), 43-53.

2888.  Wilson, Raymond.  "The Writing of Ohiyesa--Charles
       Alexander Eastman, M. D., Santee Sioux." SDH,
       6:1 (Winter 1975), 55-73.

2889.  Wissler, Clark.  "The Whirlwind and the Elk in the
       Mythology of the Dakota." JAFL, 18 (October 1905),
       257-268.  More on Sioux philosophy than literature.

2890.  Wright, Robert C.  "The Myth of the Isolated Self
       in Manfred's Siouxland Novels." See entry no.
       2810, pp. 110-118.

2891.  Wroth, Lawrence C.  "The Indian Treaty as Litera-
       ture." YR, 17 (July 1928), 749-766.  Mainly about
       treaty conferences.

2892.  Wylder, Delbert E.  "Manfred's Indian Novel." SDR,
       7 (Winter 1969-70), 100-109.  About Conquering
       Horse; see entry no. 663.

2893.  Wylder, Delbert E.  "Thomas Berger's Little Big
       Man as Literature." WAL, 3 (Winter 1969), 273-
       284.

2894.  Yoder, Jon A.  "Miscegenation in Our Virgin Land."
       SDR, 12 (Winter 1974-75), 102-110.


                        WARFARE AMONG TRIBES


2895.  Babcock, Willoughby M. Jr.  "Radiograms of Min-
       nesota History:  Sioux Versus Chippewa." MHB,

6:1 (March 1925), 41-45.    Radio address delivered March 17, 1924.

2896.  Babcock, Willoughby M., Jr.  "Sioux Versus Chippewa."  MiH, 6 (March 1925), 41-45.

2897.  Baird, Elizabeth T.  "Indian Customs and Early Recollections."  CWHS, 9 (1882), 303-326.  She remembered customs and intertribal warfare.

2898.  Bassett, Samuel Clay.  "This Sioux-Pawnee Battle-- Letters."  NH, 16 (July-September 1935), 156-70.

2899.  Blaine, Garland James, and Martha Royce Blaine. "Pa-re-su A-ri-ra-ke:  The Hunters That Were Massacred."  NH, 58:3 (Fall 1977), 342-358.  A party of 350-400 Pawnee were hunting August 5, 1873--men, women and children--and some were killed by Sioux.

2900.  Blegen, Theodore C., ed.  "Armistice and War on the Minnesota Frontier:  The Sioux and the Chippeways."  By Ezekiel G. Gear.  MiH, 24 (March 1943), 11-25.  Letter by Gear to his brother from Fort Snelling, July 19, 1839.

2901.  Brennan, Mary R.  "Some Devil's Lake Notes." CHSND, 1 (1906), 476-478.  About the killing of Sioux soldiers by Ojibway.

2902.  Briggs, John E.  "Implacable Foes."  Palimpsest, 8:9 (September 1927), 306-314.  Fighting between Sacs and Foxes embroiled the Sioux.

2903.  Brisbois, B. W.  "Recollections of Prairie du Chien."  CWHS, 9 (1882), 282-302.

2904.  Clark, Julius Taylor.  The Ojibwa Conquest:  An Indian Epistle.  n. p., 1898.  123 pp.  A souvenir edition, published in 1850 under the name George Conway, to whom the original author had given his manuscript with permission to publish.

2905.  Draper, Lyman C.  "Early French Forts in Western Wisconsin."  CWHS, 10 (1888), 321-372.  Much on intertribal engagements.

2906.  Enmegahbowh, or John Johnson.  En-me-gah-bowh's
       Story:  An Account of the Disturbance of the Chip-
       pewa Indians at Gull Lake in 1857 and 1862 and
       Their Removal in 1868.  Minneapolis, MN:  Wom-
       an's Auxiliary, St. Barnabas Hospital, 1904.  56
       pp.

2907.  Ewers, John C.  "Intertribal Warfare as a Precursor
       of Indian-White Warfare on the Northern Great
       Plains."  WHQ, 6:4 (October 1975), 397-410.

2908.  Forbes, Allan.  "The Plain Agon--A Gross Typology."
       PlA, 17:56 (May 1972), 143-155.  There were seven
       district types of military operations among Plains
       Indians.

2909.  Freeman, Winfield.  "The Battle of Arickaree."
       TKHS, 6 (1900), 346-357.  Roman Nose was killed
       during this encounter, in which Sioux and other
       tribes participated in September of 1868.

2910.  Hazen, R. W.  "The Pawnee Indian War, 1859."
       PNSHS, 3 (1892), 279-286.  War between the
       Pawnee and Sioux during July of 1859, in which the
       Pawnee were defeated by the Sioux and the United
       States Army.

2911.  Hitchcock, Ida J.  "Chippewa Fought the Sioux for
       Possession of Minnesota."  AI, 5:3 (1931), 14-15.

2912.  Landes, Ruth.  "Dakota Warfare."  SJA, 15:1 (Spring
       1959), 43-52.  About honors, bravery, and the dis-
       grace of committing suicide in warfare, or failing
       to participate in combat.

2913.  Mahan, Bruce E.  "The Great Council of 1825."
       Palimpsest, 6:9 (September 1925), 305-318.

2914.  Mooney, James.  "The Indian Congress at Omaha."
       AA, 1:1 (January 1899), 126-149.  Many tribes, in-
       cluding the Sioux, were there.

2915.  Neill, Edward D.  "Battle of Pokeguma:  As Narrated
       by an Eye Witness."  CMHS, 1 (1872), 177-182.
       On war between Sioux and Ojibwa.

2916.  Newcombe, W. W., Jr.  "A Re-examination of the

Causes of Plains Warfare. " AA, 52:3 (July-
September 1950), 317-330.  On war between Plains
tribes, including Sioux.

2917.  Nichols, Roger L.  "The Black Hawk War:  Another
View. "  AIo, 36:7 (Winter 1963), 525-533.  Includes information about the Sioux.

2918.  O'Meara, Walter A.  The Sioux Are Coming.  Boston:
Houghton Mifflin, 1971.  105 pp.  About an Ojibwa
family's flight from the Sioux.

2919.  Pond, Samuel W.  "Indian Warfare in Minnesota. "
CMHS, 3 (1880), 129-138.  About battles fought by
eastern Sioux in the period 1835-1845, while Pond
served in Minnesota as a missionary and farm in-
structor.

2920.  "Prairie du Chien Documents, 1814-15. "  CWHS, 9
(1882), 262-281.  Material on the Sioux.

2921.  Ramsey, Jarold, ed.  "Fish-Hawk's Raid Against the
Sioux. "  As told by Gilbert Minthorn to Morris
Swadesh.  Alcheringa, 3:1 (1977), 96-99.

2922.  Schoolcraft, Henry Rowe.  "War Between the Chippewas and the Sioux.  A Peculiar Mode of Negotiation
Between Them by Means of Pictography, or De-
vices Inscribed on Bark. "  In School, Pt. VI, pp.
387-392.

2923.  Sibley, Henry H.  "Sketches of Indian Warfare, by
Hal, A Dakotah. "  Spirit of the Times, 18:3 (1848),
25.

2924.  Smith, Marian W.  "The War Complex of the Plains
Indians. "  PAPS, 78 (1937), 425-464.  Contends
that warfare was a principal concern among Great
Plains tribes.

2925.  [Snelling, William Joseph].  "Running the Gauntlet:
A Thrilling Incident of Early Days at Fort Snelling. "  CMHS, 1 (1872), 439-456.  Snelling is
credited with this anonymous article about a battle
between the Sioux and the Ojibwa.

2926.  Street, Joseph M.  "Sioux and the Black Hawk War. "
CWHS, 5 (1868), 310-314.

2927.  Strong, Moses M.   "The Indian Wars of Wisconsin."
       CWHS, 8 (1879), 241-286.

2928.  "Talk of Peace."  Palimpsest, 8:9 (September 1927),
       315-326.  Verbatim account of the Indian Peace
       Council at Washington, D. C. between the Sioux
       and their Sac and Fox, and Iowa, neighbors, re-
       printed from Miles National Register, 53 (1837).

2929.  Taylor, William Z.   "The Last Battle of the Pawnee
       with the Sioux."  PNSHS, 16 (1911), 165-167.

2930.  Warren, William W.   "Sioux and Chippewa Wars."
       MA, 12 (October 1946), 95-107.

2931.  Watrall, Charles R.   "Virginia Deer and the Buffer
       Zone in the Late Prehistoric-Early Prehistoric
       Period in Minnesota."  PIA, 13:40 (May 1968), 81-
       86.

2932.  Williamson, John W.   The Battle of Massacre Canyon:
       The Unfortunate Ending of the Last Buffalo Hunt of
       the Pawnees, An Account of the Last Battle by In-
       dians.  Trenton, NB:  Republican Leader, 1922,
       1930.  16 pp.


                       WARS OF THE EAST

2933.  Babcock, Willoughby M.   "The Minnesota Indian and
       His History."  MA, 19:3 (July 1954), 18-25.

2934.  Baker, Miriam Hawthorn.   "Inkpaduta's Camp at
       Smithland."  AIo, 39:2 (Fall 1967), 81-104.  Baker's
       great grandfather was visited by Inkpaduta before
       the Spirit Lake Uprising.

2935.  Baker, Robert O.   The Muster Roll:  A Biography of
       Fort Ripley, Minnesota.  St. Paul, MN:  H. M.
       Smyth Co., 1971.  206 pp.

2936.  Barness, John, and William Dickinson.   "The Sully
       Campaign of 1864."  Montana, 16:3 (July 1966), 23-
       29.

2937.  Beau, Geraldine.   "General Alfred Sully and the North-

west Indian Expedition. " NDH, 33:3 (Summer
1966), 240-259.

2938. Berghold, Alexander. The Indians' Revenge: Or,
Days of Horror. San Francisco: P. J. Thomas,
Printer, 1891. 240 pp.

2939. Blegen, Theodore C. , ed. "The Unfinished Autobiography of Henry Hastings Sibley. " MiH, 8:4 (December 1927), 329-362; rpt as The Unfinished Autobiography of Henry Hastings Sibley, Together with
a Selection of Hitherto Unpublished Letters from the
Thirties. Minneapolis, MN: Voyageur Press,
Fred Totten Phelps, 1932. 75 pp.

2940. Brackett, George A. A Winter Evening's Tale. New
York: Printed for the Author, 1880. 31 pp.

2941. Brown, George A. "The Settlement of Cherokee
County. " AI, 36:7 (Winter 1963), 539-556. Be-
ginning with February 1856, deals with the Spirit
Lake Uprising and other activities of the Sioux.

2942. Brownell, Charles De Wolf. The Indian Races of
North and South America. Hartford, CT: American Publishing Company, 1873. Includes some information about the Minnesota Sioux War.

2943. Cade, James E. Indians and Rebels. New York:
H. L. Lindquist Publications, 1963. Includes letters of J. E. Cade, from Stamps, 7 September
1963, pp. 346-348, 350, describing Cade's service
with the 8th Minnesota Volunteers against the Sioux
and the Confederacy during the Civil War.

2944. Camp Release Monument, Erected in 1894 by the State
of Minnesota, at Camp Release, Lac Qui Parle
County, Minnesota, in Accordance with an Act of
the Legislature, Approved April 11, 1893. Monte-
video, MN: Hoard and Henry, Printers, 1894.
26 pp.

2945. Churchill, Caroline Nichols. Active Footsteps.
Colorado Springs, CO: Mrs. C. N. Churchill,
1909. 256 pp.

2946. Clark, Dan E. "Frontier Defense in Iowa, 1850-1865. "

IJHP, 16:3 (July 1918), 315-386.   Largely on the
Sioux; includes the Minnesota Sioux War of 1862.

2947.   Collins, Loren Warren.   The Expedition Against the
Sioux Indians in 1863,  Under Gen. Henry H. Sibley.
St. Cloud, MN:   Journal Press Print. , 1895.   22
pp.

2948.   Cooke, David Coxe.   Fighting Indians of the West.
New York:   Dodd, Mead, 1954.   208 pp.   Includes
a biography of Little Crow, and a description of
the Sioux War of 1862.

2949.   Cooke, David Coxe.   Fighting Indians of America.
New York:   Dodd, Mead, 1966.   226 pp.

2950.   Cray, Lorin.   "Experiences in Southwestern Minnesota, 1859 to 1867. "   CMHS, 15 (1915), 435-454.
An account of a raid by the Sioux on August 11,
1864, between Shelbyville and Vernon, which was
the last raid, except for a skirmish on May 2 in
Blue Earth County.

2951.   Daniels, Arthur M.   A Journal of Sibley's Indian Expedition, During the Summer of 1863.   Winona, MN:
Republican Office, 1864.   52 pp.   Prepared by a
soldier in Company H, 6th Regiment.

2952.   Davis, Jane S.   Guide to a Microfilm Edition of the
Henry Hastings Sibley Papers.   St. Paul:   Minnesota Historical Society, 1968.   27 pp.   About Sibley's career as a fur trader and military leader
during the Sioux War.

2953.   Dearborn, Alva.   Gen. Sibley's Expedition Against
Sioux Indians 1863.   St. Paul:  n. p. , 1924.   Photo-
stat of originals held by the Minnesota Historical
Society.

2954.   Eastman, Enoch.   "Portions of the Diary of Enoch
Eastman, Co. E, Hatches Battalion Minnesota Vols. ,
With Sibley's Expedition in 1863. "   Ed. Dana
Wright.   NDHQ, 1:3 (April 1927), 41-45; 1:4 (July
1927), 12-13; 2:2 (January 1928), 127-128.

2955.   Ebbell, Bendix Joachim.   De Som Drog Ut:   Av Den
Norske Utvandrings Historie.   Oslo:   Byldendal,
Norsk Forlag, 1925.   118 pp.

2956.  Ellis, Richard N.   "Civilians, the Army and the In-
       dian Problem on the Northern Plains, 1862-1866. "
       NDH, 37:1 (Winter 1970), 20-39.   Deals with cam-
       paigns against the Sioux.

2957.  Ellis, Richard N.   "Political Pressures and Army
       Politics on the Northern Plains, 1862-1865. "   MiH,
       42 (Summer 1970), 43-53.   Largely about the Sioux.

2958.  Ely, Edmund Franklin.   "Battle of Lake Pokeguma. "
       Minnesota Historical Society Transactions (1879),
       pp. 9-17.

2959.  English, Abner.   "Dakota's First Soldiers:   History
       of the First Dakota Cavalry, 1862-1865. "   CHSSD,
       9 (1918), 241-307.   English was First Sergeant in
       Company A, 1st Dakota Cavalry.   He served during
       engagements with the Sioux.

2960.  Flandrau, Charles E.   "The Ink-Pa-Du-Ta Massacre
       of 1857:   A Paper Read Before the Minnesota His-
       torical Society, December 8, 1879. "   CMHS, 3
       (1889), 386-407.

2961.  Flandrau, Charles E.   "Narrative of the Indian War
       of 1862-1864, and Following Campaigns in Minne-
       sota. "   In Minnesota in the Civil War and Indian
       Wars, 1861-1865, pp. 728-818.

2962.  Foot, Solomon R.   "The Sioux Indian War. "   IHR, 10
       (1896), 132-137; 11 (1897), 323-329.

2963.  "Frontier Fear of the Indians. "   AI, 29:4 (April 1948),
       315-322.   Contains Frontier Guard correspondence
       and other letters about fear after the Spirit Lake
       Uprising.

2964.  George, Alice Mendenhall.   The Story of My Child-
       hood, Written for My Children.   Whittier, CA:
       W. A. Smith, 1923.   88 pp.

2965.  Goodwin, Carol G.   "The Letters of Private Milton
       Spencer, 1862-1865:   A Soldier's View of Military
       Life on the Northern Plains. "   NDH, 37:4 (Fall
       1970), 232-269.   A Private in the 6th Iowa Cavalry
       in the years 1863-65 tells about garrison life and
       campaigns against the Sioux in Dakota Territory.

Contains long excerpts from Spencer's letters plus a picture of Yanktonai Two Bears.

2966.   Hanson, Joseph M.   With Sully into the Sioux Land. Chicago: McClurg, 1910.   Tells of General Sully's experiences as he pursued the Sioux into the Black Hills.

2967.   Hargrave, Joseph James.   Red River.   Montreal: Printed for the Author by J. Lovell, 1871.   506 pp. Deals with the Minnesota Sioux War of 1862-63.

2968.   Heard, Isaac V. D.   History of the Sioux War and Massacres of 1862 and 1863.   New York: Harper, 1865; rpt. Chicago: Library Resources, 1971, New York: Kraus Reprint, 1975.   354 pp.   Heard, a young lawyer and court recorder, wrote the best first-hand account of the trials of the Sioux following the Minnesota Sioux War, and of the general course of the War.

2969.   Heilbron, Bertha L.   "Documentary Panorama." MiH, 30 (1949), 14-23.

2970.   Herriott, F. I.   "The Aftermath of the Spirit Lake Massacre, March 8-15, 1857."   AIo, 18:6 (October 1932), 434-470; 18:7 (January 1933), 483-517; 18:8 (April 1933), 597-631.

2971.   Herriott, F. I.   "Dr. Isaac H. Herriott, One of the Victims of the Spirit Lake Massacre, Killed on the Evening of Sunday, March 8, 1857."   AIo, 18:4 (April 1932), 243-294.   A long account of the Minnesota Sioux War, with quotes from the correspondence of Herriott.   Author was a professor at Drake University.

2972.   Herriott, F. I.   "The Origins of the Indian Massacre Between the Okobojis, March 8, 1857."   AIo, 18:5 (July 1932), 323-382.   Continuation of the account presented in source cited above.

2973.   Hilger, Nicholas.   "General Alfred Sully's Expedition of 1864:   Battle with the Combined Tribes of Sioux Indians Among the Bad Lands of the Little Missouri, From the Diary of Judge Nicholas Hilger."   CHSMo, 2 (1896), 314-322.

2974.   Hill, Alfred J.   History of Company E, of the Sixth
        Minnesota Regiment of Volunteer Infantry.   St.
        Paul, MN:   Pioneer Press Company, 1899.   45 pp.

2975.   Hoffman, Charles F.   Wild Scenes in the Forest and
        Prairie.   2 vols.   1842; rpt.   Upper Saddle River,
        NJ:   Gregg Press, Inc., 1970.

2976.   Hoover, Sgt. Harris.   "The Relief Expedition."
        Palimpsest, 38:6 (June 1957), 253-264.   About the
        Spirit Lake Uprising.   Reprinted from Hamilton
        Freeman, August 20, 27, 1857.

2977.   Howe, Orlando C.   "The Discovery of the Spirit Lake
        Massacre."   AIo, 11:6 (July 1914), 408-424.

2978.   Hughes, Thomas.   "Causes and Results of the Ink-
        paduta Massacre."   CMHS, 12 (1908), 263-282.

2979.   Hughes, Thomas.   "Discovery of the Skeltons of
        Many Sioux Killed in War, Buried Near Fort L'Huil-
        lier."   CMHS, 12 (1908), 287-290.

2980.   Ingham, Harvey.   The Northern Border Brigade:   A
        Story of Military Beginnings.   Des Moines, IA:
        Privately Printed, 1926.   96 pp.

2981.   Ingham, Harvey.   "Sioux Indians Harassed the Early
        Iowa Settlers."   AIo, 34:2 (October 1957), 137-141.
        Gives names of some of the Sioux chiefs during
        raids in the 1840's and 1850's.

2982.   Jacobson, Clair.   "The Battle of Whitestone Hill."
        NDH, 44:3 (Summer 1977), 4-14.   With General
        Sully in command, this has been called the bloodi-
        est battle ever fought on North Dakota soil.

2983.   Johnson, Roy P.   "The Siege at Fort Abercrombie."
        NDH, 24:1 (January 1957), 4-79.   Beginning August
        20, 1862, it lasted nearly two months.

2984.   Jones, Robert Huhn.   The Civil War in the North-
        west:   Nebraska, Wisconsin, Iowa, Minnesota, and
        the Dakotas.   Norman:   University of Oklahoma
        Press, 1960.   216 pp.   Deals with the impact of
        the Minnesota Sioux War of 1862-63.

2985.   Judd, A. N.   Campaigning Against the Sioux ...
        Being Extracts from a Diary Kept During One of
        Three Expeditions Participated in by the Author
        Against the Sioux, Under General Alfred Sully in
        1863-4-5.   Watsonville, CA:   Press of the Daily
        Pajaronian, 1906; rpt New York:   Sol Lewis, 1973.
        45 pp.

2986.   King, James T.   "The Civil War of Private Morton. "
        NDH, 35:1 (Winter 1968), 8-19.   The letters of
        Pvt. Thomas F. Morton of Company C, 7th Minne-
        sota Volunteer Infantry, from the period July-
        August 1863, on the expedition of Henry H. Sibley.

2987.   Kingsburg, David L.   "Sully's Expedition Against the
        Sioux in 1864. "   CMHS, 8 (1898), 449-462.   Kings-
        bury was a Lieutenant in Sully's army.

2988.   Kinney, Newcombe.   Reminiscences of the Sioux In-
        dian and Civil Wars.   Transcribed by Mrs. John
        Mahan.   n. p. , 1916.   9 pp.

2989.   Kunz, Virginia.   Muskets to Missiles:  A Military
        History of Minnesota.   St. Paul:  Minnesota State-
        hood Centennial Commission, 1958.   198 pp.

2990.   Kunz, Virginia.   "Sergeant Ramer's Indian War. "
        Ramsey County History, 1:2 (Fall 1964), 16-22.

2991.   Laut, Agnes Christina.   "Daughters of the Vikings--
        Guri Endreson:  Heroine of Kondiyohi. "   OM, 52
        (July 1908), 413-423.

2992.   Lawson, Victor Emanuel.   "The First Settlements in
        the Kankiyohi Region and Their Fate in the Indian
        Outbreak. "   Swedish Historical Society of America,
        10 (1925), 19-44.

2993.   Lovering, N.   "The Spirit Lake Stockade. "   IHR, 3:
        4 (October 1887), 568-575.

2994.   Lingk, Ray W.   "The Northwestern Indian Expedi-
        tion ... the Sully Trail. "   NDH, 24:4 (October
        1957), 181-199.   On Sully's punitive expedition of
        1864.

2995.   McCullough, Boyd.   The Experience of Seventy Years.

Minneapolis, MN:   The Tribune Job Printing Co.,
1895.   199 pp.

2996.   McKenzie, John H.   "Capture of Little Six and Grey
Iron in 1864.   Statement of John H.   McKenzie and
Onisime Giguere. "   Printed by the Minnesota State
Legislature, February 1, 1867.   11 pp.

2997.   McKusick, Marshall.   The Iowa Northern Border Brigade.   Iowa City:   University of Iowa Office of
Archaeologist, 1975.   172 pp.

2998.   McLaren, Robert N.   Diary of Colonel Robert N.
McLaren in Sully's Expedition Against the Sioux,
1864.   Typewritten Manuscript available at the Minnesota Historical Society.

2999.   Marking the 120th Anniversary of the Battle Between
the Chippewa and Sioux Near Nielsville, Minnesota.
n. p. , 1939.   18 pp.

3000.   Marshall, William R.   Journal of Sibley Expedition
from Camp Pope to the Missouri River and Return
to Fort Snelling, June, July and August, 1863.
Typewritten manuscript available at the Minnesota
Historical Society.

3001.   Marshall, William R.   "Portions of the Journal of the
Military Expedition Against the Sioux Indians from
Camp Pope in the Summer of 1863 Under Command
of Brigadier General Henry Hastings Sibley. "   Ed.
Dana Wright.   NDHQ, 1:3 (April 1927), 38-40; 1:4
(July 1927), 11; 2:2 (January 1928), 126-128.

3002.   Merritt, Leonidas.   "An Incident at Old Fort Sully. "
CHSSD, 5 (1910), 415-416.   While a member of
Company B, Brackett's Battalion of the Minnesota
Cavalry, he was almost captured by Sioux in 1864
on a trip from Fort Snelling to Sioux City.

3003.   Minnesota.   Board of Commissioners on Publication
of History of Minnesota in Civil and Indian Wars.
Minnesota in the Civil and Indian Wars, 1861-1865.
2 vols.   St. Paul, MN:   Pioneer Press Company,
1890-1893.   Published at the order of the Minnesota
legislature April 16, 1889.   Contains a roster of
citizen soldiers as well as Charles E.   Flandrau's

description of the Minnesota Sioux War, a narrative
by Thomas P. Gere, and others.

3004. Mooers, Calvin. "Indian Warfare in the Red River
Country, 1862-1866. " Detroit Society for Genea-
logical Research Magazine, 20 (1957), 139-141.

3005. Morton, William Lewis. "The Battle at the Grand
Coteau, July 13 and 14, 1851. " In Papers of the
Historical and Scientific Society of Manitoba, Winni-
peg. Ser. 3, No. 16 (1960), 37-49.

3006. Musgrove, Richard Watson. Autobiography. Bristol,
NH: Musgrove Printing House, 1921. 230 pp.
About the Minnesota Sioux War of 1862-63.

3007. Nichols, David A. "The Other Civil War: Lincoln
and the Indians. " MiH, 44:1 (Spring 1974), 2-15.

3008. Nicolay, John G. "The Sioux War. " CMo, 3:2
(February 1863), 195-204.

3009. Nix, Jacob. Der Ausbruch der Sioux-Indianer in
Minnesota, im August 1862. New Ulm, MN: Verlag des Verfassers, 1887. 71 pp.

3010. Nix, Jacob. Capt. Nix Tells Story of Indian Outbreak
in Book. New Ulm Review, September 1, 8, 15,
22, 1949. Translation of 2993 by Gretchen Stein-
hauser, a granddaughter.

3011. Pattee, John. "Dakota Campaigns. " CHSSD, 5 (1910),
273-350.

3012. Petersen, William J. "Massacre on the Okobojis. "
Palimpsest, 38:6 (June 1957), 221-235; rpt. Palimpsest, 43:10 (October 1962), 433 ff.

3013. Petersen, William J. "Troops and Military Supplies
on Upper Mississippi River Steamboats. " IJHP,
33:3 (July 1935), 260-286.

3014. Pettijohn, Jonas. Autobiography, Family History and
Various Reminiscences of the Life of Jonas Petti-
john Among the Sioux or Dakota Indians. Clay Cen-
ter, KS: Dispatch Printing House, 1890. 104 pp.
About the causes of the Minnesota Sioux War, and
Pettijohn's escape in August, 1862.

3015.   Pfaller, Fr. Louis.   "The Peace Mission of 1863-
        1864. "   NDH, 37:4 (Fall 1970), 292-313.   Attempts
        by Fr. Alexis Andre and Major Joseph Brown to
        bring peace between Sioux and non-Indians during
        the Sibley-Sully campaigns.   Contains a photograph
        of Sisseton Chief Standing Buffalo, who subsequently
        moved to Canada to found a reservation near Ft.
        QuAppelle.

3016.   Pfaller, Fr. Louis.   "Sully's Expedition of 1864 Fea-
        turing the Kildeer Mountain and Badland's Battles. "
        NDH, 31:1 (January 1964), 25-77; rpt. Bismarck:
        State Historical Society of North Dakota, 1964.   54
        pp.

3017.   Potter, Theodore Edgar.   "Captain Potter's Recollec-
        tions of Minnesota Experiences. "   MiH, 1:8 (Novem-
        ber 1916), 418-521.   Covers the period 1855-1876,
        and deals with the Minnesota Sioux War.

3018.   Pritchett, John Perry, ed.   "On the March with Sib-
        ley in 1863:   The Diary of Private Henry J. Haga-
        dorn. "   NDHQ, 5:2 (January 1931), 103-129.

3019.   Pritchett, John P.   "Sidelights on the Sibley Expedi-
        tion from the Diary of a Private. "   MiH, 7:4 (De-
        cember 1926), 326-335.   Contains material from the
        Hagadorn Diary, which he kept from June 11 to
        August 31, 1863.

3020.   Prucha, Fr. Francis Paul.   Broadax and Bayonet:
        The Role of the United States Army in the Develop-
        ment of the Northwest, 1815-1860.   Lincoln:   Uni-
        versity of Nebraska Press, 1967.

3021.   Richards, Charles R.   "The Spirit Lake Expedition--
        1857. "   IHR, 7:1 (January 1891), 18-34.   A Captain
        in Company A of the Volunteers, he went to relieve
        the settlements.

3022.   Robertson, Thomas A.   "Reminiscence of Thomas A.
        Robertson. "   CHSSD, 20 (1940), 559-608.

3023.   Roddis, Louis H.   The Indian Wars of Minnesota.
        Cedar Rapids:   Torch Press, 1956.   311 pp.   Writ-
        ing almost exclusively on the Sioux, the author
        traced Indian conflict from the Spirit Lake Massacre

to the Sully campaigns following the Minnesota
Sioux War.   Interesting book by a Captain in the
Medical Corps.

3024.   Rothfuss, Hermann E.   "German Witnesses of the
Sioux Campaigns. "   NDH, 25:4 (October 1958), 123-
133.   On the years 1962 to 1964.

3025.   Sander, John.   "Fifty Years Ago in Minnesota, "
Young Folks, September 28, October 12 and 26,
November 23,  1912.

3026.   Seelye, W. E.   "Early Military Experiences in Da-
kota. "   CHSND, 3 (1910), 242-246.   A soldier at
Fort Snelling describes the retreat of Sioux into
Canada, etc.

3027.   Sergeant, Elizabeth Shepley.   Short as Any Dream.
New York:   Harper and Brothers, 1929.   244 pp.
Pioneer at St. Cloud describes the Minnesota Sioux
War of 1862.

3028.   Shortridge, Wilson P.   "Henry Hastings Sibley and
the Minnesota Frontier. "   MiH, 3:3 (August 1919),
115-125.

3029.   [Stambaugh, Benjamin F. ,  ed. ]   "Iowa Troops in the
Sully Campaigns. "   IJHP, 20:3 (July 1922), 364-
443.   Material from the diaries and letters of
Henry J. Wieneke, Amos R. Cherry, and Josiah F.
Hill.

3030.   Starkey, J.   Reminiscences of Indian Depredations.
The Sunrise and Other Expeditions.   St. Paul, MN:
D. Ramaley and Son, 1891.   25 pp.

3031.   Street, Joseph M. ,  et al.   "Indian Affairs of the
Iowa Region, 1827-1830. "   AIo, 16:1 (July 1927),
25-42.

3032.   Sully, Langdon.   No Tears for the General:   The
Life of Alfred Sully, 1821-1879.   Palo Alto, CA:
American West Publishing Co. , 1974.   255 pp.
Much on the campaigns against the Sioux in
1863.

3033.   Taylor, James W.   The Sioux War:   What Has Been

Done by the Minnesota Campaign of 1863:  What
Should Be Done During a Dakota Campaign of 1864.
St. Paul, MN:  Press Printing Co., 1863.  16 pp.
Reprint of papers that appeared in the St. Paul
Daily Press during August and September, 1863.

3034.   Taylor, Joseph H.  "Inkpaduta and Sons."  NDHQ,
4:3 (April 1930), 153-164.  About the Spirit Lake
Massacre.

3035.   Teakle, Thomas.  The Spirit Lake Massacre.  Iowa
City:  State Historical Society of Iowa, 1918.  336
pp.  Best account.

3036.   Throne, Mildred, ed.  "Iowa Troops in Dakota Territory, 1861-1864:  Based on the Diaries and Letters
of Henry J. Wieneke."  IJHP, 57:2 (April 1959),
97-190.  On Indian treatment of captives.

3037.   Thurn, Karl F.  Guri Enderson:  A True Story of
Pioneer Courage.  Willmar, MN:  Thicket Press,
1956.  40 pp.

3038.   U. S. Army.  Copies and Extracts of All the Corres-
pondence Between the Commanding Officers of the
United States Troops in Minnesota and the Resident
Governor of Hudson's Bay Company at Red River
Respecting a Tribe of Sioux Indians Who Were
Refugees Within the British Territory.  London:
n.p., 1864.  18 pp.

3039.   U. S. War Department.  Pembina Settlement.  Washington, DC:  Government Printing Office, 1850.
55 pp.  A letter from the Secretary of War transmitting a report from Major Wood about his expedition to the Pembina settlement, and the condition
of affairs in the northwest, from House Exec. Doc.
51, 31 Cong., 1st Sess., March 19, 1850.

3040.   Van Osdel, A. L.  Indian War History:  Reminiscences of Early Days in the Two Dakotas.  Mission
Hill, SD:  A. L. Van Osdel, 1912-1913.

3041.   Wall, Oscar G.  "Portions of the Diary of Oscar G.
Wall, Company B 5th Minnesota Volunteer Infantry,
With the Sibley Expedition of 1863."  Ed. Dana
Wright.  NDHQ, 1:3 (April 1927), 40-41; 1:4 (July
1927), 11-12; 2:2 (January 1928), 128.

3042. Warming, Irene B. , ed.  Minnesotans in the Civil
      and Indian Wars, An Index to the Rosters in Min-
      nesota in the Civil and Indian Wars, 1861-65:
      Compiled as a W. P. A. Project for The Minnesota
      Historical Society Under the Direction of Irene B.
      Warming, Reference Assistant. St. Paul: The
      Minnesota Historical Society, 1936.  488 pp.

3043. Wellman, Paul E.  Death on the Prairie:  The Thirty
      Years' Struggle for the Western Plains.  New York:
      Macmillan Co. , 1934.  298 pp.  Contains informa-
      tion about the Minnesota Sioux War, and other ma-
      terial on the Sioux and their leaders.

3044. Widen, Albin.  Svenskarna Och Siouxupproret.  Oma-
      lag Och Techningar:  Gunnar Olofsson.  Stockholm:
      Lindqvist, 1965.  170 pp.

3045. Williams, William.  "Report of Major Williams. "
      Palimpsest, 38:6 (June 1957), 265-272; rpt. Palimp-
      sest, 43:10 (October 1962), 433 ff.  On the Spirit
      Lake Uprising.

3046. Wright, Dana.  "The Sibley Trail of 1863. "  NDH, 29:
      4 (October 1962), 282-296.  Conducted to punish
      tribes responsible for the Minnesota Sioux War.

3047. Wright, Dana.  "The Sibley Trail in North Dakota. "
      NDHQ, 1:3 (April 1927), 30-37; 1:4 (July 1927), 5-
      11; 2:2 (January 1928), 120-126.


                        WARS OF THE WEST

3048. "The Affair at Slim Buttes. "  CHSSD, 6 (1912), 491-
      590.  The defeat of American Horse and Crazy
      Horse on September 9 and 10, 1876, by General
      Crook's forces.

3049. Anderson, Harry H.  "The Battle of Slim Buttes. "
      WBB, 22 (September 1965), 49-56.

3050. Anderson, Harry H.  "A Sioux Pictorial Account of
      General Terry's Council. "  NDH, 22 (July 1955),
      87-96.

3051. Arthur, M. Elizabeth.  "General Dickson and the Indian Liberating Army in the North." <u>OH</u>, 62 (September 1970), 151-162.

3052.   Athearn, Robert G. "The Fort Buford 'Massacre'."
        <u>MVHR</u>, 41:4 (March 1955), 675-684. In the spring
        of 1867 a newspaper report of a massacre at Fort
        Buford, which never took place, stirred public opin-
        ion about western Indian affairs.

3053.   Athearn, Robert G. "War Paint Against Brass: The
        Army and the Plains Indians." <u>Montana,</u> 6:3 (July
        1956), 11-22.

3054.   Athearn, Robert G. "A Winter Campaign Against the
        Sioux." <u>MVHR</u>, 35:2 (September 1940), 272-284.
        Materials from Major Alfred L. Hough's unpublished
        autobiography concerning the period after the Great
        Sioux War of 1876.

3055.   Bailey, Ralph E. <u>Indian Fighter: The Story of Nel-
        son A Miles.</u> New York: William Morrow and
        Co., 1965. Juvenile literature.

3056.   Baird, G. W. "General Miles's Indian Campaigns."
        <u>Century,</u> 42 (May-October 1891), 351-370.

3057.   Bates, Charles Francis. <u>Commanding Officers:
        Civil War and Sioux War.</u> New York: National
        Highway Assoc., 1927.

3058.   Benchley, Nathaniel. <u>Only Earth and Sky Remain
        Forever.</u> New York: Harper and Row, 1972.
        About Dark Elk and the invasion of the Black Hills.

3059.   Bland, Thomas Augustus. <u>A Brief History of the
        Late Military Invasion of the Home of the Sioux.</u>
        Washington, DC: The National Indian Defense
        Assn., 1891. 32 pp.

3060.   Blankenburg, William B. "The Role of the Press in
        an Indian Massacre, 1871." <u>JQ</u>, 45 (1968), 61-70.

3061.   Bordeaux, William. <u>Conquering the Mighty Sioux.</u>
        Sioux Falls, SD: n. p., 1929.

3062.   Bourke, John G. <u>On the Border with Crook.</u> 1891;
        rpt. Los Angeles: Westernlore Press, 1969; West-
        port, CT: Greenwood Press, Inc., 1970.

3063.   Bradley, James H.   "The Sioux Campaign of 1876
        Under the Command of General John Gibbon. "
        CHSMo, 2 (1896), 140- 226.

3064.   Brady, Cyrus T.   Indian Fights and Fighters.   1904;
        rpt. Lincoln:   University of Nebraska Press, 1971.
        423 pp.   A popular book, reprinted many times,
        describes the Sioux War of 1876-77 from documen-
        tary sources with editorial assistance from partici-
        pants in the War.

3065.   Brininstool, E. A.   "The Fetterman Disaster (Offi-
        cial Report of Col. Henry B. Carrington). "   OTT,
        2:1 (May-June 1941), 19- 29.

3066.   Brininstool, E. A.   "The Fetterman Massacre. "   TB,
        2:7 (July 1916), 667- 669, 683- 688, 691- 693.

3067.   Brininstool, E. A.   Fighting Red Cloud's Warriors.
        1926; rpt. New York:   Cooper Square, 1974.

3068.   Brininstool, E. A.   "The Wagon Box Fight. "   TB, 1:
        8 (August 1915), 186- 201.

3069.   Brown, Dee.   Action at Beecher Island.   New York:
        Modern Literary Editions Publishing Co. , 1967.
        237 pp.   A nine-day siege of Forsyth's Scouts by
        Plains Indians at Beecher Island in September of
        1868.

3070.   Brown, Dee.   Galvanized Yankees.   Urbana:   Univer-
        sity of Illinois Press, 1963.

3071.   Brown, Dee.   The Westerners.   New York:   Holt,
        Rinehart and Winston, Co. , 1974.

3072.   Brown, Lisle G.   "Yellowstone Supply Depot. "   NDH,
        40:1 (Winter 1973), 24- 33.   Reveals the enormous
        effort to subdue the Sioux.

3073.   Brown, Mark H.   "A New Focus on the Sioux War. "
        Montana, 11:4 (October 1971), 76- 85.

3074.   Brown, William C.   "Reynolds' Attack on Crazy
        Horse's Village on Powder River, March 17, 1876. "
        News Record, 5 April 1934.

3075.   Buckskin and Blanket Days:   Memoirs of a Friend of

the Indians Written in 1905 by Thomas Henry Tib-
bles. Lincoln: University of Nebraska Press,
1969. 336 pp.

3076. Burdick, Usher L. Jacob Horner and the Indian Campaigns of 1876 and 1877. Baltimore: Wirth Bros.,
1942. 30 pp.

3077. Burdick, Usher L. The Last Battle of the Sioux
Nation. Stevens Point, WI: Worzalia Publishing
Co., 1929. 164 pp.

3078. Burdick, Usher L. The Marquis de Mores at War
in the Bad Lands. 1929; rpt. Seattle, WA: Shorey
Publications, 1970.

3079. Burdick, Usher L. Tales from Buffalo Land: The
Story of Fort Buford. Baltimore: Wirth Brothers,
1940.

3080. Burdick, Usher L. Tragedy in the Great Sioux Camp.
Baltimore: The Proof Press, 1936. 15 pp.

3081. Byrne, P. E. Soldiers of the Plains. New York:
Minton, Balch and Co., 1926. 260 pp. Covering
the Period 1868-1877, contains information about
Red Cloud, Crazy Horse, Gall, Sitting Bull and
others, as well as the Battle of the Little Big Horn.

3082. Camp, W. M. "Discovery of the Lost Site of the
Slim Buttes Battle." CHSSD, 9 (1918), 55-68.
Maps included.

3083. Carleton, James Henry. 1844-1845: The Prairie
Logbooks. Dragoon Campaigns to the Pawnee
Villages in 1844, and to the Rocky Mountains in
1845. Ed. Louis Pelzer. Chicago: The Caxton
Club, 1943. 295 pp.

3084. Carrington, Frances C. Army Life on the Plains.
Philadelphia: J. B. Lippincott, 1910.

3085. Carrington, Henry B. The Indian Question. An
Address ... at Bristol, 1875. Rpt. Boston: De-
Wolff & Fiske Co., 1909. 32 pp. Official report
of the Fort Phil Kearny Battle.

3086.   Cash, Joseph H.   "Prelude to Tragedy:   The Indians
        and the Military in Dakota in 1889."   CHSSD, 35
        (1975),   59-68.

3087.   Colby, L. W.   Report of Brig. General L. W. Colby,
        Commanding of Nebraska Guard in the Indian Cam-
        paign of 1890-91 to the Adjutant General, N. N. G.
        Lincoln, NB:   Calhoun and Woodruff, 1891.   23 pp.

3088.   Colby, L. W.   "The Sioux Indian War of 1890-'91."
        PNSHS, 3 (1892), 144-190.   Includes ethnological
        information, an account of the assassination of
        Sitting Bull and of the Massacre at Wounded Knee.
        Also has biographical sketches of Young-Man-Afraid-
        of-His-Horses, Little Wound, Two Strike, Kicking
        Bear, Little Chief, Rocky Bear, Crow Dog, Amer-
        ican Horse, William Vlandry, and Big Road.

3089.   Cook, James H.   "The Art of Fighting Indians."
        AMe, 23 (May 1931), 170-179.   On fighting the
        Sioux and other Indians.

3090.   Cox, John E.   "Soldiering in Dakota Territory in the
        Seventies:   A Communication."   NDHQ, 6:1 (Octo-
        ber 1931), 63-81.   By a Sergeant in Company K,
        1st U. S. Infantry, describes service in Dakota in
        the period 1874-1877.   Tells of attempts by the
        Army to keep prospectors out of the Black Hills.

3091.   Crook, George.   General George Crook:   His Auto-
        biography.   Ed. Martin F. Schmitt.   Norman:   Uni-
        versity of Oklahoma Press, 1960.

3092.   Daniel, Forrest W.   "Dismounting the Sioux."   NDH,
        41:3 (Summer 1974), 8-13.   About the confiscation
        of ponies on Standing Rock Reservation in 1876.

3093.   Davis, H. L.   "The Last Indian Outbreak:   1906."
        AMe, 30 (September 1933), 50-57.   A band of Utes
        marched into the Cheyenne River Reservation in
        1906, remained for nearly two years, then went
        home.

3094.   DeLand, Charles Edmund.   "The Sioux Wars:   Minne-
        sota Outbreak; Red Cloud and other Wars of 1867;
        Little Bighorn; Wounded Knee."   CHSSD, 15 (1930),
        9-730; 17 (1934), 177-551.

3095.    Dobak, William A.    "Yellow-leg Journalists:  En-
        listed Men as Newspaper Reporters in the Sioux
        Campaign, 1876. "   JW, 13:1 (1974),  86-112.

3096.    Downey, Fairfax.   The Buffalo Soldiers in the Indian
        Wars.   New York:   McGraw-Hill Co. ,  1969.   Ju-
        venile literature.

3097.    Downey, Fairfax.   The Indian Wars of the United
        States Army, 1776-1885.   New York:   Doubleday
        Doran Co. ,  1965.   248 pp.

3098.    Downey, Fairfax, and Jacques N. Jacobsen.   The Red
        Bluecoats:   The Indian Scouts,  U. S.  Army.   Fort
        Collins, CO:   Old Army Press,  1973.   204 pp.
        Thin but interesting narrative which describes scouts
        from Sioux and other tribes that served with the
        U. S. Army from the 1860's to the 1940's.

3099.    Drum, Richard C.    "Reminiscences of the Indian
        Fight at Ash Hollow, 1855. "   PNSHS,  16 (1911),
        143-151.   General Harney attacked Brules, Oglalas,
        Minneconjous and Northern Cheyenne on September
        3,  1855.

3100.    Drum, W. F.   Sioux Indian Troubles Dept-Dakota,
        1890-91.   n. p. ,  n. d.   The Commander at Fort
        Yates wrote the Assistant Adjutant General, De-
        partment of Dakota, St. Paul, on February 27,
        1891 to describe events of December 12-15,  1890,
        that led to the death of Sitting Bull on Grand River.

3101.    Dudley, Edgar S.    "Notes on the Early Military His-
        tory of Nebraska. "   PNSHS,  2 (1887),  166-186.
        Covers the period 1803-1871; much information
        about the Sioux.

3102.    Dunn, J. P.   Massacres of the Mountains:   A His-
        tory of the Indian Wars of the Far West,  1815-1875.
        1880; rpt.  New York:   Archer House, Inc. ,  1965;
        New York:   G. P. Putnam's Sons,  1969; Gloucester,
        MA:   Peter Smith,  1971.

3103.    Eastman, Elaine Goodale.    "Indian Wars and War-
        riors. "   The Cosmopolitan,  16 (1894),  409-414.

3104.    Ege, Robert J.    "Legend Was a Man Named Keogh. "
        Montana,  16:2 (Spring 1966),  27-39.

3105.  Eggleston, Edward. "George W. Northrup: The Kit
       Carson of the Northwest. The-Man-That-Draws-
       the-Handcart." Ed. Fr. Louis Pfaller. NDH, 33:
       1 (Winter 1966), 4-21. Had many experiences
       with the Sioux before they killed him in the Battle
       of Kildeer Mountain on July 28, 1864.

3106.  Engles, F. J. "Last Battle:   Battle of Massacre
       Canyon, August 5, 1873." Hobbies, 48 (May 1943),
       97-98.

3107.  Ewert, Theodore. Private Theodore Ewert's Diary
       of the Black Hills Expedition of 1874. Ed. John
       M. Carroll and Lawrence A. Frost. Piscataway,
       NJ:   Consultant Resources, Inc., 1976.   131 pp.

3108.  Finerty, John F. War-Path and Bivouac:   Or the
       Conquest of the Sioux. Chicago:   M. A. Donohue
       and Co., 1890; rpt. Norman:   University of Okla-
       homa Press, 1961; Ed. Milo M. Quaife.   Lincoln:
       University of Nebraska Press, 1966.   375 pp.   On
       the Bighorn and Yellowstone Expedition of 1876,
       and about the campaign on the Canadian border in
       1879.

3109.  Garber, Vie W. "The Site of the Wagon Box Fight."
       OTT, 2:2 (July-August 1941), 17-20.

3110.  Gatchell, T. J. "The Battle on the Red Fork." OTT,
       3:2 (July-August 1942), 29-36, 45.   The last en-
       gagement of the Sioux War of 1876.

3111.  Gibbon, John. "Expedition of 1876 Against the Sioux."
       American Catholic Quarterly, 2 (October 1877),
       271, 665.

3112.  Gibbon, John. Gibbon on the Sioux Campaign of 1876.
       Belleview, NB:   Old Army Press, 1969.   64 pp.

3113.  Gibbon, John. Last Summer's Expedition Against the
       Sioux and Its Great Catastrophe. Philadelphia:
       n.p., 1877.

3114.  Goble, Paul, and Dorothy Goble, eds. Brave Eagle's
       Account of the Fetterman Fight. New York:   Pan-
       theon Books, 1972.   Indian viewpoint of the Fetter-
       man fight.

3115.  Greene, Jerome A. "The Hayfield Fight: A Reap-
       praisal of a Neglected Action." Montana, 22:4
       (October 1972), 30-43.

3116.  Greene, Jerome A. , ed. "'We Do Not Know What
       the Government Intends to Do....' Lt. Palmer
       Writes from the Bozeman Trail, 1867-68." Mon-
       tana 28:3 (July 1978), 16-35.

3117.  Gressley, Gene M. "A Soldier with Crook: The Let-
       ters of Henry R. Porter." Montana, 8:3 (July 1958),
       33-47.

3118.  Hampton, H. D. "The Powder River Expedition of
       1865." Montana, 14:4 (October 1964), 2-15.

3119.  Hanson, Joseph M. The Conquest of the Missouri:
       Being the Story of the Life and Exploits of Captain
       Grant Marsh. Chicago: A. C. McClurg and Co.,
       1909. 458 pp. From steamboat navigation on the
       Missouri to the wars of the western Sioux.

3120.  Harvey, Robert. "The Battle Ground of Ash Hollow."
       PNSHS, 16 (1911), 152-164. Where General Harney
       battled Brules, Oglalas, and Minneconjous.

3121.  Hilman, Fred W. "The Wagon Box Monument." OTT,
       2:2 (July-August 1941), 22.

3122.  Howe, George F., ed. "Expedition to the Yellowstone
       River in 1873: Letters of a Young Cavalry Offi-
       cer." MVHR, 39:3 (December 1952), 519-534.
       From Lt. Charles W. Larned, who served under
       George Custer; deals with Custer and the Sioux in
       the period April-August 1873.

3123.  Huggins, Eli L. "Letters of an Army Captain on the
       Sioux Campaign of 1879-1880." Ed. Francis
       Haines. PNQ, 39:1 (January 1948), 39-64.

3124.  Hutchins, James S. "Poison in the Pemmican: The
       Yellowstone Wagon Road and Prospecting Expedi-
       tion of 1874." Montana, 8:3 (July 1958), 8-25.
       Describes a fight with the Sioux on Grass Lodge
       Creek, and other incidents.

3125.  Keenan, Gerald. "The Seventeenth of June." NDH,

26:1 (Winter 1959), 25-31.  Date of the battle of
the Rosebud between the forces of Crazy Horse
and Crook.

3126.   Keenan, Jerry.  "The Wagon Box Fight. "  JW,  11:1
(1972),  51-74.  A victory over the Sioux and their
allies.

3127.   Keim, DeBenneville Randolph.  Sheridan's Troopers
on the Borders:  A Winter Campaign on the Plains.
London:  George Routledge, 1885; rpt.  Chicago:
Library Resources, 1971.

3128.   Keirnes, Helen R.  "Final Days of the Indian Campaign of 1876-1877:  Aftermath of the Little Big
Horn. "  CHSSD, 37 (1972), 445-523.

3129.   King, Charles.  Campaigning with Crook and Stories
of Army Life.  1890; rpt.  Norman:  University of
Oklahoma Press, 1964; Ann Arbor, MI:  University
Microfilms, 1966.

3130.   King, Charles.  Starlight Ranch and Other Stories of
Army Life on the Frontier.  1890; rpt.  New York:
Books for Libraries, Inc. ,  1970.

3131.   King, James T.  "General Crook at Camp Cloud
Peak:  'I Am at a Loss What to Do. '"  JW,  11:1
(January 1972),  114-127.  After his defeat at the
Battle of the Rosebud,  he retreated to Goose Creek
on the Tongue River in Wyoming.

3132.   Knight, Oliver.  Following the Indian Wars:  The Story
of the Newspaper Correspondents Among the Indian
Campaigners.  Norman:  University of Oklahoma
Press, 1960.  248 pp.  Contains much material on
the Sioux for the period 1866-1891.

3133.   Kroeker, Marvin E.  Great Plains Command:  William B. Hazen in the Frontier West.  Norman:
University of Oklahoma Press, 1976.  216 pp.

3134.   Leckie, William H.  The Buffalo Soldiers:  A Narrative of the Negro Cavalry in the West.  Norman:
University of Oklahoma Press, 1967.

3135.   Leonard, Thomas C.  "Red, White and the Army Blue:

Empathy and Anger in the American West. " AQ,
26:2 (May 1974), 176-190.

3136.   Leonard, Thomas C.   "The Reluctant Conquerors:
How the Generals Viewed the Indians. " AH, 27:5
(August 1976), 34-41.

3137.   "Locating the Site of the Wagon-Box Fight. " TB, 2:
7 (July 1916), 663-666.

3138.   Longstreet, Stephen.   War Cries on Horseback:   The
Story of the Indian Wars of the Great Plains.   Garden City, NY:   Doubleday and Co. , 1970.

3139.   Lowe, Percival G.   Five Years a Dragoon ('49 to
'54):   And Other Adventures on the Great Plains.
Intro. and notes Don Russell.   Norman:   University
of Oklahoma Press, 1965.   336 pp.

3140.   Luce, Edward S. , ed.   "The Diary and Letters of
Dr. James M. DeWolf, Acting Assistant Surgeon,
U. S. Army; His Record of the Sioux Expedition of
1876 as Kept Until His Death. " NDH, 25:2 and 3
(April-July 1958), 33-81.   Begins with departure
from Fort Totten March 10, 1876, and concludes
June 24, 1876 (just prior to his death July 28).

3141.   Lyons, R. D.   "Big Injun Wagon-Box Fight. " Com-
monweal, 4 July 1941, pp. 249-251.

3142.   McCracken, Harold.   The Winning of the West.   New
York:   Doubleday Doran, 1970.

3143.   McDermott, Louis M.   "The Primary Role of the
Military on the Dakota Frontier. " SDH, 2:1 (Winter 1971), 1-22.

3144.   McKnight, Charles.   Our Western Border, Its Life,
Combats, Adventures, Forays, Massacres, Captiv-
ities, Scouts, Red Chiefs, Pioneer Women, One
Hundred Years Ago, Carefully Written and Com-
piled.   1876; rpt. New York:   Johnson Reprint
Corp. , 1971.

3145.   Malm, Einar.   Dodsdans i Dakota.   Stockholm:   Ra-
ben and Sjogren, 1961.   257 pp.

3146. Malm, Einar. Siouxindianernas sista Strid, med
      lojtant Ragnar Ling-vannerus; falt mot Sitting Bull
      under andedansoroligheterna; Dakota 1890-91.
      Stockholm: P. A. Norstedt and Soners, 1929.
      203 pp.

3147. Mattison, Ray H., ed. "The Fisk Expedition of 1864:
      The Diary of William L. Larned." NDH, 36:3
      (Summer 1969), 208-274. About the Sioux siege of
      a wagon train under James Fisk in 1864, which
      lasted fourteen days. Larned's journal covers the
      period June 29-December 31, 1864.

3148. Mattison, Ray H. "The Indian Frontier on the Upper
      Missouri to 1865." NH, 39:3 (September 1958),
      241-266.

3149. Mattison, Ray H. "The Military Frontier on the Up-
      per Missouri." NH, 37:3 (September 1956), 159-
      182.

3150. Meddaugh, S. L. Diary of S. L. Meddaugh, 6th U. S.
      Infantry, Covering the Indian Campaign Along the
      Yellowstone River, From May to September, 1876.
      Los Angeles: n. p., 1924. 14 pp.

3151. Miles, Nelson A. Personal Recollections and Obser-
      vations of General Nelson A. Miles. Chicago: The
      Werner Co., 1896; rpt. New York: Plenum, 1971.
      Although Miles erred occasionally while recording
      facts and forming judgments about culture, he left
      a useful record of campaigns against the Sioux in
      the 1870's, and about Sioux military forces and
      leadership.

3152. Miles, Nelson A. Serving the Republic. New York:
      Harper and Bros., 1911. Contains information
      about battles with the Sioux.

3153. Miller, George L. "The Fort Pierre Expedition."
      PNSHS, 3 (1892), 110-118. An expedition to deal
      with the Sioux in 1855.

3154. Miller, George L. "The Military Camp on the Big
      Sioux River in 1855." PNSHS, 3 (1892), 119-124.
      Deals more with General Harney's concern about
      logistics than with his attitudes about the Sioux.

3155.  Mills, Anson. "Address by General Anson Mills,
       U. S. Army Ret. , on 'The Battle of the Rosebud. ' "
       Proceedings of The Annual Meeting of the Order of
       Indian Wars of the United States (1917), pp. 17-33.

3156.  Mishkin, Bernard. Rank and Warfare Among the
       Plains Indians. Seattle: University of Washington
       Press, 1940; rpt. 1966 and 1973. 66 pp. Deals
       primarily with Kiowas, although it contains informa-
       tion on other tribes, as well.

3157.  Munn, Fred M. "Fred Munn, Veteran of Frontier
       Experiences, Remembered Days He Rode with Miles,
       Howard and Terry. " Montana, 16:2 (Spring 1966),
       50-64. As told to Robert A. Griffin.

3158.  Museum of Anthropology. Military Engagements Be-
       tween United States Troops and Plains Indians.
       Documentary Inquiry by the U. S. Congress: Part
       I: 1854-1876. Greeley: University of Northern
       Colorado, 1972. 245 pp. Two monographs.

3159.  Museum of Anthropology. Military Engagements Be-
       tween United States Troops and Plains Indians.
       Documentary Inquiry by the U. S. Congress: Part
       II: Report of the Secretary of War on the Inquiry
       into the Sand Creek Massacre. Greeley: Univer-
       sity of Northern Colorado, 1974. 328 pp. Two
       monographs.

3160.  Museum of Anthropology. Military Engagements Be-
       tween United States Troops and Plains Indians.
       Documentary Inquiry by the U. S. Congress: Part
       III: Report of the Secretary of the Interior Regard-
       ing the Origin and Progress of Indian Hostilities on
       the Frontier. Greeley: University of Northern
       Colorado Press, 1973. 103 pp.

3161.  Museum of Anthropology. Military Engagements Be-
       tween United States Troops and Plains Indians.
       Documentary Inquiry by the U. S. Congress: Part
       IV: 1872-1890. Greeley: University of Northern
       Colorado, 1973. 150 pp.

3162.  Myers, Frank. Soldiering in Dakota, Among the In-
       dians, in 1863-4-5. Huron, Dakota Terr. : Huronite
       Printing House, 1888; rpt. Pierre, SD: State His-

torical Society, 1936; Facsimile ed. New York:
Books for Libraries, 1976; New York: Arno Press,
1978.

3163.  Nebraska State Historical Society.  Sioux Memorial
Issue.  Lincoln:  Nebraska State Historical Society,
1941.  145 pp.

3164.  Northrup, Henry Davenport.  Indian Horrors:  Or,
Massacres by the Red Men.  Being a Thrilling Narrative of Bloody Wars with ... Savages, Including
a Full Account of the Daring Deeds and Tragic
Death of ... Sitting Bull, with Startling Descriptions
of Fantastic Ghost Dances; Mysterious Medicine Men
... etc., the Whole Comprising a Fascinating History of the Indians from the Discovery of America
to the Present Time.  Augusta, ME:  J. F. Hill
and Co., 1891; Philadelphia:  National Publishing
Co., 1891.  600 pp.  Of value largely as an example of the emotional, racist writing of the late
19th Century on Great Plains Indian warfare.

3165.  Nye, Wilbur S.  Plains Indian Raiders:  The Final
Phases of Warfare from the Arkansas to the Red
River.  Norman:  University of Oklahoma Press,
1968.  418 pp.

3166.  O'Daffer, Floyd C.  American Indian Wars Sixteen
Twenty One--Eighteen Ninety.  New York:  Carlton
Press, 1970.

3167.  Olson, James C.  "The 'Lasting Peace' of Fort Laramie:  Prelude to Massacre."  AW, 2:1 (1965),
46- 53.

3168.  Palmer, H. E.  "History of the Power River Indian
Expedition of 1865."  PNSHS, 2 (1887), 197-229.

3169.  Parkhill, Forbes.  The Last of the Indian Wars.  New
York:  Crowell-Collier Press, 1962.  127 pp.

3170.  Pennick, Isaac B.  Diary of Sergeant Isaac B. Pennick.  Los Angeles:  Typewritten Copy, 1924.  67
pp.  Company I, 11th Kansas Cavalry fought at
Platte Bridge Station, July 26, 1865, while on the
Wind River Expedition.  Also contains an account
of an Indian attack on a wagon train led by Sergeant
Custard the same day.

3171.   Remington, Frederic. "Sioux Outbreak in South Da-
        kota. " HW, 24 January 1891, pp. 57, 64-65.

3172.   Richardson, E. M. "The Forgotten Haycutters at
        Fort C. F. Smith. " Montana, 9:3 (1959), 22-33.
        About the Wagon Box Fight.

3173.   Rickey, Don. "Bullets Buzzing Like Bees." Mon-
        tana, 11:3 (July 1961), 2-10. About Sioux wars.

3174.   Rickey, Don. Forty Miles a Day on Beans and Hay:
        The Enlisted Soldier Fighting the Indian Wars.
        1963; rpt. Norman:   University of Oklahoma Press,
        1966.

3175.   Riley, Paul D. "The Battle of Massacre Canyon. "
        NH, 16:3 (1935). Entire issue.

3176.   Robinson, Doane. "A Relic of the Great Sioux War. "
        CHSSD, 12 (1924), 184-185. A rusted leg-iron.

3177.   [Robinson, Doane.] "The Slim Buttes Battlefield. "
        CHSSD, 9 (1918), 47-54. Correspondence about
        and discussion of the location of the battlefield, an
        introduction to entry no. 3082.

3178.   Rowen, Richard, ed. "The Second Nebraska's Cam-
        paign Against the Sioux. " NH, 44:1 (March 1963),
        3-53. Material from the journal of Col. Robert
        W. Furnas, diaries of Henry W. Pierce and Pvt.
        George P. Belden.

3179.   Russell, Don. "How Many Indians Were Killed?
        White Man Versus Red Man:   The Facts and the
        Legend. " AW, 10:4 (1973), 42-47, 61-63.

3180.   Russell, Don. "Tongue River Indian Fight. " OTT,
        1:3 (September-October 1940), 13-15.

3181.   Schmitt, Martin F. , and Dee Brown. Fighting In-
        dians of the West. New York: Scribners, 1948;
        rpt. New York:   Bonanza, 1969. 362 pp. Contains
        many photographs.

3182.   Schreibeis, Charles D. "The Tragedy of Fort Philip
        Kearny. " OTT, 1:6 (March-April 1941), 5-20.
        About the Fetterman fight.

3183.   Schreibeis, Charles D.   "The Wagon Box Fight."
        OTT, 2:2 (July-August 1941), 4-12, 21.

3184.   Schreibeis, Charles D.   "The Wagon Box Fight."
        OTT, 3:1 (May-June 1942), 5-14, 16-19.

3185.   Secoy, Frank R.   Changing Military Patterns on the
        Great Plains.   New York:   J. J. Augustin Publisher,
        1953.   112 pp.   About the effects of culture and en-
        vironment upon military affairs.

3186.   Sheridan, P. H.   Record of Engagements with Hostile
        Indians within the Military Division of the Missouri,
        from 1865 to 1882.   Washington, DC:   Government
        Printing Office, 1882; rpt. facsimile ed.   Bellevue,
        NB:   The Old Army Press, 1969.   112 pp.

3187.   Sinclair, F. H.   "White Men's Medicine Fight:   An
        Account of the Fort Phil Kearney 'Wagon Box Bat-
        tle.'"   Montana, 6:3 (July 1956), 1-10.   Red Cloud
        called this the "White Men's Medicine Fight."

3188.   Sinclair, Harold.   The Cavalryman.   New York:
        Harper and Row, 1958.   Based upon the campaign
        against Sioux in 1864, as Civil War veterans pur-
        sued Indians through the Badlands.

3189.   Sprague, Marshall.   Massacre:   The Tragedy at White
        River.   New York:   Little, Brown and Co., 1957.

3190.   Springer, Charles S.   Soldiering in Sioux Country,
        1865; rpt. Los Angeles:   Nash Publishing Co.,
        1971.

3191.   Stroud, Harry A.   The Conquest of the Prairies.
        Waco, TX:   Texian Press, 1970.

3192.   Sturgis, Thomas.   Common Sense View of the Sioux
        War, with True Method of Treatment, as Opposed
        to Both Exterminative and the Sentimental Policy.
        Waltham, MA:   Hastings Sentinel Office Print.,
        1877.   45 pp.

3193.   Taunton, Francis B.   Sidelights of the Sioux Wars.
        London:   English Westerners' Society, 1967.   78 pp.

3194.   Terrell, John U., and G. Walton.   Faint the Trumpet

Sounds: The Life and Trial of Major Reno. New
York: David McKay Co., 1966.

3195. Todd, John Blair Smith. "The Harney Expedition
Against the Sioux: The Journal of Captain John
B. S. Todd." Ed. Ray H. Mattison. NH, 20:2
(June 1962), 89-130.

3196. Traub, Peter Edward. Sioux Campaign--Winter of
1890-91. Proceedings of The Annual Meeting of the
Order of Indian Wars of the United States (1926),
pp. 28-70.

3197. Trobriand, Phillippe Regis Denis de Keredern, Comte
de. Army Life in Dakotas: Selections from His
Journal. Trans. George Francis Will. Ed. Milo
M. Quaife. Chicago: Donnelley, 1941.

3198. Trotter, George A. From Feather, Blanket and
Tepee: The Indians' Fight for Equality. Deer
Park, NY: Brown Book Co., 1970.

3199. U. S. Army. Department of California. Report of
the Part Taken by the Troops of the Department of
Dakota in the Sioux Indian Campaign During the Latter Part of 1890 and the Early Part of the Present
Year. San Francisco, n. p., 1891. 4 pp.

3200. U. S. Congress. House. Committee on Military Affairs. Military Expedition Against the Sioux Indians. July 15, 1876. Washington, DC: Government Printing Office, 1876. 63 pp. House Exec.
Doc. No. 184, 34 Cong. 1st Sess.

3201. U. S. Congress. Senate. "Report of Lieutenant G. K.
Warren to Brevet Brig. Gen. W. F. Harney, U. S.
Army, Commanding Sioux Expedition." CHSSD, 11
(1922), 60-133. Reprint of Senate Exec. Doc. No.
76, Serial 822, 34 Cong. 1st Sess.

3202. Utley, Robert M. "A Chained Dog: The Indian-
Fighting Army. Military Strategy on the Western
Frontier." AW, 10:4 (1973), 18-24, 61.

3203. Utley, Robert M. Frontiersmen in Blue: The United
States Army and the Indian, 1848-1865. New York:
Macmillan, 1967.

3204.  Van Ostermann, George Frederick.  The Last Sioux
       Indian War.  San Antonio, TX:  Palm Tree Press,
       1942.  27 pp.

3205.  Vaughn, Jesse.  The Battle of Platte Bridge.  Nor-
       man:  University of Oklahoma Press, 1963.  132
       pp.  Sioux and Cheyenne vs. the U. S. Army.

3206.  Vaughn, Jesse W.  Indian Fights:  New Facts on
       Seven Encounters.  Norman:  University of Okla-
       homa Press, 1966.  250 pp.  On Cheyenne Fort,
       Fetterman, Hayfield, Rosebud, Major Reno, Heck
       Reel's Wagon Train, and Slim Buttes.

3207.  Vaughn, Jesse W.  The Reynolds Campaign on Powder
       River.  Norman:  University of Oklahoma Press,
       1961.  239 pp.

3208.  Vaughn, Jesse W.  With Crook at the Rosebud.  Har-
       risburg, PA:  Stackpole Books, 1956.

3209.  Wade, Arthur P.  "The Military Command Structure:
       The Great Plains, 1853-1891."  JW, 15:3 (July
       1976), 5-22.  Contains material on the Sioux and
       Wounded Knee Massacre.

3210.  Ware, Eugene F.  The Indian War of Eighteen Sixty-
       Four.  Ed. Clyde C. Walton.  New York:  St.
       Martin's Press, 1960; rpt. Lincoln:  University of
       Nebraska Press, 1963.  483 pp.

3211.  Warren, Governeur K.  Explorations in the Dakota
       Country, in the Year 1855.  Washington, DC:
       A. O. P. Nicholson Printer, 1856.  Information on
       the Battle of Ash Hollow, September 3, 1855, and
       other Sioux conflicts.

3212.  Watson, Elmo Scott.  "'The Bravery of Our Bugler
       Is Much Spoken of.'"  OTT, 1:6 (March-April 1941),
       21-24.  On the Fetterman Fight.

3213.  Wellman, Paul L.  Death on Horseback:  Seventy
       Years of War for the American West.  1934; rpt.
       Philadelphia:  Lippincott, 1947, as The Indian Wars
       of the West.  New York:  Modern Library Editions
       Publishing Co., 1971.

3214.   Welty, Raymond L.   "The Frontier Army on the Mis-
        souri River, 1860-1870. "   NDHQ, 2:2 (January 1928),
        85-99.

3215.   White, Lonnie J.   "The Battle of Beecher Island:
        The Scouts Hold Fast on the Arickaree. "   JW, 5:1
        (1966), 1-24.   Involved Sioux under Spotted Tail.

3216.   Whitman, S. E.   The Troopers:  An Informal History
        of the Plains Cavalry, 1865-1890.   New York:
        Hastings House, 1962.

3217.   Wild Life on the Plains and Horrors of Indian War-
        fare.   1891; rpt. St. Louis, MO:   Continental Pub-
        lishing Co. , 1971.   592 pp.

3218.   Willits, Vie [Mrs. A. L. Garber].   "Facts Concern-
        ing the Bozeman Trail and Adjacent Territory. "
        TB, 2:8 (August 1916), 722-731; 2:9 (September
        1916), 767-778.   Contains summaries of battles with
        the Sioux in the area.

3219.   Wilson, G.   "Sioux War. "   Nation, 8 January 1891,
        pp.  29-30.


                    WOUNDED KNEE I AND II
                      (1890 AND 1973)

3220.   "Behind a Modern-Day Indian Uprising:  Sioux Mili-
        tancy. "   U. S. News, 12 March 1973, p. 36.

3221.   "Behind the Second Battle of Wounded Knee. "   Time,
        19 March 1973, p. 18.

3222.   Bermant, G. , ed.   "Notion of Conspiracy Is Not
        Tasty to Americans:  Use of Social Science Tech-
        niques in Wounded Knee Trial Jury Selection:  In-
        terview. "   PT, 8 (May 1975), 60-61.

3223.   Bonham, Barbara.   The Battle of Wounded Knee:
        The Ghost Dance Uprising.   Chicago:  Reilly and
        Lee Books, 1970.   169 pp.

3224.   Bosma, Boyd.   "An Interview with Jim Mesteth. "
        InH, 11:2 (Spring 1978), 18-21.   Mesteth, ninety-

        six years old at the time of the interview, re-
        membered Wounded Knee 1890.

3225.   Brown, Dee. Bury My Heart at Wounded Knee. An
        Indian History of the American West. New York:
        Holt, Rinehart and Winston, Co., 1970. 487 pp.

3226.   Brown, Dee. "The Ghost Dance and the Battle of
        Wounded Knee." AHI, 1 (December 1966), 5-16;
        rpt. in The American Indian: Past and Present.
        Ed. Roger L. Nichols and George R. Adams.
        Waltham, MA: Xerox College Publishing Co., 1971.
        pp. 221-229.

3227.   Brown, Dee. Wounded Knee: An Indian History of
        the American West. New York: Dell, 1975.

3228.   "Clean Up Wounded Knee." NaRe, 13 April 1973, pp.
        405-406.

3229.   Colby, L. W. "The Sioux Indian War of 1890-'91."
        PNSHS, 3 (1892), 144-190. On Wounded Knee, by
        a Brigadier General.

3230.   Cole, David L. "The Second Tragedy at Wounded
        Knee: A Reader's Comments." AW, 10:6 (Novem-
        ber 1973), 48.

3231.   Collier, P. "Wounded Knee: The New Indian War."
        Ramparts, 11 (June 1973), 25-29.

3232.   "Death at Wounded Knee." Time, 7 May 1973, p. 28.

3233.   Dilley, R. "NCC's Role at Wounded Knee." ChC,
        90 (4 April 1973), 400-402.

3234.   Dollar, Clyde. "The Second Tragedy at Wounded
        Knee." AW, 10:5 (September 1973), 4-11, 58-61.

3235.   Eastman, Elaine G. "The Ghost Dance and Wounded
        Knee Massacre of 1890-1891." NH, 26:1 (January
        1945), 26-42.

3236.   Feaver, Eric. "Indian Soldier, 1891-95: An Experi-
        ment on the Closing Frontier." Prologue, 7:2
        (Summer 1975), 109-118. About the aftermath of
        Wounded Knee 1890.

3237.   Flying Cloud, Chief (Francis B. Zahn). The Crimson
        Carnage of Wounded Knee. Bottineau, ND: Ed-
        ward A. Milligan, 1967. 12 pp. Author is Sioux.

3238.   Geyer, Alan. "Wounded Knee and My Lai." ChC,
        88:3 (January 1971), 59.

3239.   Ghost Dancers in the West--The Sioux at Pine Ridge
        and Wounded Knee in 1891. 1891; rpt. Ramona,
        CA: Acoma Books, 1976.

3240.   Giese, Paula. "Birthing a New Indian Nation." NCA,
        No. 12 (July-August 1974), pp. 10-19.

3241.   Giese, Paula. "Spread the Word About Wounded
        Knee." NCA, No. 11 (May-June 1974), pp. 20-23.

3242.   Giese, Paula. "Wounded Knee: The Government on
        Trial." NCA, No. 10 (February-March 1974), pp.
        5-13.

3243.   Gold, V. "Of Fallen Trees and Wounded Knees:
        New Coverage." NaR, 27 April 1973, pp. 464-
        465.

3244.   Greene, Jerome A. "The Sioux Land Commission of
        1889: A Prelude to Wounded Knee." SDH, 1:1
        (Winter 1970), 41-72.

3245.   Hanlon, W. T. "Whose Ox Was Gored at Wounded
        Knee?" America, 16 March 1974, pp. 190-192.

3246.   Hawthorne, Harry L. Lieut. Hawthorne's Vivid De-
        scription of Warpath Life. n. p., n. d. 3 pp.
        How Big Foot's band concealed weapons as long
        as possible, and when this failed, the fight at
        Wounded Knee occurred.

3247.   Helm, June. "Deloria on Wounded Knee." FN, 14:
        6 (1973), 13-14.

3248.   Hill, Ann. "Wounded Knee: Refusing to Be Invisi-
        ble." Freedomways, 13:4 (1973), 324-330.

3249.   Huntley, Allan. "Massacre at Wounded Knee." AI,
        1:1 (1963), 33.

3250.   Jones, Douglas C.   A Creek Called Wounded Knee.
        New York:   Scribner's,   1978.

3251.   Karp, Walter.   "Wounded Knee Between Wars. "   AH,
        25:1 (December 1973),   34-35,   101.

3252.   Kelley, William F.   "The Indian Troubles and the
        Battle of Wounded Knee. "   PNSHS,   4 (1892),   30-50.

3253.   Kelley, William F. , and Pierre Bovis, eds.   Pine
        Ridge, 1890:   An Eye Witness Account of the Events
        Surrounding the Fighting at Wounded Knee.   San
        Francisco:  P. Bovis, 1971.   267 pp.   Published
        originally in Nebraska State Journal,  November 24,
        1890-January 16,  1891.

3254.   Kentfield, S. D. C.   "Dispatch from Wounded Knee:
        Pine Ridge Reservation. "   New York Times Maga-
        zine,   15 October, 1967, pp.  28-31.

3255.   LaBlanc, Tom, and Rick McArthur.   "Reprisals
        Against Indians/After Wounded Knee. "   NCA,  No.
        8 (October-November 1973),  pp.  44-45.

3256.   Lyons, T. D.   "Preparedness, 1890:  Governor of
        the Dakota Territory Chose Guns and the Sioux
        Were Lost. "   Commonweal,  20 September 1940,
        pp.  443-445.

3257.   McCormick, L. S.   Wounded Knee and Drexel Mis-
        sion Fights:  December 29 and 30, 1890.   Fort
        Leavenworth, KS:   n. p. ,  1904.   20 pp.

3258.   McGregor, James H.   The Wounded Knee Massacre
        from the Viewpoint of the Sioux.   Baltimore:
        Wirth Brothers, 1940.   140 pp.   Strongly pro-
        Indian.   Contains testimony by a substantial num-
        ber of Indians who were there.

3259.   Marquis, A.   "Those Brave Boys in Blue at Wounded
        Knee. "   JRe,  13 (May 1974),  26-27.

3260.   Mattes, Merrill.   "The Enigma of Wounded Knee. "
        PlA,  5:9 (May 1960),  1-11.   Deals with the causes
        of Wounded Knee 1890.

3261.   Milligan, Edward A.   Wounded Knee 1973 and the Fort

Laramie Treaty of 1868. Bottineau, ND: Bottineau Courant Print., 1973.

3262.  "Not with a Bang." Newsweek, 21 May 1973, pp. 31-32.

3263.  One Feather, Vivian. "View from Wounded Knee." Sr Schol, 14 May 1973, pp. 10-11. Author is Sioux from Pine Ridge Reservation.

3264.  "Raid at Wounded Knee: Sioux Protesters." Time, 12 March 1973, p. 21.

3265.  Remington, Frederic. Incidents of the Wounded Knee Battle Described by Injured Soldiers. n. p., 1891. 3 pp.

3266.  "Return to Wounded Knee: Sioux Militants Confrontation with Federal Authorities." Newsweek, 12 March 1973, p. 27.

3267.  Richardson, Wilds Preston. "Some Observations upon the Sioux Campaign of 1890-91." Journal of the Military Institution of the United States, 18 (1896), 512-536.

3268.  Schultz, T. "Continuing Massacre at Wounded Knee: Election for Presidency of the Tribal Council." H, 248 (June 1974), 30.

3269.  Scott, E. D. "Wounded Knee: A Look at the Record." Field Artillery Journal, 24 (1939).

3270.  "Siege of Wounded Knee." Newsweek, 19 March 1973, pp. 22-23.

3271.  Sievers, Michael A. "The Historiography of 'The Bloody Field ... that Kept the Secret of the Everlasting Word': Wounded Knee." SDH, 6:1 (Winter 1975), 33-54.

3272.  Smith, Rex Alan. Moon of Popping Trees. New York: Reader's Digest Press, 1975. 219 pp. Romanticized account of Wounded Knee 1890, based upon weak scholarship.

3273.  Spindler, Will H. Tragedy Strikes at Wounded Knee.

Gordon, NB: Gordon Journal Publishing Co., 1955.
80 pp.

3274. "Suspenseful Show of Red Power: Sioux Protest."
Time, 19 March 1973, pp. 16-18.

3275. Talbert, Carol. "Experiences of Wounded Knee."
HO, 33 (Summer 1974), 215-217.

3276. Tilsen, Kenneth E. "Great Stand at Wounded Knee."
NCA, No. 6 (June-July 1973), pp. 6-8.

3277. Tilsen, Kenneth E. "Struggle at Wounded Knee."
NCA, No. 5 (April-May 1973), pp. 54-57.

3278. "Trap at Wounded Knee: Television Coverage of
Sioux Protest." Time, 26 March 1973, p. 67.

3279. "Twin Stalemates: Sioux Protest." Time, 26 March
1973, p. 32.

3280. U. S. Congress. House. Annual Report of the Secretary of War 1891-92. H. Exec. Doc. No. 1,
Serial 2921, 52 Cong., 1st Sess., 1892. Military
account of Wounded Knee 1890, and causes.

3281. U. S. Congress. House. Subcommittee on Indian Affairs. Sioux Indians: Wounded Knee Massacre.
Washington: Government Printing Office, 1938.
49 pp. Hearing Before the Subcommittee on H. R.
2535, March 7 and May 12, 1938.

3282. U. S. Congress. House. Subcommittee on Indian Affairs. To Liquidate the Liability of the United
States for the Massacre of Sioux Indian Men, Wom-
en, and Children at Wounded Knee on December 29,
1890. 75 Cong. 2nd Sess., March 7, 1938, hearing
on H. R. 2535.

3283. U. S. Congress. Senate. Committee on Interior and
Insular Affairs. Subcommittee on Indian Affairs,
of the Committee on Interior and Insular Affairs.
Hearings June 16, 1973, Pine Ridge, South Dakota;
June 17, 1973, Kyle, South Dakota. Washington,
DC: Government Printing Office, 1974. 506 pp.

3284. U. S. Congress. Senate. Committee on the Judiciary.

Wounded Knee Massacre: Hearings Before the Judiciary ... on S. 1147 and S. 2900 ... February 5 and 6, 1976. Washington, DC: Government Printing Office, 1976. 596 pp.

3285. U. S. Department of the Interior. Report ... on H. R. 2535, Dated April 28, 1937, Recompensing Sioux Indians for Injuries Suffered at the Massacre of Wounded Knee. Washington, DC: Government Printing Office, 1937. 1 p.

3286. Van Every, Dale. The Day the Sun Died. New York: Little, Brown, Co., 1971. 348 pp. A novel about Wounded Knee 1890.

3287. Voices from Wounded Knee, 1973, in the Words of the Participants. Rooseveltown, NY: Akwesasne Notes, 1974.

3288. West, Jim. "Inside Wounded Knee ... and Beyond." Youth, 24:11 (November 1973), 2-13.

3289. Wilson, George. "The Sioux War." The Nation, 8 January 1891, pp. 29-30.

3290. "Wounded History? U. S. Army Report." Newsweek, 12 January 1976, p. 34.

3291. "Wounded Knee Goes On." NCA, No. 9 (January 1974), p. 50.

3292. Youngkin, Stephen D. "Prelude to Wounded Knee: The Military Point of View." SDH, 4:3 (Summer 974), 333-351.

3293. Zimmerman, Bill. Airlift to Wounded Knee. Chicago: Swallow Press, 1976. 348 pp. Alternate chapters describe the historical background to Wounded Knee 1973 and the relief air lift that took place to feed its participants.


## THESES AND DISSERTATIONS

3294. Adams, Katherine Jean. "The Santee Treaties of 1851." M. A. Thesis. University of Oklahoma, 1970.

3295.  Ala, Viola. "The Problems Related to the Assimilation of the Indian of South Dakota." M. A. Thesis. University of South Dakota 1949.

3296.  Albers, Patricia C. "The Regional System of the Devil's Lake Sioux: Its Structure, Composition, Development and Functions." DAI, 35:11 (May 1975), 6860A. University of Wisconsin, Madison 1974. 537 pp.

3297.  Anderson, Gary C. "The Santee Sioux: A Study of Sovereignty and Economic Dependency." DAI, 39: 6 (December 1978), 3767A-3768A. University of Toledo 1978. 286 pp.

3298.  Asmussen, Johannes Mary. "Visual-Motor Perception of Sioux and Chippewa Children and the Normative Population on the Bender Gestalt Test Using the Koppitz Scoring System." DAI, 37:11 (May 1977), 7012A-7013A. University of Northern Colorado 1976. 70 pp. 488 subjects studied: 202 non-reservation children ages 5 to 10 and 286 reservation children in the same age group. No statistically significant differences between tribal children.

3299.  Bailey, John W. "General Terry and the Decline of the Sioux, 1866-1890." DAI, 36:1 (July 1975), 469A-470A. Marquette University 1974. 383 pp. Terry tried to give fair treatment to the Sioux and to persuade the federal government to be fair-- unsuccessfully.

3300.  Bass, Mary Anna Owen. "Food and Nutrient Intake Patterns on the Standing Rock Reservation, North and South Dakota." DAI, 33:5 (November 1972), 2171B. Kansas State University 1972. Based on interviews with 94 Indian women during the summer of 1970.

3301.  Beaulieu, David Leonard. "An Analysis of Differences in the Perception of Information Needs Among American Indian Students in Two Selected Indian Reservation Communities." DAI, 34:1 (May 1974), 6936A. University of Minnesota 1973. 235 pp. Study of secondary students on the Standing Rock Sioux and the St. Regis Akwesasne Reservations.

3302.  Buel, Francis Elizabeth. "Sioux Reaction to Govern-
       ment Policy, 1868-1906." M. A. Thesis. Univer-
       sity of South Dakota 1943.   87 pp.

3303.  Carlson, Richard George. "From the Sun Dance to
       the Ghost Dance:  A Social and Intellectual History
       of the Lakotas, 1868-1890." Ph. D.  University of
       Virginia 1973.  Abstract not available.

3304.  Carter, Edward Russell. "The Adjustments of the
       Dakota Indians in Rapid City, South Dakota." M. A.
       Thesis.  University of Kansas 1950.

3305.  Carter, Richard T., Jr.  "Teton Dakota Phonology."
       DAI, 35:9 (March 1975), 6120A.  University of New
       Mexico.  314 pp.

3306.  Clow, Richmond Lee.  "The Rosebud Sioux:  The Fed-
       eral Government and the Reservation Years 1878-
       1940."  DAI, 38:6 (December 1977), 3677A-3678A.
       University of New Mexico 1977.  277 pp.

3307.  Couture, James A.  "Indian Student Informational
       Needs as Perceived by Teachers:  An Analysis of
       Those Perceptions." DAI, 35:12, Pt. 1 (June
       1975), 7548A.  University of Minnesota 1974.  160
       pp.  Students were Standing Rock Sioux, Mohawk,
       and Navajo.

3308.  Cwach, Elmer Duane.  "A History of the Yankton In-
       dian Agency During the Nineteenth Century." M. A.
       Thesis.  University of South Dakota 1958.

3309.  Davis, Lawrence J.  "The Socio-Cultural Changes in
       the Cheyenne River Sioux Indians as a Result of
       Contact with White Civilization." M. A. Thesis.
       University of Southern California 1944.

3310.  Dellebovi, Charles J.  "Hostilities in the Dakota Ter-
       ritory, 1862-1866." M. A. Thesis.  University of
       South Dakota 1976.  95 pp.

3311.  Denman, Murrie.  "Art in the Life of the Sioux In-
       dian." M. A. Thesis.  University of South Dakota
       1953.

3312.  Dugan, Kathleen Margaret. "The Vision Quest of the

Plains Indians:  Its Significance. "  DAI,  38:1  (July 1977),  333A.   Fordham University 1977.   306 pp. Primarily on the Sioux and Cheyenne.

3313.  Estes, Frank C.   "A Study of Selected Factors Which May Be Associated with the Imminent Migration of Individuals from the Lower Brule Indian Reservation. "  M. A. Thesis.   South Dakota State University 1961.

3314.  Fitzgerald, Sr. Mary Clement.  "Bishop Marty and His Sioux Missions, 1876-1896. "  M. A. Thesis. University of Notre Dame 1940; published in CHSSD, 20 (1940),  523-558.

3315.  Forbes, Bruce D.   "Evangelization and Acculturation Among the Santee Dakota Indians, 1834-1864. "  DAI, 38:4 (October 1977),  2193A-2194A.   Princeton Theological Seminary 1977.   364 pp.   On the work of missionaries.

3316.  Forsee, Frances Aylesa.   "Policy of the United States Government Towards the Sisseton Sioux Indians, 1871-1931. "   M. A. Thesis.   University of Colorado, Boulder, 1931.

3317.  Fox, Sandra J.   "An Evaluation of the Eight Reading Programs Implemented for Indian Students in North and South Dakota. "  DAI,  37:11 (May 1977),  7095A. Pennsylvania State University 1976.   96 pp.   Primarily on Chippewa and Sioux children who were pre- and post-tested during the school year 1973-74. Tests show significant change in reading ability as a result of the Title I program.

3318.  Girton, Polly W.   "The Protestant Episcopal Indian Missions of Dakota Territory. "   M. A. Thesis. University of South Dakota 1960.

3319.  Goto, Kent Asa.   "A Study of Problems in Recruiting Minority People into Industrial Arts for the Western States of Colorado, Montana, North Dakota, South Dakota, Utah and Wyoming. "   DAI,  38:8 (February 1978),  4625A-4626A.   University of Northern Colorado 1977.   90 pp.

3320.  Gribskov, Margaret E.   "A Critical Analysis of Text-

book Accounts of the Role of Indians in American
History. " DAI, 34:6 (December 1973), 3301A.
University of Oregon 1973.

3321.  Grinnell, Ira H.  "The Tribal Government of the Oglala Sioux Tribe of Pine Ridge, South Dakota. " M. A.
Thesis.  University of South Dakota 1959.  133 pp.

3322.  Grobsmith, Elizabeth S.  "Lakhota Bilingualism:  A
Comparative Study of Language Use in Two Communities on the Rosebud Sioux Reservation. " DAI, 37:
12, Pt. 1 (June 1977), 7830A-7831A.  University of
Arizona 1976.  363 pp.  On the Antelope and Spring
Creek settlements where functional bilingualism exists.  Lakota is used for ritual activities, English
for official transactions.

3323.  Hagen, Shirley T.  "Descriptive Analysis of the Attitudes of Sioux Indian Women Towards Birth Control
and Family Planning. " M. A. Thesis.  University
of South Dakota 1971.  28 pp.

3324.  Hakes, Judith Ann.  "Elements of Social Culture in
Teton Folktales. " DAI, 35:4 (October 1974), 2146A.
University of Colorado 1974.  222 pp.  Studies 178
folktales from five major collections.

3325.  Hall, Robert E.  "A Comparison of Characteristics of
Sioux and Non-Sioux Teachers:  Teacher Perceptions
Which Help Determine Educational Exceptionality in
a Bisocial Setting. " DAI, 35:4 (October 1974),
2081A-2082A.  George Washington University 1974.
163 pp.

3326.  Harrold, Paul T.  "A Program to Assist in the Improvement of the Economic Conditions of the United
Sioux Tribes of South Dakota. " DAI, 36:11 (May
1976), 7684A.  University of Northern Colorado
1975.  240 pp.  The Sioux need time to adjust to
the need for accepting assistance in these areas.

3327.  Hauck, William C.  "A Study of American Indian
Graduates of Black Hills State College. " DAI, 32:9
(March 1972), 4982A-4983A.  University of South
Dakota 1971.  A study of 48 graduates of this west-
ern South Dakota College between 1948 and 1970.

3328.   Hill, Thomas W.   "'Feeling Good' and 'Getting High':
        Alcohol Use of Urban Indians." DAI, 37:6 (Janu-
        ary 1977), 445A.   University of Pennsylvania 1976.
        243 pp.   On the drinking problems of "everyday"
        Winnebago and Santee Dakota of Sioux City, Iowa.

3329.   Jackson, John.   "State Jurisdiction of Indian Affairs
        in South Dakota." M. A. Thesis.   University of
        Iowa 1938.

3330.   Jahner, Elaine.   "Spatial Categories in Sioux Folk
        Narrative." DAI, 36:11 (May 1976), 7561A-7562A.
        Indiana University 1975.   120 pp.   Based on the nar-
        ratives of eight different story-tellers, collected
        during four years of field work.

3331.   Keeble, Blossom Iris.   "An Investigation in the Sioux
        Language Teaching of the Effectiveness of Language
        Pattern Practice Drill Techniques on the Fifth and
        Sixth Grade Levels in Second Language Training."
        DAI, 36:2 (August 1975), 757A-758A.   University of
        South Dakota 1974.   Testing 40 subjects from among
        Sioux Indian students at St. Paul's Mission School,
        Marty, South Dakota, in the spring of 1974.   Au-
        thor is Sioux.

3332.   Kohoutek, Fred J.   "A History of the Lake Traverse
        Indian Reservation." M. A. Thesis.   University of
        South Dakota 1939.

3333.   Koss, Allen B.   "The Use of the Vocational Prefer-
        ence Inventory with a North Dakota Indian Popula-
        tion." DAI, 32:12, Pt. 1 (June 1972), 6761A-
        6762A.   University of North Dakota 1971.   Tested
        161 high school juniors and seniors enrolled at
        Turtle Mountain Community School at Belcourt and
        the Standing Rock Community School at Fort Yates.

3334.   Kuske, Irwin L.   "Psycholinguistic Abilities of Sioux
        Indian Children." M. A. Thesis.   University of
        South Dakota 1969.   118 pp.

3335.   Lass, William E.   "Stanley J. Morrow, Frontier
        Photographer." M. A. Thesis.   University of South
        Dakota 1954.

3336.   Lawrence, Duane L.   "A Study of the Variables Related

to Satisfaction of North Dakota Students in Higher
Education. " DAI, 36:2 (August 1975), 759A. University of North Dakota 1974. 134 pp. On North
Dakota students in colleges and universities in that
state funded through the Bureau of Indian Affairs
grants during the academic year 1970-71.

3337. Leach, Duane M. "A History of the Santee Sioux,
1860-1890. " M. A. Thesis. University of South
Dakota 1959.

3338. Leatham, Raymond C. "A Study of the Relationship
Between Self-Concept Variables and Different Lengths
of Sobriety for Male American Indian Alcoholics and
Male American Indian Non-Alcoholics. " DAI, 37:6
(December 1976), 3523A. University of South Da-
kota 1975. 124 pp. Deals with 80 subjects.

3339. Lebow, Ella C. "Transition of Indian Education from
Federal to State Schools on the Rosebud Indian
Reservation, Rosebud, South Dakota, 1942-1955. "
M. A. Thesis. University of South Dakota 1958.
Author is Sioux.

3340. Lind, Robert W. "Familistic Attitudes and Marriage
Role Expectations of American Indian and White
Adolescents. " DAI, 32:9 (March 1972), 5288B.
Florida State University 1971. 122 pp. Studied
150 whites and 135 Indians in Montana, including
Crow, Northern Cheyenne, Flathead, Sioux, and
Assiniboin.

3341. McAreavey, James P. "An Analysis of Selected Educationally Handicapped South Dakota Sioux Indian
Children's Responses to the Wechsler Intelligence
Scale for Children and Wide Range Achievement
Test of Reading. " DAI, 36:8 (February 1976),
5154A-5155A. University of Colorado 1975. 136
pp. Tested 100 educationally handicapped Indian
children.

3342. McCluskey, Murton Leon. "An Analysis of Selected
Attitudes Toward School and Knowledge of Indian
Culture Held by Indian Students Enrolled in Grand
Forks, North Dakota, Public Schools. " DAI, 37:
5 (November 1976), 2702A. University of North
Dakota 1975. 175 pp. Tested 130 Indian students

K-12 and 120 non-Indian K-12. Indian students
know very little about their culture. They have a
high self-concept.

3343. Marsden, Michael T. "A Selected, Annotated Edition
of Henry Rowe Schoolcraft's Personal Memoirs of
a Residence of Thirty Years with the Indian Tribes
on the American Frontiers." DAI, 33:7 (January
1973), 3593A-3595A. Bowling Green State University 1972. 555 pp.

3344. Marshall, Daniel W. "Classroom Climate as Related
to Alienation, Attitude Toward School, and Achievement Motivation Among Oglala Sioux Pupils." DAI,
33:5 (November 1972), 2174A. University of Denver 1972. 221 pp. Tested 192 pupils taught by 7
teachers.

3345. Melody, Michael E. "The Sacred Hoop: The Way of
the Chiricahua and Teton Lakota." DAI, 37:3 (September 1976), 1772A. University of Notre Dame
1976. Material on Sioux cosmogony and a suggested
interpretation of the Sun Dance and a collation of
descriptions of the dance.

3346. Miller, David R. "Charles Alexander Eastman: One
Man's Journey in Two Worlds." M. A. Thesis.
University of North Dakota 1975. A biographical
study.

3347. Nelson, Thurston D. "Efforts to Rehabilitate the
Standing Rock Sioux." M. A. Thesis. North Dakota State University 1968. 94 pp.

3348. Peterson, Susan Carol. "Two Twentieth Century Mission Newspapers." M. A. Thesis. University of
South Dakota 1976. 84 pp.

3349. Pike, William A. "A Study of Self Concept as a Fac-
tor in Social Groupings of Three Indian Social
Groups in Sioux City." DAI, 36:8 (February 1976),
5158A. University of South Dakota 1975. 113 pp.

3350. Pipal, Bert G. "A History of Standing Rock Indian
Agency, 1868-1880." M. A. Thesis. University
of South Dakota 1962. 62 pp.

3351. Pourier, James Emery E. "A Comparison of Values Among Indian High Schools, Indian Dropouts, and Non-Indian Teachers." DAI, 37:9 (March 1977), 5710A. University of South Dakota 1976. 50 pp. Investigation of value differences between Indian students, Indian dropouts, and non-Indian high school teachers of the Oglala Community High School on the Pine Ridge Reservation. Author is Sioux.

3352. Riner, Reed D. "Attitudes Toward Federal Education Among American Indian Parents and Students in Six Communities." DAI, 38:7 (January 1978), 4241A-4242A. University of Colorado, Boulder, 1977. 298 pp. Besides two communities among the Blackfeet and two among the Navajo, he examined the St. Francis Mission and Eagle Butte communities in South Dakota.

3353. Robbins, Webster S. "The Administrative and Educational Policies of the United States Federal Government with Regard to the North American Tribes of Nebraska from 1870 to 1970." DAI, 37:5 (November 1976), 2687A. University of Nebraska 1976. 422 pp.

3354. Ross, Kenneth G. "The Relationship of Bilingualism to Selected Indicators of Indian Cultural Identity as a Variable in the Administration of Indian Education." DAI, 34:5 (November 1973), 2239A-2240A. University of Minnesota 1973. 167 pp. Studies adults and students on the Standing Rock Sioux Reservation. Author is Sioux.

3355. Ryan, Loye Marie J. "A Study of Personality Traits and Values of American Indian and Non-American Indian Counselors Trained at the University of South Dakota." DAI, 37:6 (December 1976), 3427A-3428A. University of South Dakota 1976. 93 pp. Study of fifty Indian and non-Indian counselors in the M. A. program. There are differences, and the American males are the most different.

3356. Shaw, Patricia A. "Dakota Phonology and Morphology." DAI, 39:4 (October 1978), 2226A-2227A. University of Toronto, Canada, 1976. Considers two Canadian dialects--Santee of Sioux Valley, Manitoba, and the Stoney dialect of Morley, Alberta, not previously described.

3357. Stanislaus, John. "Contact Negotiation and Conflict: An Ethnohistory of the Eastern Dakota, 1819-1839." DAI, 35:8 (February 1975), 4775A-4776A. University of Texas, Austin, 1974. 267 pp.

3358. Swanson, Duane P. "The Northern Pacific Railroad and the Sisseton-Wahpeton Sioux: A Case Study in Land Acquisitions." M. A. Thesis. University of Delaware 1972. 88 pp.

3359. Talley, Tyra. "A Multifaceted Inquiry into the Personality Factors and Academic Achievement of Indian High School Students." DAI, 36:8 (February 1976), 5063A-5064A. University of South Dakota 1975. 84 pp. Tested 124 students from immediately adjacent high schools in central South Dakota: 31 male Indians, 31 female Indians; 31 male non-Indians and 31 female non-Indians. Author is Sioux.

3360. Thomas, Darlene Kay. "Time Concept in North American Indian Mythology." DAI, 33:8 (February 1973), 3438B. University of Colorado 1972.

3361. Tuebner, Johanna E. "Fourth Grade Creativity of Urban, Rural, and Indian Children in an Experimental Program." DAI, 33:12, Pt. 1 (June 1973), 6602A-6603A. University of North Dakota 1972. 85 pp. Study of 237 Fourth graders.

3362. Van Der Beets, Richard. "The Indian Captivity Narrative: An American Genre." DAI, 34:4 (October 1973), 1873A. University of the Pacific 1973. 199 pp.

3363. Wanberg, Larrie Dale. "The Relationship of Policy Preferences and Value Orientations Among Indian Tribal Leaders and Anglo Administrators on Four North Dakota Reservations." DAI, 34:7 (January 1974), 4420A. University of Denver 1973.

3364. Werden, Patricia Lucille K. "Study of Health Needs of Oglala Sioux Indian Students." 2 vols. DAI, 34:5 (November 1973), 2104B-2105B. University of Northern Colorado 1973. 442 pp.

3365. Wescott, Jane R. "The Effect of the Distar Reading Program on Selected Disadvantaged Children in South Dakota." DAI, 35:11 (May 1975), 6954A.

University of South Dakota 1974. 138 pp. Fifth
grade students on the Rosebud Reservation in South
Dakota were tested to find the effects of the Distar
Reading Program.

3366. Williams, John R. "A Comparison of the Self-
Concepts of Alcoholic and Non-Alcoholic Males of
Indian and Non-Indian Ancestry in Terms of Scores
on the Tennessee Self Concept Scale. " DAI, 36:9
(March 1976), 5844A-5845A.    University of South
Dakota 1975.    127 pp.    One hundred subjects were
tested.

3367. Wilson, Raymond. "Dr. Charles Alexander Eastman
(Ohiyesa), Santee Sioux. " DAI, 38:6 (December
1977), 3688A.    University of New Mexico 1977.
278 pp.    Says he wrote his books with the assistance of his wife, Elaine Goodale Eastman.

# NAME INDEX

Abbott, Frederick H. 417
Abel, Annie H. 968
Abel, Midge B. 2752
Aberle, David F. 2244
Aberle, Sophie D. 474
Abernathy, Alonzo 1465
Abourezk, James 1466
Abrahall, John Hoskyns 1883
Ackermann, Gertrude W. 747, 1720
Acuera 1809
Adams, Alexander B. 1721
Adams, Mrs. Ann 2614
Adams, Jacob 786
Adams, Katherine Jean 3294
Adams, Moses N. 1965, 2219
Adler, Mildred Scott 946
Ala, Viola 3295
Albers, Patricia 2245, 3296
Alberts, George B. 2423
Albright, Samuel J. 969
Aldrich, Vernice M. 2089
Alexander, Hartley B. 158, 2753
Alinder, Jim 162
Allanson, George G. 428
Allen, Charles W. 1723
Allen, Clifford 970
Allen, Helen N. 2424
Allen, Louis 1548
Allen, Patricia 1286
Allen, Paula Gunn 1317-1322, 2754-2756
Allen, Thomas E. 1286
Allis, Samuel 2090
Allison, Edward H. 1549, 1724, 1725
Ambrose, Stephen E. 1726

American Board of Commissioners for Foreign Missions 67, 68
American Horse 1450, 3048
Ames, J. H. 971
Amiotte, Arthur 159
Amon, Aline 1550
Anderson, Beverly L. 558
Anderson, Fred 2425
Anderson, Gary C. 3297
Anderson, Grant K. 1467, 1727
Anderson, Harry H. 160, 698, 699, 748, 749, 787, 972-974, 1468, 1966, 2015, 3049, 3050
Anderson, John A. 161, 162, 207, 238
Anderson, LaVere 1728
Anderson, Myrtle M. 163, 629
Anderson, Rufus 2091
Andreas, Alfred Theodore 975
Andrews, H. A. 2
Andrews, Ralph W. 1729, 2584
Andrist, Ralph D. 976, 1967
Andros, F. 1287
Aquila, Richard 2246
Armstrong, Moses K. 1056
Armstrong, Robert Plant 2757
Armstrong, Thomas R. 2585
Armstrong, Virginia I. 1884
Arneson, Harry E. 98
Arthur, M. Elizabeth 3051
Artichoker, John 470, 559

# SUBJECT INDEX

Alcoholism and drinking   1291, 1296, 1301, 3328, 3366
Algonquian   1675, 2262
Allotment   1191, 2433
Anthropometry   541
Appraisals   91, 100-102, 107, 109-112, 114, 116
Arapaho Indians   809
Archeology   114-150
Arikara Indians   404, 837, 1108, 2909, 2913
Ash Hollow Battle   3099, 3120
Astorians   750
Athapascan   1600
Atkinson-O'Fallon Expedition   776
Autobiographies   386-416, 2586, 2598, 2667, 2833, 2940,
      3006, 3014, 3091


Badlands   2606, 2690, 2691
Beadwork   290, 291
Beacher Island Fight   3069, 3215
Birch Coulee   989, 990, 1974, 1984, 1985, 2001
Black Hawk War   2917, 2926
The Black Hills   1190, 1228, 1246, 1253, 1467, 1523, 1538,
      1620, 1945, 2617, 2631, 2634, 3058
Brule   207, 1011-1013, 1267, 1269, 1495
Bureau of Indian Affairs   1428, 1429
Burial Mounds   122, 124, 126, 128-130, 132, 133, 141, 144,
      145, 152, 153, 2406
Burials   2262, 2419, 2420


Caddoan   1570, 1674, 1675, 2262
Canadian Sioux   417-427, 1313, 1506, 1959, 2339, 3356
Captivity literature   43, 428-469, 1960, 2758, 2827, 3362
Catholic Church   2104, 2107, 2126, 2127, 2141, 2173, 2175,
      2216, 2243
Cessions   103-106, 108
Cheyenne Indians   333, 406, 787, 809, 1244, 1354, 3205
Cheyenne River Reservation   116, 575, 625, 699, 1312, 1375,